the
Britons

The Peoples of Europe

General Editors: James Campbell and Barry Cuncliffe

This series is about the European tribes and peoples from their origins in prehistory to the present day. Drawing upon a wide range of archaeological and historical evidence, each volume presents a fresh and absorbing account of a group's culture, society and usually turbulent history.

Already published:

The Etruscans
Graeme Barker and Thomas Rasmussen

The Normans
Marjory Chibnall

The Norsemen in the Viking Age
Eric Christiansen

The Lombards
Neil Christie

The Basques*
Roger Collins

The English
Geoffrey Elton

The Gypsies
Second Edition
Angus Fraser

The Bretons
Patrick Galliou and Michael Jones

The Goths
Peter Heather

The Franks*
Edward James

The Russians
Robin Milner-Gulland

The Mongols
David Morgan

The Armenians
A. E. Redgate

The Britons
Christopher A. Snyder

The Huns
E. A. Thompson

The Early Germans
Malcolm Todd

The Illyrians
John Wilkes

In preparation:

The Scilians
David Abulafia

The Irish
Francis John Byrne and Michael Herity

The Byzantines
Averil Cameron

The Serbs
Sima Cirkovic

The Spanish
Roger Collins

The Romans
Timothy Cornell

The Scots
Colin Kidd

The Picts
Charles Thomas

* Denotes title now out of print

the

Britons

Christopher A. Snyder

Blackwell
Publishing

350 Main Street, Malden, MA 02148,USA
9600 Garsington Road, Oxford OX4 2DQ, UK
550 Swanston Street, Carlton South, Melbourne, Victoria 3053, Australia
Kurfürstendamm 57, 10707 Berlin, Germany

First published 2003 by Blackwell Publishing Ltd

Library of Congress Cataloging in Publication Data

Snyder, Christopher A. (Christopher Allen), 1966–
    The Britons / Christopher A. Snyder.
        p.   cm. — (The peoples of Europe)
    Includes bibliographical references and index.
    ISBN 0–631–22260–X (alk. paper)
    1. Britons. 2. Great Britain—Civilization—To 1066. 3. Great
Britain—Antiquities, Celtic. 4. Great Britain—History—To 449. 5.
Celts—Great Britain. 6. Druids and Druidism. 7. Arthur, King. I.
Title. II. Series
DA140 .s73 2003
941′.004916—dc21
                                                              2002011113

A catalogue record for this title is available from the British Library.

Picture Research by Judy Lehane

Set in 10 on 12 pt Sabon
by Ace Filmsetting Ltd, Frome, Somerset
Printed and bound in the United Kingdom
by T. J. International Ltd, Padstow, Cornwall

For further information on
Blackwell Publishing, visit our website:
http://www.blackwellpublishing.com

To my King
this service is rendered

Contents

Plates

Figures

Maps

Tables

Preface

For satisfaction and therefore for delight – and not for imperial policy – we are still 'British' at heart. It is the native language to which in unexplored desire we would still go home.

J.R.R. Tolkien, "English and Welsh"

Many readers of this book may be aware of another work of similar title written in 1992 by the Yale historian Linda Colley.[1] This well-received cultural history explores the ways in which many English, Irish, Welsh, and Scottish citizens of the United Kingdom came to accept a unifying label – Britons – as a response to foreign wars and economic opportunities during the eighteenth century. At that time it was assumed, by scholar and politician alike, that there had once been an ancient people called the Britons who had inhabited the entire island of Britain. The popular adoption of the terms Britons and British following the 1707 Act of Union certainly heightened interest in the ancient Britons, but it also unleashed a legion of fanciful myths about them (e.g. the Druids' connection with Stonehenge) and obscured the real contributions of their medieval descendants in Brittany, Cornwall, Wales, and northern Britain.

The present book is, in part, an attempt to remind the reader of the legacy of these medieval Britons. But to do so we must examine the ancient origins of the Britons, and question those eighteenth-century assumptions about a unified, widespread, and concretely defined British people. In other words, where Colley worked to construct a British identity we must begin by deconstructing one. In doing so I am hardly breaking new ground, for the last two decades have witnessed a flurry of academic skepticism regarding not only the myths that have become attached to the Britons (especially that of King Arthur) but also the assumption that the ancient Britons were part of a larger 'Celtic' world. At the same time there has emerged a tremendous popular interest in the history and legends of the Britons, an interest which should be addressed seriously by scholars and educators but is not.

I am most grateful to the editors of Blackwell's Peoples of Europe series

1 Linda Colley, *Britons* (New Haven and London: Yale University Press, 1992).

for inviting me to write a book that bridges this gap between enthusiast and skeptic. It was most encouraging to hear their comments and others' describing the need for a survey of the Britons, not just in this series but also in general. I thank Tessa Harvey for her support of the project, and especially Barry Cunliffe for his warmth and generosity. The following individuals have read various parts of the book and lent their critical insights: Richard Abels, James Campbell, Craig Cessford, Rees Davies, Deanna Forsman, Martin Grimmer, Bruce O'Brien, and Michelle Ziegler. My appreciation goes to Gail Flatness and the inter-library loan staff of Reinsch Library for their help in obtaining material, and my love to Renée and Carys for their patience with me during the whole process.

One participant at a recent conference on ethnography in early medieval Britain remarked (half-seriously), 'Mountain inhabitants tend to be more stubborn [about ethnic identity] than city people.' Though he wasn't referring to me, I happen to hail from a Welsh settlement in the Mountain State (West Virginia), which has no town population over 100,000 and whose motto is *Montani semper liberi*, 'Mountaineers are always free.' I shall, however, try not to be too stubborn in the following pages in asserting the case for ethnic identity among the early Britons.

Christopher A. Snyder
Marymount University

Abbreviations

BAR	British Archaeological Reports
BBCS	*Bulletin of the Board of Celtic Studies*
CMCS	*Cambrian Medieval Celtic Studies*
ECMW	*The Early Christian Monuments of Wales*, ed. Nash-Williams
EH	Bede, *The Ecclesiastical History of the English People*
HB	*Historia Brittonum*
HF	Gregory of Tours, *History of the Franks*
LPRIA	Late Pre-Roman Iron Age
MGH	*Monumenta Germaniae Historica*, ed. Mommsen
OED	*Oxford English Dictionary*
RIB	*Roman Inscriptions in Britain*

1
Who are the Britons?

In the film *Monty Python and the Holy Grail*, Graham Chapman's King Arthur identifies himself to a peasant woman as 'King of the Britons.' His unimpressed subject retorts, 'King of the who? Who are the Britons?' When Arthur informs her that she is in fact a Briton, that 'We are all Britons,' the audience – especially modern Britons – is expected to laugh at this ethnic confusion. It is a funny scene, but it is also a poignant reminder of how truly complex is the subject of ethnic identity in the Middle Ages.

It is not that we are unfamiliar with the word Britons. It is not an obscure term, like Picts, which requires immediate explanation. On the contrary, we have used 'Britons' and 'British' for so long that we automatically accept their validity and assume that our audience knows what we mean. Yet these words in their various forms have meant many different things to different ages. Modern usage of these terms to describe, after 1707, citizens of the United Kingdom is a distorted reflection of ancient and medieval usage. Modern scholars studying the early Britons have in turn been influenced by this modern political usage of the term, and occasionally by political motives as well. Even when we have been able to divorce ourselves from these influences we are, because of the limitations or the evidence, closer to the confusion of the peasant woman than to the assertiveness of Arthur.

Britons and the Great Celtic Debate

I certainly hope that we can be a little less confused, and that we can agree on a sensible definition of Britons for scholarly and educational purposes. But before such a thing can be advanced there are serious criticisms that must be addressed. These are, in question form, as follows:

Did these people ever see themselves as Britons?
Were they ever a unified group with a single, identifiable culture?
How were they distinct from their neighbors?

The last question will be addressed throughout this book, but the first two must be considered before such a study as this can even begin. It seems to me that these issues are related to the current debate over Celtic identity. Though there were some earlier skeptics like Tolkien,[1] this debate has really taken shape in the last 20 years and is an explicit response from specialists to the growing popularity of things Arthurian and Celtic. The general public, complain the critics, are buying books which uncritically perpetuate old romantic myths about the Celts, and profit-seeking authors and publishers are allowing these myths to form current racial and political sentiments that are untrue and potentially dangerous.

I don't want here to rehearse every detail of the Celtic debate, and indeed there are signs that scholars are growing weary of it,[2] but a book on the Britons should acknowledge where these attacks are coming from and what, if any, ramifications they will have on future perceptions of the Celtic peoples. Most of the argument is emanating from archaeologists who study the European Iron Age. They are now questioning the association of Hallstatt and La Tène cultures with Celtic-speaking peoples,[3] and whether the specifically continental term *Keltoi* (or *Celtae*) should be used to describe the Iron Age inhabitants of Britain and Ireland.[4] Greek and Roman writers were inconsistent in their usage of the term, they say, and 'Celt' was never used to describe a person from the British Isles prior to the seventeenth century.

Some Iron Age archaeologists and art historians have responded to the criticisms,[5] but a greater number of scholars have been converted to what has been described as a 'politically correct' skepticism of things Celtic. Medievalists have not been as quick to jump on this bandwagon. While a few have attacked the notion of a uniform Celtic Church,[6] most have continued to use Celtic to describe – and lump together – the peoples and cultures of medieval Ireland, Scotland, Wales, and Brittany. These lands are often referred to together as the medieval 'Celtic fringe'.

Those medievalists and archaeologists who are critical of the Celtic la-

---

1   Tolkien, 1963.
2   For example, Pittock, 1999. See, however, the laudable *Celticity Project* <http://www.aber.ac.uk/awcwww/s/p5_cartref.html>.
3   See e.g. Merriman, 1987; Hill, 1993; Hill, 1996; Graves-Brown, Jones, and Gamble, 1996; Collis, 1996; and Collis, 1997.
4   See James and Rigby, 1997; and James, 1999.
5   Megaw and Megaw, 1996; idem, 1998; Cunliffe, 1997.
6   See discussion of the Celtic churches in Chapter Six below.

bel have drawn upon recent anthropological research to back their skepticism. They have especially used the work of Malcolm Chapman,[7] whose criticisms of the 'Celtic myth' are little known outside this circle of specialists. Chapman and his followers[8] traced the genesis of Celtic identity to the early eighteenth century, when early philologists like Edward Lhuyd borrowed the Classical term *Celtae* to describe a language group that included ancient Gaulish and Brittonic as well as contemporary Goidelic and Brythonic tongues. It is significant, they point out, that Lhuyd's theory of the relationship of the Celtic languages was published in 1707, the very year in which 'Briton' was being officially imposed as a unifying label over English and 'Celtic' peoples.

Crucial to the anthropological critique of the Celts is the Greco-Roman construct of the barbarian 'Other' and the outmoded racial theories that pervade popular studies of the Celts, both of which impose uniformity on diversity. When Greek and Roman authors use labels like Celts and Britons, they ignore tribal or regional diversity in order to contrast for their audiences the exotic/uncivilized barbarians with the familiar/civilized Mediterranean peoples. This kind of stereotype was perpetuated by modern imperialists, and is reflected in nineteenth-century racial theory. But since anthropology no longer believes in race theory nor in uniform and static 'cultures' (which had virtually defined Iron Age archaeology), such constructs as the Celts are no longer tenable.

There is much that is sensible in these provocative critiques. But why have the Celts been chosen as the target? Are not such 'mongrel nations' as the Romans, the Germans, the English, the French – not to mention the Russians and the Americans – equally susceptible to such criticism? Each of these peoples has long possessed a diversity of languages, cultures, and races within the larger group. If we follow to the letter current anthropological theory on ethnic identity, can we make any generalization of peoples? If all identity is locally or even individually determined, can we write any group history?

In order to do just this, to produce histories of peoples or pre-modern 'nations,' many historians and archaeologists have resorted to the theory of 'ethnogenesis.' Simply stated, this is the belief that in early societies a very small number of elites (political, military, or intellectual) can impose an ethnic identity upon the larger group. To return to our Monty Python analogy, Arthur and his knights can impose their ethnic label 'Britons' upon the peasant population, which before had only identified itself in

---

7   Especially Chapman, 1992.
8   Most notably Sims-Williams, 1986; and James, 1999. See also the essays in Brown, 1996.

family or community terms. Individual or local history can thus be transformed into ethnic or national history through the sheer will of elites like kings and chroniclers.

After about two decades of success in helping us to understand the formation of the Germanic peoples, the ethnogenesis theory is starting to receive some criticism from medievalists. In any case it does not work as well in explaining the Britons' ethnic origins. For, unlike such peoples as the Goths and the Anglo-Saxons, the Britons were disrupted in the process of forming Iron Age identities by the Romans, who introduced (or imposed) other identities: Roman (cultural Romanization), *civis* (political citizenship), and eventually (for some) Christian. Then, with the Roman political and military apparatus withdrawn *c.*410, the Britons were forced once more into reexamining their identity, this time in the face of Germanic invaders/settlers. Some Britons became 'Germanicized' (by choice or necessity) and melted into the nascent English state; others resisted – through arms and prejudice – and clung to a new Brittonic identity that contained Iron Age, Roman, and Christian elements.

I make no claims to being well versed in either Classical ethnography or modern cultural anthropology. But it seems to me common sense that any historian attempting to discuss any pre-modern people would have three questions in mind when dealing with ethnic identity:

> Do we know what the people called themselves?
> What terms did their literate neighbors apply to them?
> What terms do modern scholars (historians, archaeologists, linguists) use to describe them?

If the answer to the first question is simple, unequivocal, and consistent throughout their history then we could simply end the discussion there. Of course, for most pre-modern peoples it is not (see Table 1.1 below). Rather, the first question is likely to elicit several equally valid answers for each group of people; i.e. pre-modern peoples chose to identify themselves in several different ways: by family, extended family (tribe), local community or town, state, or trans-local religion or culture. Conversely, the second question may yield a more simple answer, for written evidence shows that neighboring peoples often simplify and overlook regional variation and diversity – they stereotype.

Modern scholars have often been accused of doing the same, of oversimplifying complex identities and overlooking cultural variation within a large group. Archaeologists are just as guilty of doing this as are historians, though the former may use labels derived from material culture rather than written evidence (e.g. 'Beaker people' rather than Britons).

Table 1.1   Identity terms for some pre-modern peoples.

What do they call themselves?	Family/tribal identities: Iceni, Dumnonii, etc.	Family/tribal identities: Bacchiadae, Lacedaemonians	Family/tribal identities: Julii, Pompeii, etc.	Family/tribal identities: Wulfingas, Angel, Seaxan, Frisan, etc.
		City-state identities: Athenians, Spartans, etc.		
	Britanni/ Brittones, Brythoniaid, Cymry.		Romani.	
		Hellenes.		
What do their neighbors call them?	Britanni (Roman neighbors); Wealh (Germanic neighbors).	Graeci (Roman neighbors).	Romoi, Walchen, etc. Greek and Germanic neighbors).	Anglii, Saxones, etc. (Roman neighbors).
What do modern scholars call them?	Britons	Greeks.	Romans.	Anglo-Saxons, English.

But such generalizations and stereotypes, as long as they are founded on good material or written evidence, *are absolutely necessary* if we are to advance scholarly discussion beyond the level of micro-history and biography.

Polybius observed that, after Alexander conquered the Persian Empire and Rome defeated Carthage, history was no longer local. Like other Iron Age peoples in Europe and Asia, the British tribes were shocked into this realization by the expansionist power of Rome. The Britons' failure to conform to a single political and military entity resulted in a weak resistance to (and in some cases a compliance with) the conquests of Caesar and Claudius. Faced much later with a second external threat – rebellious Germanic mercenaries and their North Sea compatriots – many Britons rallied behind a single religious and cultural identity and vowed to resist this threat to their political sovereignty of the island, as they saw it. While some in the lowlands failed or gave in, those in northern Britain, Wales, Cornwall, and Brittany struggled to maintain an independent ethnic identity that we see most clearly in their language, poetry, and history.

Historiography and Methodology

This book is an attempt to tell the story of these Britons and to examine their culture through the fragmentary written *and* material evidence. It was not a monolithic or static culture, any more than was that of the Celts, the Romans, or the English. But it will be shown that these geographically dispersed peoples did share much in common, not least a vision of past unity and a persistent hope for future delivery. Bringing these members of the medieval Celtic fringe together, in a single study, is a novel approach that will not go without some criticism. My only defense is that I was led along this path by the voices of the Britons themselves – by Patrick and Gildas, by the poets and the rebel Glyn Dŵr, and by the not so famous who are remembered only in their stone epitaphs – and have followed their itinerant monastic saints as they traversed the scattered Brittonic lands with relative ease, showing us kinship bonds and a cultural continuum.

While there has been no great non-antiquarian tradition of writing historical surveys of the ancient and medieval Britons, there has indeed been a great deal of modern scholarship concerning the various topics and periods which this book covers. Britain in the Late Pre-Roman Iron Age is well represented within the scholarship of the European Iron Age. This is a field, of course, dominated by archaeologists, though recently numismatists have contributed important work on Celtic coinage in the years between the Caesarian and Claudian invasions. Archaeologists are also devoting more attention to rural settlement during the Roman occupation of Britain, and British burial practices are being illumined by recent studies of intra-mural and extra-mural cemeteries. Late Roman Britain has developed virtually as a separate publishing industry, with no shortage of books on the end of Roman rule and the coming of the Anglo-Saxons (though the British dimension has gained little attention outside of 'Arthurian' publications).

In the last 20 years several important works on early medieval Wales have appeared, and a few on the origins of Brittany, but medieval Cornwall and Brittonic northern Britain have remained nearly untouched by historians. Important excavations have occurred in all these areas, mostly focusing on hill-forts and other defended settlements and a few major religious sites. The study of both pottery and inscriptions found at these sites testifies to trade with the Mediterranean and extensive contacts between the Britons and Gaul in the early Middle Ages.

Scholarship on the Brittonic lands during the Viking Age (*c.*800–1100) is hardly impressive. Nevertheless, important studies have been done on both the Welsh laws and Breton charters attributed to this period. The involvement of Bretons in the Norman Conquest of England, and the Welsh campaigns of both the Norman and Plantagenet kings, have garnered some interest. Especially relevant to this study are several essays which have recently appeared on English and French attitudes toward their Welsh and Breton neighbors in the twelfth and thirteenth centuries. And then there are the rebels – especially Owain Glyn Dŵr, who was the subject of two substantial works in the last five years.

But it has been the literary figures and myths of the Britons, rather than their history, which have most often captured the public's attention. Stonehenge and the Druids, Celtic paganism, Arthur and Merlin. . . . Such subjects have inspired artistic creations, pop histories, and scholarly critiques. The fascinating aspect of this for a historian is that these subjects have their origins in history, and figures like Arthur and Merlin may have even been real persons who took on mythic and literary identities. Medieval Britons used these Arthurian myths for political purposes; with political devolution underway in Britain, might they return as such again?

Anyone familiar with the symbolism of the red dragon on the Welsh flag knows that, in a sense, they never went away.

Part I
Romans and Britons

2

The Late Pre-Roman Iron Age

Another Briton who has been appropriated – some would say misappropriated – for political purposes is Boudica. The ancient queen, known as Boadicea to her Victorian admirers, exudes power and dignity from her bronze war chariot on the bank of the Thames. In the nineteenth and early twentieth centuries she stood for a British Empire greater than the Roman; presently she is, for many Celtophiles, a symbol of feminine power and those oppressed by empires. She may be the most famous ancient Briton – she is certainly one of the few we know by name – and written sources give us glimpses of her physical appearance and fiery personality. What forces and processes in the Iron Age shaped the character, status, and worldview of this woman? Can historical and archaeological evidence answer this question and give us a broader picture of British society before the domination of Rome?

The Late Pre-Roman Iron Age (LPRIA) is the first period in which a significant quantity and diversity of evidence emerges for the Britons. For all previous ages – Stone, Bronze, and Iron – we are forced to rely entirely on archaeological evidence, much of which has proven at best challenging to the archaeologist and of little use for the historian.[1] But in the Late Iron Age the archaeological evidence increases and is joined by coin inscriptions and extensive written accounts by Julius Caesar, Strabo, and other Classical observers.[2] While we still have no written account from a British hand, it is in this period that the Britons truly emerge as a distinct people recognized as such by their neighbors and capable of some military and political unity.

---

1   For a general overview of prehistoric Britain, see the essays in Cunliffe, 1998; for the Bronze Age, see the chapter on Britain in M. Coles and A. F. Harding, 1979.

2   For a discussion of the written evidence, see Rankin, 1987.

The Earliest Britons

We do not know what the earliest inhabitants of Britain were called, either by others or their own terms. Self-identification was probably familial, perhaps tribal. Outsiders, literate and with broader geographic knowledge, left the first recorded names for Britain and its inhabitants. The earliest appear in a *periplus* ('circumnavigation'), or sailing manual, written by a mariner from Massilia (Marseilles) in the sixth century BC. Though we do not possess this manual, it was used (along with information from the Carthaginian admiral Himilco) by the Roman writer Avienus in his poem *Ora Maritima* ('The Maritime Shores') *c.*AD 400. While describing the ancient trade route along the Atlantic coasts from Cadiz to Brittany, Avienus mentions 'the Sacred Island' inhabited 'by the race of Hiberni' ('sacred' being a common Greek interpretation of the Irish word *Ierne*) and the nearby 'island of the Albions (*insula Albionum*).' The earliest Greek explorers seem to have identified the inhabitants of Britain geographically, that is by naming them after an island they knew as 'Albion.'[3]

This enigmatic name for Britain, revived much later by Romantic poets like William Blake, did not remain popular among Greek writers. It was soon replaced by Ρρεττανια and Βρεττανια (Britain), Βρεττανος (a Briton), and Βρεττανικος (the adjective British). From these words the Romans derived the Latin forms *Britannia*, *Britannus*, and *Britannicus* respectively. Again, this is a geographic rather than a cultural or political designation, for αι Βρεττανιαι, 'the Brittanic Isles,' included Ireland.

We do not know if the Britons themselves suggested or accepted these labels. The term *Albiones* is enigmatic but appears to be a very early Celtic word and may date to the Bronze Age 'celticization' of the insular vocabulary. Ρρεττανοι derives from a Gallo-Brittonic word which may have been introduced to Britain during the P-Celtic linguistic innovations of the sixth century BC.[4] It is remarkably similar to both *Priteni*, the Britons' term for the Picts, and *Prydein*, the Welsh word for Britain, and thus the Greeks may have picked up (probably from the Gauls) an insular name that the Britons called themselves or a particular British tribe. The medieval etymologist Isidore of Seville, perhaps influenced by the negative portrayal of Britons in Latin sources, wrote that *Britto* (an alternate form of *Britanni*) derived from *brutus*, 'unwieldy or dull.'[5]

Another way to pose the question is when do Britons first appear as a

---

3   'Albion' and 'Albiones' also appears in the works of Pseudo-Aristotle, Pseudo-Agathemerus, Marcian, Stephanus, Eustathius, and Pliny.   See Hawkes, 1977, and Rivet and Smith, 1979.

4   Cunliffe, 1997, 154–6.

5   Matthews, 1999, 16.

distinctive group in the archaeological record? Stone Age Britons were constantly receiving innovations from the continent. This certainly continued in the Bronze Age, which saw settled agricultural communities expand through the use of new technologies. Bronze metallurgy, which came to Britain from Ireland *c.*1800 BC, has often been associated with the so-called 'Beaker culture' (named from the form of their funerary pottery) found throughout northwestern Europe. Now it is no longer believed that there was an 'invasion' of Beaker People who overcame Stone Age Britons with their superior metal weapons, but rather a more gradual adoption of Beaker culture attributes over a long period of time.

Bronze weapons did, however, lead to military elites who demanded prestige goods and prestigious burials (replacing earlier communal burial), most notably with the Wessex culture. Without written records, however, we have no knowledge of the political arrangements of these Britons or how they viewed kinship and cultural ties. By the Middle Bronze Age we see evidence of significant social organization in the landscape. While late Neolithic peoples in Britain had organized themselves to construct megalithic ritual monuments, Bronze Age Britons were dividing and organizing the land (through 'reaves' of drystone walls and timber fences) in order to grow more and better crops and to minimize social conflict.[6] Ditched enclosures appear on prominent hilltops, serving as central places for religious festivals, feasting, and the exchange of goods.

Hallstatt and La Tène

The British goods that were being manufactured and exchanged, especially prestige goods like weapons, begin in the Late Bronze Age to show stylistic and decorative characteristics of a continental style known as Hallstatt. Named after excavated cemeteries in Austria, the Hallstatt culture covered much of northwestern Europe from the Late Bronze Age to the Early Iron Age (see chart 2.2). It is defined by the first appearance of 'hill-forts,' richly adorned inhumations, distinctive weapons, and decorated objects, and the first significant contacts with the Mediterranean world. It is also clear, from Greek sources and continental placenames, that most Europeans who possessed a Hallstatt material culture were in lands where Celtic languages were spoken.

Does this mean that the Britons were Celts? In their nomenclature Greek writers distinguish between Βρεττανοι and Κελτοι, though both are described as barbarians with similar cultural attributes. There is now some

6   Cunliffe, 1995, 27.

Dates bc/ad	Europe		
1300			
	Bronze D		
1200		Late Bronze Age A1	
	Hallstatt A1		
1100			
	Hallstatt A2	Late Bronze Age A2	
1000			
	Hallstatt B1	Late Bronze Age B1	
900			
	Hallstatt B2	Late Bronze Age B2	
800			
	Hallstatt B3	Late Bronze Age B3	
700			
	Hallstatt C	Late Bronze Age C	Earliest Iron Age
600			
	Hallstatt D		
500			
	La Tène Ia		Early Iron Age
400			
	La Tène Ib		
300			Middle Iron Age
	La Tène Ic		
200			
	La Tène II		
100			
	La Tène III		Late Pre-Roman Iron Age
0			
100			
200			Roman

Figure 2.1   Subdivisions of the European Bronze and Iron Ages.

Plate 2.1   La Tène objects from Britain. (British Museum, London.)

debate among archaeologists as to whether Britain and Ireland were really a part of the Hallstatt culture. In the seventh century, long bronze
slashing swords, stylistically Hallstatt, begin to appear in Britain, followed
by iron swords and daggers, bronze harness fittings, and male jewelry in
the sixth and fifth centuries. Once thought to signal Hallstatt invaders
from the continent, these finds are now interpreted as diplomatic gifts
between warrior elites on both sides of the Channel.[7]

A similar debate exists with La Tène, the Iron Age material culture
most closely identified with the Celts. Named after the site of an excava-

7 Cunliffe, 1991, 419-43; Cunliffe, 1995, 23.

tion beneath Lake Neuchâtel, in Switzerland, La Tène culture is characterized by curvilinear art displayed on weapons, jewelry, and pottery. Such items are found in abundance throughout northern Europe, including both Britain and Ireland (see plate 2.1), though British examples often display some variation from continental styles. Again, most archaeologists now prefer to see La Tène objects and practices in Britain as continental imports or emulation rather than signs of a large-scale invasion.

A conservative approach taken by many archaeologists is to simply avoid the terms Celts, Hallstatt, and La Tène when discussing Britain and Ireland. Instead, many scholars speak of local cultures (e.g. Woodbury, Aylesford–Swarling, Arras), specific hoards, or simply Early/Middle/Late Iron Age. Barry Cunliffe has emphasized the regional variation in Iron Age Britain, suggesting a division of the island into cultural 'zones' corresponding to influences coming from Ireland and the Continent. The lands that will become the medieval 'Celtic fringe' (Ireland, Brittany, Cornwall, Wales, Cumbria, Scotland) comprise, in this model, an Atlantic Zone, while the lowlands that will become England comprise a Channel Zone which emphasizes their links – then and now – with technologically innovative and economically potent lands stretching across northern France and Germany to the Po Valley.

The Belgae

Britain's most important contacts for most of the Iron Age were with Gaul, the English Channel serving more as a highway than a barrier. Commercial trade between Britain and Gaul, and the less structured transferal of ideas and customs, began in the Paleolithic period and witnessed few interruptions in the Bronze and Iron Ages. As we have noted, British innovations that were once explained by invasions from the continent are now attributed to less violent commercial contacts and kinship links. But in the LPRIA we finally have written evidence of a significant group of invaders: the Belgae. In his most famous commentary, *The Gallic War*, Julius Caesar gives this description of British origins:

> The inland regions of Britain are inhabited by people whom the Britons themselves claim, according to oral tradition, are indigenous. The coastal areas belong to people who once crossed from Belgium in search of booty and war: almost all of these inhabitants are called by the same national names as those of the states they originally came from. After waging war they remained in Britain and began to farm the land. Population density is high, and their dwellings are . . . very like those of the Gauls.[8]

8   Caesar, *The Gallic War*, 5.12 (trans. Carolyn Hammond).

There is much to substantiate Caesar's account of the Belgae. For example, the names of such British tribes as the Parisi, Brigantes, and Atrebates can be found in Gaul as well, and Gallo-Belgic coins begin appearing around the Thames estuary in the second century BC. Archaeologists, beginning with Arthur Evans in the late nineteenth century, found other links. Evans discovered a cremation cemetery in Aylesford, Kent, which displayed characteristics of Gaulish burial rites and funerary objects.[9] Swarling, another Kentish cemetery, was later also found to have similar commonalities with Southern Belgic culture.[10] This Aylesford–Swarling culture, encompassing a large part of eastern Britain, was explained as the result of a significant invasion from northern Gaul.

A similar interpretation was attached to the discovery, in East Yorkshire, of large ditch-enclosed cemeteries containing peculiar 'vehicle burials.'[11] These consist of large graves in which disassembled two-wheeled vehicles (carts or chariots) covered the remains of men and women who, because some were accompanied by prestige goods (e.g. chain mail, swords, ornate mirrors), were identified as members of local nobility. These elite burials of the Arras culture, as it came to be called, have close parallels with La Tène burials throughout northern Europe.

These finds alone, however, do not prove massive migrations. Many of the cremation cemeteries, for example, have now been dated to after Caesar's British invasion. Archaeologists in recent years have preferred to see the cremations and graves as evidence for close ties between military elites on both sides of the Channel, as indeed Caesar says there were, with British nobles copying the arms and funerary rites of their near neighbors and kin in Gaul. Still, all but the most skeptical archaeologists admit to some movement of warrior groups from northern Gaul to eastern Britain, where they may have intermarried with the native aristocracy.[12] The timeframe for such movements is difficult to work out, but clearly by the LPRIA these contacts – as well as the commercial links – were intensifying and resulting in important innovation and change among the Britons of the Channel Zone.

Oppida and Proto-urbanism in Britain

One continental phenomenon, closely associated with La Tène or Celtic culture in Gaul, that is clearly to be seen in Iron Age Britain is the prolif-

9   James and Rigby, 1997, 12.
10   Cunliffe, 1995, 66–7.
11   Cunliffe, 1991, 499–504.
12   A modified 'limited invasion' hypothesis is put forward in Harding, 1974.

eration of hill-forts. The first hill-forts proper appear in the sixth century BC and serve, it has been suggested, as 'means of demonstrating dominance over the land by a controlling group.'[13] These early hillforts were lightly defended, and, as has been shown by a recent geophysical survey of Wessex, contained little or no permanent settlement.[14]

In the Middle Iron Age there was a veritable explosion of hill-fort construction, particularly in central southern Britain, indicating a massive intensification of the social and economic systems of many Britons. These developed hill-forts were multivallate (i.e. defended by multiple ramparts and/or ditches) and sported complex entrances, serving not only as stronger refuges but also as symbols of the increasing prestige of the communities. These later, heavily defended hill-forts were often intensively occupied as well, with a dense collection of houses, granaries, and religious shrines. Danebury and Maiden Castle are two of the most impressive excavated examples.[15] In timber-impoverished northwestern Britain, complex round houses like the picturesque brochs in the Orkneys were built similarly to impress and served as centers of power.

Archaeologists believe that the appearance of these new centers of power, and an increasing population overall,[16] led to the emergence of tribal groupings in Britain. There is no written evidence to corroborate this, and of course large extended families had always been present in the island, but burial and settlement patterns seem to indicate that the entity which anthropologists call the 'simple chiefdom' appeared in most parts of Britain by the second century BC.[17] Once again, it is the Channel Zone which was first to innovate, but by the LPRIA tribal chiefdoms appear to be the norm throughout Britain.

The south continued to innovate in the second and first centuries BC, though hill-fort construction came to a halt in this area and many were abandoned in favor of new settlements. An economic explanation can be found in the change in trading patterns due to the expansion westward of the Roman state.[18] Two significant moments in this expansion were the establishment of the province of Transalpina in southern Gaul, in 124 BC, and Julius Caesar's conquest of Gaul from 58 to 50 BC. The first event led to the commercial exploitation, by Roman merchants, of the old overland trade route which had for centuries brought British tin to Mediterranean

13   Cunliffe, 1995, 35.
14   *British Archaeology*, 39 (1998).
15   Danebury: Cunliffe, 1983; Cunliffe, 1984.   Maiden Castle: Wheeler, 1943; Sharples, 1991.
16   Cunliffe, 1995, 25, estimates that Britain reached a population high point of 3–6 million in the second century BC.
17   Collis, 1997, 19 and 173.
18   See the essays in Macready and Thompson, 1984.

ports. Now Roman wine travelled (as demonstrated by finds of Dressel amphoras) over the Carcassone Gap to Toulouse, then via the Gironde to Brittany and the Channel Islands, and finally to the principal British harbors of Hengistbury Head and Poole Harbor, where it was exchanged for metals, shale, and probably slaves.

The second event, Caesar's conquests, disrupted this Atlantic trade route and reoriented commerce in the middle of the first century BC. A serious blow came with Caesar's destruction of the fleets of the Veneti, the Gallic tribe who had acted as middlemen in trade with Britain. At the same time, commercial links were being developed across the Channel on the Seine–Solent and Somme–Thames axes. Both Caesar and Strabo describe these short crossings, which were utilized by both merchants and Gallic nobles fleeing from the Roman legions. When Caesar finally conquered northern Gaul the contacts did not cease; rather, Roman and Gallic merchants took advantage of the now complete Roman control of the overland routes to further exploit the potential of the British markets.

These shifting trade routes transformed the native British economy, many would argue, introducing a true market/currency system and leading to the development of Britain's first towns.[19] Scholars call these proto-towns *oppida*, borrowing the term used most often by Roman writers to describe major Gallic and British settlements.[20] The first British *oppida* appear in the middle of the first century BC, guarding river crossings and major land routes. They are relatively small, enclosed by at least one earthwork, and contain a formally planned layout of roads, rectangular timber buildings, and storage facilities. These were joined at the end of the century by huge territorial *oppida*, consisting of complex linear earthworks surrounding vast tracts of land. British *oppida* show clear signs of true urban activity, including centralized kingship, formal cemeteries, and the minting of coins that bear the names of these settlements. It is telling that when the Romans later took over such British *oppida* as *Verlamion* (St. Albans), *Calleva* (Silchester), and *Camulodunon* (Colchester) they continued to use them as the administrative centers of the local tribes.

Caesar and the Britons

The Britons, then, on the eve of Caesar's expeditions, were developing towns, a market economy, and complex chiefdoms (at least in the core Channel Zone). They had also developed two other features which par-

19 Cunliffe, 1995, 68–74.
20 For discussion of the definition and function of *oppida*, see Collis, 1984.

ticularly caught Caesar's attention: impressive military tactics and complex religious practices. The latter, of course, are represented by the Druids, an 'extra-tribal brotherhood' found in Gaul as well as the British Isles.[21] Classical writers describe the Druids as intermediaries between their communities and the gods, performing sacrifices and other religious rites as well as settling legal disputes. Caesar states that the training to become a Druid took as long as 20 years, and that the education was rigorous and required initiates to commit vast amounts of information to memory (Druids usually prohibited writing amongst their own ranks).[22] He also remarked that Druidism originated in Britain and was later brought to Gaul, with those Gallic Druids wishing to continue their education making the trip across the Channel.

Archaeologically the Druids have left few traces in Britain. There has been much excitement over the discovery and analysis of Lindow Man, the well-preserved body of a 2000-year-old Briton found in a Cheshire peat bog in 1984.[23] Apparently the victim of ritual sacrifice, Lindow Man was found with mistletoe pollen in his stomach, recalling the image described by Pliny of Druids harvesting sacred mistletoe with a golden sickle. While there is no explicit evidence of Druidism in Britain, there is plenty of evidence of ritual and worship.[24] Bog bodies like Lindow Man seem to validate Caesar's testimony of human sacrifice in Britain, while skeletons found at the bottom of disused storage pits at Danebury indicate propitiatory burials. More often ornate weapons and jewelry are found in pits and pools, offerings to unknown gods. Only from later written evidence do we hear the names of these gods, though clearly the Iron Age Britons were polytheistic and worshiped a variety of mostly local deities.

According to Caesar the Druids were held in high standing in their communties; in Gaul they were the equal of the warrior caste, and could themselves wield great political power. But it was the combat methods of the British warriors that most intrigued the Roman general.[25] British tribal armies contained infantry, cavalry, and chariot divisions and were capable of fighting both pitched battles and guerrilla warfare. From written descriptions, warrior burials, and depictions on native coinage we have a clear picture of the accouterment of a LPRIA British warrior (see plate 2.2). Caesar was amazed at these Britons' abilities to handle (often in rough terrain) and fight from chariots, though typically the warrior would

---

21 The phrase is Cunliffe's (1995, 105). Standard works on the Druids are Chadwick, 1966; Piggott, 1985; and Green, 1997.

22 Caesar, *The Gallic War*, 6.13–14.

23 See Stead et al., 1986; and Turner and Scaife, 1995.

24 See Ross, 1996; and Wait, 1985.

25 See Caesar, *The Gallic War*, 4.24 and 33.

dismount after discharging missiles and fight on foot. 'Thus,' remarks Caesar, 'they provide the flexible mobility of cavalry and the stability of infantry in battle.'

Caesar had two opportunities to observe such British warriors, during expeditions to the island in the autumn of 55 BC and again in the spring of 54. Not much has changed in our understanding of Caesar's British cam-

Plate 2.2   An artist's reconstruction of an Iron Age British warrior and his wife based upon archaeological finds and the descriptions of Classical authors. (Photo: AKG London/Peter Connolly.)

paigns.[26] During his campaigns in Gaul, Caesar often observed British contingents fighting against him alongside the Gallic armies. The Britons had also given refuge to Belgic nobles who had fled Gaul when their anti-Roman policies failed to persuade their kinsmen. One Gallic noble, a powerful Belgic king named Diviciacus, is credited by Caesar with controlling parts of Gaul *and* Britain 'within living memory.'[27] Then there were the Druids, political agitators in Gaul who would later feed anti-Roman sentiment in Britain. If Britain was, as he claimed, the revered home of their brotherhood, controlling (or wiping out) the British Druids could weaken the Gauls' urge to rebel and eliminate their abominable practice of human sacrifice.

Caesar also had purely political reasons for his British expeditions. As part of the First Triumvirate, Caesar needed new and spectacular military successes to keep pace with his colleagues (especially Pompey) and to keep his name before the people in Rome. By extending the Gallic campaigns to Britain Caesar would also retain his commission – that is, his troops – and would not have to return as a civilian to face his political enemies in Rome.[28] Roman merchants certainly had an interest in Caesar bringing both sides of the Channel under control and establishing new ties with British rulers. Finally, pure ambition and curiosity could have driven the Roman general to the mysterious island that lay at the end of the world.

The first expedition was only minimally successful and was nearly a complete disaster for Caesar.[29] After sending a Gallic noble named Commius to Britain to show British leaders the wisdom of cooperation with Rome, Caesar gathered about 100 ships to transport his 'reconnaissance' force of two legions plus cavalry and auxiliaries. The main force left Boulogne and landed at Deal, while the cavalry was forced by the tide back to Gaul. The Roman infantry at first hesitated before the assembled British cavalry and chariots, but rallied by the courageous standard-bearer of the Tenth Legion they waded ashore, fell into formation, and routed the Britons. Without his cavalry, however, Caesar could not follow up on this initial success. He did receive the submission of several British chiefs, and some hostages, but another disaster struck. A storm prevented another attempt by the Roman cavalry to reach Caesar and severely damaged all of his transport ships in Britain. The Britons attacked his camp, but were beaten back by the legions and a small force of about 30 cavalrymen led by Commius. Caesar demanded twice the number of hostages from the British chiefs, but left for Gaul as soon as his ships were repaired.

---

26   For secondary literature to supplement Caesar's account, see Webster, 1980.

27   Caesar, *The Gallic War*, 2.4.

28   Salway, 1993, 19.

29   The account is in Caesar, *The Gallic War*, 4.20–36.

If the first expedition was a successful reconnaissance with a narrow escape, the second was an attempt at the conquest and submission of central southern Britain.[30] It is this part of Britain that Caesar describes as 'the most civilized,' where 'the way of life [of these Britons] is much the same as that of the Gauls.' He had good information about the settlements and tribal chiefdoms of this area, whereas the rest of the Britons, distant from the Channel Zone, he dismissed as pastoralists who 'live on milk and meat and clothe themselves in animal skins.'[31] This time Caesar assembled more than 800 vessels to carry a force that included five legions and 2,000 cavalry, enough to make good any threats he had made the previous year. But he was also accompanied by a multitude of civilians, including many merchants in private ships who hoped to profit from further Roman conquest.

Carried south by the tides, Caesar was forced to beach at the same site of the previous year's unfortunate landing. This time no enemy army met him on the beach, and he had time to build a fortification on the shore to protect his fleet, which had anchored offshore. Another storm hit, however, damaging many of his ships before he could beach them and forcing him to recall his first detachment. This gave the Britons more time to muster their forces, now a confederacy from various tribes placed under the command of one war leader, Cassivellaunus. Abandoning civil discord, the Britons joined together in a formidable army with which Cassivellaunus was able to directly threaten Caesar's camp. One thrust from the Britons reached the legionary standards, but was repelled with difficulty by the Romans. Cassivellaunus tried several tactics against Caesar, but eventually he dismissed the confederate infantry and retained only his own army – 4,000 charioteers – to harass Caesar's march toward the Thames.

The decisive point in this second expedition was a native dispute which Caesar worked to his advantage. Mandubracius, a young British prince of the Trinovantes, whose father the king had been allegedly killed by Cassivellaunus, had come to Caesar in Gaul as a political exile. Now his kinsmen in the Trinovantes were offering to surrender to Caesar in return for help against Cassivellaunus and the return of Mandubracius as king. Caesar graciously accepted, and soon other minor tribes from southern Britain were also defecting. Caesar chose this time to strike at Cassivellaunus' 'stronghold,' whose whereabouts (now unknown) were betrayed by British defectors. During the siege Cassivellaunus sent word to the four kings of Kent to attack Caesar's beach camp. This attack

---

30   The account of the second expedition is in Caesar, *The Gallic War*, 5.8–23.
31   Caesar, *The Gallic War*, 5.14.

failed, and Caesar's troops took Cassivellaunus' stronghold. The British war leader was forced to surrender. Caesar demanded hostages from the British chiefs and an annual tribute to be paid to the Roman state. He ordered Cassivellaunus not to harm the Trinovantes – the first of several British tribes to become a protectorate of Rome – and then returned to Gaul.

British Tribes and the Rise of the Catuvellauni

While Caesar's British expeditions had hardly been a thorough military conquest, their results for the Britons were manifold. We have already seen how the conquest of Gaul shifted trade patterns so that the majority of Mediterranean goods no longer traveled the Atlantic route but rather came overland to northern Gaul and then across the Channel to south-eastern Britain. While this strengthened pre-existent political and economic ties between Britons and Gauls in the Channel Zone, it also may have led to communities of Roman merchants residing long-term in Britain. The minting of multiple denominations of coins by British tribes in this area indicates an emulation of the Roman market system operating in Gaul. These developments resulted in a shift of trading patterns within Britain, with raw materials and slaves being taken to southeastern Britain to be exchanged for wine and other Roman luxuries. Archaeologists have expressed this with a simple Core–Periphery model (see map), and we may now use these terms to describe areas of LPRIA Britain between the invasions of Caesar and Claudius.

Accompanying these economic developments were even greater changes in the socio-political structure of Britain. The cessation of hill-fort construction and the rise of *oppida* in the Core Zone in the middle of the first century BC signaled the centralizing of government which we can now discern in the literary and numismatic record. Through archaeological finds we can also see some of these trends filtering into tribes of the Periphery, while other changes were occurring in the now solidifying peoples of the Outer Zone whose names are finally appearing in historical sources.

Caesar considered the peoples of Kent (*Cantium*), sometimes called the Cantiaci, to be the most civilized Britons, and at the time of his second expedition they were ruled by four kings or possibly magistrates.[32] To their west were tribes that had come under Belgic political and cultural influence, most notably the Atrebates, the Belgae, and the Regni. Just

32   Salway, 1993, 33.

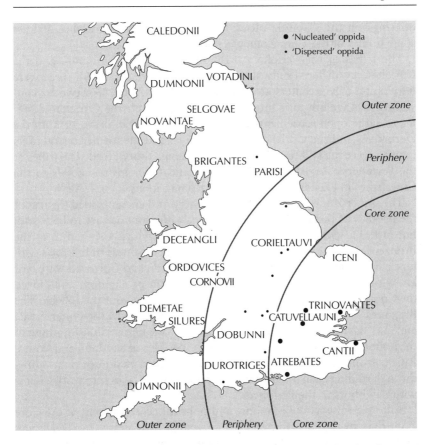

Map 2.1 Political map of Britain in the Late Pre-Roman Iron Age, showing the names of known tribes and major settlements, and illustrating the Core–Periphery model.

north of the Thames were two powerful Core tribes which eventually merged into one kingdom – the Catuvellauni and the Trinovantes – and the Iceni, a bit isolated in Norfolk but nonetheless influenced by their more powerful neighbors. While these peoples of the Core Zone shared many similarities both with each other and their Gallic neighbors across the Channel, a few traits made them distinct from their fellow Britons. Most minted their own coins, which bore the name of their king and/or their urban center. Some, like the Trinovantes, could increase their power and prestige in Britain by claiming the protection of Rome. Two kings, Tincommius of the Atrebates and Dubnovellaunus of Kent, appeared before Augustus in Rome as suppliants and others traveled to Rome to make offerings on the Capitol.[33] Rich burials and hoards show that at least some nobles of the Core Zone were adopting a Roman lifestyle.

The tribes of the Periphery – the Durotriges, the Dobunni, and the Corieltauvi – differed only slightly from the Core tribes. All three were developing urban centers at the end of the LPRIA, the first two by converting massive hill-forts into enclosed *oppida* while the Corieltauvi preferred large open settlements like Dragonby and Old Sleaford. Both the Durotriges and the Corieltauvi struck coins, and the former operated its mint to serve the still functioning port at Hengistbury Head. The tribes of the Periphery thrived by trading slaves and other insular goods to the Core tribes in exchange for coins and Roman items.

The Outer Zone lay beyond the Periphery and encompassed the rest of the peoples of Britain. Here neither *oppida* nor coin use are to be found, but rather a variety of cultural traits many of which survived from the Bronze Age. Most of these peoples possessed a multitude of hill-forts with no clear political center. The Dumnonii of Devon and Cornwall were best known to Classical authors because of their tin production, and indeed their port of Mount Batten continued in use throughout the LPRIA. The Brigantes of northern England were the largest tribe of the Outer Zone, and may have been a confederacy of peoples. We know almost nothing of the political structure and economy of the peoples of Scotland and Wales. Rulers from all these areas, however, tended to maintain their status through raiding each other's territory and trading slaves for prestige items with neighbors in the Periphery.

So powerful was the economy and political centralization of the Core Zone that, by the early first century AD, a single British state was emerging under the leadership of the Catuvellauni. The appearance in Essex *c.*15 BC of the coinage of the Catuvellaunian king Tasciovanus may signal their merger with the Trinovantes, while the suppliant kings recorded in the *Res Gestae* were likely refugees from Catuvellaunian expansion. The hegemony of the Catuvellauni was completed by a prince of the house of Tasciovanus named Cunobelinus, Shakespeare's Cymbeline. His coinage appears in AD 7 at Colchester, the new capital of the consolidated kingdom, and soon afterwards he is minting coins at St. Albans as well.[34] A century later Suetonius described him as *rex Britanniarum*, 'King of the Britons.'[35]

Most scholars have sought an economic explanation for the rise of the Catuvellauni.[36] According to the leading theory, the Catuvellauni came to

---

33   Augustus, *Res Gestae*, 32; Strabo, 4.5.3.
34   Salway, 1993, 41.
35   Suetonius, *Lives of the Caesars*, 4.44.
36   See, for example, Cunliffe, 1995, 73; and Salway, 1993, 41–4.

possess a virtual monopoly on trade with Roman Gaul following their merger with the Trinovantes. Archaeologically this is noticeable when fewer and fewer Roman goods enter Britain through Hengistbury Head, while in the written sources we have the diplomatic favors granted the Trinovantes by Caesar in 54 BC. Strabo mentions both prestige items – gold, slaves, hunting dogs – and military supplies – grain, cattle, iron – imported from Britain. When Cunobelinus came to control most of the southeast coast of Britain, including the Thames estuary, he was in a position to supply the vast Roman army in Gaul with British goods, as well as the nobility of several British tribes with the Roman luxury items with which they maintained their high status. It is no coincidence that, when the Roman legions returned to Britain in AD 43, they captured Colchester and made it the capital of their new province.

In conclusion, a few trends can be deduced from the available evidence and recent scholarly literature for LPRIA Britain:

1   We do not know what Iron Age Britons called themselves. Greek writers usually employed the term Βρεττανος, from whence Latin writers developed *Britannus*. From Caesar and native coinage we know that LPRIA rulers at least employed tribal terms.

2   The Britons maintained close contacts with continental Europeans, especially the inhabitants of Gaul, from the Stone Age to the Roman occupation. These contacts have resulted in important continental influences on the language and culture of the Britons.

3   The popular theory of Celtic invaders from the continent has recently fallen out of favor among scholars, especially archaeologists. It is now believed that the presence of Celtic languages in Britain, as well as Hallstatt and La Tène material cultures, can be explained through trading contacts and emulation among élite groups.

4   In many parts of Iron Age Britain the hillfort emerged as an impressive place of refuge and royal power. By the end of this period, however, centralizing tendencies led to the development of proto-towns called *oppida*. These humble beginnings of urbanization in Britain were tied closely to economic and political developments spurred on by Roman expansion into Gaul.

5   Political and economic ties between eastern Britain and northern Gaul intensified during Caesar's Gallic campaigns and played an important role in his decision to come to Britain. The most dramatic results of Caesar's British expeditions were economic rather than military, for they heightened the desire of many British elites for Roman goods, especially wine. A few British chieftains were able to capitalize on this new consumer demand to raise their personal status and expand their kingdoms. Ultimately the Catuvellauni created a monopoly in this market and formed the first British state.

6 Archaeologists have recently argued against a monolithic British culture, as might be inferred from Classical accounts, and opted instead to
   view Iron Age Britain as consisting of changing cultural zones or regions. Most important, according to this theory, is the cultural dichotomy
   between southeastern Britain, with its many ties to Gaul and Roman
   trade, and the rest of Britain.

From these trends one can see the emphasis shifting from a static and
monolithic view of the ancient 'Celtic' Britons to the diversity and muta-
bility of Iron Age culture(s) in Britain. In this shifting paradigm, however,
let us not overlook the enormous energy, creativity, and innovative nature of these Iron Age Britons. From the complexity of the stone architecture in the Orkneys to the intricate details of the gold jewelry in southern
Britain, and from the amazing stunts of the chariot fighters to the esoteric
learning of the Druids, these Britons living at the western edge of the
world captured the attention of faraway Greeks and Romans just as they
continue to capture the attention of modern museum-goers and book-
buyers. The scholarly community has recently chosen to look at broader
socio-economic processes and patterns, and at the farmers and peasants
whose simpler duties supported the more easily observable culture of the
military and religious élites. Hopefully this will prove an enhancement
rather than a detriment to popular interest in the Britons.

3
The Roman Period

There has been no shortage of books on Roman Britain. Both good scholarly surveys[1] and attractive 'coffee-table' books have proliferated as publishers continue to tap into the subject's commercial potential. Many modern Britons, seemingly, long for the days when their island was part of a great Mediterranean empire. Roman achievement in art, architecture, and engineering can still be glimpsed in the ruins which dot the British landscape and in many remarkable museum collections. While less spectacular than the Roman structures of France and the Mediterranean lands, Britain still possesses one monument – Hadrian's Wall – which has stood for centuries as the most recognizable symbol of Roman military accomplishment and the concrete delineation between *cives* and barbarians.

This chapter will not be yet another survey of the Romans in Britain. Rather, it will focus on the native population during the years of Roman rule. In the initial phase of Roman conquest, some Britons cooperated with the Romans while others resisted. As rebellion subsided, Romanization accelerated.[2] Yet even after 212, when all provincials were made Roman citizens by decree of the emperor Caracalla, the majority of Britons continued native practices of farming, husbandry, religion, art, and countless other areas of their culture which had been slowly evolving since the Bronze Age. Given this, and the fact that many Britons in Cornwall, Wales, and Scotland never had any substantial contact with Roman ways, it is hardly surprising that scholars once spoke of a 'Celtic Renaissance' in the post-Roman period. While this concept is now seen as a bit simplistic, it is hardly radical, given the tenor of current research, to state that native

---

1 See especially Frere, 1987; Todd, 1981; Wacher, 1978; Salway, 1981; Salway, 1993; and Millet, 1995.
2 Millet, 1990, surveys the successes of Romanization.

British culture played a far greater role in Roman Britain than our 'text-book image' of the period has allowed.

The Claudian Conquest

We have seen that, on the eve of the Roman conquest, both urbanization and state formation were building in central southern Britain, an area then under Catuvellaunian hegemony. Several tribes in this region were also minting their own coins and, due to the stimulus of Roman traders, moving toward a market economy. A 'developed' British state so close to their still rebellious Gallic provinces may have legitimately concerned Roman authorities. Yet many scholars believe that the Romans considered Britain an already half-conquered possession in the years between the expeditions of Caesar and Claudius. The Roman authors are ambivalent on this issue,[3] though a general anticipation of full conquest during the principate of Augustus is neatly expressed in a contemporary ode by Horace:

> May you [the goddess of Fortune] preserve our Caesar soon to go against the Britons, furthest of earth's peoples.[4]

Augustus contemplated a British campaign that would have made him even more convincing as Caesar's heir, but was distracted by Marc Antony and other matters. Tiberius contented himself with continuing the diplomatic relations with British rulers which we saw in Augustus' reception of the British princes described in his *Res Gestae*. Gaius 'Caligula' also received a suppliant British prince in AD 40. Adminius, who had been banished from Britain by his father Cunobelinus, submitted himself to Caligula in Gaul along with a few of his followers. In an infamous incident, a triumphant Caligula then ordered his soldiers to collect seashells from the beach as 'the spoils from the Ocean owed to the Capitol and Palatine' for the conquest of Britain.[5]

But it was Claudius who would be able to celebrate a real conquest of the island. There are several reasons why this particular emperor would have undertaken such a venture.[6] Claudius survived a senatorial coup in AD 42 (just a year after the Praetorian Guard assassinated his predecessor)

---

3   Ireland, 1996, 37–43, has conveniently collected the references to Britain.
4   Horace, *Odes* 1.35.29f (*c.* 26 BC, trans. Ireland).
5   The incident is described in Suetonius, *Caligula*, 44 and 46; and Dio Cassius 59.25.1–3.
6   Discussed in Salway, 1993, 49–54; and Webster, 1993, 84–5. The pertinent Roman sources are collected in Ireland, 1996, 44–50.

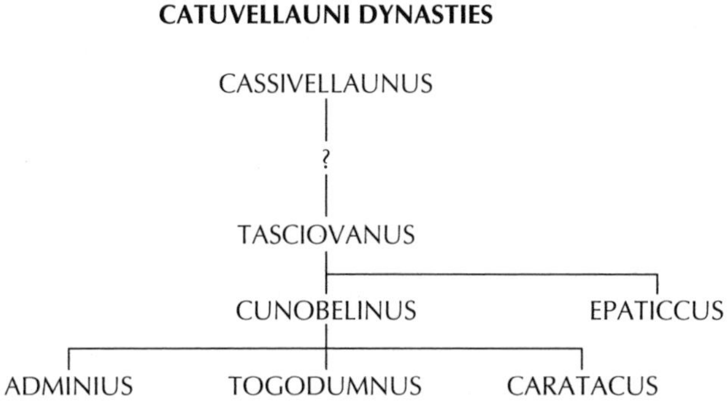

CATUVELLAUNI DYNASTIES

CASSIVELLAUNUS
|
?
|
TASCIOVANUS
|
CUNOBELINUS   EPATICCUS
|
ADMINIUS   TOGODUMNUS   CARATACUS

Figure 3.1   The Catuvellaunian kings of the Late Pre-Roman Iron Age, featuring the family of Cunobelinus.

and realized the need to gain the loyalty and respect of the army. This was best achieved by a dramatic military victory and the rewarding of booty to the soldiers. Caligula had spent extravagantly, and Claudius looked for a conquest that could create new markets and provide needed natural resources and slaves. Iron and lead were certainly two natural resources that Rome expected to gain from bringing Britain into the empire.

The most compelling reason, however, may be a recent shift in British politics with the rise of anti-Roman forces in the southeast. This began during the early years of Cunobelinus' reign and accelerated after the Catuvellaunian king's death. In the last decade of the first century BC, the Roman ally Tincommius, King of the Atrebates, was expelled by a cousin of Cunobelinus named Epillus. After reigning for a short while at Calleva (Silchester), Epillus moved into east Kent and expelled another pro-Roman ruler, Dubnovellaunos (both Tincommius and Dubnovellaunos appeared before Augustus in Rome as suppliants).[7]

Epillus' successor among the Atrebates, Verica, became an ally of Rome and thus reestablished a brief equilibrium between pro- and anti-Roman forces in the south. Around AD 10 this was upset by Epaticcus, a brother of Cunobelinus, who seized control among the Atrebates, minting coins from Calleva that have been found throughout the southeast. Verica was able to regain his throne and expel the usurper by the year 37. Two years later, however, Adminius, who was then ruling in east Kent, was expelled by his father and sought help from Rome. Whether or not this signaled a shift in the aged Cunobelinus' attitude toward Rome, it became clear with

7   Webster, 1980, 65.

the great king's death (between AD 40 and 43) that the anti-Roman forces among the Catuvellauni held the greatest power. Two of his sons, Togodumnus and Caratacus, joined forces to extend Catuvellaunian power at the expense of pro-Roman rulers. While the elder brother consolidated his power north of the Thames (including a western extension into Dobunnic territory), Caratacus, with the assistance of western Britons like the Durotriges, deposed Verica and seized control of the lands of the Atrebates and the Cantiaci.

While the Catuvellauni demanded from Rome the return of the political refugees, Verica is said to have encouraged Claudius to invade the island. The emperor made his move in AD 43, commissioning the senator Aulus Plautius (the Plautii had close ties to the Imperial family) to lead an invasion force of four legions plus an equal number of auxiliaries, probably 40,000 men in all (and including two future emperors).[8] Of course, we don't have comparable information about the British forces that awaited the Roman landing in Kent. A long delay by the Romans (Dio says the soldiers were reluctant to cross the Channel) caused the British levies to disperse.

After some cajoling from Narcissus, Claudius' Secretary of State, the Romans disembarked from Boulogne in three divisions. Though details are lacking, the Roman landing was later commemorated at Richborough (see plate 3.1), where a small harbor guarded the newly created Wansum channel that took small ships into the Thames Estuary. It is possible that part of the Roman forces landed further south, in Bosham Harbor, where the Roman ally Cogidubnus would later support the southwestern advance of Vespasian. Caratacus and Togodumnus reassembled their personal retinues to face Plautius, the brothers trying to slow down the Roman advance to the Medway River while their own allies returned. Unfortunately one ally, a segment of the Dobunni that had been subject to the Catuvellauni, offered their submission to Rome.

As the Romans marched up the Pilgrims Way the Britons assembled rather casually along the west bank of the Medway, believing that the Romans could not make a crossing without a bridge. Dio writes that the battle lasted two days, and began with surprise attacks from the Romans. Plautius' first move was to send a group of Batavians swimming across the river downstream, where they could sneak up on the Britons and maim their chariot horses. In the ensuing chaos, Vespasian and his brother Sabinus crossed the river upstream with two legions and established a bridgehead. The Britons rushed up to attack, but the Flavian brothers

---

8   The only substantial account of the invasion is that of Dio Cassius (60.19–23), with a few additional remarks supplied by Suetonius. The most detailed military discussion is in Webster, 1993.

Plate 3.1   The still standing walls of the Roman fort at Richborough, landing place for the Claudian invasion of Britain. In the foreground is the base of the triumphal arch erected in memory of Claudius' conquest. (Photo: Christopher A. Snyder.)

held firm and allowed the rest of the Roman army to cross. The main battle took place the next day and was fierce, with the Roman legionaries pushing their wedge-shaped columns into the British ranks. It was indecisive until the Roman commander Hosidius Geta broke through and encircled the Britons. Many of the native troops were slaughtered, but Caratacus and Togodumnus managed to extricate themselves and fled toward the Thames.

Plautius chased after the retreating Britons, who had found a safe spot to cross the Thames. Once again Plautius first sent the Batavians swimming across, while the main body found (or constructed) a bridge upstream, possibly near Westminster. Their objective was to march on the Catuvellaunian *oppidum* Camulodunum. Togodumnus seems to have died (from injuries suffered at the Medway?) at this point, forcing his brother to rally the Britons for a desperate defense. Caratacus attacked the Romans after their crossing, but was once again forced to withdraw. But instead of pursuing the Britons, Plautius paused near London and sent word to the emperor that his presence was 'needed' to capture Camulodunum. This prearranged move caused a six-week delay, allowing Caratacus and his family to escape to the west, though Plautius may have dispatched Vespasian in the meantime to campaign against the Durotriges in the southwest.

Claudius traveled to Britain accompanied by a section of the Praetorian Guard and war elephants. Suetonius states bluntly, 'he received a part of the island without a single battle or any bloodshed.'[9] Dio, however, writes that Claudius defeated Britons who had gathered to defend Camulodunum (Caratacus was not amongst them), 'won over numerous tribes,' and was saluted Imperator on several occasions. In 16 days Claudius received five salutations and received the submission of 11 British rulers before returning to Rome where the Senate awarded him a triumph and the title Britannicus. The capital of the great Cunobelinus now became the capital of Rome's newest province, and Aulus Plautius its first governor.

British Client Kings

While Caratacus was rallying support in western Britain, it is interesting to see the political moves of the other powerful British rulers. Cartimandua (her name means 'sleek filly'), queen of the Brigantes, made an early alliance with Rome. Along with a diplomatic marriage to Venutius, ruler of a tribe to the north, the alliance with Rome helped Cartimandua consolidate power in northern Britain. It worked both to her advantage and that of Rome to have a dependable ruler with hegemony over the diverse northern tribes, and Cartimandua did indeed remain loyal to Rome through several subsequent trials. The most threatening of these came when she took as her lover Venutius' armor-bearer, Vellocatus.[10] Roman troops narrowly prevented Venutius from deposing his queen, though in 69 he was successful in doing so and openly rebelled against Rome.

It is not clear what happened to Cartimandua after this incident (though we know Venutius was eventually defeated), nor is it exactly clear how she came to power in the first place. Tacitus says she exercised great power over the Brigantes 'by virtue of her noble birth,' but we do not know whether she came to the throne with Roman help or prior to the Claudian invasion. The alliance with Rome brought her 'wealth and the self-indulgence of success,' according to Tacitus, and both the alliance and her scandalous behavior seems to have cost her the allegiance of the Brigantes.

Another Roman ally from this period whom we have some information about is Prasutagus, king of the Iceni in East Anglia. The king of the Iceni at the time of the Claudian conquest may have been one Antedios, whose

---

9   Suetonius, *Claudius*, 17.
10   Tacitus narrates these events in *Annals*, 12.40, and *Histories*, 3.45.

name is found on coins of the Iceni and the Dobunni.[11] Of Cunobelinus' generation, Antedios was likely deposed by Rome when the Iceni rose in rebellion in AD 47. They and other friendly tribes had been allowed by Plautius to retain their arms after the conquest, but in that year the new governor Ostorius Scapula reversed policy and tried to disarm the Iceni. The outraged Iceni and their allies put up a stiff fight, but the revolt was suppressed by Scapula's auxiliary troops.[12]

The details are unclear, but it seems that at this point Prasutagus came to power. He acquired a reputation for great wealth. If he minted coins, however, none have been found. This fact, and the terms of his will (see below), suggest that Prasutagus was placed on the throne by Rome and kept under tight control.

The third of the known client kings is the controversial figure Cogidumnus, or Cogidubnus as he came to be known. His origins are, like those of Cartimandua and Prasutagus, not easy to ascertain. In the region that he came to dominate, the lands of the Atrebates and the Regni, there had been many kings of which Verica was the most powerful in the pre-conquest period. Presumably Verica regained his kingdom in 43, but since there is no more record of him he may have either died soon after or been supplanted by another ruler. In any case, his lands and other 'civitates were assigned to Cogidubnus as king' after they had been suppressed by Plautius' southern forces.[13] It is indeed possible that Cogidubnus was Verica's son.[14]

The unusual status of Cogidubnus is further complicated by epigraphic evidence. An inscription from Chichester provides startling evidence about this man:

> [This temple is dedicated] on the authority of Tiberius Claudius Cogidubnus, Great King (rex magnus) in Britain.[15]

That Cogidubnus was rex magnus simply verifies Tacitus' information that he was given control over vast lands; a stature matched by the grand villa of Fishbourne which he came to inhabit. But even more remarkable is his use of the Roman tria nomina, a proclamation of Roman citizenship. That he obtained citizenship from Claudius seems likely, given that he had adopted the emperor's name, but it may rather have come later from Nero.[16] In any event, here we have clear evidence of a British king

11   Birley, 1980, 24–5.
12   Tacitus, Annals, 12.31.
13   Tacitus, Agricola, 14.
14   Braund, 1984, 39–40.
15   RIB 1.91 (trans. Ireland). For discussion, see Birley, 1980.
16   Braund, 1984, 40.

given land and citizenship by Rome, adopting a Roman lifestyle, but ruling as a semi-autonomous monarch on the fringe of the Roman province. Can we expect that other native monarchs who chose friendship with Rome, but whose names have not survived, received similar treatment?

Caratacus

What we do know is that this was not an option considered by Caratacus. The British king's retreat westward was actually a good strategic move, for by winning the allegiance of western Britons he was able to prevent Plautius' attempt at creating client kingdoms along the Severn valley.[17] But Plautius was well prepared to deal with Britons who were not willing to come to peaceful terms with Rome. While waiting for Claudius' arrival, he had dispatched Vespasian to begin a series of campaigns in the southwest. From Suetonius and Tacitus we learn that Vespasian commanded the *Legio II Augusta*, fought 30 battles, overcame two hostile tribes (likely the Durotriges and part of the Dobunni), and took more than 20 *oppida* in addition to the Isle of Wight.[18] For *oppida* we should read hill-fort, and excavations have revealed that such hill-forts as South Cadbury, Maiden Castle (see plate 3.1), and Hod Hill fell to Vespasian or else in the campaigns of 48 and 61.

In the winter of 47 Aulus Plautius returned to Rome and was replaced by Publius Ostorius Scapula. The new military governor of Britain prepared for campaigning in Wales by disarming the Britons east of the Trent and Severn rivers. This, as we have seen, included the Iceni, who resisted vigorously before being suppressed by Roman auxiliaries (probably within one of their own hillforts). Scapula then felt secure enough to begin campaigning westward, first and successfully against the Deceangli in Cheshire, though a Brigantian disturbance forced him to return south in 48.[19] It was at this time, Tacitus tells us, that a Roman veteran colony was founded at Camulodunum, while the legion stationed there – the XX – was moved to Kingsholm, on the Welsh front, where it could be deployed against Caratacus.

The leader of the British resistance had won the trust of the Silures, whose 'innate ferocity' was unleashed against the Romans in southeast Wales. However, while Scapula aimed his attack against Caratacus in

---

17 Webster, 1993, 115.
18 Suetonius, *Vespasian*, 4.
19 Scapula's western campaigns are narrated in Tacitus, *Annals*, 12.31–9.

Plate 3.2   The ramparts of Maiden Castle, a massive Iron Age hill-fort taken by the Romans during their early years of campaigning against the Durotriges. (© Crown copyright. NMR.)

Silurian territory, Tacitus tells us that the British prince quickly left his southern stronghold and drew the Romans into the land of the Ordovices. Here not only did his numbers increase, but more important, he had the advantage of a rough terrain for his last stand. Scapula's two legions were forced to maneuver a narrow pass and face the British forces that were protected by hills, stone ramparts, and a river 'with a precarious crossing.'[20] The Romans, however, made the crossing, dismantled the rampart (under heavy missile fire), and pushed the Britons uphill. At close quarters the Britons, lacking sufficient armor, were cut down. Caratacus' wife, daughter, and brothers surrendered, but the prince himself escaped.

20   The most extensive analysis of the battle is Webster, 1981, 28–32.

The next events in the dramatic life of Caratacus are of theatrical pro-
portions. After a devastating defeat, the deflated prince fled to the north,
where he sought the protection of the Brigantes in 51. Since, however, as
Tacitus says 'there is no security in misfortune,' Caratacus was arrested
by Queen Cartimandua, whom he had tried to persuade to join the resistance. Whether out of loyalty to Rome, tribal rivalry, or simply to protect
her own power and possessions, Cartimandua seemingly deceived
Caratacus, bound him in chains, and turned him over to Roman authorities.

Caratacus was brought to Rome, preceded by his reputation, which
had left many curious to see the guerrilla leader. Moving through the
throngs of spectators in the capital, Caratacus allegedly marveled at the
Roman architecture and uttered, rhetorically, 'When you have all this,
why do you envy us our poor hovels?'[21] As the prince and his family
approached the emperor and his Praetorian troops, gold torcs, ornamen-
tal bosses, and other captured treasures were displayed to the public. Most
of the British captives immediately pleaded for their lives, but Caratacus
is said to have approached Claudius with silent dignity, then delivered the
following speech:

> 'If I had been as moderate in success as my noble birth and rank are great, I
> should have entered this city as a friend rather than as a captive . . . My
> present lot is as much a source of glory to you as it is degrading to myself. I
> had horses, men, arms, wealth; what wonder then if I regret their loss. If
> you wish to rule the world, does it follow that everyone welcomes servi-
> tude? If I were being dragged before you as one who had surrendered at the
> outset, neither my own downfall nor your glory would have become fa-
> mous: oblivion would have been the consequence of my punishment. If on
> the other hand you spare my life, I shall always be a memorial to your
> clemency.'[22]

These words fit well with Tacitus' rhetoric and republicanism. Yet they
also are necessary to display Claudius' *clementia*, and given that this
was a very public display it is unlikely that Tacitus simply invented the
speech. Caratacus, with his aristocratic pride and bearing, appears on
the stage of history as the first Briton whom we can know in a significant way. Both Claudius and Tacitus required him to play the role of
'noble savage,' yet it is the nobility of Caratacus that has so captured the
modern observer.

---

21   Dio Cassius, 60.33.
22   Tacitus, *Annals*, 12.37 (trans. Ireland).

Boudica

While Claudius and the citizens of Rome were apparently celebrating, with the capture of Caratacus, the final stage of the conquest of Britain, events in Britain would prove this to be premature. The Silures, hearing a rumor that the Romans planned on exterminating them or else shipping them off to Gaul, reinvigorated their attacks and began coaxing neighboring tribes into rebellion. Scapula suffered serious losses to his forces, then died prematurely in Britain in 52. Aulus Didius, the new governor, faced in addition to the hostilities of the Welsh tribes the rebellion of Venutius against Cartimandua. Didius went to Cartimandua's aid and held his ground in southern Wales, founding a few new forts. But with the death of Claudius and accession of Nero in 54, Rome halted expansion in Britain and focused instead on support of the new cities in the province, with the new emperor and his tutor Seneca themselves investing the capital.

Of these new cities Colchester received the most attention, for it served as both provincial capital and *colonia*. When Rome decided to turn Colchester into a colony for army veterans, many of the Trinovantes were evicted from their farms and their lands were seized by the government. The veterans of Colchester treated their new British neighbors badly – in fact as slaves, according to Tacitus – and some of the Trinovantian nobles were forced to take out loans to pay for the grandiose temple of Claudius being built in the city.[23] Such loans were made at extravagant interest rates, and the British chiefs, who also had to pay heavy taxes to Rome, were perplexed at the capitalistic machinations (Claudius had dispensed money as gifts rather than loans) and outraged by the government's behavior.

But the outrage that truly united Britons against Roman rule occurred after the death of Prasutagus in AD 60.[24] The Icenian king and ally of Rome left, in his will, half his lands to his young daughters and half to Nero. The emperor, however, declared that the whole kingdom belonged to Rome, standard imperial practice after the death of a client king. The imperial procurator, Catus Decianus, badly mismanaged the affair, sending a gang of veterans and slaves to seize Icenian lands and confiscate all royal property. These men grabbed the estates of the Icenian nobles and treated them like slaves. When the widowed queen Boudica resisted, she was publicly stripped and flogged by the procurator's slaves while her two daughters were raped.

---

23 Tacitus, *Annals*, 14.31. Tacitus says that the Britons saw the new temple as 'a stronghold of eternal tyranny.'
24 Our information for the Boudican revolt comes from Tacitus, *Annals*, 14.29–39; idem, *Agricola*, 5.15–16; and Dio Cassius 62.1–12.

The enraged Britons held a council, with the disgruntled Trinovantes joining the disenfranchised Iceni, and they chose Boudica as their leader. Dio Cassius gives us a memorable description of the warrior queen:

> In stature she was very tall, in appearance most terrifying, in the glance of her eye most fierce, and her voice was harsh; a great mass of bright red hair fell to her hips; around her neck was a great twisted golden torc; and she wore a tunic of divers colors over which a thick mantle was fastened with a brooch. She waved a massive spear to strike fear into all who watched her.[25]

Boudica (Boudīcā, though Tacitus spells it Boudicca) is a feminization of a common Celtic word for 'victory,' thus making the queen's name the Brittonic equivalent of Victoria (see plate 3.3). Though she became the undisputed leader of the British rebellion, whether she would have succeeded her husband as ruler of the Iceni or whether she 'had greatness thrust upon her' by the events may never be determined. What is clear, however, is that by publicly humiliating the queen and her daughters the Romans thought to destroy the authority of the royal house of the Iceni. They saw the queen and her daughters as simply the spoils of war, an attitude that would cost the Romans many lives and nearly the entire province.

In the year of Prasutagus' death the new governor of Britain, a seasoned military man named Caius Suetonius Paullinus, had begun a second season of campaigning in Wales. The expedition of AD 60 was aimed at wiping out the Druid sanctuary on the island of Mona, modern Anglesey. Not only were the Druids stirring up rebellious sentiment there, but they were also harboring dissidents on the remote isle.[26] Defended by a motley crew of warriors, praying Druids, and shrieking priestesses, Mona eventually fell to Paullinus' troops, who burnt the sanctuary to the ground. With Paullinus far away and occupied, Boudica chose this as the moment for rebellion.

The first target was the hated veterans colony at Colchester. As soon as Paullinus heard of the uprising, he dispatched the IX Legion to deal with the situation. But by the time that the legion was regrouped from its various posts, Boudica's army had already taken possession of Colchester. The 200 or so veterans stationed at Colchester could not keep the elated Britons from marching through the town and destroying everything in their path. The frightened citizenry retreated within the massive walls of the Temple of Claudius, hoping to hold off the rebels until the IX Legion could arrive.

---

25 Dio Cassius 62.2.
26 Jane Webster (*British Archaeology*, 39) suggests that the Druids were 'prophets of rebellion' and as such were more dangerous than Pliny and Tacitus would admit.

Plate 3.3   Queen Boudica (here 'Boadicea'), recast by the Victorians as a symbol of the British Empire, rides her war chariot on the banks of the Thames near Westminster. (Bridgeman Art Library, London.)

Boudica had not overlooked strategy in her vengeance. On the road approaching Colchester, she had stationed troops waiting in the woods to ambush the legion. The Roman troops were caught completely off guard. The entire infantry was slaughtered by the Britons, with only a handful of their cavalry escaping alive back to their fort. Meanwhile, Boudica's frenzied warriors had completely destroyed the temple and murdered the remaining citizens. Over 2,000 Romans lost their lives in the first flames of the British resistance.

Paullinus raced back with his cavalry as soon as he could. But by this time Colchester had already been taken, and Boudica's scattered forces were busy pillaging the pro-Roman settlements in the surrounding countryside. Therefore he headed for the next likely target, the new commercial center of Londinium. London had been the site of a small British settlement before the invasion. But because of its location on the Thames, the Romans had begun to turn it into the major commercial and transportation center in the south. On the riverbanks were a crowd of houses, shops, and military supply depots; but as yet there were no defensive walls or army settlements. Paullinus surveyed the situation there, and it was obvious that the only option was to evacuate the city and wait for the rest of his army to return from Wales.

Some of the Roman residents and merchants of London joined Paullinus' escort as it hastily pulled out of the doomed city. Remarkably, the majority of the citizens stayed put, in disbelief of the seriousness of the revolt. Defenseless Londoners stood helplessly in their streets and homes as Boudica's avenging horde swept across the city. The awesome destruction unleashed upon London by Boudica's host has left the city with scars that can still be seen today. Detached skulls found in the Roman stream-bed of the Walbrook may represent some of Boudica's victims.[27] About 20 feet below the city's surface lies more convincing evidence: a thick layer of ash and blackened Neronian pottery, the remains of buildings consumed by Boudica's fires.[28]

Boudica pursued the Roman general as he retreated, but on the path between them lay the Roman *municipium* of Verulamium. Though inhabited mostly by native Britons, the citizens of Verulamium had been staunchly pro-Roman and belonged to the Catuvellauni, rivals of the Iceni. This was all that was needed for the rebels to make Verulamium the third city to fall victim to their swords. The rebellion had now claimed the lives of as many as 80,000 people. The euphoric Britons then made a tactical mistake. Paullinus lead Boudica's host into a clearing which was flanked on either side by high ground, and which tapered as it came nearer to the road.[29] This meant that the massive army would come at the Roman ranks as if they were passing through a funnel. To make things worse, the Britons had brought their families to the battle loaded in huge carts and wagons. These wagons, laden with supplies and civilians, were arranged in a semicircle behind the army, creating a third wall and cutting off any possibility of retreat.

Retreat, of course, was not in the mind of the confident queen. The total destruction of the IX Legion, Colchester, London, and St. Albans would have created expectations of absolute victory in the hearts and minds of the rebels. There are two accounts of the preliminary activities. Tacitus depicts Boudica in a war chariot, accompanied by her two daughters, riding up and down the ranks exhorting each clan to avenge the wrongs done to her family and her people.[30] Dio attributes to the queen

---

27   Hall and Merrifield, 1986, 6–7.
28   Webster, 1978, 120–1.
29   The exact location is not known, though estimates place it along Watling Street between St. Albans and Mancetter. The most detailed analysis of the battle is in Webster, 1978.
30   Tacitus, *Annals*, 14.35.

an even longer battle speech, followed by a divination in which Boudica releases a wild hare from beneath her cloak, in hopes that it will run to the side of the victor.[31] It is perceived favorably, and Boudica gives thanks to a goddess named Andraste, who will grant the Britons victory over the Romans, whom she/Dio characterizes as effeminate 'slaves to a lyre-player – and a bad one at that'!

The battle commences with the British army rushing forward in a tremendous and terrifying wave. But the disciplined Roman ranks held their positions and cut down the Britons. In their retreat the Britons were trapped against their own supply wagons, women and children meeting the same violent deaths as the warriors. Even the oxen that had pulled the wagons were slaughtered by the legions. Most of the estimated 100,000 Britons who had come to the battle were slaughtered by the Roman army that day; less than 1,000 Roman soldiers perished.[32] On the fate of Boudica herself we have conflicting accounts. Tacitus states that Boudica took poison, seemingly to avoid falling into the hands of the Romans. Dio says simply that the queen fell sick and died after the battle, with her mourners giving her a lavish funeral.

Paullinus, however, was not satisfied with simply chasing down the few rebels that had escaped. Instead, he began a ferocious campaign of extermination in the territories of the rebel tribes and adjacent lands. Backed by reinforcements from Germany and most of the provincial army, Paullinus marched through southeastern Britain burning all farms and crops in his path, creating famine conditions which led to the deaths of untold numbers of Britons. At South Cadbury and Thetford excavations have revealed uncovered bodies, weapons, and signs of destruction that may be attributed to Paullinus' campaign. So terrible was the revenge he enacted that the new Roman procurator, Julius Classicianus, asked the emperor to have Paullinus replaced.

Military Expansion and Romanization

Our picture of Britain in the second half of the first century is colored overwhelmingly by the writings of Tacitus. The great historian describes the governors who replaced Paullinus as lazy men whose vices grew with their military inactivity. This description was required to contrast their characters with that of his father-in-law, Gnaeus Julius Agricola, who

31 Dio Cassius 62.6.
32 Dio likely exaggerated the size of the armies (he gives the Britons 230,000 warriors), Tacitus the number of casualties (80,000 Britons to 400 Romans).

served as a military tribune in Britain under Paullinus and returned as provincial governor in AD 77 or 78. Tacitus' biography of Agricola, with its laudatory descriptions of Agricola's military accomplishments, tends to overshadow his predecessors' victories in Wales and northern Britain, which included the establishment of the legionary fortress at York and the final defeat of the Brigantian rebel Venutius.

Nevertheless, the energetic Agricola went into action immediately upon his return.[33] He took the XXth Legion into Wales where he annexed Anglesey and nearly exterminated the Ordovices. In the next campaigning season Agricola took his forces north, consolidating Rome's hold over the Brigantes by building numerous forts. The following season he marched his troops, in two columns, through Corbridge and Carlisle (where fortresses were built), meeting up at the River Tay, where he harassed the local tribes continually through the winter. In the fourth season Agricola advanced to the Forth–Clyde isthmus in Scotland, driving the natives northward; in the fifth he garrisoned the southwestern coast of Scotland, in hopes of a future invasion of Ireland. The confident general, having received an exiled Irish prince in his camp, allegedly confided to his son-in-law that Ireland 'could be conquered and held with one legion and a small number of auxiliaries,' a conquest which would then remove liberty from the sight of the Britons.[34]

In the summer of 82 Agricola made a bold attempt at removing liberty from the entire island. By land and by sea he pushed further north, establishing camps as far as the mouth of the River Spey. The enemy, described in the sources as Caledonians (*Caledonii*, probably a confederation rather than a single tribe), harassed his forts and proved elusive. Finally, early in the campaigning season of 83, Agricola brought his troops accompanied by British allies to a spot called Mons Graupius, where some 30,000 Caledonians had drawn up to face him. The exact location of Mons Graupius is unknown, and one of the most contentious subjects in the historiography, though most locate it on the northern edge of the Grampian Mountains. Before describing the battle, Tacitus once again relates speeches allegedly made by the two commanders before their troops. The most famous is that spoken by Calgacus – 'who among many leaders was preeminent in bravery and ancestry':

> I have great confidence that this day and your union will be the beginning
> of freedom for all Britain . . . Plunderers of the world, after [the Romans],
> laying everything to waste, ran out of land, they search out the sea: if the

33   For details of Agricola's campaigns, see Tacitus, *Agricola*, 18–38, supplemented by Dio Cassius 66.20.1–3. For modern analysis, see Hanson, 1987.
34   Tacitus, *Agricola*, 24.

enemy is wealthy, they are greedy; if he is poor they seek prestige; men whom neither the East nor West has sated, they alone of all men desire wealth and poverty with equal enthusiasm. Robbery, butchery, rapine they call empire by euphemisms, and when they produce a wasteland, they call it peace.[35]

While Tacitus did have access to information from Agricola, his hearing and understanding a speech made in the Caledonian camp is most unlikely. More trustworthy are his details of the actual battle (though the size of the armies given carries a caveat). The Caledonians, like the southern Britons, utilized chariots to bring infantry to the field. Agricola relied upon a large contingent of auxiliary cavalry and infantry, which he led himself on foot. After an exchange of missile fire both infantries engaged, while the Roman cavalry went after the British chariots. As the British army descended down the slope, the Roman horses broke through their ranks and encircled them. Tacitus gives the figures of 10,000 Caledonian casualties – to 360 Roman – while the remaining 20,000 Britons disappeared into the night, presumably returning to the Highlands.

Agricola did not pursue these Highlanders, and thus never completed his conquest of the north. He did, however, establish a defensive system along the southeastern edge of the Highlands to protect the Scottish lowlands, centered on the never finished legionary fortress at Inchtuthil. He intended further northern campaigns, and even sent a Roman fleet to circumnavigate the island. But at this point, in the spring of 84, he was recalled to Rome. 'Britain was completely conquered,' laments his son-in-law, 'and immediately let go.'[36]

It is appropriate at this point to evaluate this statement. Was Britain ever 'completely conquered'? Was Rome committed to making the island Roman, and, more important for this study, what was the Britons' attitude toward Romanization? Martin Henig has recently made the provocative statement that Rome didn't have to conquer southern Britain because client kings like Cogidubnus, who stood to profit most from the invasion, willingly Romanized it.[37] Tacitus invented the conquest of Britain, writes Henig, in order to magnify the accomplishments of Agricola. Tacitus in fact goes so far as describing Agricola as *the* catalyst for Romanization of the Britons:

In order that men who were scattered and uncivilized and for this reason easily moved to wars might become accustomed to peace and quiet through pleasures, [Agricola] encouraged individuals and assisted communities to

35   Tacitus, *Agricola*, 30 (trans. Benario).
36   Tacitus, *Histories*, 1.2.
37   *British Archaeology*, 37 (September 1998).

build temples, fora and homes . . . Furthermore, he educated the sons of chieftains in the liberal arts and gave higher marks to the talents of the Britons than to the studied skills of the Gauls . . . Then too our manner of dress became stylish and there was widespread use of the toga; and gradually they gave in to the attractions of vices, porticoes and baths and the elegance of banquets. And this was called civilization among those who did not know better, although it was part of [their] slavery.[38]

As we saw in the last chapter, there were kings in Britain who were already adopting elements of Roman culture decades before the Roman invasion. Indeed, the Romanization of the southern Britons is part a larger continuum of continental influences on British tribes in the so-called Channel Zone (see p. 16). Northern and western Britain, however, have shown a more isolated and conservative character throughout the Iron Age. It should not surprise us, then, that it is these areas which harbored rebellion and on which Rome expended so much military effort. Three legions remained in Britain at the end of the first century, and they were stationed at Caerleon, Chester, and York. The presence of two legionary fortresses and more than a dozen smaller forts in Wales in the Flavian period signals an aggressive occupation of the west and disarmament of the still dangerous Welsh tribes.

The great symbol of Roman military might in the north is, of course, Hadrian's Wall. Constructed over an approximately ten-year period following the emperor Hadrian's visit to Britain in AD 122, the great Wall stretches some 73 miles (117 kilometers) from the bridge crossing the Tyne at Newcastle to the Solway estuary. The retreat of the frontier to the Tyne–Solway line is the clearest indicator that Rome had abandoned all plans of a total occupation of the island. Troop withdrawals from the Highlands after Agricola's recall forced a less-ambitious scheme of controlling the region between the Forth and the Tay with a series of forts and watchtowers – the so-called Gask 'frontier.' The need for troops in Wales and the Pennines made even holding the Forth–Clyde line untenable, and Hadrian declared the irregular system of forts constructed along the Stanegate road under Trajan too vulnerable to hostile northern tribes. Originally planned as an addition to the Stanegate forts, the Wall system came to include 15 attached forts and 80 milecastles regularly placed and separated by two turrets.

It is important to stress that, at this point in time, Hadrian's Wall did not represent the physical limit of Roman control in Britain, separating Roman from barbarian in the province. Rather, as the many forts north of the Wall attest, Hadrian's strategy was to divide the Britons with a

38   Tacitus, *Agricola*, 21 (trans. Benario).

physical barrier that made control on both sides easier. Antoninus Pius' turf wall along the Forth–Clyde line, constructed c.143 but abandoned ten years later, was a similar attempt at controlling the Britons of southern Scotland. Ambitious military emperors would continue to campaign in Scotland until the early fourth century, and the area would provide recruits for the Roman army to be used in other frontier regions.[39]

Recruitment of natives is only one aspect of military and civilian relations in Britain. The construction of the two walls and their associated forts stimulated the local economy and – like modern imperialism – also transformed it. Roman soldiers married native women, soldiers' families settled near the northern forts, and merchants came to provide Roman goods and services. As in other parts of the Roman frontier, small civilian settlements (*vici*) began to appear alongside the forts, as did one large town – Carlisle, near the largest of the Wall forts, Stanwix – which came to acquire significant political and military status in the Late Empire.[40]

Organizing the Britons

This does not mean that the division between Roman and native simply disappeared in northern Britain. In 1973 archaeologists provided us with a wonderful glimpse of daily life in this area around AD 100. Excavations directed by Robin Birley at Vindolanda, a fort just south of Hadrian's Wall, resulted in the discovery of over 200 wooden writing tablets.[41] These documents from the soldiers and their families range from letters of recommendation to supply requisitions, and even include an invitation to a birthday party! Besides telling us that the soldiery was consuming impressive quantities of *cervesa* – Celtic beer – one tablet also reveals the unflattering nickname which at least one Roman soldier had for the natives: *Brittunculi*, 'wretched little Britons.'

It should be expected that intermarriage and Romanization would have varying degrees of success and also vary according to region. Britons recruited into the army would have acquired Latin, engineering and other trade skills, and of course Roman citizenship. Many would have returned to Britain after serving in the army and started families where these Roman cultural traits would have been passed on. Other Roman soldiers who had served in Britain would also have started families and retired in the island. While only officers were legally permitted to marry before the third century, many soldiers would have nevertheless taken wives from

39   Salway, 1993, 147.
40   Salway, 1993, 134.
41   Birley, 1990; Bowman, 1983; Bowman and Thomas, 1983.

among the local peasantry and slaves. Memorial stones found along Hadrian's Wall attest to this, and it is likely that the attached merchant communities would have witnessed a similar phenomenon.

This type of Romanization would have most affected the militarized districts in northern Britain and Wales. Elsewhere cities took the lead in Romanizing the province, especially among the native aristocracy. The creation of towns in Roman Britain proceeded soon after the conquest and concurrently with the establishment of military bases. Three *coloniae* – Colchester, Lincoln, and Gloucester – were deliberately founded for veterans, while a fourth – York – was raised to *colonia* status in the third century.[42] Two other large urban settlements – Chester and Caerleon – grew out of permanent legionary fortresses, though never attained *colonia* status like York. London, the major trading center which later became the provincial capital, held a unique status, reflected in its fourth-century name Augusta, while Verulamium is the only certain instance of a *municipium*. All of the above were chartered towns governed from the beginning by Roman citizens.

The majority of the large towns, however, were *civitates peregrinae*, formed along tribal lines and governed by the increasingly Romanized native aristocracy. This eastern city-state model was adapted to the British environment by finding a large tribal settlement – whether hill-fort, *oppidum*, or trade center – and transforming it into a Mediterranean-style city with all the typical Roman civic amenities: fora for markets, basilicas for government, baths and theaters for recreation. Local nobles who had already developed a taste for Roman comforts would have steered their sons toward the classical education required for the local magistracies. Sons of Roman allies were likely given citizenship status and soon this class was dominating the local *ordo* or *curia*, the town council of 100 members called decurions and headed by two magistrates (*duoviri*).

This transformation of a non-literate, warrior aristocracy into a Latin-speaking, toga-wearing urban curial class could not have been an instant and all-inclusive metamorphosis. But the problem is a lack of evidence for the fate of Britain's tribal aristocracy. Tacitus describes for us the process of Romanization and gives us glimpses of some British nobles, but then they virtually disappear from the written sources. Where Ausonius and other Gallic sources give us a picture of Gallo-Roman nobles, only a few inscriptions yield British personal and tribal names from the second to fourth centuries. Those Britons following the example of Cogidubnus built Roman-style villas – some very near the towns, others remote and rural – where they lived and managed their agricultural lands. Evidence from

---

42   Salway, 1993, 391–3.

British villas, however, shows a unique pattern of joint occupancy, indicating extended families continuing native domestic arrangements.[43]

Farming and Rural Settlement

All of this evidence for Romanization, such as it is, is based on the native aristocracy and their dependents. But what of the vast majority of Britons, farmers and laborers who never came to inhabit the Roman towns nor enter the Roman army? There was, to be sure, a reciprocal relationship between town and country, where meat and agricultural produce were sold in the urban markets and sustained the urban populations.[44] Many rural estates were also controlled by the urban aristocracy or else owned by the imperial government whose officials operated in the cities. But apart from the hundreds of Roman villas in Britain, there is a much greater number of native farmsteads less easily recognizable in the archaeological record and thus less studied by modern scholars. Here we must place the vast majority of Britons, for even the major towns of Roman Britain had relatively small populations (see map 3.1).[45]

Written sources are not much help in discussing rural concerns. Recently archaeologists have shifted away from the traditional focus on urban sites and are becoming increasingly interested in rural and extra-mural settlements. These studies have revealed a variety of rural settlement types (villages, compounds, single farms) as well as building types (round houses, aisled houses, corridor houses) in the Roman period.[46] Once again, it appears that the native 'kindred' model of domestic arrangement, with its extended families derived from polygamy and household retainers, was more common in these settlements than the Roman monogamous, nuclear family. Iron Age building types are also commonly used in Roman period construction, while intensive farming continued an Iron Age trend in Britain rather than reflecting a Roman innovation.

Language in Roman Britain

Along with these signs of continuity we should also remember that many native Iron Age settlements – for example the Ty Mawr hut-group, on

---

43 Hingley, 1989, 6.
44 The major towns often acted as parasites on the countryside: see Fulford, 1982.
45 The native farmstead to villa ratio may have been as high as 100:1 (100,000 farmsteads to 1,000 villas), while only an estimated 5 percent of the population of Britain lived in towns: see James, 1993, 147.
46 See Hingley, 1989.

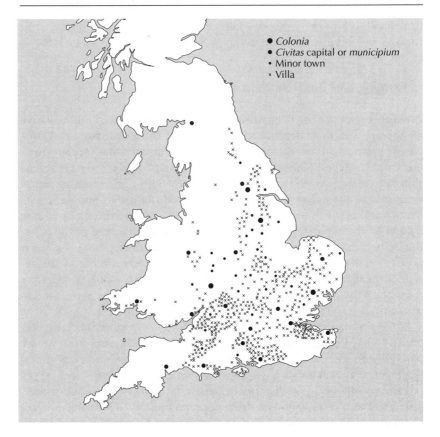

Map 3.1   The Romanization of Britain, as measured by the density of towns and villas.

Holyhead (see plate 3.4) – continued to be occupied into the Roman period, with little or no contact with Roman ways. That so much of the population of Roman Britain was rural and culturally isolated leads one to wonder about two important indicators of cultural identity: language and religion. Did the Roman conquest of Britain have any real and lasting impact on the language spoken by Britons, and upon their religious beliefs and practices?

The Brythonic (or Brittonic) Celtic language spoken in Iron Age Britain did not assume written form, apart from short inscriptions on coins and perhaps some religious records which have not survived. Latin, on the other hand, survives in countless and often lengthy inscriptions on stone, pottery, metal, wooden tablets, and other materials that make it clear that

Plate 3.4   The Ty Mawr hut-group, on the southern slopes of Holyhead Mountain, Anglesey, Wales. Situated beneath an ancient hill fort, Ty Mawr continued to be occupied in the Roman and early medieval periods. (Photo: Christopher A. Snyder.)

the language was used commonly in Britain for both everyday business and in important religious and political contexts. Some scholars have argued that most Britons learned their Latin in school and thus spoke a Vulgar Latin which, isolated from continental developments, sounded more archaic than elsewhere in the empire. Whatever the case, it is clear that Latin became the *lingua franca* for a culturally diverse Roman Britain.

Does this mean that Latin replaced the language of the natives, as it did (eventually) in Roman Gaul? The survival of Brythonic – in the form of Welsh, Cornish, Cumbric, and Breton – into the Middle Ages and later clearly refutes this. Latin *was* needed for political administration, most commerce, and in the army. But Latin lacked words to describe many objects and concepts in the Celtic-speaking world, and thus borrowed heavily from both Gaulish and Brythonic, just us Welsh and other surviving Celtic languages have Latin loan words as well. In the geographic language of Roman Britain, the vast majority of the words – for towns, rivers, forts, islands – are Celtic, and this goes for new settlements as well as age-old features in the landscape.[47]

47   See Rivet and Smith, 1979, passim; and Jones and Mattingly, 1990, 37–42.

Another area in which we see preference for the native tradition is personal names. Native British (and occasionally Gaulish) names continue to appear in records throughout the Roman period. If the predominantly aristocratic Britons commemorated on tombstones and in formal texts bear Celtic, Latinized Celtic, or hybrid names, what should we expect among the masses of unremembered or unnoticed Britons? The conservative nature of naming children, most noticeable among the aristocracy, resulted in the names of British grandees like Caratacus surviving five or six centuries to appear again in early medieval forms like Coroticus and Cerdic.

Religion

British names for native gods and goddesses also survive the centuries of Roman occupation. Roman religion was itself syncretistic – going back to its original borrowings from the Etruscans and the Greeks – and thus it should not surprise us to see Celtic and Romano-Celtic deities being worshiped even in state-operated shrines. Romans conflated local deities with their classical gods, while Britons adopted Roman practices like written dedications and representational sculpture to worship their local gods. Indeed, the extremely local nature of Celtic religion, with its multitude of deities, meshed well with the Roman practice of worshiping multiple aspects or attributes of their Olympian gods.

It is also commonly taught that the Romans were 'tolerant' of the religions of their conquered subjects, as seen in both societal attitudes and in political policy (the latter influenced by Stoic philosophy). There are three known exceptions to this tolerance – Druids, Jews, and Christians – and in each case extreme forms of suppression were used to eliminate potential political threat. The Druids, as we have seen, were linked with the native independence movement in Britain, and were all but wiped out between the revolts of Caratacus and Boudica. Officially, the Romans claimed that the Druids were suppressed throughout the empire because of their abhorrent devotional practices, especially human sacrifice. Given the evidence for some survival of Druidism in later Roman Gaul, it is likely that Druids did not entirely disappear in Britain and may be equated with the 'wizards' who later served the Pictish kings.[48]

But with the organizational structure which the Druids would have provided gone from Roman Britain, the Roman state seemed only too willing

---

48   Green, 1997, points out the presence of 'Druid's Egg' amulets and ritually deposited cauldrons in Scotland during the Roman period.

to help with the promotion of local cults. New temples, shrines, and even religious resorts like Bath (dedicated to the hybrid deity Sulis Minerva) and Lydney (dedicated to Nodens, a native healing god) were constructed in classical style with government funds. Agricola sponsored such projects as a way to Romanize the Britons, but it may rather have strengthened the power of local cults and practices.[49] The native religious practice of votive shafts, some containing dog and baby burials, continued into the Roman period, and the Roman authorities may have even looked the other way to allow occasional human sacrifice, if the evidence for a continuing severed head cult (e.g. at Wroxeter) is any indicator. With votive shafts and sacred groves appearing close to Roman towns and forts in Britain, what rites must the Britons of the countryside and remote areas of the island have been practicing?

It is evident that Romanization as a whole was most successful in south and eastern Britain, with native 'Celtic' patterns continuing much stronger and longer in northern Britain, Wales, and the southwest. This corresponds roughly to the Iron Age trends discussed in the last chapter, with the English Channel Zone innovating along continental lines while the rest of Britain remained more culturally conservative. The politically and economically powerful states of the Channel Zone were divided by pro- and anti-Roman factions on the eve of the Claudian conquest, and this cost them their political autonomy and trade monopolies. Some princes chose cooperation and were amply rewarded by the Romans, becoming the first instruments of Romanization in Britain. But neither client kings nor military conquest could ensure the Romanization of Britain. Ancient and deeply embedded social practices continued among the Britons, as did their language and religious practices, through the last years of the Roman occupation and beyond.

---

49 Webster, 1986, emphasizes the continuity of Celtic religion in Britain; Henig, 1984, emphasizes the Romanization of native religious practices.

4
Late Roman Britain

In the year 212 the *Constitutio Antoniniana*, issued by the emperor Caracalla, granted Roman citizenship to almost all free inhabitants of the empire. Those newly arriving at this status took the emperor's *nomen gentilicium* – Aurelius – and it quickly became one of the most common names in the empire. Of the 227 native Britons who recorded Roman *gentilicia* in inscriptions, 83 were Aurelii.[1] Should we assume then that, after 212, Romanization was so successful that most Britons began thinking of themselves as Roman citizens (*cives*) and adopting Roman names?

Epigraphic evidence indicates the continuing popularity of Celtic personal names in Late Roman Britain, and suggests that it was mostly foreigners stationed in Britain who proclaimed their citizenship status. In the later years of Roman rule, those Britons at home and abroad who left us Latin inscriptions often described themselves as *Brittanus* (or *Britto*), and if they proclaimed citizenship status it was as *cives* of a British tribe or of a *patria* ('homeland') that was *Britannia*, not *Roma*.[2] Ironically Latin – which Tacitus predicted would be most successful in Romanizing the natives – actually gave the Britons a written medium in which they could express, for the first time, a sense of national identity.

Military and Political Events

Several military and political events in the last two centuries of Roman rule prevented the kind of transformation which Agricola had envisioned for the Britons. Northern Britain continued to be a problem, and a drain on imperial resources. A revolt by the Brigantes in the mid second century

---

1 Birley, 1980, 18, 29.
2 See Snyder, 1998. Civic pride did emerge in Roman Britain, but it never reached the levels attained in both Gaul and the Mediterranean provinces.

necessitated the withdrawal of troops from Germany to bolster the three legions in Britain.[3] Late in that century both Marcus Aurelius and Commodus committed more military resources to wars in northern Britain, the most interesting move being the transfer in 175 of 5,500 Iazyges (Sarmatian) armored cavalry from Pannonia to aid the Legio VI Victrix.[4] These Sarmatians settled, as veterans, in Bremetenacum (Ribchester); the *praefectus* of the Legio VI was named Lucius *Artorius* Castus.[5]

The often discussed 'Crisis of the Third Century' resulted in large part from synchronous losses to the barbarians, undisciplined and rebellious troops, and imperial usurpations. This pattern is evident as early as 185 in Britain, where soldiers mutinied against the Praetorian Prefect Perrenius.[6] Commodus sent to Britain his eventual successor, Pertinax, but the British troops balked at his strict discipline and called for his resignation.[7] When Commodus was assassinated in 192, Pertinax replaced him and Britain was under the control of an aristocrat named Decimus Clodius Albinus. Albinus claimed the imperial title when Pertinax was killed a year later, and his most serious rival was a military man from North Africa named Septimius Severus. After four years of civil war, Severus emerged as victorious and Albinus fell in battle near Lyons.

Septimius Severus, the last successful military emperor until Valerian, is uniquely linked to Britain. In 197 he brought Britain back into the empire, but divided it into two provinces – Britannia Inferior and Britannia Superior – reflecting the need to handle the north and south differently. At the turn of the century Roman Britain was threatened by an alliance of two northern British confederations, the Caledonii and the Maeatae.[8] Fearing that he could not stop such an alliance from crossing Hadrian's Wall, the governor of Britain bribed the Maeatae with a large sum and in exchange received a few captives. But this proved to be only a temporary stop. In 208 the emperor himself came to Britain, transplanting his entire household to York (which was then elevated to the status of *colonia*), and launched a serious northern campaign.

The Roman sources claim that Severus certainly wanted to add conquests in Britain to his successes in the east, but his most dire need was to remove his two unruly sons from Rome and employ them in a disciplined military environment.[9] Geta he sent to administer justice in southern

---

3   Pausanius, *Description of Greece*, 8.43.3–4.
4   Dio Cassius 71.16.2.
5   See Linda A. Malcor, 'Lucius Castus,Part I' *The Heroic Age* 1 (Spring 1999), <http://www.mun.ca/mst/heroicage/issues/1/halac.htm>; and chapter 5 below.
6   Dio Cassius 72.9.
7   *Historia Augusta*, Pertinax, 3.5–10.
8   Dio Cassius 75.5.4.
9   The accounts of Severus' activities in Britain are Herodian 3.14 and Dio Cassius 76.11-15.

Britain, while Caracalla was kept by his father's side as the emperor launched a campaign in Scotland. Severus' route was very similar to Agricola's, skirting the eastern flank of the Grampian Mountains, but unlike the latter he was not able to bring the Britons out into a pitched battle.[10] A temporary peace was made, but the Caledonii joined the Maeatae in rebellion in 210 and Severus seems to have planned a punitive total conquest of Scotland. Command was given to Caracalla, but the planned conquest fizzled with the death of Severus at York in 211. Not only would Rome have to abandon any hope of conquering Scotland, but Severus' aggression had forced the northernmost Britons into dangerous confederations and alliances that would prove impossible to control.

With Scotland temporarily pacified and permanently abandoned, Caracalla proceeded to assassinate his brother before leaving Britain for a short and inauspicious reign. A shortage of written sources and inscriptions from Britain has left us with the impression of stagnation in third-century Britain. Barbarian incursions along the Danubian and Persian frontiers were not answered by any serious barbarian threat in Britain. Military rebellions continued, however, and Britain was removed entirely from imperial control along with the other northwestern provinces to form the so-called Gallic Empire in 260. Britain may have been one of the healthiest parts of this breakaway Roman state, which lasted some 13 years.[11] When the emperor Aurelian put an end to the barbarian threat and to the Gallic Empire in 274, Britain returned to Roman control and may have actually benefited from Roman losses in Gaul (if an increase in British villa construction can be linked to the flight of Gallic aristocrats and capital).

Following Aurelian's death in 275, however, rebellion returned to the empire and involved Britain on several occasions. In 277 the governor of Britain revolted and caused the emperor Probus to settle Burgundians and Vandals in Britain to guard against further usurpation.[12] Probus' successor Carus sent his own son, Carinus, to fight barbarians in the western provinces in 282, from which he took the title 'Britannicus Maximus,'[13] as did Carinus' successor, Diocletian. These latest barbarian attacks seem to have come from the sea, in particular the English Channel, and both Diocletian and his western colleague Maximian were kept busy defending the coasts of Brittany and northern Gaul (Britain is not specifically mentioned) from Saxon and Frankish raiders. To combat this Maximian placed

10   Salway, 1993, 168–9.
11   Salway, 1993, 190–1.
12   Zosimus 1.66–8.
13   Salway, 1993, 196.
14   Aurelius Victor, *Liber de Caesaribus*, 39.20–1; Eutropius 9.21.

an officer named M. Mauseus Carausius in charge of the Channel forts and the *classis Britannicus*, the British fleet. Carausius had great success against the pirates, but there was a rumor that he was in collusion with them and was keeping some of the recovered plunder. When Maximian ordered his execution in 286, Carausius seized Britain and proclaimed himself emperor.[14]

Falling only 16 years after the demise of the Gallic Empire, independence from Rome must have again become 'an attractive memory' for the British troops who supported Carausius' regime.[15] There are signs, too, that Carausius actively sought British support by playing on native interests. In his coinage, he depicts himself as the *restitutor Britanniae* ('Restorer of Britain') welcomed by the *genius Britanniae*, the 'guardian spirit' of the island.[16] Diocletian needed help to remove Carausius. The Roman Principate – rule of one emperor – had by this point given way to the Tetrarchy created by Diocletian, where two emperors, each bearing the title Augustus, ruled together with two junior colleagues, who bore the title Caesar. After Maximian failed to defeat Carausius in a naval encounter, Diocletian turned to the new Caesar, Constantius Chlorus.

Carausius' land forces were no match for those of Constantius. In 293 Carausius was assassinated and succeeded by his finance minister Allectus, who in turn fell in battle against Constantius' generals while the Caesar himself sailed triumphantly into London.[17] After rescuing the city from Frankish pirates, Constantius set about strengthening the defenses on the northern frontier. It was also at this time that Britain was exposed to Diocletian's administrative reforms, which had begun in the rest of the empire while Britain was under the control of Carausius. Britain had been divided by Severus into two provinces; now, the 'Diocese of the Britains' consisted of four provinces: *Britannia Prima, Britannia Secunda, Flavia Caesariensis*, and *Maxima Caesariensis* (see map 4.1). Each province had a capital city and a civilian governor (*praeses* or *rector*) who was responsible to the *vicarius Britanniarum* in London. He in turn reported to the praetorian prefect in Gaul, making Britain's inclusion in the "Prefecture of the Gauls" a clear sign that her future would from now on be linked with events happening across the Channel, militarily and otherwise.

Constantius returned to Britain in 306, accompanied by his son Constantine, and began a military campaign in the north. A victory is recorded over the Picts, who make their first appearance at this time in the historical sources, replacing the Caledonians as the most hostile of the

---

15   Salway, 1981, 289.
16   See Salway, 1981, 297; Frere, 1978, 327; and Casey, 1994, 58, 65.
17   Eutropius 9.22.2.   See also *Panegyric on Constantius Caesar* (delivered AD 297), 8.13–20.

Map 4.1 The Diocese of the Britains, showing political, military, and ecclesiastical offices.

northern peoples.[18] When Constantius returned to York from his victory he died quite suddenly, and his army, encouraged by the Germanic 'king' Crocus, proclaimed Constantine as Augustus.[19] This unconstitutional succession launched Constantine into 18 years of civil war and political maneuvering until he finally emerged as sole emperor in 324. Britain appears favorably in the panegyrics as the starting point of the emperor's ascension, and Constantine himself took the title *Britannicus Maximus* around 315.[20]

18 *Panegyric on Constantius*, 8.11; *Panegyric on Constantine*, 6.7.1–2.
19 Aurelius Victor, *Liber de Caesaribus*, 40.2–4; Eutropius 10.1.3 and 2.2; Zosimus 2.8.2 and 9.1.
20 Eusebius, *De Vita Constantini*, 1.8 and 25. See also Casey, 1978; and Snyder, 1998, 8.

Constantine (later, for his championing of the Christian cause, given the epithet 'the Great') effectively completed the separation of military and civil offices in the provinces that had begun with Diocletian. He answered Diocletian's great administrative reforms with sweeping military reforms of his own. Stationary frontier generals were given the rank of *dux*, and new mobile commands were given to men who held the higher rank *and* title (for it was given also to high officials at his court) of *comes*. This was translated in Britain as three major commands: the *dux Britanniarum* who commanded the garrison troops (*limitanei*) along Hadrian's Wall; the *comes litoris Saxonici* who probably commanded troops along both the southeast (the so-called 'Saxon Shore') and northwest coasts of Britain; and the *comes Britanniarum*, a later addition given (perhaps temporarily) to the mobile command of crack cavalry units (*comitatenses*).[21]

The Count of the Saxon Shore remains the most enigmatic of these posts.[22] This was probably originally a *dux* who was later elevated to the rank of *comes*, perhaps with the inclusion of command of the Welsh coast. The title first appears in the *Notitia Dignitatum* (written *c*.423–5), and while some of the Shore forts date back to the early third century, they did not become a unified system under a single command until much later.[23]

It is still debated whether *litus Saxonicum* means the shore was attacked by Saxons or settled with Saxons.

The material evidence (villa construction and renovation, new mosaics, road repairs) suggests that Britain enjoyed prosperity under Constantine's rule. This prosperity began to slip only gradually with the succession of his sons, Constantine II, Constans, and Constantius II. The emperor Constans made an official visit to Britain in 343 (in midwinter) for some unknown reason, though victory over barbarians seems to have been one result.[24] Shortly after this visit the elder Gratian, father of the emperor Valentinian I, was appointed to Britain with the command and status of *comes rei militaris*.[25] The reason again is obscure, but this is probably the first sign of unrest in the north. Constans had more serious trouble at home, however, for in 350 he fell victim to a palace plot and rule in the West went to a usurper named Magnentius

---

21   See the western portion of the *Notitia Dignitatum*.
22   On the origins of the Saxon Shore forts, see Salway, 1981, 320–1; idem, 1993, 182, 299, 332; Johnson, 1976; idem, 1980, 98ff.; D. E. Johnston, 1977; Maxfield, 1989; and Esmonde Cleary, 1989, 52ff.
23   Wood, 1990, has suggested that the command was created by Stilicho *c*.395.
24   Julius Firmicus Maternus, *De Errore Profanum Religionum*, 28.6; Libanius, *Oration*, 59.141; Ammianus Marcellinus 20.1.1.
25   Ammianus 30.7.3.

(who was said to have had a British father). After three years of rule, Magnentius was defeated in battle by the eastern emperor Constantius II. Constantius then sent the imperial notary Paulus Catena (Paul 'the Chain') to Britain to suppress the conspirators, and the savagery with which the supporters of Magnentius were hunted down in Britain suggests that they were loyal and many.[26]

Britain again appears in the sources with the Gallic campaigns of Julian, Constantius' Caesar and ultimately his challenger. In 359 Julian organized a fleet of 600 ships to transport grain from Britain to support his army, seemingly an attempt to reopen an important supply route that had ceased to function.[27] A year later he was informed that the Picts and the Scots had broken a truce and were raiding the northern frontier lands of Britain.[28] This was spreading alarm throughout the British provinces, and the morale of the army was said to be very low. Julian decided not to go himself, but sent his *magister equitum* Lupicinus to Britain with four units of his field army. Lupicinus waited out the winter in London, and was soon after recalled by Julian and arrested under trumped-up charges. While Julian was making his own play for power, the situation in Britain was growing steadily worse.

Ammianus Marcellinus records that in 364 Britain was constantly being harassed by four peoples: Picts, Saxons, Scots, and 'Attacotti.'[29] The Picts and the Scots were, by now, the traditional threat in the north, while the Saxons are here, for the first time, linked specifically with Britain.[30] The Attacotti, perhaps hailing from Ireland or the Western Isles, were described as cannibals by the credulous St. Jerome.[31] We do not know what the Roman response was to these attacks, for they occurred shortly after the confusion surrounding Julian's death. But Ammianus gives a detailed account of the more serious attacks of 367, which he calls the 'barbarian conspiracy.'[32] The news reached the emperor Valentinian, while he was suffering from a serious illness, that several groups of barbarians had conspired together to launch a joint attack: Picts, Attacotti, and Scots devastated much of Britain, while Franks and Saxons ravaged the coast of Gaul. Under promises of

26   Ammianus 14.5.6–8.
27   Julian, *Letter to the Athenians*, 279D; Ammianus, 18.2.3; Libanius, *Oration*, 18.82–3; Eunapius, frag. 12; Zosimus, 3.5.2. See Salway, 1993, 359–60.
28   Ammianus 20.1.
29   Ammianus 26.4.5.
30   See, however, Bartholomew, 1984.
31   Jerome, *Adversus Jovinianum*, 2.7.48: *atticotos, gentem Britannicam, humanis vesci carnibus*.
32   Ammianus 27.8 and 28.3.

booty, the *areani* – frontier spies – had abandoned their duty and had allegedly allied themselves with the barbarians.[33] Thus the enemy attacked without warning and ambushed the *dux Britanniarum*, Fullofaudes, who was taken prisoner. At the same time Nectaridus, the '*comes* of the maritime region' (which probably included the 'Saxon Shore' and the forts on the west coast of Britain, possibly those on the Gallic coast as well), was killed. After these disasters, the barbarians split up into small bands and pillaged the provinces at will. Desertions from the army were numerous, and armed thugs roamed the land unchecked.

The presence of Franks and Saxons on the coast of Gaul may have delayed the news from Britain as well as the Roman response. The emperor did not come himself but sent his commander of the guard to assess the situation.[34] He was soon recalled and four units of the field army were dispatched to Britain in 368 under the command of the *comes rei militaris* Theodosius, the father of the future emperor of the same name. Count Theodosius landed at Richborough and advanced with his army to London, cutting down the bands of marauders who were laden with booty. At London he established a new *vicarius* (aptly named Civilis) over the diocese of Britain and issued a general pardon to those who had deserted from the British garrisons. When Theodosius took to the field he routed the barbarians and even pursued them on the seas.[35] Subsequently, he had to deal with a serious revolt led by a rich exile named Valentinus, who may have been luring frontier troops away from their post with promises of booty.[36] Theodosius quickly dealt with the rebellion (Valentinus was executed, his supporters pardoned) and the recovered lands were organized into a fifth British province, *Valentia*.[37]

Ammianus also tells us that Theodosius 'restored the cities and forts' in the British provinces. One new area of construction was Britain's northeastern coastline, where a series of well-fortified watch-towers were built at this time to warn nearby forts of seaborne Pictish raids. Similar stations built on the northwest coast had gone out of service in the second century, but there is archaeological evidence that some of the Cumbrian coastal

33   Ammianus 28.3.8.
34   Ammianus, 27.8.2.
35   The panegyrics praise Theodosius' victories over Picts, Scots, and Saxons: see Pacatus, *Panegyric on Theodosius*, 2.5.2.; Claudian, *Panegyric on the Third Consulship of Honorius*, 51–6, and idem, *Panegyric on the Fourth Consulship of Honorius*, 24–33.
36   Johnson, 1980, 122-3.
37   For varying views on the location of Valentia, see Salway, 1981, 392–6, 411; Frere, 1987 200; and Bartholomew, 1984, 185.

forts were rebuilt at this time to protect against raids coming around the other side of the Wall.[38]

One of Count Theodosius' lieutenants in Britain was a soldier from the Hispanic provinces named Magnus Maximus.[39] Maximus was sent back to Britain in the early 380s to organize defenses, whether as *dux Britanniarum* or *comes* is unclear. He is credited with a victory over the Picts and Scots in the north in 382, and some historians have further attributed to Maximus the settlement of tribal protectorates in Wales to control Irish infiltration.[40] Around 383 Maximus' British troops declared him emperor of the West.[41] The usurpation began with Maximus taking his army (perhaps from the garrisons in Wales) into Gaul, where he defeated and killed the young emperor Gratian. Maximus established his court at Trier and was baptized as a Catholic, securing the blessings of the Church and the western frontier at the same time.[42] The eastern emperor, Theodosius (son of the Count), was forced to recognize Maximus' control of the West. Five years later, Maximus crossed the Alps and was defeated in Pannonia by Theodosius, who seized the usurper at Aquileia and beheaded him.[43]

The effect Maximus' bid for power had on Britain is uncertain. Gildas states that Britain promised submission to Roman rule, and in exchange a legion was sent by sea to drive out the Scots and the Picts.[44] The panegyricist Claudian records that in 398, while Stilicho was busy suppressing revolt in Africa, Britain was suffering from attacks by Saxons, Scots, and Picts.[45] Stilicho, the Vandal-born *magister militum* (chief military commander) of the western emperor Honorius, is given credit for a victory over these barbarians, though he may not have been himself in Britain.[46] Claudian says that in 402 Stilicho withdrew from Britain 'a legion, protector of the furthest Britons,' an assumed reference to a garrison from Hadrian's Wall.[47]

Though the sources are a bit unclear, it appears that Stilicho's 'Pictish War' occurred in 398, while measures for new fortifications in Britain

---

38   See Salway, 1981, 383–4; Johnson, 1980, 127–30; and chapter 10 below.
39   For the survival of Maximus in Welsh genealogy and literature, see chapter 12 below.
40   *The Gallic Chronicle of 452, sub annum* 382. The migration of Cunedda to Gwynedd, however, is now disputed: see Dumville, 1977, 181–2; Johnson, 1980, 83, 131; and Salway, 1981, 404.
41   Zosimus 4.35.2-6 and 37.1–3; Orosius, *Adversum Paganos*, 7.34.9–10.
42   See Mathews, 1975; and idem, 1983, 431.
43   Sozomen 7.13; Orosius 7.35.3–4. For the role of Maximus' troops in the legend of the founding of Brittany, see chapter 7 below.
44   *De Excidio*, 15.2.
45   Claudian, *Against Eutropius*, 1.391-3.
46   Claudian, *On the Consulship of Stilicho*, 2.247–55.
47   Claudian, *Gothic War*, 416–18.   See Salway, 1981, 423–4; and Frere, 1978, 355.

were ordered in 399 and the *legio* was ordered overseas in 401 or 402.[48] The last Roman coins that appear in Britain in large numbers also date to around 402, and it has been suggested that Stilicho had either stripped Britain of most of its garrison or that the impoverished imperial government could no longer pay the troops.[49] Either situation could explain the insular unrest that led to the dramatic events of 406–10 and British independence.

Towns Great and Small

In 410, following the Visigothic sack of Rome, the western emperor Honorius wrote to the cities (πολεις) of Britain telling them to organize their own defenses.[50] In the next chapter we will look in detail at the events leading up to the so-called 'Rescript of Honorius.' First, however, let us look at some of the individual ingredients of Britain's troubles and subsequent revolt against Rome, starting with the towns. A theory that has recently gained in popularity is that, by about 350, the cities of Britain had been reduced to mere villages, and all signs of true urban life had disappeared.[51] This is based mainly on archaeological evidence, which shows a lack of expenditure on public buildings such as the forum and basilica in the fourth century. What we do see is a tremendous amount of military construction in and around the cities. Ditches were widened and external towers were added to the city walls to provide fighting platforms, which could also support catapults and *ballistae*.[52] These improvements actually helped the towns to outlive the forts, which were constantly being stripped of manpower.

The critics would say that these expenditures merely prove that the cities had ceased to be centers of urban activity and had become walled fortresses. The *Notitia* shows that even the civilian *vicarius* in London had command of some troops. Still, it would be closer to the truth to say that urban life had not *ceased* in the fourth century, but rather that it had *changed*. Lincoln, for example, remained economically active in the late fourth century, attested not only by coin finds and house occupation, but also by a recently identified food-processing industry which included an active commercial butchery and heated grain stores.[53] At York, military

---

48   Miller, 1975.
49   Salway, 1981, 425.
50   Zosimus 6.10.2.
51   See Reece, 1980.
52   Johnson, 1980, 123–5; Salway, 1981, 387–9.
53   See *British Archaeology*, 5 (1995).

buildings were carefully demolished to make way for commercial exploitation, in this case both metal-working and the large-scale slaughtering of sheep and cattle.[54] Analyses of ceramic and faunal assemblages from fourth-century London indicate diminution of population.[55] Layers of dark loam – the so-called 'black earth' – found overlaying masonry structures at many Romano-British towns have been interpreted as wind-blown debris indicating the end of urban occupation. But 'black earth' is one of the most controversial elements in the debate over the fate of Romano-British towns. Its presence in some towns and forts (e.g. Segontium) clearly indicates rubbish disposal.[56] Others have argued that 'black earth' is the decayed remnants of simple earth and wattle structures, and indicates dense, low-status occupation in fourth-century towns.[57] Some have even interpreted it as landscaping topsoil used by urban aristocrats to adorn their town houses.[58]

Martin Millet has constructed a model which best explains these changes in Romano-British towns.[59] The crisis of the third century, according to Millet, led to the decline of the *civitas* capitals in Britain, the emergence of the small towns (*pagi*), and the decentralization of the economy to the periphery. The *pagi* came under the control of local magnates (*possessores*) who owned villas nearby and who turned increasingly to these small towns as markets for their goods. The cities 'were no longer principally economic foci but rather defended centres for their districts' containing large private houses.[60] These were most likely the residences of the magnates who, though maintaining their status as *decuriones* (town councillors), relied on the *pagi* as their personal power bases.

Rural settlements and small towns, which represented the majority of the population despite being under-represented in the archaeological record, were isolated from much that was 'Roman' about Romano-British society and may have felt little need for the adoption of Roman cultural attributes.[61] If the *possessores* were relying increasingly on the resources of the small towns, it should not surprise us to see these magnates 'going native' and rejecting the imperial administration.

---

54   See *British Archaeology*, 7 (1995).
55   Davies and Kirby, 1995.
56   Davies and Kirby, 1995.
57   Dark, 1993; idem, 1996.
58   Dixon, 1992.
59   Millet, 1990, 149–51.
60   Millet, 1990, 221.
61   Hunter-Mann, 1993, 69.

Hill-forts and the Native Aristocracy

In the previous chapter we observed that a significant number of tribal aristocrats began filling city magistracies in Britain soon after the Roman conquest. These British aristocrats virtually disappear as a distinct group in the subsequent documentary evidence. We must assume that they made up the bulk of the curial families in Late Roman Britain, and were thus subject to such trends as those just discussed. In the Late Empire, many of the *possessores* of Roman Gaul retired to great rural estates where, protected by private military forces, they could defy government agents and organize their own local defense against barbarians.[62] If the British magnates followed their lead, we should look for them in two places: villas and hillforts.

Villas have been seen as one of the hallmarks of Romanization in the provinces. Yet patterns in Britain suggest that the roots of villa development lay in pre-Roman Iron Age farming communities, and illustrate the economic success of native elites rather than colonials.[63] While large imperial estates, with their palatial houses, declined in the fourth century, several smaller villas show, through the installation of industrial objects (especially corn-drying ovens) in their last phase, a self-reliance that took precedence over older luxuries.

Archaeological evidence also points to a revival of hill-forts in Late Roman Britain.[64] Part of the Claudian conquest, especially the campaigns of Vespasian, had been aimed at seizing control of fortified hilltops where resisting British tribes took refuge. Once the hill-fort was taken, the surviving population was disarmed and resettled in the nearest Roman town. Beginning in about the third century, however, a large number of Roman items appear at many of the British hill-forts. These items are associated with newly constructed Romano-Celtic temples, Roman villas and manses, native round houses and huts, and cemeteries. Datable evidence (including Roman coins and pottery) indicates that reoccupation continued to the very end of the Roman period, and in many cases beyond.

One way to interpret this evidence is to envision the Roman authorities allowing a small number of natives to return to the hill-forts once the area was no longer deemed a military threat. In some cases we can see the return of a local magnate, perhaps reclaiming his ancestral home, constructing a rural estate with Roman or hybrid buildings. At other hill-forts the Roman authorities apparently sponsored the construction of native

---

62   The phenomenon is described in Salvian, *De Gubernatione Dei*. See Matthews, 1975; and Jones, 1996a, 169.
63   Jones and Mattingly, 1990, 244–6.
64   For general discussion, see Burrow, 1981; Dark, 1994.

shrines and cemeteries to serve as focal points for the community. These pagan temples went out of use or were dismantled by the beginning of the fifth century, and in some instances they were replaced by small Christian churches.[65] At more than a dozen hill-forts in Wales and the southwest there was even more intensive occupation in the fifth and sixth centuries, characterized by new or strengthened fortifications.[66] The traditional explanation of this refortification is that these hill-forts were serving as places of refuge for British communities facing the barbarian threat.

Forts and *Foederati*

The question remains, however, just how serious were barbarian attacks on Britain in the last decades of Roman rule? The written accounts portray an island suffering from constant attack by the most savage of peoples, who foray unhindered into the British countryside and terrorize the vulnerable cities. Some years are singled out (296, 367, 398) as worse than others, usually because of joint attacks, and Britain is only narrowly saved by the heroic efforts of an imperial general. Archaeologists have, in the past, taken these years as historical landmarks in their search for signs of destruction and decay. In recent years, however, both historians and archaeologists have cautioned against automatically attributing all archaeological signs of fire, demolition, and reconstruction to these landmark dates.[67] 'The ineffectiveness of Roman defensive arrangements was exposed not by a single disastrous raid,' remarks Stephen Johnson, 'but by the cumulative effect of a series of such raids.'[68]

Part of the controversy involves the role of the Saxons, who raided (along with the Franks) in the Channel in the fourth century and who established permanent settlements in Britain by the mid fifth century.[69] Were some Saxons hired as mercenaries by Roman authorities as early as the fourth century? Such barbarian mercenaries appear throughout the Late Roman world as *laeti*, who served in auxiliary units in Roman armies, or *foederati*, larger groups fighting (under their own kings) for Rome in exchange for land and supplies (*annona, epimenia*). An older theory held that Germanic mercenaries began to be used extensively in Britain during the calamities of the fourth century, in particular to man city garrisons and protect rural estates.[70] Sonia Chadwick Hawkes and other ar-

65   See discussion in chapter 6 below.
66   See discussion in the next chapter.
67   E.g. Salway, 1981, 312, 380; Frere, 1978, 353.
68   Johnson, 1980, 123.
69   See Bartholemew, 1984; and Jones, 1996.
70   Based on slight evidence in the *Notitia* and Ammianus 29.4.7.

chaeologists cited chip-carved style belt-buckles and other military items in Britain, comparable with Germanic equipment used by the *laeti* stationed along the Gallic frontier, as evidence for Germanic mercenaries in Britain.[71] It was assumed that these Germans, or their descendants, were the Saxons who rebelled in the early fifth century and the first to assume power as Roman control collapsed in Britain. This theory has recently been discredited. Such 'Germanic' equipment was not used exclusively by *laeti*: it was worn by regular Roman soldiers along the frontier as well as by provincial civilians with 'ethnic' tastes, and was used occasionally as insignia by the civil administration.[72] Evidence now suggests that not until the early fifth century should we expect to find barbarian federates under separate command in Britain.[73]

While the defense of Britain still probably depended upon the Roman forts in the late fourth century, the character of the occupation within those forts may have been changing significantly. Michael Jones has suggested that, due to the observable stability of Roman units stationed along the Wall in the fourth century, these soldiers may have served more as military police than imperial army units, eventually merging into the 'Celtic social world' of war-band and clan.[74] A recent study of fourth-century Caerleon confirms the difficulty in distinguishing military from civilian in Late Romano-British military sites. 'Some units,' writes Andrew Garner, 'based in a particular place for a long time, identify more with the community in which they live than the larger community of the army.'[75]

The Picts and the Scots

The most serious barbarian threat to Britain in the fourth and early fifth centuries was from the Picts and the Scots. On this the written sources all agree. These two peoples are often linked in written accounts of raids on Late Roman Britain, which allege occasional combined efforts. So worried were the Britons at this threat that they would eventually hire Germanic mercenaries to beat back the Picts and the Scots, and thus the latter were in part responsible for the creation of Anglo-Saxon England.

---

71 See S. C. Hawkes and G. C. Dunning, 'Soldiers and Settlers in Britain, fourth to fifth century,' *Medieval Archaeology*, 5 (1961): 1–70; and C. J. Simpson, 'Belt-Buckles and Strap-Ends of the later Roman Empire,' *Britannia*, 7 (1976): 192–223.
72 See Johnson, 1980, 125–6; and Salway, 1981, 386–8.
73 See Salway, 1981, 418; Esmonde Cleary, 1989, 191–204; Welch, 1994; and chapter 5 below.
74 Jones, 1996b, 48.
75 Garner, 1999, 414.

The Picts make their first appearance (under this name) in the historical sources at the time of Constantius' British campaigns.[76] 'Picts' seems to denote yet another a tribal confederation, one that included *Caledones* and various tribes living north of the Forth–Clyde valley. Evidence indicates that, by the fourth century, there were two large confederations in Scotland, both of which Latin authors describe as *Picti*. When Severus campaigned in central Scotland in the early third century, he was opposed by two allied tribes, the Caledonii and the Maeatae. Archaeological evidence suggests that, at around this time, the broch-dwellers of Caithness and the Orkney and Shetland Isles clashed with these southern tribes, who were based on hill-forts and thus more closely resembled their British neighbors. Ammianus describes the fourth-century Picts as composed of two groups, the Dicalydones (surely related to the *Calidones*) and the Verturiones.[77] This may represent the north/south distinction we see in the archaeological record as well as in later written sources. Bede, for example, saw the Picts as one nation (*natio*) inhabiting distinct provinces, with a southern branch and one 'across the mountains,' that is, northwest of the Grampians.[78]

The term *Picti*, 'painted ones,' is as controversial and enigmatic as the people themselves. The word is probably a reference to the common Celtic practice of warriors painting or tattooing their naked bodies before going into battle. *Priteni*, related to both *Britanni* and *Prydein* (the Welsh word for Britain) and meaning 'people of the forms,' is the vernacular equivalent used by southerners to describe the barbarians beyond the Antonine Wall. Thus *Picti* is unlikely to be a tribal name, but rather a term describing yet another confederation of hostile northern tribes.

On the other hand, *Picti* may be related to what these people actually called themselves. The linguist Kenneth Jackson developed a theory that the Pictish language, which survives only in placenames and a few inscriptions, is Celtic and belongs to the P-Celtic branch (that is, it is related to the ancient British tongue which has become modern Welsh). But Jackson also noticed similarities between Pictish and the language spoken by the ancient Celtic inhabitants of Gaul. This is most noticeable in placenames beginning with *Pit-*, such as Pitcairn. The Pictish language developed differently from British, it has been suggested, because the Picts intermingled with the indigenous natives of Scotland and borrowed from their non-Indo-European language.

It may have been hard for the Romans – and indeed for us – to distin-

---

76   In the panegyrics and in *Laterculus Veronensis* (AD 300), in Riese (ed.), *Geographi Latini Minores*, p. 128.
77   Ammianus 27.8.5.
78   *EH*, 3.4.

Plate 4.1   A hoard of Roman silver discovered at Traprain Law, in the territory of the Votadini in southern Scotland. It contains both Roman military ornaments and cut and folded tablewares; scholars remain unsure whether this was booty from a raid or an official payment made for political or military purposes. (National Museums of Scotland.)

guish the Picts from the free Britons living north of Hadrian's Wall, such as the Votadini and the Selgovae. The tribes of central and southeastern Scotland, for example, inhabited both hill-forts and crannogs – artificial islands built on platforms over a lake – a type of habitation adopted by northern Britons and also found in Ireland. It has been suggested that the Romans had established diplomatic relations with some northern British tribes so that they could act as a buffer between the Picts and the Roman settlements near the Wall. Roman items have been found in the Scottish Lowlands (see plate 4.1), but these may be the product of diplomacy, peaceful trade, or unfriendly raiding.

The Irish were involved in both trading with and raiding Late Roman Britain. Though usually called *Hibernii* by Greek and Latin authors, the Irish who began raiding Britain in the fourth century were called *Scoti* (also *Scotti*). This semantic confusion between Irish and Scots, made famous by Sellar and Yeatman in *1066 and All That* ('a memorable history of England' first published in 1930), is at least as old as Ptolemy. The Greek geographer drew a map of the peoples and places of the British Isles around the year AD 100. One of the peoples on Ptolemy's map, the *Cruithin*, inhabit both Ireland and Scotland. According to medieval Irish tradition, the *Cruithni* – which is the term used in some Irish sources for the Picts – invaded Ireland from Scotland. *Scoti* may derive from an Irish verb meaning 'to raid,' and of course raiding (especially of cattle and slaves) was endemic in early Irish society. But the Irish also came to Britain as colonists. Their most lasting settlement, in Argyll, came to be known as *Scotia*, or 'Scot-land.' For some reason, medieval Latin authors continued to use the term *Scoti* to describe Irish living in both Scotland and Ireland.

While Romans traded with the Irish, and may even have established a trading post near Dublin, Roman imports never made a real impact on Ireland until the arrival of Christianity in the early fifth century. Ptolemy's map shows that Ireland at this time was the home of a variety of tribes, and the names which he ascribes to them reflect many of the families or clans which would dominate Irish politics in the early Christian period (e.g. the Ulaid and the Érainn). While Irish raiding was clearly aimed at removing portable wealth from Roman Britain, it is less clear why some of the Irish stayed in Britain. Some historians have suggested that Roman authorities invited some Irish, as *laeti* or *foederati*, to settle in western Britain to guard the coasts from Scottish and Pictish raids. It does appear that, from epigraphic and genealogical evidence, substantial numbers of Irish settled in Wales and the southwest.[79] The most significant Irish settlement is that of the Dál Riata of Antrim, who made the short crossing to Argyll and founded the kingdom of Dalriada. These Scots became on-again off-again enemies of the northern Britons.[80]

Britons Abroad

The Irish weren't the only ones emigrating in the fourth and fifth centuries. There are actually more Britons known by name living abroad in this period than living in Britain itself. Partly this is due to the lack of written sources for Britain; but it also clearly reflects a trend among Britons – especially clerics – to leave their troubled island and seek new homes and career advancement in other parts of the Roman Empire.

The first of these British expatriates to enter the historical record is Pelagius, and many of the fifth-century British émigrés were clerics with ties to Pelagianism. We will examine this phenomenon in detail in a later chapter.[81] But it should be pointed out here that Pelagius' enemies, especially Jerome and Orosius, frequently slung barbarian stereotype insults at Pelagius because of his British origin.[82] He was called a 'a big man . . . fleshy,' 'a huge Alpine hound,' 'a monstrous Goliath with . . . a thick neck,' 'thoroughly stolid, weighed down by Scottish porridge.'[83] Even more

---

79   See chapters 8 and 9 below.
80   See chapter 10 below.
81   See chapter 6 below.
82   See Birley, 1980, 154–4; and Jones, 1987.
83   These slurs, and the identification of Pelagius as a Briton, can be found in the *Letters* of Augustine and Jerome, Orosius' *Adversum Paganos*, and Prosper's *Chronicle*.

biting is the description of a British poet named Silvius Bonus, written
c.382 by the rhetorician Ausonius of Bordeaux:

> 'Who is Silvius?' 'He is a Briton.' 'Either this Silvius is no Briton, or he is
> Silvius "Bad."'
> Silvius is called Good and called a Briton. . . .
> No good man is a Briton.[84]

Michael Jones and other historians have seen this as evidence of clear
cultural prejudice, a recognition by the *literati* in other parts of the Empire that Romanization had failed in Britain. Apart from one knight and
possibly a fifth-century usurper or two, no high-ranking imperial bureau-
crat, general, or statesman is known to have been British. Britons traveling
abroad could not escape this prejudice – not even erudite Britons like
Pelagius – while civil servants like Victorinus, returning to the continent
from a tour in Britain, could speak of 'the wild Britons' as late as 417.[85]

The British Tyrants

In Bethlehem the great Jerome, titillated by news of barbarians and usurpers
in far-off Britain, wrote that 'Britain is a province fertile with tyrants.'[86]
Carausius, Constantine, and Magnus Maximus are just three noteworthy
examples of usurpation in the island, and the fifth century would provide
several more. What was it about Britain and 'the wild Britons' that made
an otherwise unnoteworthy Roman province so prominent in the political events of the Late Empire?
  The revolt of Maximus, like other imperial usurpations in the third and
fourth centuries, was seen by his supporters as necessary to meet local
defense and administrative needs to which a distant and harassed emperor could not attend.[87] At the same time the landed elite of Britain, no
longer depending on the Roman government for advancement, turned
increasingly to patron–client relationships to build a loyal body of supporters with which they eventually seized control of their districts.[88] In
the fifth century they stepped out of the shadows to take the reins of
government in independent Britain, engineering a successful separation
from the Empire and ushering in the Brittonic Age.

---

84   Ausonius, *Epigrammata*, 107–12.
85   In Rutilius Namatianus, *De Reditu Suo*, 1.500. See Birley, 1980, 11, 56–7; and Snyder,
1998, 71.
86   Jerome, *Epistolae*, 133.9.14.
87   Mathews, 1983, 431.
88   See Evans, 1990, 98.

Part II
The Brittonic Age

5
Britons and Saxons

Some scholars have recently suggested that it was the Roman invasion of Britain which sparked an ethnic awareness among the Britons.[1] Faced with being incorporated into a multinational empire, and subsequently classified as a single province by Rome, native Britons could finally contrast themselves to other provincials and use a Greco-Roman concept – *Britannus* – to express a common ethnic identity. Ironically, it was a second external military threat – the barbarians, and particularly the *Saxones* – that solidified Brittonic identity. At the end of the ancient world and the beginning of the Middle Ages, it was the British political and ecclesiastical elites who defined Brittonic identity, and defined it, at least in part, by what the Britons were not: namely, pagan and English.

The fifth and sixth centuries AD were the most crucial period for the formation of Brittonic identity and Brittonic culture. Furthermore, by the year 600 the three 'nations' of Britain – England, Scotland, and Wales – began their slow emergence as separate political entities. Yet the period is plagued by two problems: the lack of a name and the lack of evidence. For centuries scholars have either ignored this era or treated it as a 'transition' or 'interlude' between two better-understood periods, Roman Britain and Anglo-Saxon England.[2] More recently, specialists have adopted the labels post-Roman and sub-Roman Britain. Post-Roman is obviously vague in its terminus, while sub-Roman, used first by pottery experts to describe ceramics that had degenerated from Roman norms, is downright offensive. In popular works Arthur's Britain or the Arthurian Period are often employed as labels, but these have serious flaws (as we'll examine below) and will never convince many academics.

I have suggested the Brittonic Age as a label for the fifth and sixth

---

1 See Matthews, 1999, 29; and James, 1999.
2 I have surveyed this attitude in Snyder, 1998.

centuries, whether one is talking about England, Scotland, or Wales.[3] It derives from the ethnic term used by contemporary British writers (especially Patrick and Gildas), and after all, only the Britons of the island's peoples produced writings in the fifth and sixth centuries. Furthermore, most scholars agree that the Britons remained the majority population throughout Britain in this period, and in most areas the politically dominant one as well. Though using the label Brittonic Age might strike some as partisan, it makes more sense than continuing to view the fifth and sixth centuries as Early Anglo-Saxon England when we have no contemporary English written sources and the material evidence for the Saxons prior to 600 is therefore difficult to interpret.

Sources and Evidence

The scarcity of evidence – literary, epigraphic, and archaeological – remains the biggest problem for scholars of the Brittonic Age, whether they are examining the natives or the immigrants. For the beginning of the period there are a few mentions of Britain by Greek and Latin chroniclers writing in other parts of the empire.[4] For the most part, however, these writers are only interested in the activities of the British tyrants who made bids for the imperial crown in 407–11. Events in Britain after 411 are described by two Gallic witnesses: the so-called Gallic Chronicles (written in 452 and 511), and Constantius of Lyons's *Life of St. Germanus of Auxerre* (written *c*.480). The value of the British evidence from these Gallic sources remains controversial, but they must be used in any attempt to construct a chronology of events in fifth-century Britain.[5]

The remainder of the historical evidence comes from British writers, and two in particular. 'If we wish to learn about sub-Roman Britain there is little we can do,' writes Ian Wood, 'other than investigate the cultural and social worlds of Patrick and Gildas.'[6] Detailed discussion of these two famous Britons will follow in the next chapter, on the British Church. Here it will suffice to say that controversies surround the dating of these two authors and their works, though much good work has been done recently by specialists and we can feel a bit safer in using their epistles to write our histories of the period, albeit tentatively.[7] For the sixth century other 'Celtic'

3   Snyder, 1998, 252.
4   E.g. Claudian, Olympiodorus, Orosius, Sozomen, Zosimus, and Procopius. For detailed discussion of the written evidence, see Snyder, 1998, ch. 3.
5   See Bartholomew, 1982; Muhlberger, 1983; Thompson, 1984; Wood, 1987; Jones and Casey, 1988; idem, 1991; and Burgess, 1990.
6   Wood, 1987, 260.
7   See Lapidge and Dumville, 1984; and Dumville et al., 1993.

sources – the Llandaff Charters, the *Historia Brittonum* and the *Annales Cambriae*, early Welsh and Irish penitentials, Welsh genealogies and saints' lives – have often been used by historians, but they are not contemporary and will be mostly avoided in this chapter. The same can be said for the English sources, especially Bede's *Ecclesiastical History* and the *Anglo-Saxon Chronicle*, which may reflect some trends in early English expansion but tempt us toward unsubstantiated narrative.

Inscriptions, on the other hand, can be used without such temptation. The epigraphic record of Roman Britain was by no means extensive, as compared to other imperial provinces. But it did set a precedent for the Britons of the fifth and sixth centuries, who also took clues from the Christian memorial inscriptions popular in post-Roman Gaul.[8] In both Latin and Ogam (an imported Irish script) dozens of Britons proclaimed their names, genealogy, faith, professions, and even patriotism in stone inscriptions.[9] The epigraphic evidence has been a little-used resource for writing the history of early medieval Britain, but there are some signs that this is beginning to change.[10]

As for the material evidence of the Brittonic Age, most attention has been focused on excavation of towns, hill-forts, and cemeteries.[11] Other important areas, less well investigated, include forts, villas, farmsteads, and coin hoards. Problems, however, beset excavators at most period sites.[12] Neither the Britons nor the first Saxon settlers used stone much in their structures, preferring materials like timber and thatch, which are ephemeral and difficult for most excavators to observe. Even more serious is the lack of datable artifacts. For the most part, Roman coins ceased arriving in Britain around 410, as did datable Roman ceramics (local wares are notoriously difficult to date). Germanic pottery and jewelry in Saxon graves, ceramics and glass imported from Gaul and the eastern Mediterranean beginning in the late fifth century, and an occasional radiocarbon date are all the material evidence we have for building chronologies in the Brittonic Age.

It has been said often that the Britons became 'archaeologically invisible' after 410, with no distinctive material culture of their own. 'But, "invisible" though they may be,' comments Peter Fowler, 'the British are there.'[13] Anglo-Saxon remains have heretofore dominated discussion of

8   See, for example, Knight, 1996.
9   For discussion and sources, see Snyder, 1998, 47–8; and the 'Celtic Inscribed Stones Project' on the Internet <http://www.ucl.ac.uk/archaeology/cisp/database/>.
10   See, for example, Thomas, 1994.
11   In general see Alcock, 1971; idem, 1987; and Snyder, 1997.
12   See Snyder, 1996, 6–9.
13   Fowler in Hines, 1997, 168.

the archaeological record. Weapons and other grave goods abound in Saxon cemeteries, and in the case of Sutton Hoo provide spectacular testimony to the material culture of early medieval Britain. To uncover the Britons' culture we must look harder, and the evidence is more often subtle than spectacular.

An Historical Narrative?

I have said, and still maintain, that it is impossible to write a true historical narrative of Britain in the fifth and sixth centuries, given the present state of our evidence. A cultural history of the Britons, derived from specific terms used by their writers and from their material remains, is more easily achievable. Nevertheless, a few political and ecclesiastical events can be glimpsed in the written sources and will now be related to provide a skeleton chronology on which to hang the cultural evidence.[14]

Our quasi-narrative begins with the political and military crises which mark the last years of Roman Britain. We saw in the previous chapter that problems in Italy between the Roman *magister* Stilicho and the Gothic federates under Alaric necessitated the withdrawal of troops from Britain in 401 or 402. Gildas, predictably, makes it a dramatic event: 'They [the Romans] then bade the Britons farewell, as if intending never to return.'[15] Though Britain was not left completely unprotected, its security was more than ever tied to the precarious defense of the western provinces, which was centered in Gaul. Disaster struck there on the last day of December 406, when Alans, Vandals, and Sueves crossed the frozen Rhine and overran the Gallic provinces of Gaul. Zosimus states that the invasion of Gaul terrorized the troops in Britain, who, fearing that the barbarians would cross the Channel next, responded by electing their own emperors to solve the frontier problems.[16]

The first to be elected was a soldier named Marcus, but he was soon put to death when he failed to please the soldiery. Their second choice is more interesting. He was a civilian named Gratian, described by Orosius as a *municeps* (civilian official).[17] According to Zosimus, the soldiers bestowed upon Gratian the imperial garb – purple robe and crown – and 'formed a bodyguard for him as they would an emperor.'[18] But the results

---

14   For a more detailed discussion, see Snyder, 1998, ch. 2.
15   Gildas, *De Excidio*, 18.3.
16   Zosimus, 6.3.1.
17   Orosius, 7.40.4.
18   Zosimus, 6.2.

of this usurpation were the same: failing to please his supporters, Gratian was killed after a four-month reign. The third candidate proved to be longer lived. Constantine – who became Constantine III – was chosen from the ranks of the military solely, we are told, on the basis of his name.[19] Cashing in on the reputation of Constantine the Great, who had also been declared emperor by the troops in Britain exactly 100 years before, the new usurper carried the propaganda even further by renaming his sons Constans and Julian. He then followed the example of that other British tyrant, Magnus Maximus, by taking British troops across to Gaul to secure the western frontier.

The fascinating moves of Consantine III, Alaric, Stilicho, and Honorius belong to the realm of Late Roman politics, and are best dealt with elsewhere.[20] Here it will suffice to relate Constantine's British connections and his political fate as it relates to the situation in Britain. After crossing to Gaul, the two generals Constantine appointed as his *magistri* were slain by Stilicho's *magister*. His new appointees included a Briton named Gerontius, who was sent to Spain with Constans (now carrying the title Caesar) to guard the Pyrenees while Constantine garrisoned the Alps. After initial successes Constans returned to his father in Gaul, entrusting Spain to the *magister* Gerontius. In 409, after concluding successful negotiations with Honorius, Constantine prepared to send his son back to Spain accompanied by a new *magister* to replace Gerontius. Somehow Gerontius got wind of these developments and proclaimed one of his own dependents, a man ironically named Maximus, as emperor. Zosimus states that Gerontius was able to win his soldiers' support for Maximus and even incited the barbarians in Gaul to revolt against Constantine, who, denuded of his Spanish troops, 'allowed the barbarians over the Rhine [i.e. Vandals, Sueves, etc.] to make unrestricted incursions' into Spain.[21]

These same 'barbarians from beyond the Rhine' (though here the confused Zosimus likely means other trans-Rhine barbarians, such as the Saxons) also harassed the inhabitants of Britain and some of the Gallic peoples (probably the Armoricans), forcing them to take up arms (illegally) and rebel against Rome.[22] 'The revolt of the provinces of Britain and Gaul occurred during Constantine's tyranny,' comments Zosimus, 'because the barbarians took advantage of his careless government.'[23]

Constantine responded to the crisis by making Constans his colleague, as Augustus, and sent him along with a new praetorian prefect to subdue

19   Orosius, 7.40.4; Sozomen, 9.11.
20   See, for example, Thomas S. Burns, *Barbarians Within the Gates of Rome* (1994).
21   Zosimus, 6.5.2. Cf. Orosius, 7.38–40; and Sozomen, 9.12.
22   Zosimus, 6.5.2–3. Cf. the *Gallic Chronicle of 452*, 281.17.
23   Zosimus, 6.6.1.

Spain. Constantine himself seems to have led an army across the Alps to meet Honorius in 410, perhaps to be defeated by Alaric, but soon returned to Gaul as Alaric turned south and sacked Rome. While Honorius was safely tucked away in fortified Ravenna, for Constantine the end was indeed near. Constans was repulsed by Gerontius and his allies in Spain, and returned to Constantine at Arelate. Constantine then sent his son in 411 to Vienna, but Constans was intercepted and killed by Gerontius.[24] Gerontius then marched on Arelate and besieged Constantine there. Honorius finally decided to rid himself of the usurper, and sent an army to Gaul under the command of Stilicho's successor, Constantius. Upon seeing the imperial army, Gerontius fled to a friend's estate, where he was himself besieged by his own troops and ultimately took his own life.[25] The besieged and despairing Constantine then laid down his power and took refuge in a church, where he was hurriedly ordained a priest. The city gates were then opened, and Constantine's troops turned the usurper and his young son Julian over to Constantius' army.[26] While the prisoners were being transported back to Italy, Honorius sent a band of assassins to meet them, and they were beheaded near the River Mincio.

The contemporary sources are quick to point out the negative impact that the actions of these 'tyrants' (as they were labeled) and their barbarian allies had on Britain, Gaul, and Spain. Zosimus records that fear of barbarian invasions is what drove the Britons to support Constantine's ambitions in 406.[27] But according to the Gallic Chronicles, while Constantine was busy 'oppressing' Gaul, he left Britain defenseless against a devastating attack by the Saxons in 408 or 410.[28] Piracy in the English Channel was endemic in the Late Roman period. For most of the third and fourth centuries the Franks posed the most serious threat to the western Roman provinces, though only attacks on the coast of Gaul are specifically mentioned in the sources.[29] By the late fourth century Saxon pirates begin to eclipse the Franks, and the first unambiguous references to Saxon raids on Britain appear c.400.[30] It may be to this date that we affix the official naming of the 'Saxon Shore,' in which case it was most likely a creation of Stilicho's.

24   Sozomen, 9.12–13; Orosius, 7.42.4.
25   Sozomen, 11.13.
26   Sozomen, 9.15; Orosius, 7.42.3.
27   Zosimus, 6.3.1.
28   Gallic Chronicle of 452, under Honorius XVI (410). For the dating controversy, see Thompson, 1977; Bartholomew, 1982; Muhlberger, 1983; Wood, 1984; and Jones and Casey, 1988.
29   Wood, 1990, 94.
30   Wood, 1990; Bartholomew, 1984.

Zosimus records another Saxon attack on Britain in 409, which deserves quoting in full:

[Constantine III] allowed the barbarians over the Rhine to make unrestricted incursions. They reduced the inhabitants of Britain and some of the Gallic peoples to such straits that they revolted from the Roman empire, no longer submitted to Roman law, and reverted to their native customs. The Britons, therefore, armed themselves and ran many risks to ensure their own safety and free their cities from the attacking barbarians. The whole of Armorica and other Gallic provinces, in imitation of the Britons, freed themselves in the same way, by expelling the Roman magistrates and establishing the government they wanted.[31]

The actions taken by the Britons and Armoricans in successfully freeing themselves from the empire were revolutionary, illegal, and unprecedented. Procopius tells us that, after the revolt of Constantine III, 'the Romans were no longer able to recover Britain, which from that time on continued to be ruled by tyrants.'[32] An entry in a mid-fifth-century Roman chronicle, describing events in 410, confirms this: 'The British provinces were removed from Roman authority forever.'[33] Even later writers like Bede preserve the tradition that the year 410 marks the end of Roman rule in Britain.[34]

One further piece of significant evidence that has been seen by many to signify the official end of Roman rule in Britain is the so-called Rescript of Honorius. This survives in a passage in Zosimus, who, while describing Alaric's activities in Italy in 410, writes: 'Honorius sent letters to the cities [πόλεις] in Britain, urging them to fend for themselves.'[35] This Rescript may have been in response to an appeal for help from some party in Britain, and it is significant that Honorius addressed his letters to the cities in Britain. One would expect such letters to be sent to the *vicarius* or some such imperial representative; the implication is that the municipal authorities were the only officials to survive the tumultuous events of 406–10.[36]

While it is commonly agreed that the British revolution and the Rescript of Honorius are significant events, interpretations have varied

31   Zosimus, 6.5 (trans. Ridley).
32   Procopius, *De Bello Vandalico*, 1.2.31 and 38.
33   *Narratio de imperatoribus domus Valentinianae et Theodosianae* (*MGH, Chronica Minora*, bk. 1, 629, my translation).
34   See, for example, Bede, *EH*, 1.11; *Historia Brittonum*, 28; and *The Anglo-Saxon Chronicle* (A, Parker Chronicle), sa 409.
35   For controversies surrounding the Rescript, see Bartholomew, 1982; Thompson, 1982; and idem, 1983.
36   See Biddle, 1976, 104.

enormously.[37] I have argued that the events of 409–11 can best be interpreted as an aristocratic coup staged by Britons who were faced with serious barbarian raids in Britain and the news of Constantine III's failures on the continent.[38] Gildas, Zosimus and other observers state that the Britons (or at least a faction of them) expelled Roman officials and reverted to native laws and local rulers.[39] To take up arms against the barbarians threatening their cities, the Britons would by necessity have had to disobey Roman law and those responsible for enforcing it: Constantine's officials. Those remaining to defend and govern Britain, who rejected Roman government and now truly saw themselves as Britons, were those with most at stake in the island: civic officials and local aristocrats who had land, wealth, and retainers. These are the tyrants of sub-Roman Britain, the forerunners of the dynastic kings of the early Middle Ages, and we will return to them later in this chapter.

The only detailed description of events in Britain after 410 comes from Constantius of Lyons, who described two visits of St. Germanus to Britain in 429 and c.440.[40] A chronicler tells us that Germanus, then bishop of Auxerre, was sent by Pope Celestine to Britain 'to confound the [Pelagian] heretics and guide the Britons to the Catholic faith.'[41] Though this is described as a papal mission, Germanus may also have been sent to implement laws against Pelagians created by Honorius after Britain was separated from Rome.[42] Pelagianism was a real presence in fifth-century Britain (as we'll see in the next chapter), but it is stretching the evidence to infer (as some scholars have done)[43] that Pelagians were the leaders of the political revolt of 410.

Constantius, of course, describes both of Germanus' visits to Britain as successes. The bishop defeats the Pelagians in debate; heals a blind girl who is the daughter of a 'man of tribunician power'; visits the shrine of the British martyr St. Alban (presumably at Verulamium); baptizes British soldiers and leads them to victory against Picts and Scots (the famous 'Alleluia! Victory'); and, on the last visit, healed the son of one 'Elafius, chief man of that region.'[44] Unfortunately, our Gallic author is vague about geographical details in Britain, and does not give us any real picture of the political climate on the island in the middle of the fifth century.

---

37   See, for example, Myres, 1960; Morris, 1965; Thompson, 1977; Thomas, 1981a, 57–60; and Wood, 1984.
38   Snyder, 1998, passim.
39   See, for example, Gildas, *De Excidio*, 13–14; and Zosimus, 6.5.3.
40   The second date is controversial: see Thompson, 1984, 55–70; and Wood, 1984.
41   Prosper of Aquitaine, *Chronicon*, sa 429.
42   Higham, 1992, 74–5.
43   See Myres, 1960; Morris, 1965; and Wood, 1984.
44   Constantius, *Life of St. Germanus*, 3.14–15 and 5.25–7.

Other Gallic witnesses, however, do make a couple of bold statements on the political situation at this time:

In the eighteenth and nineteenth years of the reign of Theodosius II, the British provinces, which to this time had suffered from various disasters and misfortunes, are reduced by the power of the Saxons.[45]

In the sixteenth year of Theodosius II and Valentinian III, the British provinces, lost to the Romans, yield to the power of the Saxons.[46]

Studies have assigned both of these entries to the year 441. On the surface, this would appear to be concrete evidence for the end of sub-Roman Britain and the beginning of Anglo-Saxon England in 441.[47] However, given that Bede and other sources clung to the year 449 as the *beginning* of the Saxon migrations, and given that the archaeological evidence for Saxon settlement in Britain prior to 450 is very slight, it seems unlikely that any more than a small (eastern) portion of British lands had come under Saxon control by 441. Our Gallic witness, writing in the later fifth century (possibly with Frankish informants), may be giving us a distorted and exaggerated view of the political realities in Britain.[48]

In any event, the Britons were feeling seriously threatened by barbarians at this time. They (or specifically a pro-imperial party in Britain)[49] sent an appeal to the Roman general Aëtius, who was conducting military operations in Gaul in the 430s, asking for aid:

'To Agitius [sic], thrice consul, the groans of the British . . . The barbarians push us back to the sea, the sea pushes us back to the barbarians; between these two kinds of death, we are either drowned or slaughtered.'[50]

No Roman aid came. From this it seems that it may have been the Picts and the Scots, rather than the Saxons, who were the most serious threat. Further weakened by famine and civil war, the Britons decided to convene a council to address national security issues. Led by the 'proud tyrant' – *tyrannus superbus*, named in some accounts as the British king *Vortigern* – the council decided to hire Saxon mercenaries to wage war in Britain against 'the peoples of the north.'[51] These Saxons came to Britain

45   *The Gallic Chronicle of 452.*
46   *The Gallic Chronicle of 511.*
47   See Jones and Casey, 1988.
48   See Burgess, 1990.
49   See Wood, 1987, 261.
50   Quoted in Gildas, *De Excidio*, 20.1.
51   Gildas, *De Excidio*, 22–3.

in their *keels* (warships) and were settled 'on the east side of the island' under a formal treaty which gave them regular payments and food supplies in exchange for their service. Gildas' information accords well with established Roman military policies regarding barbarian federates.

The Saxon federates were apparently successful in keeping the Picts at bay. They asked for more supplies, and at the same time called for reinforcements from their continental homelands. Then, complaining that their payments were insufficient, they broke their treaty and began plundering British towns:

> All the major towns were laid low by the repeated battering of enemy rams; laid low, too, all the inhabitants – church leaders, priests and people alike, as the swords glinted all around and the flames crackled. It was a sad sight. In the middle of the squares the foundation stones of high walls and towers that had been torn from their lofty base, holy altars, fragments of corpses, covered . . . with a purple crust of congealed blood . . . There was no burial to be had except in the ruins of houses or the bellies of beasts and birds.[52]

In the wake of these devastations, some Britons fled to the mountains and to hill-forts, others 'made for lands beyond the sea.' Those Britons who stayed put finally found a leader, Ambrosius Aurelianus, described by Gildas as a gentleman (*vir modesto*), 'perhaps last of the Romans,' whose parents 'had possibly worn the purple.'[53] Ambrosius challenged the Saxons in battle, and won some victories. The pendulum swung back and forth until 'the siege of Badon Hill (*mons Badonicus*),' a major victory for the Britons attributed in later sources to Arthur.[54] Gildas dates Badon to the year of his birth, with 44 years passing until the writing of the De Excidio. Though a matter of much scholarly debate, current opinion favors a dating of Badon to around 485–500.[55]

Badon marked the beginning of a period of relative peace (perhaps a legal truce) between Briton and Saxon. The archaeological record shows consolidation rather than expansion of English-controlled areas, and an increase of imported luxuries at British high-status sites. Gildas says that the Britons were distracted by political and ecclesiastical corruption and civil war in this period. He gives the names (and sins) of five British rulers – Constantinus, Aurelius Caninus, Vortipor, Cuneglasus, and Maglocunus – but is vague about the territory they controlled. More sixth-century

---

52   Gildas, *De Excidio*, 24.3–4.
53   Gildas, *De Excidio*, 25.2–3.
54   Gildas, *De Excidio*, 26; *Annales Cambriae*, s.a. 518.
55   Dumville, 1984; Jones, 1996a, 46; Snyder, 1998, 45. See, however, Higham, 1994; and Wiseman, 2000.

British rulers are known from memorial stones: e.g. Voteporix (Irish *Votecorix*) in Carmarthenshire, King Cadfan and Maglos 'the Magistrate' in Gwynedd, and the *Princeps* Iuriucus in Dumnonia.[56] We don't know exactly when this stalemate between Britons and Saxons ended. Later sources, like the *Anglo-Saxon Chronicle*, mention significant English victories in the west in the late fifth century which would have isolated the British. For example, the Battle of Dyrham (*c.577*), in which the British towns of Gloucester, Cirencester, and Bath fell to the West Saxons, cut off the Britons of Dumnonia from those in Wales, just as the Battle of Chester (*c.615*), in which the English slew a host of British soldiers and priests, would have isolated the Welsh from the northern Britons (dissecting the kingdom of Powys). The Battle of Catraeth (*c.572*), commemorated in the British poem *Y Gododdin*, saw the Deirans wipe out an entire war-band of the Votadini (Britons from around Edinburgh), and perhaps paved the way for the creation of the English kingdom of Northumbria.[57]

A New Model for the *Adventus Saxonum*

Heroic poetry and propagandistic chronicles penned centuries after the events are not the best material for writing an accurate history of the British–Saxon wars. Bede's *Ecclesiastical History of the English People*, written in 731, has for centuries provided the narrative framework for our understanding of the English conquest of the Britons. Now, however, Anglo-Saxonists are relying more on archaeological evidence to construct their models. What follows is a survey of current scholarly thought on the creation of Anglo-Saxon England, and my own model for what has come to be called the *adventus Saxonum*, the coming of the Saxons.

Angles and Saxons begin appearing in Roman sources around the time of Tacitus and Ptolemy. Saxon soldiers fought under Roman commanders in the East in the mid-fourth century, and Ambrose records that Saxon troops played an important part in Theodosius' victory over Magnus Maximus in 388.[58] We don't know when or how the first Saxons came to settle in Britain, though as we have seen they appear as sea raiders in the late fourth century. From archaeological and placename evidence it has been observed that the earliest Anglo-Saxon settlements in Britain lay in close proximity to Roman settlements and roads, and that these new

56   ECMW nos. 138 and 103. See Thomas, 1997, 77; and Snyder, 1998, 118.
57   See Dumville, 1989; and chapter 10 below.
58   See Bartholomew, 1984.

settlements often corresponded to Roman estate boundaries.[59] All this suggests that, until the late fifth century, Anglo-Saxon settlement was being controlled by Romano-British authorities.[60]

Bede's account of the advent of the English peoples in Britain has become legendary (and indeed may have derived from legends):

> They came from three very powerful Germanic tribes, the Saxons, Angles, and Jutes. The people of Kent and the inhabitants of the Isle of Wight are of Jutish origin . . . From the Saxon country, that is, the district now known as Old Saxony, came the East Saxons, the South Saxons, and the West Saxons. Besides this, from the country of the Angles, that is, the land between the kingdoms of the Jutes and the Saxons, which is called *Angulus*, came the East Angles, the Middle Angles, the Mercians, and all the Northumbrian race (that is those who dwell north of the river Humber) as well as the other Anglian tribes.[61]

Rather than discard it, archaeologists have provided a complement to Bede's settlement account based upon the distribution of identifiable continental pottery types, metalwork, and burial rites in England (see map 5.1).[62] Though not without criticism of some of its details, it does offer a broad and useful picture: settlers from Anglian Schleswig-Holstein and Fyn were in the Midlands and northeastern England from the early fifth century, those from western Norway reaching Norfolk and Humberside in the late fifth century, Saxons from between the Wesser and the Elbe in northern Germany settling in the Thames Valley, Wessex, and Sussex in the middle of the fifth century, about the same time that some Jutes migrated from Jutland to Kent. Other small groups of Germanic immigrants, distinguished by their material culture, include Franks in southeastern England (fifth/sixth century) and Scandinavians from southern and western Norway who settled on the east coast in the last quarter of the fifth century. Frisian immigration to Britain has recently been dismissed.[63] In all, some 30 tribal groupings were identified in Anglo-Saxon England by a seventh-century survey known as the Tribal Hidage.

An ongoing controversy is recorded in opinions on the scale of the migrations. The conventional view, based mainly on the evidence of Gildas and Bede, would have massive numbers of Germanic immigrants overwhelming the British population in a series of bloody wars – the 'burn

---

59   Hodges, 1989, 25.
60   Yorke, 1992, 5, 7–8.
61   Bede, *EH*, 1.15 (trans. Colgrave).
62   See Evison, 1981, 166; Hines, 1990; Welch, 1993, 11; Hines, 1994; and Arnold, 1997, 23.
63   Bremmer, 1990.

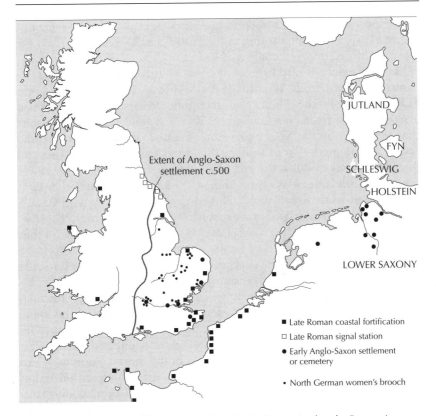

Map 5.1   The continental homelands of the Anglo-Saxons and early Germanic settlement in Britain.

and slaughter' model. The minimalist position, which is currently gaining a lot of adherents, sees the 'conquest' as the work of a relatively small number of warrior elites from the continent who impose their language and material culture on the Britons. Michael Jones, leaning toward the latter explanation, estimates that the total numbers for the Anglo-Saxon migrations c.410–550 were between 10,000 and 20,000.[64] The high number of weapons in early Anglo-Saxon burials suggests that the movement was highly militarized, though weapons clearly played a symbolic role in pagan Germanic burial rites.[65] Böhme has suggested a date of c.420 for the beginning of the Saxon advent, based on associated metalwork (especially brooches) in the earliest Anglo-Saxon cremation cemeteries

64   Jones, 1996a, 27.
65   Härke, 1989; Jones, 1996a, 32

(Dorchester-on-Thames, Milton Regis, Mucking).[66] These may represent Germanic *laeti* set up by someone like Stilicho or Constantine III in the waning years of imperial control of Britain.

Material evidence also gives us the best picture of settlement and expansion patterns.[67] The handful of Anglo-Saxon settlements dated pre-450 lie between the Thames and Humber rivers, with southward expansion into Kent, Sussex, Surrey, Wiltshire, and Hampshire occurring by *c*.475. By the 520s expansion occurred westward, toward the Severn and along the Trent, and northward in Yorkshire to the Tees and the Tyne. From *c*.520 to the end of the Migration Period, *c*.560, there was no significant extension of Anglo-Saxon territory, but rather consolidation of lands already held. This corresponds roughly with Gildas' description of relative peace in the first half of the sixth century. 'Clearly,' writes Michael Jones, 'for Gildas and his contemporaries the Saxons pose no imminent threat.'[68]

It should be noted that this archaeological picture shows us basically the beginnings of an Anglicization of Britain's 'Channel Zone.'[69] This east central portion of the island, which would eventually become England, was according to Cunliffe the most innovative region of the island in the Iron Age, frequently absorbing new ideas from the continent. With the fall of the Catuvellaunian state in AD 43, native British identity asserted itself in the Roman period usually in the more conservative Atlantic Zone and in the far north. This roughly corresponds with Britain's medieval 'Celtic fringe' – Cornwall, Wales and Man, Cumbria, and Scotland. While the newcomers in England continued to be influenced by trends in northern Gaul and southern Scandinavia, the Britons in this northern and western fringe continued to develop contacts with the Atlantic regions of northwest Spain, Brittany, Ireland, and the Western Isles of Scotland.

It is now possible to posit a new model for the Saxon advent, one that takes into account both the latest archaeological evidence as well as our current understanding of the written sources.[70] Most historians and archaeologists are in surprising agreement with Gildas on the arrival of the first Saxons. They came to Britain – in small numbers at first – as military recruits, mercenaries (*laeti* or *foederati*) who had served Roman commanders along the Rhine. In the mid-fifth century they responded to a particular invitation of the British council and the *tyrannus superbus*. These British

66   Böhme, 1986.
67   See, for example, Hines, 1990, 26–8.
68   Jones, 1996a, 51.
69   See discussion in chapter 2.
70   See also Snyder, forthcoming.

authorities settled the Saxon recruits (according to a treaty which gave them regular rations of food and other supplies) in the north and east of Britain, mainly to protect the British towns and rich lowland farmlands from the sea-borne raids of the Picts and assorted North Sea pirates. Specifically, they were billeted in or near towns, from the Wash and Humber estuaries down through the Thames river valley, perhaps joining earlier Germanic mercenaries established by the last imperial authorities in Britain.[71]

During this time, in the middle of the fifth century, the Saxons increased their numbers through an influx of women and children from their continental homelands. We can glimpse this in the archaeological record, which shows desertion of low-lying coastal communities in Germany and Denmark c.450 (perhaps necessitated by rising sea-levels) and the appearance of north German women's brooches in eastern Britain (see map 5.1 above). After some successful fighting against the Picts, the Saxon mercenaries turned against their British employers in a revolt that involved the pillaging of the towns of lowland Britain. It will be shown below that most of these eastern towns, where Saxon sunken-floored huts have been found inside or just outside city walls, fell completely out of use by c.500. Yet few if any of these towns have revealed incontrovertible evidence of fire and destruction, as Gildas depicts in his account. Gildas also writes that plague and famine led to the destruction of urban life in Britain. While the plague did visit the British Isles in the late sixth century, there is no strong evidence of it playing a catastrophic role in the years preceding the Saxon revolt.[72]

I believe that a desertion model best fits the material and historical evidence.[73] A large-scale depopulation, and especially evacuation, in the towns of eastern Britain supports Gildas' testimony and explains the lack of destruction layers at most excavated towns. In most Romano-British towns, the material evidence argues for abandonment and deliberate dismantling rather than destruction.[74] (The *Anglo-Saxon Chronicle* does not record the conquest of a single British town until the Battle of Dyrham in 577, when the three cities that were taken are in the west.) Furthermore, Gildas describes Britons fleeing these ravaged towns for lands across the sea. He says that they sang psalms (rather than chanteys) aboard the ships as they left Britain, suggesting that they were Christians led by their clergy.[75]

71   Welch, 1994, 175; Eagles, 1980.
72   Todd, 1977.
73   For a more detailed discussion, see Snyder, forthcoming.
74   See Russo, 1998, 51–2 and 83.
75   Gildas, *De Excidio*, 25.1.

This may explain the numerous literary references to British clergy in Gaul – indeed, more expatriate Britons are known by name than their kin in fifth-century Britain.[76]

For the leaders of the evacuation we should look to the British bishops. The bishops would have had the administrative ability to organize an evacuation of the towns and to resettle their congregations in free communities throughout Brittany and Galicia, where we have the names of British clergy on record.[77] Meanwhile, the Christians remaining in Britain sought increasingly places of worship farther removed and better protected from the pagan Saxons. (In the next chapter we'll look at the impact British Christians had on their English neighbors as the latter were becoming converts.) This fit well with the ascetic spirit of British monasticism, which grew rapidly after 500.[78] Rural villas became monasteries, while hermitages were established in caves and on islands. From excavations and from hagiography we get a clear picture of a British Church moving rapidly and irreversibly from towns to rural and even isolated sites.

When the Roman missionary Augustine crossed from Gaul to Canterbury in 597, he dealt not with British bishops but with English kings who had established kingdoms throughout the east and trade agreements with their Frankish counterparts across the Channel. Richard Hodges has suggested that it was these new trade contacts with the Franks that incited the Saxons into expansion in Britain, for wars against the Britons would enable Anglo-Saxon elites to acquire slaves and prestige items to trade with Frankish merchants.[79] These trade contacts were followed, especially in Kent, by inter-dynastic marriages and ecclesiastical connections, to the point that Merovingian kings made claims of hegemony over much of southern England.[80] These and more ancient kinship ties with the Saxons led Frankish chroniclers in the sixth century to ignore the British princes and prelates who still held sway over most of the island (and it was Gaul who most often informed Rome and Constantinople of western affairs).

Though not all archaeologists accept the minimalist view of the scale of the Saxon advent, few if any support the notion that the British population of 'England' was completely wiped out.[81] King Ine's laws (*c.*700) clearly show that *wilisc* and *englisc* – British and English – are living side-

---

76   See Snyder, 1998, 70.
77   See chapter 7 below.
78   See Thomas, 1981a, 347–55.
79   Hodges, 1989, 33.
80   Wood, 1990, 96.
81   See Richards, 1995, 56–7.

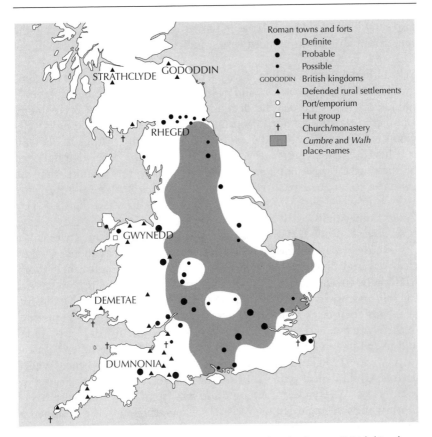

Map 5.2 Britain in the fifth and sixth centuries AD, showing known British kingdoms and settlements. Shaded areas indicate regions that came under English control by the end of the Brittonic Age but contained a high density of placenames indicating surviving British communities.

by-side within Wessex. Archaeologists have proposed two 'Saxon-free zones' – around Leeds, which became the kingdom of Elmet, and in the Chilterns – where British polities may have survived for some time surrounded by English kingdoms. Two such English kingdoms in the north – Bernicia and Deira – have names of British origin, while the names of other English polities like Kent and Lindsey preserve British elements.[82] Kenneth Jackson suggested that this was the result of bilingual Britons transmitting Celtic toponyms to English-speaking immigrants. Studies have

82   Bassett, 1989, 5.

also shown that field boundaries in East Anglia and the Midlands stay the same from Roman to modern times, indicating continuity of use in the fifth and sixth centuries.[83]

In addition to land-holding patterns, other signs of continuity of Brittonic practices in Anglo-Saxon England include placenames and building types.[84] Frequently discussed are the dozens of English towns like Brettenham, Cumberworth, Wallingford, Walton, etc. which contain Old English elements – *Brettas*, *Walas*, and *Cumbre* – that designate Britons.[85] These, it is believed, are names given by the English to communities characterized by their large British populations. We now know, furthermore, that the common rectangular timber buildings once called 'Saxon houses' derive at least in part from Romano-British rural structures (see figure 5.1).[86] Large timber halls excavated at Yeavering and Cowdery's Down have been described as a fusion of Romano-British and Germanic styles.[87]

Nevertheless, in northern and western Britain there was an increasingly clear cultural divide between the Britons and their English neighbors. Materially, this is apparent in, for example, the British elites' preference for hillforts, their exclusive trade contacts with the eastern Mediterranean, and their large regional cemeteries (see below).[88] It is also apparent in the written sources from both sides of the hostile divide, with Gildas and 'Nennius' on one side and Aldhelm and Bede on the other.[89] In the early Anglo-Saxon laws the Old English word *wealh*, from whence 'Welsh' derives, could denote either a Briton or a slave. '[This] shows,' observes John Hines, 'a very clear contempt and a sense of the very low status of those who were regarded as Welsh.'[90] The surprisingly low number of Celtic loan-words in the English language has been interpreted as strong linguistic evidence against intermarriage between Britons and Saxons.[91]

David Dumville has, alone among recent historians, been consistent in stressing this cultural divide. He writes, in the context of the British element in Northumbria, that

> Anglo-British relations in the fifth, sixth and seventh centuries were of course largely characterized by hostility. There seems no reason to regard the course of events in the North as essentially different from that in the Midlands or

83   Esmonde Cleary, 1995.
84   See Richards, 1995, 57; and Hooke, 1998, passim.
85   See, for example, Thomas, 1981a, 257.
86   Dixon, 1982; Hodges, 1989, 34–6; Arnold, 1997, 30.
87   Yorke, 1992, 9.
88   Hodges, 1989, 32.
89   See chapter 12 below.
90   Hines in Dumville, 1995, 214. See also Härke, 1997.
91   Härke, 1997, 149.

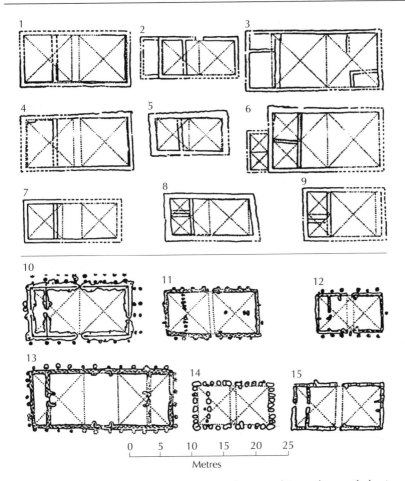

Figure 5.1   Comparison plans of Late Roman (above) and Saxon houses (below).

the South. As Wendy Davies reminded us in her Oxford O'Donnell Lectures, English aggression is a constant theme in Anglo-British relations: talk of treaties, and of continuity of institutions and population between British and English rule, cannot wish that away.[92]

The Historical Arthur Debate

The most recognizable symbol of the enmity between Briton and Saxon is the Britons' legendary war leader, King Arthur. Yet the most famous of

92   Dumville, 1989, 219.

all Britons is, regrettably, the most elusive to historians.[93] There is no contemporary written evidence for the existence of Arthur; nor is there any concrete physical evidence linked specifically with the king, despite the claim of the Glastonbury monks in 1190 that they had uncovered his grave.[94] Yet there is enough circumstantial evidence to have launched a veritable publishing industry around historical Arthur theories. When, in the early 1970s, two well-respected scholars released serious books building a case for an Arthurian Age, a few academics responded with a vigorous skepticism that has now become orthodoxy.[95]

I agree with the skeptics that we cannot, or should not, construct our historical models of the Brittonic Age using Arthur.[96] The earliest mentions of Arthur are in vernacular poetry and chronicles written centuries after the Battle of Badon Hill, a British victory usually attributed to him. Nor is the linguistic and placename evidence for Arthur's existence any stronger than the historical and archaeological. He was, without a doubt, an important figure (usually heroic, but sometimes tyrannical) to the Britons throughout the Middle Ages, lending his name to dozens of geographical features across Britain and serving, along with his knights, as the subject of several Welsh and Breton tales which in turn inspired the great French romances of the twelfth and thirteenth centuries.[97] But academic historians, playing by the strict rules of our discipline, can say little of value about Arthur.[98]

I disagree, however, with those skeptics who believe there is proof that Arthur is pure fabrication. Theories that trace his origins to mythology and folklore are as unconvincing as those that 'prove' his historicity. We cannot dismiss Arthur as an ancient god remembered as a man nor as a folkloric hero created by an imaginative bard. He must, for now at least, remain both a mystery and a possibility. Rather than asking how Arthur defined this period in British history, let us use our resources to define the culture of this period that may or may not have been home to an historical Arthur, but did nevertheless launch his legend.

Towns and Hill-forts

The quest for Arthur took on an archaeological dimension in the late 1960s with a highly publicized excavation at South Cadbury hill-fort,

93   For full discussion see Snyder, 2000.
94   See chapter 11 below.
95   Alcock, 1971, and Morris, 1973. The seminal essay from the skeptics is Dumville, 1977.
96   See Thomas, 1981a, 245; and Snyder, 1998, appendix B.
97   See chapter 12 below.
98   See Charles-Edwards, 1991.

known locally since at least the sixteenth century as 'Camelot.' These excavations, directed by Leslie Alcock, focused scholars' attention on the re-occupied hill-forts throughout northern and western Britain which were an important part of British culture in the fifth and sixth centuries AD. At about the same time archaeologists began to wonder about the fate of Roman towns in the post-Roman years, suggesting that there may have been more continuity of urban occupation than had been previously assumed. Together, the recent excavation of towns and hill-forts provides us with the largest body of material evidence in discussing Brittonic culture.

The first strong evidence for urban continuity came from the cities of Bath, Silchester, and Verulamium (St. Albans).[99] Cunliffe's excavations at Bath revealed a small town whose population actually increased in the fourth century while other urban populations were, allegedly, decreasing.[100] Activity was so intense at the baths complex that its floors had to be repaved a total of six times after the year 350, with three of those pavings belonging to the fifth century; even the last floor slabs showed considerable wear from the passage of feet. At least one new domestic structure was built in the fifth century, and literary evidence suggests that Bath was a major British settlement (and perhaps the residence of a king) when it was taken by the advancing West Saxons in the late sixth century.

Silchester likewise has shown signs of new structures and renovations in the fourth century, with economic activity continuing in the forum and elsewhere, confirmed by the presence of fifth-century coins, jewelry, pottery, and glass.[101] Most interesting of all was the discovery of a late fourth-century basilican church and accompanying baptismal font, the first Christian church to be identified in Roman Britain. A series of massive earthen dykes in the area (Grim's Bank being the most substantial) may have been an attempt by the Britons to mark the boundaries of their kingdom or *civitas*, centered around Silchester, which held out against the Saxons until the seventh century.

A 'Saxon-free zone' has also been argued for Verulamium, which (according to *The Anglo-Saxon Chronicle*) fell to the Saxons after the Battle of Bedcanford in 571. Sheppard Frere's excavations revealed a diversity of both public and private activity in sub-Roman Verulamium, including a 22-room town house built c.380 with subsequent extensions, new mosaics, and the installation of a corn-drying oven.[102] When this house was

99   For a more extensive discussion of sub-Roman towns see Snyder, 1998, 138–63.
100   See Cunliffe and Davenport, 1985; and Snyder, 1997.
101   See Fulford, 1985; and Snyder, 1997. The Silchester excavations have not yet been fully published.
102   See Frere, 1983; and Snyder, 1997.

demolished *c*.460, it was replaced by a large hall or barn, disturbed at an even later stage by the laying of a wood and iron water-pipe. Mosaics and water-pipes signal the survival of Roman artistic and engineering skills in the fifth century, not to mention a still-functioning Roman aqueduct. A healthy fifth-century economy is confirmed by the presence of imported Mediterranean pottery at Verulamium, and intensive activity is also apparent at the shrine of St. Alban located beneath the later Anglo-Saxon church.

Although it is now clear that British occupation continued into (at least) the sixth century at Silchester and Verulamium, neither of these towns became significant Anglo-Saxon settlements. Of course, most of the large towns of Roman Britain – e.g. London, York, and Lincoln – *did* become important English towns, mainly because of episcopal organization. London has shown some signs of fifth-century activity, especially at the Tower and along the waterfront.[103] At a town house near Billingsgate, for example, under-floor heating and a private bath suite continued in use well into the fifth century, while its occupants were buying eastern Mediterranean imports. London likely remained an important British center until the end of the fifth century, when, vulnerable to raids up the Thames, it was probably abandoned (no major Saxon settlement occurred until the time of Alfred).

Slight archaeological finds in Lincoln (e.g. a wooden church and a sub-Roman cemetery in the forum courtyard) suggest a fifth-century Christian community in the city, which has produced no archaeological evidence of early English settlers (they seem to have settled two miles to the north of the modern city limit).[104] The royal genealogy of Lindsey records a sixth-century king with the unmistakably British name of Caedbad, and when in the late seventh century the English took over Lincoln its ruler bore the title *praefectus Lindocolinae civitas*.[105] In the previous chapter we noted that industrial activity continued at York well after it had ceased to be an important Roman fortress. A small pig horizon, found under the collapsed roof of the Legionary Basilica, and African amphoras found in the centurion's quarter of Barrack 2, suggest large-scale specialist consumption by a fifth-century potentate.[106] 'The implication is that,' writes Steve Roskams, 'surplus could still be taken from the countryside, and on a considerable scale.'[107]

103   See Perring, 1991; and Snyder, 1997.
104   See Gilmour, 1979; and Snyder, 1997.
105   See Eagles, 1989.
106   Martin Carver in Phillips and Haywood, 1995, 187–97.
107   Roskams, 1996, 283-4.

The most talked-about urban construction in the Brittonic Age is that discovered by Philip Barker's team at Wroxeter (see plate 5.1).[108] Specifically, the area of the baths basilica at Roman Wroxeter saw careful demolition and subsequent rebuilding in the fifth and sixth centuries. The basilica roof was dismantled and the interior was used first as an open-air market, with some nearby industrial activity. This was followed by a carefully planned complex of multi-storied timber houses, market stalls, and boardwalks. The largest structure resembled a tower-façade villa, probably the residence of a civic magnate or *tyrannus*. An alternative recently suggested is that Wroxeter formed the center of a still active Catholic diocese with an 'episcopal villa' constructed at its heart in the sixth century.[109] The fact that the *frigidarium* remained intact has led some to interpret its reuse as a small church (the plunge pool serving as a baptismal font) with accompanying cemetery (12 burials were found in the surrounding hypocaust).

The Wroxeter timber complex is an exceptional find, but one wonders how many Romano-British towns may have possessed such sub-Roman wooden structures, the slight remains of which were overlooked by early excavators. More durable artifacts, like pottery and metalwork, have helped archaeologists identify sub-Roman continuity at many other British towns: Carlisle, Worcester, Gloucester, Caerwent, Cirencester, Dorchester, Exeter, Winchester, Chichester, Canterbury, Chelmsford.[110] It should be noted that most of these towns are in the west, while eastern towns like Colchester, Caistor, and Aldborough do not show us material evidence for fifth-century Britons, but instead show signs either of abandonment or intense early English occupation.

The northern part of Roman Britain had not been highly urbanized. Gildas, though a bit confused in his northern geography, seems to suggest that the Hadrianic frontier continued to function after 410 in a Brittish defense against the Picts.[111] New structures at Birdoswald and South Shields (including timber halls and gatehouses), and an assortment of weapon finds, support this scenario.[112] Pollen analysis suggests that reforestation along Hadrian's Wall began in the mid-fifth century, probably an indicator that agricultural lands whose chief purpose was to sustain the large Roman military population had gone out of use.[113] The armies of the

---

108   See Barker et al., 1997.
109   Barker et al., 1997, 238.
110   See Snyder, 1998, 138–63.
111   See Jones, 1996b, 52.
112   See K.R. Dark, 1992; Snyder, 1998, 168–73.
113   Jones, 1996b, 50–5; S.P. Dark, 1996.

Plate 5.1 Reconstruction drawing of the timber complex at Wroxeter. After most of the the masonry baths basilica was carefully dismantled, classical-style timber buildings were erected on the site in the later fifth and sixth centuries. (© English Heritage.)

Brittonic Age are clearly much smaller, but they are there in the north and were likely still using some Roman military installations. The same can be said of the forts of the Saxon Shore, whose still standing massive walls would have made them attractive to sub-Roman kings, though their eastern location and susceptibility to sea raiders explains why many fell early to the English.[114]

The threat to the forts and walled towns of southern Britain would have sent many Britons in search of alternative places of refuge. In Wales and the southwest the most attractive candidates were Iron Age hill-forts and other defensible hilltops and promontories. Though the early Roman campaigns were aimed at capturing hill-forts and resettling their inhabitants, archaeological evidence suggests that the Roman administration must have permitted Britons to reoccupy some rural hill-forts by the third century AD if not earlier.[115]

An early, and perhaps the most important, discovery came in the 1930s with Ralegh Radford's excavations at Tintagel 'Island,' a steep-cliffed promontory in Cornwall.[116] Beyond the inner ward of Tintagel's Norman castle, Radford uncovered the remains of several small rectangular structures made of stone and slate, as well as thousands of sherds of imported Mediterranean pottery, then termed 'Tintagel ware.' Many of the sherds came from wine and oil containers datable to the fifth to seventh centuries, leading Radford to interpret this settlement as a 'Celtic' monastery. Subsequent excavations at Tintagel have revealed many more structures and associated pottery, though now the prevailing interpretation is that Tintagel served as a princely stronghold, perhaps occupied seasonally, where goods were exchanged at many levels.

Tintagel's impressive commercial activity proved that the Britons were hardly isolated in the fifth and sixth centuries. On the contrary, new trade relations were opened with Gaul, North Africa, and the eastern Mediterranean in which British commodities (most likely tin and slaves) were exchanged for luxury goods. 'Tintagel ware' (which was subsequently sub-classified)[117] soon began to be identified from pottery finds at other sites, and new excavations turned up more examples along with imported glass and jewelry. The defended hilltop settlement at Dinas Powys, near Cardiff in Glamorgan, yielded an abundance of these imports, even though its occupation area is quite small compared to Tintagel and the sub-Roman hill-forts. Leslie Alcock's excavations at Dinas Powys in the 1950s also

---

114   For discussion of individual forts, see Snyder, 1997; and idem, 1998, 164–76.
115   For fuller discussion of reoccupied hillforts, see Snyder, 1998, 176–202.
116   The best discussion of these and later excavations at Tintagel is Thomas, 1993.
117   See Thomas, 1981b.

revealed evidence of a thriving native metalworking industry, perhaps controled by local rulers who exchanged goods for military services.[118]

Alcock's excavations at South Cadbury in the late 1960s revealed the high end of high status hill-fort occupation.[119] This massive hill-fort rises 500 feet above the Somerset plains, its steep sides defended by five massive ramparts enclosing a plateau of about 18 acres. South Cadbury revealed a long sequence of activity extending from the Neolithic to the Late Saxon periods. Extensive new fortifications – including stone walls with timber fighting platforms and a sophisticated timber gateway – were made in the late fifth century AD, when a large (feasting?) hall dominated the plateau. Once again, excavators found an abundance of imported pottery along with Late Roman coins and Saxon brooches. While the much hoped-for clues to the existence of Arthur were not found at South Cadbury, Alcock did reveal a major sub-Roman settlement that was almost certainly the residence of a major British ruler.

Excavations at other high-status rural sites – Killibury, Congresbury, Dinas Emrys, Degannwy, Dumbarton, Yeavering – show this to be a widespread phenomenon in British controlled lands. Sometimes the preference is for large hill-forts that had been central places in the Iron Age, like Ham Hill and Danebury, where the last defenses included a recut ditch, and sherds of coarse grass-tempered pottery found unstratified in the interior of the hill-fort indicate sub-Roman reoccupation and redefense.[120] At other places the Britons preferred smaller, more easily defended enclosures, such as 'Cornish rounds' like Trethurgy. That most of this hill-fort reoccupation occurs in Wales and the southwest may be traced to the need to protect or control rich agricultural lands (formerly attached to villas) and small towns from adventurous Saxon war-bands decades before the organized advance of the kings of Wessex and Mercia.[121] Because of the central military and organizational role of the hill-forts, it is understandable to see them, as Ken Dark and other archaeologists have, as the new *civitas* capitals of the Brittonic Age, perhaps as direct successors to Roman towns.[122]

Kings and Tyrants

The reoccupation of hill-forts in the Brittonic Age has been linked, by Alcock and others, with the emergence of the British kings and kingdoms

118   Alcock, 1987.
119   Alcock, 1995.
120   Cunliffe, 1993, 120.
121   See Alcock, 1995, 149.
122   See, for example, Dark, 1993; and Alcock, 1995, 151.

described in the written sources. In the north this link is explicit: for example, the association of *Alt Clut* (Dumbarton) with the kings of Strathclyde. 'The hillforts [like South Cadbury],' writes Richard Hodges, 'reveal a powerfully centralized elite able to mobilize labour to repair hundreds of metres of fortifications . . . an exercise of military command quite unlike that found in south-eastern England.'[123] Dyke construction around British towns like Verulamium and Chichester also show the vast human resources that some British communities, or British lords, could still command.

'Britain has kings,' writes Gildas, 'but they are tyrants.'[124] One of the questions that has most puzzled scholars of the Brittonic Age is how we get from Roman officials governing Britain in the early fifth century to a land of kings and kingdoms by the sixth century. I have argued elsewhere that the key to this transition is the *tyrannus/tigernos*, the British tyrant that appears so frequently in the written sources.[125] In Britain imperial usurpers, city magistrates, and dynastic kings were all called 'tryants' in fifth- and sixth-century writings. The similarly sounding vernacular term *tigernos* (or *tiern*), which appears in Welsh and Breton sources and in inscriptions and meant simply 'lord,' provided Latin commentators like Gildas with a convenient rhetorical sting for rulers they disliked: to a man who boasted of being a *tigernos*, they could call him *tyrannus*. Thus a man whose very name meant 'Overlord' – Vortigern – could be described quite acerbically as a *superbus tyrannus*.

Britain's reputation for tyrants goes back at least to the time of Magnus Maximus. In the year 407 Britain launched no less than three imperial usurpers; after those men were disposed of, and Britain no longer was ruled by Rome, whatever men assumed control in Britain were viewed by outsiders like Jerome and Procopius as illegitimate tyrants. When Patrick referred to the 'tryanny' of the British warlord Coroticus, he had both illegitimacy and despotism in mind.[126] Gildas similarly describes British kings as tyrants because their wicked behavior contrasts with the virtues of the Old Testament monarchs which he extols. 'If [in Gildas' view] all present authority was illegitimate,' writes David Dumville, 'it was because of the origins of its power in rebellion against Rome and because of the current unjust exercise of its authority.'[127]

Ironically, Rome may have contributed to the rise of the British tyrants. Dumville believes that Rome had effectively ceased to govern the upland

123   Hodges, 1989, 32.
124   Gildas, *De Excidio*, 27.
125   Snyder, 1998, esp. ch. 9.
126   Patrick, *Epistola*, 6.
127   Dumville, 1995, 187.

regions in Britain in the third century, and thus native governance survived or revived in those areas.[128] This could explain the reoccupation of hill-forts before 400, as well as the many Iron Age tribal and royal names that survive into the Brittonic Age. Still this period is characterized by a mixture of Roman and native political institutions, as, for example, the many inscribed stones that commemorate local Welsh magnates with Latin titles. From the epigraphic evidence it is not always clear whether we are seeing titles or names when we encounter a TRIBVNI or a TIGERNI.[129] But by the sixth century we find individuals explicitly identified on their memorials as *rex* and *princeps*.[130]

The picture that emerges, however blurry, is one of local magnates of all sorts who assert control in Britain after 410 and eventually reestablish dynastic rule. A council still held some authority in the mid-fifth century, but it shared power with the *tyrannus superbus*, remembered in later sources as the king Vortigern. The council, if it is a remnant of Roman governance, likely included representatives of the tribal *civitates* of Britain, most of which survive as the basis of early medieval British kingdoms. That Vortigern held something like an overkingship in Britain is strongly indicated by Gildas' biblical metaphor of Pharaoh and the princes of Zoan.[131] Ambrosius may have had similar authority, unless his leadership was purely military.

Whatever guise these sub-Roman potentates took, they must have controlled both human and material resources. Many have posited a quasi-feudal model for post-Roman Britain, when a declining money economy gave way, by the middle of the fifth century, to a barter system. In such a system lords were defined by the amount of land they owned and by the number of warriors they could maintain, supporting these retainers with feasts and prestige gifts. They could also collect taxes, probably in the form of produce and livestock, from the farmers and other laborers whom their walls and war-bands protected.

Rewards to warriors and perhaps sub-kings would have come in the form of weapons and imported luxuries. These would come even cheaper if the prince could control the trade and distribution system, which has been posited for the lord of Tintagel, undoubtedly the most important port of the Brittonic Age. Michael Fulford envisions Mediterranean ships sailing to Britain in 20 to 100 voyages per year.[132] Oil, wine, fine table wares, and other yet to be discovered goods made their way from Tintagel

---

128   Dumville, 1995, 179.
129   See Okasha, 1993, 44, 97, 156, 222.
130   Snyder, 1998, 87.
131   *De Excidio*, 23.2. See Dumville, 1995, 198.
132   Fulford, 1989, 4.

to other high-status sites – South Cadbury, Glastonbury, Congresbury – where in turn some made their way to lesser landowners at places like Dinas Powys. At the high end you have kings exchanging goods with their clients, while down the socio-economic scale you have lesser lords exchanging manufactured wares for foodstuffs from their tenants.

Both written and material evidence suggests that tin – referred to in Byzantine sources as 'the Brittanic metal' – was an important commodity that the Britons traded to Gaul and the Mediterranean in exchange for these luxuries. Slaves, hunting dogs, and salt may have been other exports. Della Hooke illustrates the importance of the long-distance routes called 'saltways' in the early medieval West Midlands.[133] The salt-manufacturing center at Droitwich, which shows continuity from the Iron Age to the Anglo-Saxon period, served a wide network of communities while under British control, as well as after passing into Saxon hands.[134] Along the saltways leading southeast from Droitwich it is remarkable how many topographical features retain their British names or descriptions. Salt manufacturing at Droitwich clearly linked both British and Saxon communities in the West Midlands in an economic interdependence that remained uninterrupted by the vicissitudes of military conquest.

Presumably, Britons living in eastern parts of the island were consumers of Anglo-Saxon goods and crafts. Isolated graves and items identified as Anglian or Saxon may, therefore, need to be considered as possibly British. Conversely, Anglo-Saxon grave goods with enameling and *millefiori*, especially in border kingdoms like Mercia and Wessex, likely indicate English contacts with British craftsmen or workshops.[135] Heinrich Härke has suggested that some smaller male skeletons (buried without weapons) in Anglo-Saxon cemeteries may belong to acculturated or partly acculturated Britons, with an overall drop in male stature in seventh-century Wessex explained as large-scale assimilation of the British population in this area.[136]

But in their funerary rites the fifth-century Britons and Saxons were widely divergent. Whereas Anglo-Saxon graves and cemeteries are identified by the presence of grave goods (weapons, pottery, jewelry), British burials are often defined by the absence of such items. Archaeologists believe that most Britons preferred simple, unaccompanied inhumations, with skeletons extended on their backs, usually with their heads toward the west, as was common throughout the Late Roman world.[137] Coffins

---

133   Hooke, 1998, 2–9.
134   See Snyder, 1996, 40.
135   O'Brien, 1999, viii.
136   Härke, 1997, 150.
137   See O'Brien, 1999.

are rare, though slab-lined and long-cist inhumations are frequent vari-
ants. Because most British graves lack goods and other distinguishing characteristics, the thousands of undatable burials uncovered annually in Britain
are potentially Britons of the early Middle Ages.[138] The identification of
several intra-mural cemeteries in fifth-century towns indicates that, after
410, the Britons disregarded Roman burial law, which forbade interment
within a city.

The large British cemetery at Cannington, not far from South Cadbury,
in use from the fourth to the ninth centuries, was almost completely bereft of grave goods.[139] Some 542 burials of an estimated 2,000 were excavated in this cemetery, which probably served the community at nearby
Cannington hill-fort. Though no church was found at Cannington, most
graves were likely Christian, and were oriented west–east. A few were
crouched inhumations, indicating the continuation of Iron Age burial practices by a small minority of Britons. Even more surprising were the 15
burials accompanied by knives, which Elizabeth O'Brien suggests represent Anglo-Saxons who had become assimilated into this British community c.600.[140]

Many questions about British culture in the fifth and sixth centuries
must as yet go unanswered. While not archaeologically invisible, the material cultural of the Britons is nonetheless hard to interpret based on the
present body of evidence. The common Briton of the countryside, though
a member of the majority, is particularly hard to get at and prevents any
attempt at social history for this period. Where we can answer some questions about the Britons, however, is by looking at their religious culture.
A significant body of writings by British clergy, together with inscriptions
and some new archaeological evidence, allows us to examine the British
Church in some detail. There we can attempt to balance our picture of the
Brittonic Age.

138   See the comments of Peter Fowler in Hines, 1997, 168.
139   Esmonde Cleary, 1990, 184.
140   O'Brien, 1999, 33.

6
The British Church

In Britain, when direct Roman rule collapsed, Christianity was probably still largely confined to the declining urban communities and to the social and administrative hierarchy and their households, all of which were most strongly represented in the lowlands. It is unlikely to have had many committed recruits among the indigenes in the north and west.[1]

If this statement is true, and few scholars would dispute it, why is the period following the collapse of Roman rule known as the Age of the Saints in northern and western Britain? If few Britons had become Christian by 410, why are there so many prominent Christian Britons appearing in the following decades? Arguably the most famous early medieval saint was a fifth-century Briton, and the most significant fifth-century Christian heresy was named for a Briton. Penance – the defining medieval attitude toward sin – was first formally codified by British clergy.

Clearly the British Church was an active and productive body, despite the paucity of material evidence we possess for it and the ambivalent attitude displayed toward it by outsiders. In the fifth and sixth centuries Britons in large numbers adopted Christianity, and monastic schools in Wales trained a generation of British saints who would be venerated for centuries in Celtic-speaking lands. Though perhaps overshadowed by their Irish colleagues (many of whom they inspired), British clergy were at the center of the issues – monasticism, peregrination and missionary work, penitentials – that dominated insular Christianity in the early Middle Ages.

The Origins of Christianity in Britain

Although the Brittonic Age witnessed the grandest of its achievements, the origins of British Christianity lay – shrouded – in the early Roman

---

1   Higham, 1992, 97.

period. We possess no good historical evidence for the first Christians in Britain, though late medieval legends provide several personalities: Joseph of Arimathea, bearing the Holy Grail to Glastonbury; a second-century British king named Lucius; St. Helena, mother of Constantine the Great and alleged daughter of the British king Coel Hen ('Old King Cole'). While these, as Charles Thomas has pointed out, belong properly to 'The Matter of Britain,'[2] they may reflect the efforts of medieval Britons to fill in a void in their historical knowledge, to provide a dynamic founder of their Church who could compete with the apostles and martyrs being touted in other European nations.

The very first written mention of Christianity in Britain comes from allusions made by both Tertullian and Origen to a religion then (by AD 200) established at the very ends of the Roman world, including the westernmost province. Tertullian goes so far as to claim that Christianity can even be found 'in places of the Britons (*loca Britanniorum*) inaccessible to Romans.'[3] Thomas puts little faith in the ability of theologians in North Africa to know the state of affairs on the British frontier, but is willing to concede a slight Christian presence in Britain in the early third century.[4] By the fourth century we are on firmer ground, due to the records of now legal Christian gatherings. The proceedings of the Council of Arles in 314 list five British clergy in attendance: three bishops, representing London, Lincoln, and York, and a priest and deacon presumably from Cirencester. The British Church assented to the decisions of the Council of Nicaea in 325, and three unnamed British bishops are singled out as being 'especially poor' and in need of state support to attend the Council of Rimini in 359.[5]

Into the gap between a few unknown Christians and established British bishoprics we can place the British martyrs, a subject of much controversy. Gildas says that there were holy martyrs – 'soldiers of Christ' – of both sexes and in many parts of Roman Britain.[6] The names of five British martyrs have survived: Alban, Aaron, Julius, Augulus, and Mellonus. The best evidence is for Alban, allegedly Britain's first martyr. He was a wealthy citizen of Verulamium beheaded in the early third century, perhaps in 209 under the orders of Geta.[7] Aaron and Julius, first mentioned by Gildas, are said to have been citizens of 'the City of the Legions,' thought

2   That body of legends which would inspire the medieval Arthurian and Grail romances, treated in chapter 12 below. Thomas, 1981, 42.
3   Tertullian, *Adversos Iudaeos*, 7.4.
4   Thomas, 1981, 43–4.
5   Birley, 1980, 153.
6   Gildas, *De Excidio*, 10–11.
7   Birley, 1980, 152.

by most to be Caerleon. They probably perished during the persecutions of Decius and Valerian; Aaron's Jewish name indicates that he was likely an immigrant. Augulus, 'bishop and martyr,' is linked to the *civitas Augusta* – London – and also likely perished in the third-century persecutions.[8] Mellonus, known only from a later medieval *Life*, is said to have been a soldier born in Britain (his name is unmistakably Celtic) of wealthy parents, who was converted in Rome and went on to become the first bishop of Rouen before his martyrdom under Valerian.

The earliest physical evidence of British Christianity comes from the dozens of Roman objects – pewter ingots, silver bowls and plates, spoons, rings, lead baptismal tanks, mosaics, paintings, bone plaques – which bear the PATERNOSTER acrostic or overt Christian symbols like the *Alpha* and *Omega* and especially the *Chi-Rho*. British churches have been much harder to identify. Gildas says that, following the repeal of the persecution edicts, British Christians began rebuilding churches which had been razed as well as founding chapels dedicated to the martyrs.[9] Archaeologists agree that some British churches may have developed from Roman mausolea, as has been argued for Verulamium (the martyrium of St. Alban), Stone-by-Faversham, and Wells.[10] Placename elements may give us other clues to the location of early British churches. In Wales and Cornwall, *llan* (or *lan*) names (Llancarfan, Llanilltud Fawr, Llanbadarn Fawr, Llandegai, Langorroc, etc.) denote churches enclosed by their cemeteries and *merthyr* names (Merthyr Mawr, Merthyr Cynog) indicate a site where an early saint was buried or his or her relics were kept.[11]

The Late Roman Church

The dominant pattern of the Late Roman Church, in Britain as elsewhere in the empire, was urban and episcopal. Therefore it is to the major towns of Britain that we can expect to find the early British churches. Of all the towns of Roman Britain only 12 have yielded strong Christian evidence (see table 6.1). The Silchester basilica, one of the first to be identified, is still the strongest candidate for an intra-mural church. Canterbury and Verulamium also have contenders, while the recent discovery at Wroxeter of a large apsidal building, aligned east–west, is probably indicative of a church.[12] London's Tower Hill may have been the site of the capital city's

8   Pseudo-Jerome, *Martyrologium*.
9   Gildas, *De Excidio*, 12.
10   Higham, 1992, 99.
11   Redknap, 1995, 743.
12   See Watts, 1998, 19; *British Archaeology*, 7 (1995).

Table 6.1 The archaeological evidence for British Christianity, c.300–600.

	Location	Description	Structures	Date	Associated Burials	Reference
1	Ancaster	cemetery		4th cent.	300 inhumations, 11 limestone sarcophagi	Thomas1981; Snyder 1997
2	Ardwall Isle	monastery	timber oratory, stone altar and chapel	late 5th to 7th cents.	cemeteries	Snyder 1996
3	Bangor	monastery		early medieval	burials	Dark 1994
4	Beacon Hill, Lundy Island	monastery	enclosure	late 6th cent.	30 cist burials, 4 inscribed memorial stones	Snyder 1996
5	Brean Down	shrine	rectangular stone shrine	5th to 8th cents.	slab-lined and cist burials	Snyder 1996
6	Caerwent	chapel	apsidal room in a Roman house, Christian hoard in another townhouse	4th cent.	intramural cemetery associated with a 7th cent. church	Edwards 1996
7	Caldey Island	monastery		6th cent.	2 long-cist burials and inscribed stone	Abbot Pyro tradition
8	Chedworth Villa	baptistry	octagonal reservoir whose slates were decorated with Chi-Rhos	late 4th cent.		Thomas 1981
9	Chemsford	church	3-room house abutting stone temple	5th cent.		Snyder 1996
10	Cirencester	chapel?	Christian palindrome on the wall of a townhouse	early 4th cent.	urban cemetery with 400 inhumations (4th and early 5th cents.)	Snyder 1998
11	Colchester	church	stone basilica with apse	320 or 340	large cemetery	Salway 1993; Snyder 1996
12	Frampton	chapel	2 villa rooms, one with apse, containing Christian mosaics	4th cent.		Thomas 1981
13	Frocester Villa	monastery	timber-framed building, separate enclosure	4th cent.	burials	Dark 1994

	Site	Type	Description	Date	Burials/Features	References
14	Glastonbury Abbey	church	timber structure beneath a Saxon church, wattle "oratories," possible *vallum*	late 6th cent.	cemetery of slab-lined graves	Snyder 1996
15	Glastonbury Tor	monastery	large timber building with smaller outbuildings, 2 hearths, evidence of metalworking	5th and 6th	2 adult burials	Dark 1994; Snyder 1996
16	Hinton St. Mary	chapel	villa with Christian mosaics	4th cent.		Thomas 1981
17	Hoddom, Dumfries	baptistry	stone building beneath Anglian minster	6th cent.		Lowe 1993; Smith 1996; Jocelyn, *Life of St. Kentigern*
18	Housesteads	church	apsidal structure	c.400	single long-cist grave	Crow 1995
19	Icklingham	church and baptistry	stone foundations of a rectangular building with possible eastern apse, nearby D-shaped cistern, and 2 lead tanks with inscribed Chi-Rhos	late 4th cent.	inhumation cemetery of coffins and plain burials	Thomas 1981; Morris 1983
20	Kirkmadrine	cemetery?		c.500	memorial stone for 2 *sacerdotes*	Snyder 1996
21	Llandough	monastery	villa abandoned in the early 4th cent.	early medieval	early medieval church cemetery overlaying villa	Dark 1994; Edwards 1996; Llandaff charters
22	Llangian	churchyard	collapsed churchyard boundary, inscribed stone	c.430–670 (C14)		Edwards 1996
23	Llantwit Major	monastery	abandoned villa	early medieval	burials	Edwards 1996; hagiography
24	Looe Island	hermitage	imported pottery (B i)	mid 6th cent.		Olson 1989
25	Lullingstone	chapel	villa suite with Christian wall paintings	late 4th cent.	nearby mausoleum	Thomas 1981; Morris 1983
26	Phillack	cemetery	enclosure	c.500–c.600	east-west cist graves, nearby Chi-Rho inscription	Olson 1989; Snyder 1996

Table 6.1 cont'd

	Location	Description	Structures	Date	Associated Burials	Reference
27	Poundbury	church or baptistry, succeeded by monastery	apsidal structure	5th to 6th cent.	1000 + graves and stone mausolea	Dark 1994
28	Richborough	church and baptistry	rectangular masonry foundation, with possible eastern apse, and hexagonal stone baptismal font	late 4th to early 5th cent.		Brown 1971; Thomas 1981; Morris 1983
29	Silchester	church and baptistry	stone basilica and baptismal font	c.360 or later		Frere 1975; Morris 1983
30	South Shields	church	transformed *principia* forecourt	late 4th cent.	nearby inhumation cemetery	Bidwell and Speak 1994
31	St. Albans Cathedral	martyrium?		4th and 5th cents.		Constantius; Bede
32	St. Helen's, Scilly Isles	church	wooden church, stone chapel	early medieval		Snyder 1996
33	St. Helen's, Worcester	church		pre-680		parish charters
34	St. Kew	monastery		early medieval	burials	Dark 1994
35	St. Martin's, Canterbury	church		late 4th to 6th cents.		Thomas 1981; Snyder 1997
36	St. Mary-de-Lode, Gloucester	mausoleum	timber structure overlying a Roman house and beneath a Saxon chapel	5th or 6th cent.	single male inhumation	Snyder 1996
37	St. Pancras, Canterbury	church	rectangular nave with small apse	late 4th to 6th cents.		Thomas 1981; Snyder 1996

38	St. Paul-in-the-Bail, Lincoln	church and cemetery	apsidal structure, timber structure beneath Anglian stone church	4th and 5th cents.	5th cent. graves beneath 7th cent. Anglian church cemetery	Thomas 1981; Snyder 1996
39	Tintagel Parish Churchyard	cemetery and church	hearth, granite pillar, earthen enclosure	6th cent.	2 slate-lined graves. 2 burial mounds	Thomas 1993; Dark 1994
40	Traprain Law	church	large (96 sq. m) rectangular building with apse and narthex	post-400		Smith 1996
41	Vindolanda	church	rectangular building with western apse	mid 5th cent.		Birley 1998
42	Wells Cathedral	mausoleum	rectangular stone building underlying an early Saxon church	late 4th to 6th cents.	burial chamber	Rodwell 1980; Morris 1983
43	West Hill Uley	church	timber basilica, stone chapel and baptistry, colored window glass	c.402–600		Dark 1994
44	Whithorn	monastery	wattle buildings, stone chapel and oratory	5th and 6th cents.	cemetery with nearby inscribed stones	Hill 1998
45	Worcester Cathedral	church		c.536 and c.585	2 burials under the refectory	Snyder 1996

cathedral, for a massive masonry basilica, built between AD 350 and 400 and elaborately decorated, has recently been identified and caused some controversy.[13]

While some town houses show signs of rooms being used as Christian house-chapels (akin to their villa counterparts, discussed below), the most likely place to find urban churches is outside the walls, in cemeteries.[14] St. Alban's martyrium was most likely under the present cathedral, and St. Pancras' church may be the best candidate for the Roman church in Canterbury described by Bede. But the most recent and impressive evidence comes from the extra-mural basilica at Butt Road, Colchester, associated with a cemetery most likely in transition from pagan to Christian burial. The stone building, constructed between 320 and 340, had timber interior partitions and a rounded apse added at the eastern end.[15]

Intra-mural churches at Roman forts have long been considered, but usually these are Saxon minsters. However, Housesteads, Richborough, and South Shields have all yielded candidates for late or sub-Roman churches, and Richborough has a pretty convincing example of a baptismal font. Most recently, Robin Birley has discovered an apsed basilica constructed in the courtyard of the commander's palace at Vindolanda, perhaps in the mid-fifth century with occupation continuing into the sixth.

The difficulty in identifying British churches is due to many factors, including the incomplete excavation of most British towns and the decline of masonry construction in British towns after c.350. This becomes even more of a problem as we move into the fifth century. It could be that Britain produced churches in forms harder to recognize by archaeologists than the stone basilica model of the Mediterranean. Ian Smith has suggested that timber churches were much more prevalent than stone in sub-Roman Britain, with dressed stone taken from Roman forts (e.g. along Hadrian's Wall) controlled and dispensed by the new British political powers.[16] This need not, however, imply any lack of architectural sophistication among the Britons (witness Saxon halls and Norwegian Stave churches). Smith has also proposed several D-ended buildings in northern Britain as candidates for sub-Roman churches, believing the style to be mimicking the apsed estate churches of Late Roman Britain, such as Icklingham.

Dorothy Watts has recently argued forcefully for a significant revival of paganism in fourth-century Britain.[17] This revival she associates particu-

13   *British Archaeology*, 5 (1995).
14   See Thomas, 1981, 170–80; and Jones and Mattingly, 1990, map 9:6.
15   *Current Archaeology*, 120 (1990): 406–8.
16   Smith, 1996, 24–6.
17   Watts, 1998.

larly with the brief reign of the emperor Julian 'the Apostate,' a time which saw heightened activity at Romano-British temples. This activity came to an abrupt end at the end of the fourth century, when the Theodosian dynasty made Christianity the exclusive religion of the empire. Ken Dark has argued that militant Christians were responsible for the destruction of Romano-British paganism.[18] Pagan temples possibly converted to Christian use in the early fifth century include Brean Down, Cannington, Chelmsford, West Hill Uley, Nettleton Scrubb, Lamyatt Beacon, and Henley Wood.[19] However, absorption of pagan tradition by Christian Britons, rather than destruction, seems indicated by the written evidence.[20] In Caerwent, furthermore, pagan and Christian burials of the late fourth century are found side by side, hardly indicative of a hostile religious atmosphere.[21]

Pelagius and Pelagianism in Britain

With Christianity now the official religion of the empire, however, doctrinal disputes among Christians could and did become hostile. We know from various sources that Britain was no stranger to the Arian heresy that dominated theological dispute in the first half of the fourth century. The most interesting piece of evidence is this excerpt from a papyrus found at Bath:

> The enemy of Christ has sent Biliconus from Viriconium [Wroxeter] in order that you may take him into the sheepfold, although a dog of Arius. Pray to Christ for light.[22]

While Biliconus may be a native name, Athanasius and other contemporary writers assure us that the Britons remained by and large orthodox in the post-Nicea era. This was to change, however, in the early decades of the fifth century, when the most famous – or rather infamous – Briton in the empire was a man named Pelagius. The doctrines of Pelagius and his associates, known as Pelagianism, would in a few short years be branded heretical and would lead the papacy to become more interested in the British Isles than it had ever been before.

Pelagius was born in Britain but had moved to Rome by the early 380s

---

18   Dark, 1993.
19   See Higham, 1992, 99; and Snyder, 1998, 202–16.
20   Davies and Kirby, 1995; Jones, 1996, 177; Snyder, 1998, 236–7.
21   Redknap, 1995, 737.
22   Ireland, 1996, 206–7.

at the latest. His excellent education (his writings show a familiarity with Classical literature and philosophy as well as Christian works) must have begun in Britain. Several of his brief scriptural commentaries survive: his *Commentaries on the Thirteen Epistles of St. Paul* is the first substantial piece of literature produced by a Briton. In these works Pelagius objects to Augustine's recently stated views on divine Grace, asserting that man has free will to move toward or against salvation (though Grace can and does assist) and is theoretically capable of living without sin. This was certainly the mentality of the early eastern monastics, who followed literally the command 'Be perfect, as Our Father in Heaven art perfect,' and a view which Erasmus argued forcefully against Luther 1,100 years later.

But Pelagius' opinions bred powerful enemies, and his views may have become distorted by more extremist disciples, like Caelestius, who denied original sin. Pelagius was able to defend his views in both Rome and Jerusalem until Augustine's friends convinced both pope and emperor to condemn him and denounce Pelagianism as heretical in 418. After that date Pelagius himself disappears, probably in retirement in the east, but possibly returning to Britain, given the popularity of Pelagianism there in the 420s.

Pelagius was attacked by nearly every important Church writer of his day, including Augustine, Jerome, and Orosius. Pelagius' enemies leave us ample testimony to his physique and temperament: he was a big man, 'handsomely fleshy, with the flanks and strength of an athelete,' 'thoroughly stolid, weighed down by Irish porridge (*Scottorum pultibus*),' 'a monstrous Goliath,' built like an 'Alpine hound'; he also had a 'tilted and pointy head' and a 'bulging forehead.'[23] While these may be exaggerations of Pelagius' size, Orosius' statement that his broad shoulders and thick neck were 'nourished by baths and banquets' is purely political venom and does not fit what we know of Pelagius' ascetic beliefs. Michael Jones has argued that these are not merely attacks on a political enemy, but also racial slurs typical of Late Roman attitudes toward Britons.[24] As negative as these statements are, they are our fullest description of a Briton to date.

While Pelagius disappeared in the east, in the western provinces of Gaul and Britain his supporters gained strength. These include clergy branded as Pelagian as well as some whom we call semi-Pelagian (just as there were semi-Augustinians). Many of these men were, like Pelagius, Britons. As I have argued, the turmoil of the mid-fifth century led many British bishops to emigrate with their congregations to Gaul and western Spain. A Briton named Mansuetus, present at the Council of Tours in 461, may

23   See Birley, 1980, 155.
24   Jones, 1987.

have become bishop of Toul in northeastern France.[25] Sidonius Apollinaris corresponded with the Briton Faustus, who became bishop of Riez in 462, and his friend Riocatus (or Riochatus), a 'truly venerable . . . priest and monk' who was returning 'to his Britons' with books obtained in Gaul. At Arles, the lid of a sarcophagus bears the epitaph (dated *c*.420–60) of Tolosanus *Britannus Naione*.[26] As late as 546 there is a tombstone recording the death of a *Britto presbyter* at Mertola, in southern Portugal.

But it is the Pelagian Britons who draw most of the attention. Magnus Maximus had exiled Priscillianist heretics to Britain in the late fourth century, and it is possible that Pelagius or his associates may have fled there after his condemnation in 418. Fastidius, whom Gennadius of Marseilles describes as *Brittanorum episcopus*, was active in spreading Pelagianism in Gaul around this time.[27] A Christian socialist author of several tracts (including *De Vita Christiana*) residing in Sicily *c*.410, whom John Morris has named 'the Sicilian Briton,' may have had formal ties to Pelagianism.[28] Prosper writes, in 429, that 'Agricola, a Pelagian, son of the Pelagian bishop Severianus, [was] corrupting the churches of Britain.'[29] Though it is not stated specifically that Agricola and Severianus are Britons, Agricola at least must have had some influence in the British Church, for Prosper attributes his teachings as the impetus for Germanus' first trip to Britain.

During this visit in 429, Germanus openly debated the British Pelagians, who, writes Constantius, 'flaunted their wealth in dazzling robes,' a criticism which Gildas later levels at British clergy in general.[30] After defeating the Pelagians in debate, Germanus and his colleague Lupus visit the shrine of St. Alban, preach, and perform a series of miracles. Preceding the Allelujah Victory, Germanus and Lupus are said to have baptized many of the assembled British troops, indicating that Constantius, in the late fifth century, believed that a substantial number of British soldiers *c*.429 were unbaptized pagans.[31] Ten or 15 years later Germanus returns for a second visit, prompted by news 'from Britain that a few promoters of the Pelagian heresy were once more spreading it.'[32] This time the saint found that most of the Britons had remained faithful, but he continued to preach and perform healing miracles. Prosper judged Germanus' visits to be a success, attributing the victory over Pelagianism to Pope Celestine:

25 See Thomas, 1981, 51.
26 See Snyder, 1998, 70.
27 Gennadius, *De Scriptoribus Ecclesiasticis*, 56.
28 Morris, 1965. But see the critique by Thomas, 1981, 56–9.
29 Prosper, *Chronicon*, s.a. 429, 1301.
30 Constantius, *Vita Sancti Germani*, 3.14. See Snyder, 1998, 249.
31 Higham, 1992, 98.
32 Constantius, *Vita Sancti Germani*, 5.25.

[Celestine] removed from that hiding-place [Britain] certain enemies of grace who had occupied the land of their origin.[33]

Scholars have questioned the authenticity and date of this second visit; but, regardless, it reveals that Gallic clergy believed that Pelagianism was still a problem in Britain in the second half of the fifth century. While Patrick and Gildas have been judged to be 'orthodox' in their theology, Gildas at least reveals a strain of anti-elite social justice and a suspicion of 'faith only' doctrine.[34] Suspicions of lingering Pelagianism would continue to emanate from Rome for centuries, and would come to include Ireland as well as Britain.[35]

Patrick

From the perspective of the papacy, the spread of Pelagianism in Gaul and Britain in the second quarter of the fifth century was quite alarming. These westernmost provinces were slipping out of the control of Roman imperial armies, and threatened to slip out of the grasp of the pope as well. News of Christian converts in Ireland, probably the result of contacts with British Christians, carried the potential of heresy dominating these western isles at a time when no imperial administration could enforce orthodoxy. This, to many historians, seems to have been the impetus for Rome's new-found interest in missionary activity among the Irish. Rome's first attempt is recorded by Prosper:

AD 431. Pope Celestine sent [the deacon] Palladius to the Irish believing in Christ, ordained as their first bishop.[36]

Prosper adds elsewhere that, after Celestine expelled Pelagians from Italy, 'did he free Britain from the same plague . . . for having ordained a bishop for the Irish, while he was careful to keep the Roman island [i.e. Britain] Catholic, he also made the barbarian island Christian.'[37] Unfortunately we hear nothing more about Palladius' mission, though later medieval sources characterize it as a failure (or even that Palladius died in Britain before ever reaching Ireland), probably to strengthen the claims of the Patrician see of Armagh. Historians more recently, looking at traditions

33   Prosper, *Contra Collatorem*, 21.
34   See Gardner, 1995.
35   Dumville, 1985.
36   Prosper, *Chronicon*, s.a. 431.
37   Prosper, *Contra Collatorem*, 21. See also Thomas, 1981, 301–6.

in southern Ireland of pre-Patrician saints, are willing to see a not insignificant number of southern Irish Christians who were likely the converts of early British missionaries and who may have been organized by Palladius (who may have himself been responsible for some Irish conversions).[38]

Few would dispute, however, that the most successful missionary work in Ireland was carried out by Patrick. In his autobiographical *Confession* and his *Letter to Coroticus*, Patrick reveals a good bit about his status and origins:

> I, Patrick, a sinner, quite uncultivated and the least of all the faithful and utterly despicable to many, had as my father the deacon Calpornius, son of the late Potitus, a priest, who belonged to the town of Bannavem Taburniae; he had a small estate nearby, and it was there that I was taken captive. I was then about sixteen years old. I did not know the true God and I was taken into captivity in Ireland with so many thousands.[39]

> I, Patrick, a sinner, yes, and unlearned, established in Ireland, put on record that I am a bishop . . . I was free-born according to the flesh; my father was a decurion. I sold my good birth . . . in the interest of others. In short, I am a slave in Christ to a foreign people.[40]

Elsewhere in Patrick's writings we learn that his father's estate (*villula*) was in Britain, and that Patrick spent about six years in captivity in Ireland, tending the flocks of his master and retreating to the wilds to pray. To escape he had to travel 200 miles across Ireland before he found a ship and was able to convince its crew to take him back to Britain. Whether they sailed there directly, or (as Charles Thomas has suggested)[41] to Gaul first, Patrick was soon reunited with his parents.

Not long after this Patrick began receiving visions, calling for him to return to Ireland as a missionary. He then undertook ecclesiastical training (hindered, he constantly points out, by the interrupted schooling of his youth) and came to Ireland as bishop, where he struggled with secular authority, converted broadly, promoted monasticism, and ordained priests. He suffered threats from Irish chieftains, an attempt by the British Church to recall him (after their discovery of an unnamed boyhood sin), and raids by the soldiers of a British warlord named Coroticus, in which his Irish converts were slaughtered and sold as slaves to the Picts. Patrick wrote his *Letter* in an attempt to excommunicate Coroticus, and, in his old age,

---

38   See, for example, Thomas, 1981; and T. M. Charles-Edwards in Dumville, 1993, 1–12.
39   Patrick, *Confessio*, 1 (trans. Hood).
40   Patrick, *Epistola*, 1 and 10 (trans. Hood).
41   Thomas, 1981, 321–5.

penned the *Confession* to further explain and justify his mission in Ireland.

The gaps in Patrick's narrative, the lack of dates and imprecise geographical detail, have created plenty of room for scholarly discussion and controversy.[42] Dating Patrick has proved to be the most contentious issue, and until recently has dominated Patrician scholarship to the point of overshadowing language, theology, and other aspects of these fascinating primary sources. A sampling of suggested dating schemes is given in table 6.2. I shall not rehearse the various 'two Patricks' theories that intrigued many when they were first presented some 50 years ago.[43] The complex Patrician hagiographic tradition, beginning with Muirchú's *Life* written in the late seventh century, leads one down such slippery slopes. Rather, sticking solely to the words of Patrick himself, we can only say with certainty that the author of the *Confession* and *Letter to Coroticus* was writing in the period between 404 and 496.[44]

We can try to go one step further toward chronological precision by dating Patrick's mission in relation to that of Palladius, for which we have the firm beginning date of 431. Mario Esposito's theory that Patrick predates Palladius has recently been supported by John Koch on linguistic grounds.[45] Daniel Conneely, however, has argued that Patrick was indebted to the writings of Hilary of Arles (*c*.449) and Prosper (*c*.455), which supports the dating of Patrick's episcopate to the later half of the fifth century.[46] E. A. Thompson has made the novel suggestion that, before becoming bishop, Patrick was actually a deacon on the staff of Palladius and as such began his missionary work.[47]

To make matters even more confusing, the later Annals of Ulster give Patrick *two* death dates, 461 and 493. Nothing has been presented by Patriciologists to settle this question, and for the present study I will consider Patrick's *floruit* to be roughly mid-fifth century. A second controversy exists over Patrick's geography; that is, where exactly was Patrick's hometown (*Bannavem Taburniae*), where did he receive his ecclesiastical training, and in what part of Ireland did he establish his bishopric? Charles Thomas has devoted most attention to these questions.[48] He argues that Patrick was born on an estate near the fort of Birdoswald (*Banna*), along

---

42   An extensive bibliography is currently being prepared by Anthony Harvey, to appear as *Clavis Patricii III: An Annotated Bibliography of St. Patrick*.

43   See O'Rahilly, 1957; and Carney, 1973.

44   See Snyder, 1998, 41.

45   See Koch, 1990.

46   Conneely, 1993. See also Dronke, 1981.

47   Thompson, 1999, 175.

48   See Thomas, 1981, 307–46.

Table 6.2   The chronology of the historical St. Patrick, according to medieval and modern commentators.

	Annals of Ulster	Bury	Hanson	Thomas	Dumville	Thompson	Howlett
Patrick's birth		389	c.388–c.406	c.415			c.390
Patrick becomes bishop and returns to Ireland	432	432	c.425–c.435	c.460		431 (as deacon); 'some years after 434' (as bishop)	c.420
Patrick's death	461 and 493	461	c.460	c.492	493		461

Hadrian's Wall; that Patrick escaped from slavery in Co. Mayo and walked to Cork harbor, where a boat took him to northern Gaul; that after a few years he was back in Britain and training for the clergy in Carlisle; and that he returned to northwestern Ireland where he had been as a captive. This author is willing to accept Thomas's scheme as a plausible interpretation of the evidence found in Patrick's writing. However, the most recent excavator of Birdoswald has pointed out that Thomas's '*vicus Banna Venta* near the mountain pass (*Bernia*)' may fit Ravenglass (*Glannaventa*) better than Birdoswald, for it lies on the Irish Sea and is at the end of a Roman road running through a mountain pass.[49] Either northern location is a better fit with Patrick's description of Irish and Pictish activities than southern candidates put forward, for example, in Somerset, where Glastonbury maintained a strong Patrician tradition.[50]

Most historians now agree that Patrick's mission to Ireland was (at least in the beginning) supported and probably commissioned by the British Church. Patrician hagiography liked to link Patrick with continental luminaries like Germanus, and this has led to the belief that Patrick spent a significant amount of time in Gaul, either at Auxerre or in the monastery of Lérins. While there is no evidence that Patrick himself was a monk, his writings reveal a deep respect for the celibate life.[51] He was especially

49   Wilmott, 1997, 231.
50   See K. R. Dark in Dumville, 1993, 23; and Harry Jelley, 'Locating the Birthplace of St. Patrick,' *British Archaeology*, 36 (July 1998).
51   See Herren, 1989.

attached to the monks and nuns (*monachi et virgines Christi*) among his converts and expressed a burning desire to go visit the 'brethren' in Gaul.[52] Michael Herren points out that since celibacy was not the norm among the lower clergy in the British Church (witness Patrick's father and grandfather), the monastic ideal then popular in Gaul became Patrick's inspiration.[53] Patrick could have learned Gallic asceticism during a brief stay in Gaul, but he could also have developed a monastic interest from Gallic clergy visiting Britain.

'Patrick is writing interpretively,' reminds Richard Sharpe, 'and . . . moral truth means more to Patrick than irrecoverable factual details.'[54] While this may not be to a modern historian's liking, we must nevertheless focus more scholarly discussion on the language and themes which Patrick intended for his readers' attention. A few studies have been done on Patrick's sources, while only one now-dated analysis of his Latinity exists.[55] Most scholars agree that British was Patrick's first language, and that he had to learn successively Vulgar Latin, Old Irish, and Church Latin, a disparate and interrupted education that resulted in his self-confessed rusticity as a Latin writer. I began a preliminary enquiry into Patrick's use of geographic and political terms, like *Britanniae* and *cives*, which show his reliance upon scripture and Augustine in giving written expression to his thoughts.[56] Much more radical is David Howlett's assertion that Patrick was an accomplished Latin writer following the strict rules of 'biblical style,' a complex mathematical patterning that relies heavily upon iteration, which became quite popular among Latin authors in the medieval Celtic fringe.[57] While Howlett's 'biblical style' theory has drawn some criticism, he does rightly challenge us to not see Patrick's writing style as simply rustic.[58] The tide does seem to be turning on this issue. Charles Thomas, a believer in Howlett's theory, has gone so far as calling Patrick 'a writer of astonishing competence.'[59]

Surprisingly little attention has been paid to Patrick's theology. Though admittedly not as broad and systematic a thinker as Pelagius or Augustine, Patrick nonetheless offers us a spiritual autobiography that is honest, impassioned, and compelling. Evangelism, pastoral care,

---

52 Patrick, *Confessio*, 41–3.
53 Herren, 1989, 83.
54 Sharpe, 1987, 115.
55 See Dronke, 1981; and Mohrmann, 1961.
56 Snyder, 1998.
57 Howlett, 1994; idem, 1995.
58 See Snyder, 1996b; and the remarks by Colmán Etchingham in Thompson, 1999, xxvi.
59 Thomas, 1998, 60.

mysticism, and episcopal functions are just a few of the themes in Patrick's writings which are only now generating some scholarly attention.[60] Because Patrick the writer has been so overshadowed by Patrick the legend, very few people even within academe have actually read his works. More's the pity, for they offer us a very rare autobiographical glimpse into the life of a fifth-century missionary bishop, a Briton connected to both the receding Roman world and to the expanding western Christendom.

Gildas

Though few substantial insular writings survive from the fifth and sixth centuries, we are fortunate to have not one but two British voices. Gildas, like Patrick, called Britain his *patria*, his homeland, and like Patrick Gildas labored for – and at the same time was often critical of – the British Church. But Gildas's criticism dominated his major work, *De Excidio Britanniae* ('On the Ruin of Britain'), in which he made no attempt at either history or autobiography. It is, simply, a sermon in the form of a letter, perhaps modeled on St. Stephen's speech in Acts.[61] But it is also the most important historical source for the Brittonic Age.

> In this letter I shall deplore rather than denounce; my style may be worthless, but my intentions are kindly. What I have to deplore with mournful complaint is a general loss of good, a heaping up of bad. But no one should think that anything I say is said out of scorn for humanity or from a conviction that I am superior to all men. No, I sympathise with my country's difficulties and troubles, and rejoice in remedies to relieve them.[62]

Complaints rather than remedies dominate most of Gildas's lengthy epistle, which consists implicitly of three parts: an 'historical' preface, a 'Complaint' against British rulers, and a 'Complaint' against British clergy. As we saw in the previous chapter, Gildas's preface recounts (with little chronological precision) a long series of events including the Roman conquest of Britain, the trials and triumphs of the first British Christians, the withdrawal of the Roman legions, the raiding of the Picts and the Scots, the decision to hire Saxon mercenaries, the revolt of the Saxons and destruction of British cities, the revival of the Britons under Ambrosius and their ultimate triumph at the battle of Badon Hill. Apart from the account

---

60   See O'Donoghue, 1987; Conneely, 1993; and O'Loughlin, 2000.
61   See Gardner, 1995.
62   Gildas, *De Excidio*, 1.1 (trans. Winterbottom).

of the British martyrs, Gildas's preface offers little information about the British Church.

While the preface has captured the attention of most historians, it is the Complaint sections that betray the purpose of their author and (presumably) the interests of the original audience. Gildas complains that the British kings in his day swear false oaths before holy altars, distribute alms while amassing personal wealth, and commit a host of sins ranging from adultery to murder. One of these men, Maglocunus, is singled out because he had been taught by a 'refined master' and 'vowed to be a monk forever,' yet ended up usurping the throne by killing his uncle and marrying his own son's wife.[63]

After dispensing political advice through the words of the prophets, Gildas launches into a scathing attack on the British clergy:

> Britain has priests, but they are fools; very many ministers, but they are shameless; clerics, but they are treacherous grabbers. They are called shepherds, but they are wolves ready to slaughter souls.[64]

This colorful description is followed by a long and precise list of clerical crimes: gluttony, greed, simony, hypocrisy, lust, neglect of sacrifice, preferring the rich to the poor, indulging in sports and public entertainment. The disease is apparently throughout the clerical ranks, from deacon to bishop. Particularly galling to Gildas are those priests who buy their offices from the British tyrants or else travel overseas to seek political favors. While 'not all [British] bishops and priests are . . . stained with the disgrace of schism, pride and uncleanness,' Gildas devotes the rest of his words (the largest section of the epistle) to correcting the British clergy through Old Testament example.

As with Patrick, scholarly controversy surrounds Gildas's chronology and geography. Since Gildas records no dates, and only a handful of names and events, historians have attempted to date Gildas by using later evidence, such as the *Vitae* of Gildas (written in the eleventh and twelfth centuries) and his death date recorded in the *Annales Cambriae* (see table 6.3). Other dating schemes rely upon the regnal dates of Maelgwn Gwynedd, almost certainly Gildas's *Maglocunus*.[65] Since the only contemporary evidence for Maelgwn is the *De Excidio*, this results in circular argument.

From various internal clues, I have proposed the following scheme for both Gildas's dates and those of the events he describes in the preface:

---

63   *De Excidio*, 33–6.
64   *De Excidio*, 66.1.
65   See the cautionary remarks of Miller, 1974–6; and Dumville, 1984.

Table 6.3   The chronology of Gildas, according to medieval and modern commentators.

	Annales Cambriae	Dumville	Lapidge	O'Sullivan	Herren	Higham	M. Jones
Gildas's birth and the battle of Badon:	516 (Badon)					c.430–c.440 (Badon)	
Composition of the De Excidio:		c.550	Pre-500	c.515–20	c.500 (De Excidio) c.530–40 (Fragmenta)	479–484	beginning of the sixth century
Gildas's death:	570	570					

c.430	The Britons' appeal to Aëtius for help against the barbarians.
+25 years?	'Meanwhile,' a 'dreadful famine,' then 'a period of truce' after the Picts and Scots went home, which led to an age of 'luxury' but also 'civil war' and 'plague.'
c.455	A council was convened, and the Saxons were invited to Britain as federates.
+10 years?	'For a long time' the Saxons were satisfied with their increased payments.
c.465	Saxon rebellion, the beginning of the 'War of the Saxon Federates.'
+10 years?	'After a time' of coast-to-coast slaughter and devastation of 'town and country,' the rebels returned 'home.'
c.475	Ambrosius Aurelianus led the 'wretched survivors' to victory over the Saxons.
10 years?	A period in which victories were traded by both sides.
c.485	The year of the siege of Badon Hill and of Gildas's birth.
+44 years	'One month of the forty-fourth year since then has already passed.'
c.529	Gildas writes the De Excidio, as a contemporary of Ambrosius' grandchildren.
c.540–70	Gildas corresponds with Uinniau (or Finnio), possibly a teacher of St. Columba (c.521–97), and writes a monastic penitential.
c.547	The death of Maelgwn Gwynedd, according to the Annales Cambriae.
c.565	Gildas visits Ireland, according to the Annales Cambriae.
c.570	The death (possibly in Brittany) of Gildas sapiens, according to the Annales Cambriae.

While the last events rest on late evidence from the *Annales Cambriae*, the scheme as a whole has many advantages. It places Gildas's primary schooling in the late fifth century (following recent studies of his language) and his composition of the *De Excidio* in the first third of the sixth century, which explains his lack of familiarity with many sixth-century writers. Yet it also makes him a contemporary of Maelgwn and Saints Finnio (see below) and Columba, and allows for St. Columbanus to have known his later writings by *c*.600.

According to hagiographic tradition, Gildas was born in northern Britain and schooled in Wales. Given that he only mentions rulers of Wales and Dumnonia in the *De Excidio*, it is likely that Gildas spent most of his life in southwestern Britain, and the recent suggestions that he composed the *De Excidio* in Somerset or Dorset are most plausible.[66] Regardless, Gildas's geographic perspective in the *De Excidio* is quite broad (he is writing about the calamities of *Britannia*, not local troubles),[67] and there is no reason to doubt the later Irish and Breton traditions that Gildas was itinerant.

Some confusion remains over Gildas's exact clerical status. In many general histories he is referred to unambiguously as a monk, yet this is far from explicit in the *De Excidio*. Michael Herren believes that, at least at the time he wrote the *De Excidio*, Gildas aspired to be a monk (*sanctus*), but was probably a deacon.[68] Given his alleged authorship of monastic tracts (see discussion below) it is probable that, in the later part of his career, he joined a monastery and may have even served as abbot. Though there was likely a mixture of lay and celibate members in sixth-century insular monasteries, the *De Excidio* leads one to believe that Gildas preferred the ascetic life.

Like Patrick's writings, the *De Excidio* has been scrutinized by many Latinists who have judged Gildas the writer harshly, this despite his medieval reputation as 'Gildas *sapiens*' and as the universally respected 'historian of the Britons.' Gildas's sermonizing has never sat well with the modern secular historian, and one learned colleague of mine once proclaimed, 'There should be a book on everything Gildas *doesn't know* about sub-Roman Britain!' However, a trend in the last 15 years or so has been to resuscitate Gildas's reputation as a writer, and several specialists have shown us a Briton with advanced skills in diction, rhetoric, and rhythm.[69] It is almost certain that Gildas had received in Britain a remarkable late Classical education, from both a grammarian and a rhetor, and that he

---

66 See Dark, 1993, 260–6; and Higham, 1994, 90–117.
67 See Snyder, 1998.
68 Herren, 1990, 75.
69 See, for example, Lapidge, 1984; Kerlouégan, 1987; and Howlett, 1995.

studied Roman law as well as scripture and Classical Latin literature. 'I read how,' writes Gildas, 'because of the sins of men, the voice of the holy prophets rose in complaint, especially Jeremiah's, as he bewailed the ruin of his city.'[70] Several scholars have recently emphasized Gildas's frequent use of the Old Testament prophets, adopting the jeremiad style to critique his fellow Britons.[71] This rhetorical equation of Britons with Israelites, and the constant reference to historical catastrophes as divine plagues, shows Gildas following Eusebius and Augustine as a believer in providential history. While Augustine's *City of God* may be the most masterful of all providential histories, Gildas's *De Excidio* would firmly establish this as *the* way to view the history of early medieval Britain, profoundly influencing a string of insular writers from Bede to Geoffrey of Monmouth.

Monasticism and the Penitentials

In the *De Excidio* Gildas speaks sparingly, though with admiration, of monasticism. Yet in a letter to Pope Gregory the Great, the Irish missionary Columbanus describes Gildas as an expert on monastic discipline. British monasticism was apparently growing rapidly in Gildas's own lifetime, and one tradition maintains that Gildas took the monastic spirit to Brittany where he founded the monastery of St. Gildas de Rhuys shortly before his death. It is now time to ask when monasticism did arrive in Britain, and what was its character as practiced by Britons.

The monastic lifestyle of the Desert Fathers arrived in the Western Roman Empire in the second half of the fourth century, and two of the key figures were John Cassian and the former soldier Martin, who became bishop of Tours. Victricius, bishop of Rouen, came to Britain at the end of the fourth century – at the request of the Britons themselves – to introduce the reforms of St. Martin. Martin's attacks on paganism in Gaul and the introduction there of eastern monasticism may have crossed the Channel at this point, *c.*400. We know that Constans, the son of Constantine III, left a monastery to join his father's usurpation in 407, but we don't know whether the monastery was in Britain or in Gaul.[72] The naming of the fifth-century monastery at Whithorn *Candida Casa* is, if Bede's information is accurate, a clear homage to Martin. Still there is no clear material evidence for British monasticism in the first half of the fifth century.

Several scholars have noted the similarities between some early Chris-

---

70 *De Excidio*, 1.4.
71 See, for example, Wright, 1984.
72 Birley, 1980, 156.

tian inscriptions in western Britain and those in fifth-century Gaul.[73] Formulae like HIC IACIT and motifs like the encircled *Chi-Rho* suggest regular contact between Gaul and Atlantic Britain in the fifth and early sixth centuries. Given that these British stones are found in rural – if not isolated – areas, we are likely seeing the importation of the Gallic model (and perhaps Gallic clergy) of secular clergy assigned to rural dioceses.[74] Did these Gallic visitors also bring monasticism to western Britain?

Higham suggests that a significant number of landed aristocrats in the second half of the fifth century (including possibly Gildas) began converting their rural estates into monasteries in order to escape taxation by British lords.[75] This may have been influenced by Pelagian teachings. These villa communities – Charles Thomas calls them 'gentleman's monasteries'[76] – may be an extension of the style of worship practiced in the rural estates of Britain in the fourth century.[77] Frampton, Hinton St. Mary, and Lullingstone have revealed clear examples of aristocratic house-chapels, while Chedworth villa yielded a baptistery. Though it is not clear how long worship lasted beyond the fourth century at these particular sites, in western Britain we glimpse some continuity. At the villas of Frocester, Llancarfan, Llandough, and Llantwit Major, for example, there is evidence (some of it literary) for early medieval monasteries directly succeeding villa occupation.

Constantius does not mention monks in Britain, nor does Patrick, though he is quite familiar with monasticism (perhaps from a stay in Gaul) and actively promoted it among young men and women in Ireland. Herren sees Patrick's *monachi* as members of the lower clergy, primarily deacons and presbyters, who, along with the *virgines*, were responsible for conducting the office of psalm singing in parish churches.[78] The latest research shows that there were not many organized and exclusive monastic communities in Britain and Ireland before 600, but rather an increasing number of 'minsters' (*monasteria*) or mixed communities where clerks and monks performed pastoral duties along with the priests and bishops required for administering the sacraments.[79] Whether corruption among the secular clergy, which Patrick and Gildas certainly allude to, leads to an increasing role for monasticism in Britain depends on how much weight we want to put on their criticism of British priests and bishops.

73   See, for example, Knight, 1996; Thomas, 1998, 86.
74   Knight, 1996, 113.
75   Higham, 1992, 137.
76   Thomas, 1998, 60.
77   See Pearce, 1982.
78   Herren, 1989, 83.
79   See the Introduction in Blair and Sharpe, 1992.

Two monastic works have been attributed to Gildas: some *Fragments* of lost letters dealing with various Church issues and a *Preface On Penance*. Gildas dispenses advice in the *Fragments* on such topics as excommunication, ecclesiastical justice, and the apocalypse. But most of his concern is with asceticism and monastic discipline. As Herren has pointed out, Gildas eschews ascetic excess and severe penances in the *Fragments*.[80] Should we interpret this as a counter to a wave of ascetic extremism in the British Church?

Clearly monasticism was well established and organized in Britain by the time Gildas wrote his *Preface On Penance*. If monastic communities in Britain were following a common *regula* before this it has not survived (unless they had adopted an eastern *regula* like Cassian's). British Church leaders saw a need for rules of discipline to apply to both the celibate and secular members of their communities. Gildas, if the attribution is correct, answered this call with a short work on clerical sins and penance. A few examples will give you a flavor of this early penitential:

1   A priest or deacon committing natural fornication or sodomy who has previously taken the monastic vow shall do penance for three years . . .

2   If any monk of lower rank (does this), he shall do penance for three years, but his allowance of bread shall be increased. If he is a worker, he shall take a Roman pint of milk and another of whey and as much water as the intensity of his thirst requires.

10   If on account of drunkenness someone is unable to sing the psalms . . . he shall be deprived of his supper.

11   One who sins with a beast shall expiate his guilt for a year; if by himself alone, for three forty-day periods.

23   For good kings we ought to offer the sacrifice, for bad ones on no account.[81]

Gildas's *Preface on Penance* is widely considered the earliest of the 'Celtic Penitentials,' which in turn are the first formal guidelines on penance in Christian history. These penitentials, writes Oliver Davies, link 'the highest ascetic ideals with pastoral realism but also much that is hyperbolic and bizarre with the punctilious detailing of legal codes.'[82] A few other early penitential works are also from Britain and inspired the more famous Irish penitentials. The *Synod of North Britain*, the *Synod of the*

---

80   Herren, 1990, 70.
81   Gildas, *De Poenitentia* (trans. Bieler).
82   In Davies and O'Loughlin, 1999.

Grove of Victory, and *Excerpts from a Book of David* are brief and of unclear provenance, but an origin in sixth-century Wales seems indicated by reference to Roman measures and to penalties against those 'who afford guidance to the barbarians,' an apparent reference to British informants among the Saxons. One notable feature of the last two is that they prescribe penances for the laity as well as for the monks and other clergy.

According to Columbanus, Gildas corresponded with a man named 'Uinniau' on the topic of monastic discipline.[83] This is likely the same Uinniau (pronounced Finnio in Irish) who penned an early monastic penitential, and may be the 'bishop Finnio' under whom, according to Adomnán, Columba studied sacred scripture.[84] Uinniau is a British name, and it seems likely that this 'Finnian' was a Briton schooled in western Britain who became a teacher and abbot in Ireland. The *Penitential of Finnian* is likely the work of a Briton adapting British attitudes on penance to the legal customs of Ireland. The same can be said of an early work called the *First Synod of St. Patrick*, attributed to the bishops Patrick, Auxilius, and Iserninus. These last two works are more extensive than the British penitentials and probably represent a slightly later development of the disciplinary ideas first expressed by Gildas.

The Age of the Saints

As was pointed out earlier in this chapter, the Church of Late Roman Britain was based on urban episcopacies. With the decline and destruction of Romano-British cities in the middle of the fifth century, the role of the British bishops may have changed. Some traveled to the continent, others adapted to the new political environment in Britain. Charles Thomas has suggested that in the sixth and seventh centuries British bishops were attached to courts and royal households rather than towns with major churches.[85] There is epigraphic evidence that at least some of these bishops were married: a sixth-century memorial stone from Anglesey commemorates '*Audiva*, wife of *Bivatisus* the *sacerdos*.'[86]

In the *De Excidio* Gildas bemoaned the secularism and corruption of such priests and bishops, and both he and Patrick declared ascetics to be the new role models. From the second half of the fifth century through the end of the seventh century, Britain and Ireland produced an astonishing

---

83   Columbanus, *Letter to Pope Gregory the Great*, 1.7.
84   See the comments of Richard Sharpe (p. 11) in his introduction to Adomnán's *Life of St. Columba*.
85   Thomas, 1998, 82–83.
86   *ECMW* no. 325. See also Thomas, 1998, 85–6.

number of individuals who, because of their ascetic abilities, miracle-working, and missionary activity came to be regarded as *sancti*. Britons were well represented in the Age of the Saints, and were long remembered as founders and teachers in this extraordinary period of Church history.[87]

While many modern Christians have become increasingly enamored of these 'Celtic' saints, there are serious historiographic problems. The primary sources for most of these British saints, the *Vitae*, were produced years – sometimes centuries – after the deaths of the saints, and focus on the miraculous in order to promote the saint's cult or (less admirably) the current interests of the see or monastery. Epigraphy and archaeology, furthermore, are usually no aid in reconstructing historical biographies.

The problem is well illustrated in our quest to discover one of the first British saints, the bishop Nynia, better known as St. Ninian. Bede describes Nynia as a British bishop instructed in Rome, who established the see of Whithorn (in Latin *Candida Casa* – the 'Shining House' – named in honor of the famous church of St. Martin) and preached to the southern Picts.[88] Bede does not give us a date for Nynia, only that he operated in Scotland 'long before' the mission of St. Columba. Later in the eighth century a monk at Whithorn wrote a Latin poem called *The Miracles of Bishop Ninia*, and in the twelfth century there appeared a Latin *Life of Ninian* ascribed to Ailred of Rievaulx. In these works Nynia is a son of a British king who travels to Rome to study and visit the holy shrines. Consecrated bishop in Rome, Nynia returns to his native land, founding Candida Casa and preaching to a Pictish tribe called the Niduari while being persecuted by a local British king named Tudwal. John MacQueen has done a masterful job of sorting through these hagiographic sources, arguing for their dependence on an original Latin *Vita* produced at Whithorn *c*.550–650.[89] Still, without the discovery of that original source, the literary evidence for an historical Nynia is thin.

Peter Hill's excavations at Whithorn in the late 1980s, however, have provided some corroboration of Bede's account.[90] Galloway had previously yielded several early Christian memorial stones, and Hill's excavations revealed at least two phases of Early Christian activity at Whithorn before it was taken by the Vikings (see figures 7.1 and 7.2). Fifth- and sixth-century features of the site include small rectangular wattle buildings, a circular 'oratory,' a garden, remains of a moldboard plough, conical drinking glasses, and pottery from the Mediterranean. Hill sees

---

87 For discussion of the Welsh saints as 'Christianized folk heroes,' see Henken, 1987; idem, 1991.
88 Bede, *HE*, 3.4.
89 MacQueen, 1990.
90 Hill, 1997.

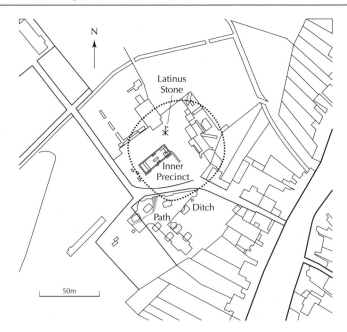

Figures 6.1 and 6.2   Plans showing the excavated features of early Christian
Whithorn in its first two phases.

Whithorn as the center of a fifth-century Christian community large enough
to warrant the provision of a bishop such as Nynia, perhaps from the
nearby Late Roman town of Carlisle.[91] Nynia's church was succeeded by
a *monasterium*, perhaps led by Gallic clergy who used sophisticated rural
technologies to build their new community around the founder's shrine.
One excavated structure, a mortared stone building, had lime-wash resi-
due, giving some credence to Bede's 'Shining House.' Around 550 the
monasterium was developed further, along the Irish model, with the construction of a double enclosure.

   This link between British and Gallic clergy can also be seen in the
hagiographic tradition of two other fifth-century British saints, Dubricius
(Dyfrig) and Illtud, said to have been disciples of Germanus.[92] Both saints
are linked to southeast Wales, both seem to have flourished around 475,
and both are mentioned in the *Life of St. Samson*. Here the *papa* Dubricius
comes to the monastery of *Eltut*, 'an illustrious *magister* of the Britons,'
to ordain Samson. Later Samson visits Bishop Dubricius on an unnamed

91   See also Thomas, 1981, ch. 11; and W. Davies, 1998.
92   See D. Simon Evans's introduction in Doble, 1971, 42, 51–5.

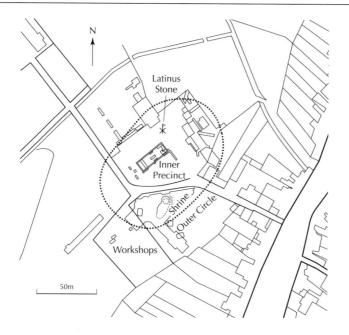

island monastery that had been built by St. Germanus, and Dubricius appoints Samson as the new abbot. Soon after he is consecrated bishop, and after years of travel, he returns to visit an aged and ill Dubricius. The author of the *Life of St. Samson* testifies that he himself 'had been in Eltut's magnificent monastery' and also on Dubricius' island home. Scholars have identified these two places as, respectively, Llantwit Major (Llanilltud Fawr) and Caldey Island, with the first identification resting on solid placename evidence and the latter relying on an Ogam inscription found on Caldey (tenuously read as 'the tonsured servant of Dubricius') and late charter evidence of land given to Dubricius at Penally, immediately opposite Caldey.

More extensive descriptions of the careers of Dubricius and Illtud can be found in their *Vitae*, both of which date from the twelfth century.[93] In these late works we learn that Germanus made Dubricius archbishop of southern Britain and that Illtud began his career as a soldier at his cousin King Arthur's court![94] Despite these claims, there is consistent evidence in earlier *Vitae* that Illtud at least was a famed head of a monastic school which produced

---

93   The *Vita Archiepiscopi Dubricii* is located in the oldest part of the *Liber Landavensis*.
94   Both the *Vita Dubricii* and the *Annales Cambriae* give Dubricius' death date as 612, which would make him nearly 200 years old.

the next generation of British saints. His disciple Samson is commemorated in what many scholars consider the earliest *Vita* of any of the 'Celtic' saints. A monk at the monastery of Dol, in Brittany, composed the *Vita Prima* of Samson, founder of Dol, based on his travels to Cornwall and information he gathered there from an elderly monk whose uncle had been Samson's companion. If this is true, the *Vita Prima* could have been written as early as the beginning of the seventh century, though recent opinion has shifted the date of composition a century or more later.[95] As we have seen, Samson is portrayed in the *Vita* as an itinerant monk who also had the sacramental and administrative abilities of a bishop. He traveled through Wales, Dumnonia, and eventually Brittany, and may be the *Samson peccator episcopus* who signed the acts of the Council of Paris in 557. As a young boy he was taught grammar by the *magister* Illtud, who used alphabetic tesserae to explain Latin letters.[96] Here in the *Vita Prima* are rare glimpses in an early work of Britons trying to keep Classical education alive in Britain nearly a hundred years after the island ceased being part of the empire.

Later hagiographic tradition named Illtud's school as the training center for the next generation of British saints, including Samson, Paul Aurelian, David, and even Gildas. Paul Aurelian, or Pol, was the son of a 'count' of Carmarthenshire, according to his *Vita* written by the Breton monk Wrmonoc in 884. After studying under Illtud, Paul traveled through Cornwall on his way to Brittany, where he is remembered as the founder of the church of St. Pol-de-Léon. Since this Paul was also called Paulinus in Breton documents, Wrmonoc appears to have combined stories of a certain Paul of Penychen, Paulinus the disciple of Illtud, and the eponymous founder of Paul near Penzance.[97] A fragmentary slab found in Carmarthenshire and dating from the sixth century commemorates a Christian Briton named Paulinus, but nothing definitive links this stone with our saint.[98]

St. David (Dewi Sant), patron saint of Wales, was almost certainly an historical figure but difficult for historians to discuss. Like Patrick, we know him best from hagiography and later medieval legends. The *Life of Saint David* was written by Rhigyfarch in about 1095, but by that time David had been featured in the *Vitae* of other British saints, and Rhigyfarch borrows from them as well as from local traditions (his father was twice bishop of St. David's). Although Rhigyfarch's finely crafted *Life* gives us some wonderful stories about David, ranging from bardic-style magical

95   Wood, 1988, suggests a late seventh-century composition date for the *Vita Prima*; Flobert, 1997, prefers a date *c.*730.
96   See Thomas, 1998, 58.
97   See Doble, 1984, 93–4, 146ff.
98   *ECMW*, no. 139: SERVATVR FIDAEI / PATRI(a)EQ(ue) SEMPER / AMATOR HIC PAVLIN/VS IACIT CVL[T]OR PIENT[I]/(s)SIM[VS AEQVI].

episodes to descriptions of great ascetic feats, the David literature tells us more about later medieval Wales than it does about the fifth and sixth centuries. Few would dispute, however, that David was likely the much-venerated founder of the large and powerful monastic see which bears his name. By about 1200 there were more than 60 churches dedicated to David in southwest Wales, and the saint had also by then become a potent symbol of Welsh nationalism.[99]

The hagiography gives us the impression that most of the British saints of this era were born or trained in south Wales and subsequently traveled to Cornwall and Brittany. Fewer traditions survive regarding northern British saints, but of these Kentigern's is certainly the strongest. In addition to a few references in the *Aberdeen Breviary* (*c*.1500), two *Vitae* of Kentigern (or Mungo, 'dear one') were written in the twelfth century, the latter, written by Jocelin of Furness, being the only complete biography. According to Jocelin, the saint was born at Culross in Fife and moved to do missionary work on the Clyde, establishing a Christian community which became modern Glasgow. He was also itinerant, fleeing Glasgow's pagan king and traveling through Dumfriesshire, Galloway, and Wales, where he became linked with saints David and Asaph. Furthermoe, Jocelin tells of a meeting between Kentigern and Columba, which took place in Tayside *c*.584, in which the two saints embraced and exchanged pastoral staves. While Adomnán never mentions Kentigern, he does say that Columba spoke with Rydderch of Strathclyde, Kentigern's patron after his return to Glasgow.

These sources for Kentigern's life are nowhere near being primary sources, though some scholars have argued for earlier Kentigern traditions circulating in Glasgow, which came to influence the hagiography. Celtic hagiography in general is seldom if ever good written evidence for the history of the fifth and sixth centuries, but it does often give us a good sense of the preoccupations and perspectives of literate Britons from the seventh to the twelfth centuries. We are drawn to the Celtic saints, I believe, because they represent a fascinating hybrid of native, Roman, and ascetic Christian traditions. Modern readers, for example, often delight in the intimate relationship that many of the saints exhibit toward their natural surroundings. It was once acceptable to attribute this quality to an enlightened indigenous or 'Celtic' attitude toward ecology. 'The Christian rite of baptism, involving purification and spiritual refreshment by water,' observes Mark Redknap, 'readily merged with pre-Christian Celtic traditions' of water and divinity.[100]

The vernacular literatures of Ireland and Wales are filled with heroic adventures often involving long voyages and quests; for example, warri-

99   See *Armes Prydein*, ll. 51, 105, 140, 196; Bradley, 1999, 46; and chapter12 below.
100   Redknap, 1995, 740.

ors traveling to the Otherworld. This, many scholars have observed, is paralleled in Celtic hagiography with the missionary saints and *peregrini*. The British *Vitae* give a consistent portrayal of itinerant saints who travel constantly between Britain, Ireland, and Brittany, with monastic foundations rather than military victories serving as the achievements of these 'soldiers of Christ.' In addition to placename evidence for British ecclesiasts founding churches on the continent, there is some written evidence for the presence of such Britons in Ireland. An entry in the Annals of Ulster (s.a. 836), for example, mentions 'Durrow of the Britons,' seemingly a British monastery in southern Ireland akin to the Saxon houses in Mayo.

We have, I think, underestimated the vitality of the British Church. Britons were without a doubt some of the most active and energetic figures in this age, an age that witnessed the preservation of Classical modes of education in the British Isles as well as the foundation of some of the most important medieval churches and monasteries. Armagh, Glasgow, Glastonbury, St. David's, and St. Gildas-de-Rhuys are just a few of the churches founded in the Brittonic Age that remembered British saints as their founders. The British influence is even greater if we consider the number of Irish and English ecclesiasts who were trained by Britons or at British establishments. As Tom O'Loughlin reminds us, Christian writers in early medieval Ireland were well aware that they had received their Christianity from British Christians.[101]

Postscript: The Synod of Whitby

Bede, while occasionally respectful of Irish saints, rarely has a good word to say about the British Church. On the contrary, he blamed the Britons' troubles against the Saxons as divine punishment for not having converted their pagan neighbors. When, for example, the pagan king Æthelfrith killed the monks of Bangor-is-Coed at the Battle of Chester, Bede felt no remorse toward this 'great slaughter of that nation of heretics.'[102] It was a just act because the Britons would not cooperate with St. Augustine in his mission to convert the English. 'Indeed,' he later adds, 'to this very day it is the habit of the Britons to despise the faith and religion of the English and not to co-operate with them in anything.'[103]

In the drama of early British history, Augustine's arrival at Canterbury in 597 signaled the beginning of the end for the Britons both politically and ecclesiastically. That Rome should choose to establish close relations

101   O'Loughlin, 2000, 1, 13.
102   Bede, *HE*, 2.2.
103   Bede, *HE*, 2.20.

with the nascent Anglo-Saxon kings rather than with British rulers was both an insult to the Britons and a signal that continental *cognoscenti* had decided upon the outcome of the struggle for control of Britain. To make matters worse, the Holy Father sent his priest Augustine to Britain with archiepiscopal powers, which meant that he and future English bishops would have control over all British clergy.

This is the context in which we should read the so-called Conference at Augustine's Oak. According to Bede, Augustine, with the help of King Æthelberht, 'summoned the bishops and teachers of the neighboring British kingdom' to a conference which would take place on the borders of the kingdoms of the Hwicce and the West Saxons (probably in the southern Cotswolds).[104] When Augustine started criticizing various British Church customs (chiefly their dating of Easter), the Britons hesitated. Finally, in 603, they sent a delegation of seven bishops and 'many learned men,' chiefly from the monastery at Bangor. On their way to the conference the British clergy asked a holy man and hermit 'whether they should forsake their own traditions at the bidding of Augustine.' He advised them that if Augustine rose to greet them at their coming, he was a humble man and should be obeyed; but if he failed to rise he was arrogant and should be ignored.

Augustine remained seated at the Britons' approach, and proceeded to inform the Britons that he would tolerate their idiosyncrasies only if they agreed to three points: to keep Easter at the proper time, to perform baptisms according to Roman rites, and to preach the Gospel to the English. The Britons refused on all three points, and said that they would not recognize Augustine as their archbishop because he was unwilling to rise at their approach. Augustine 'warned them with threats that, if they refused to accept peace from their brethren, they would have to accept war from their enemies; and if they would not preach the way of life to the English nation, they would one day suffer the vengeance of death at their hands.' Eddius Stephanus confirms that British clergy in the north at least fled from the 'hostile sword' of the English, deserting their churches.[105]

Despite Bede's claims, it is now being recognized that Britons played a major role in the conversion of their English neighbors. According to the *Historia Brittonum*, the Briton Rhun, son of Urien of Rheged, baptized some of the English inhabitants of Northumbria. In Wessex it is known that some English houses, like Glastonbury, were British foundations where, even after their transition to English governance, they continued to venerate British saints. Diane Brook's study of ecclesiastical sites on both sides of Offa's Dyke revealed a large number of curved churchyards,

104   Bede, *HE*, 2.1.
105   Eddius Stephanus, *Life of Wilfrid*, 17.

a likely indicator of British foundation, extending from the fifth to the twelfth centuries.[106] Finally, the important work of Steven Bassett on early charters and parish boundaries in the Midlands has shown the influence that British Christians had on their English neighbors in this area as the latter were becoming converts.[107] Worcester, Gloucester, Wroxeter, Lichfield, and Lincoln may all have had pre-existing episcopal churches taken over by missionaries from Canterbury, probably on papal advice and with some cooperation of the British clergy.[108]

Nevertheless, the Britons did continue to disagree with Canterbury on the timing of Easter, and the so-called 'Easter controversy' led to a showdown between 'Celtic' and 'Roman' practices at the Synod of Whitby in 664. While Bede does not mention any British clergy participating in the synod, he does relate that Wilfrid, arguing for the Roman side, slandered the Irish 'and their accomplices in obstinacy, I mean the Picts and the Britons.'[109] Colman, bishop of Lindisfarne, failed to convince those at the synod of the legitimacy of the Celtic Easter, tonsure, and 'other matters of ecclesiastical discipline.' The English clergy who had been instructed by the Irish converted to the Roman practices, while Colman and his party withdrew to Ireland to discuss the matter. Few of the Irish or British churches accepted the decision of Whitby.

The Synod of Whitby has been judged by revisionist historians as a non-event. Bede overdramatized the conflict between the Roman and Celtic sides, they say, because of his own ethnic prejudices and his obsession with calendars. This view follows on the heels of the academic skepticism concerning 'Celtic Christianity' and the 'Celtic Church.'[110] Specialists have scoffed at these romantic and thoroughly modern constructs, derived mostly from late and unreliable evidence, and have pointed out both the diversity of practices within the Celtic Churches (to use the preferred term) and their similarities to the 'Roman' practices of the English and Gallic Churches. Irish and British Christians were as orthodox as their English brethren, they rightly remind us.

But there is something distinct about the spirituality of the Celtic-speaking world.[111] Columbanus, in his letters to Pope Gregory, felt that he had to defend the strangeness of what he termed the 'western churches.'[112]

---

106   Brook, 1992.
107   Bassett, 1989; idem, 1992.
108   See Snyder, 1998, 238–9.
109   Bede, *HE*, 3.25.
110   See, for example, Hughes, 1981; W. Davies, 1992; and Bradley, 1999.
111   For a moderate counter to the skeptics, see O. Davies, 1996; and O. Davies and O'Loughlin, 1999.
112   Columbanus, *Epistolae*, 1. See also Sharpe, 1984.

This strangeness, which Bede thought heresy, is exhibited throughout the British Church. Sometime between 509 and 521, for example, three Gallic bishops sent a letter to two priests bearing British names, Louocatus and Catihernus, who likely resided in Brittany. The bishops complain:

> From the report of the man Speratus the venerable priest we have learned that bearing certain tables you do not cease to go about through the huts of your various citizens, and you presume to celebrate masses there with women present at the divine sacrifice, [women] whom you call 'fellow-hostesses' . . . [who] hold the chalices and presume to administer the blood of Christ to the people. The strangeness of this affair and the unheard of practice has saddened us not a little.[113]

Women serving Mass would have indeed struck many in the sixth century as heresy. But in most ways the Britons appear conservative rather than radical. For example, epigraphic and archaeological evidence suggests that British burial customs from the Iron Age (and earlier), such as lintel-grave and cairn burials, were condoned by the British Church, though perhaps only for aristocratic tombs.[114] The British (and Irish) zeal for ascetic and eremitic monasticism also seems to have defined the 'western Churches' while their eastern neighbors turned to other concerns, as is most clearly illustrated in the Northumbrians pleading with the Irish-educated Cumbrian St. Cuthbert to leave his hermit's cell to take up their bishopric.

The British clergy proved to be the most conservative of all the 'western Churches' in the Easter controversy, and thus became increasingly isolated from many continental developments. Wales was the last Celtic-speaking land to adopt the Roman dating system, which it did following the advice of Archbishop Elfoddw in 768. Benedictine monasticism did not take root in Wales until the eleventh century. The Britons had held out, and continued to treat their English clerical brethren with suspicion if not outright contempt, as in the claim of Aldhelm that the Dumnonian clergy had to ritually cleanse their bowls after English clergy had eaten from them.

But this conservatism had a positive side. The decision of the Synod of Whitby helped to unify the British Churches, and in turn helped strengthen British identity. Britons could for nearly four centuries be identified by their adherence to an older calendar, and could differentiate themselves from their neighbors – both Celtic and English speakers – who observed a Roman Easter. These four centuries before the Viking advent were a time of energetic monasticism, of promotion of the cults of native saints, and of looking inward by necessity to develop a sense of who they were as a post-Roman Christian nation.

113   Howlett, 1995, 66–72.
114   Higham, 1992, 102.

Part III
A People Divided

7
Brittany and Galicia

The sense of British identity developed during the Roman occupation of Britain and alongside the growing British Church was never more in need than in the years between AD 600 and 1000. The expansionist kingdoms of the English and the Scots began isolating British polities from one another in the seventh century. This isolation, and their location on the rim of the Irish and North Seas, made several British kingdoms vulnerable to Viking raids and land seizure, beginning around 800. These years saw the Britons in need of political alliances to assure their very survival, and such alliances – be they with Scots, Saxons, or Vikings – could have undermined their distinctive culture had they not developed a strong sense of British identity.

In the next several chapters we will examine the Britons as they became isolated in four distinct geographic areas: Brittany and Galicia, Cornwall, Wales and the Isle of Man, and northern Britain. While the Britons in these areas developed their own regional cultures, they also struggled to maintain their British identity through ecclesiastical contacts, itinerant bards, and occasional political alliances. One such pan-British alliance in the face of English expansion, called upon by the author of the *Armes Prydein c.*930, never fully materialized; yet it shows the power of common saints, heroes, and prejudices in holding a scattered people together against overwhelming odds. The odds would become even greater in the eleventh century, when the expansionist Norman state presented those Britons who had been able to maintain their cultural identity and political autonomy with an entirely new set of challenges.

Our discussion of the divided Britons will begin with what might be termed the 'British diaspora.' Beginning in the fifth century AD several groups of Britons left their island home and resettled on the continent, most prominently in the Roman provinces of Armorica and Gallaecia. The Armorican Britons would go on to establish the kingdom (later a duchy) of Brittany, which, despite its political and military vulnerability, maintained a Brittono-Latin culture throughout the Middle Ages and remains the only area of continental Europe where a Celtic language is actively spoken today. In the kingdom (also later a duchy) of Galicia, on the other hand, Britons remained a minority and were subsumed early on by more powerful neighbors. Still, some traces of Brittonic culture survived in the northwestern Spanish landscape throughout the medieval period.

Galicia

Contact between western Spain and the British Isles dates back at least to the Bronze Age, where archaeologists have found evidence of an extensive Atlantic coastal trade network. This trade network was still present in the Late Iron Age, when Rome completed its conquest of Spain and subsequently brought Britain into its Mediterranean-based empire. The northwestern corner of Spain was first organized into the *civitates Asturia et Gallaecia* – named for the Astures and Galaicos tribal confederations – within the province of Terraconensis.[1] By 305, the reforms of Diocletian had created a separate province of Gallaecia within the new diocese of Hispania.

The emperor Theodosius I was born in Gallaecia, which remained dominated by rural industry (especially fishing) while receiving a fair share of Romanization. It was also Christianized in the fourth century, and fell under the influence of the Priscillianist heresy *c.*385. In 411 the British tyrant Constantine III, betrayed by his general in the Pyrenees, allowed the Alans, Vandals, and Sueves to enter into Spain. Gallaecia was occupied by Asding Vandals in the east and Sueves in the west. The Sueves established an independent kingdom which was to survive until it was annexed by the Visigoths in 584. Though not Roman federates, the Sueves were saved from the Visigoths in 417 when Rome resettled the latter in Toulouse. Suevic kings preserved much of the Roman administration of Gallaecia in order to collect taxes from and enforce Roman law upon the local population. The Sueves became Arian Christians shortly after their conquest of Gallaecia, and were converted to Catholicism by St. Martin of Braga in the 550s.

Suevic kings were usually tolerant and hands-off rulers, and seem to have allowed ancient contacts between Galicia and the British Isles to continue. In the early fifth century Orosius (who was from Spain) refers to relations between *Brigantium*, the port city of La Coruña on the north-

1   There is a fairly extensive literature on Roman Galicia: see, for example, Arias Vilas, 1992.

west coast of Galicia, and Ireland.[2] In the sixth century groups of Britons, with their Catholic bishops, begin appearing in Church documents relating to Galicia. Proceedings of Church councils from the late sixth to the ninth centuries show us the formation of the diocese of Bretoña. The Council of Lugo in 567 records nine dioceses belonging to the metropolis of Galicia and a 'British see' (*sedes Britonorum*), which consisted of 'the churches which are among the Britons' (*ecclesias que sunt intro Britones*) with a *monasterium Maximi* as its center.[3] The 'monastery of Maximus' is most likely the abbey of St. Maria de Bretoña near Mondoñedo. The abbey and the presence of a bishop called Mailoc (*Mahiloc Britonensis ecclesiae episcopus*) at the Second Council of Braga in 572 are two signs of an active Brittonic community in Iberia. British bishops are also recorded at the Fourth (633), Seventh (646), and Eighth (653) Councils of Toledo as well as the Third Council of Braga (675).[4] The bishopric of Bretoña lasted until at least 830, while in the tenth century we still see references to churches in the vicinity that are *inter Britones*.

What can be made of this evidence? Mailoc is certainly a Celtic name and probably Brittonic, as are some of the names of Galician bishops attending seventh-century councils.[5] The explicit reference to a monastery, and the absence of parish names, are without parallel in other Spanish dioceses.[6] As Jonathan Wooding has pointed out, this could be because the Britons formed a Catholic pocket within the Arian Suevic kingdom, and thus Spanish Church chroniclers would have known little about them.[7] Galician monasticism has been compared to that of the Celtic Churches. The seventh-century *Life of St. Fructuosus*, for example, testifies to the ascetic and eremitic character of Galician monks, many of whom established isolated communities along the sea coast and island retreats. The form of the penitential system in Galicia is also similar to that of western Britain and Ireland, and like the insular Britons, the Galicians were late in replacing the *Vetus Latina* Bible with the Vulgate.[8] Borrowings from the Visigoths observed in Irish art may stem from ecclesiastical links between Galicia and surrounding Visigothic churches.[9]

We can supplement this with material and placename evidence. There

2   Orosius, 1.2.
3   In the *Parochiale* of the *Divisio Thiudemiri*, entry XIII. See Chandwick, 1965, 281–82; and Thompson, 1968, 202–3.
4   See Chandwick, 1965, 282.
5   See Thompson, 1968, 202–3.
6   Thompson, 1968, 203.
7   Wooding, 1996, 59.
8   Chadwick, 1969, 269.
9   Galliou and Jones, 1991, 130.

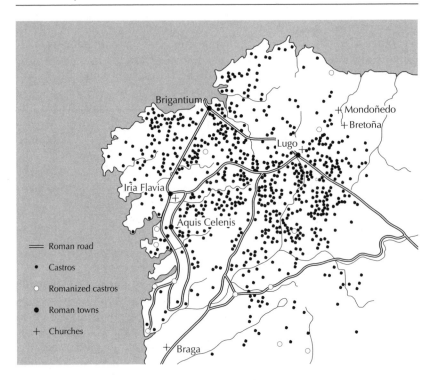

Map 7.1   Sixth-century Galicia showing Iron age *castros* and British settlements.

are over 20 names beginning in 'Brit' or 'Bret' in the Iberian Peninsula, most in the northwest, and these have been taken to denote British settlements. Ancient dykes surrounding Bretoña may have served as a monastic enclosure, with British and Irish parallels. Excavations in the 1970s suggest that the original Britons inhabited a pre-existing hill-fort in Bretoña. Iron Age Galicia was characterized by a warrior aristocracy based at hundreds of ancient fortified hilltop enclosures called *castros*. There is some evidence of the reoccupation of *castros* in the fifth and sixth centuries AD, though we do not know if Britons were among the new occupants. Galicia's rich deposits of gold and tin may have attracted British miners and craftsmen from similarly endowed Devon and Cornwall, both trading partners in the pre-Roman period.

Our information about Britons in Galicia, however, concerns purely ecclesiastical matters. We do not know the names of any British rulers in Galicia, if indeed there were any beyond the British bishops. This is not unusual, for we also lack the names of the Suevic kings who were overlords of Galicia for nearly two centuries. The diocese of Bretoña, later replaced by the diocese of Mondoñedo, seems to have stretched from Mondoñedo north to the sea, and also across the River Eo to Asturia (see map 7.1).[10] This is a sizable area, and while there is every indication that it included many British churches, no other inhabitants in the area are mentioned. Did British colonists drive out previous inhabitants? Was there some sort of organized settlement? Some have suggested that British colonization of Galicia came from Brittany rather than Britain. Unfortunately further evidence is lacking, permitting us to say only that sixth-century Galicia had a large community of Catholic Britons whose monks and bishops were able to maintain their British identity, surrounded by Arian Sueves and Vandals, for several centuries.[11]

From Armorica to Brittany

The Armorican peninsula (from the Celtic *are morico*, 'the land facing the sea') had once been part of the larger Gallic world, whose western regions – Gallia Comata – were occupied by a variety of Late Iron Age tribes. The most powerful were the Veneti, with its great fleets, who for years participated in the resistance to Roman expansion and who, like the Galaicos, maintained strong trade contacts with Britain and Ireland. After Caesar defeated the Veneti and subjugated their Gallic neighbors, Armorica became part of the Roman administrative province of Lugdunensis (see map 7.2). Five tributary *civitates* were established in the province, corresponding to the five major Gaulish tribes in the area – the Riedones, the Coriosolitae, the Osismi, the Veneti, and the Namnetes – with capitals respectively at *Condate* (Rennes), *Fanum Martis* (Corseul), *Vorgium* (Carhaix), *Darioritum* (Vannes), and *Condevincum* (Nantes). (These are amazingly reflected in the five *départements* of modern Brittany.) Amongst the ruling classes in these new cities the process of Romanization was rapid, aided by the Roman roads that soon connected these administrative centers with local ports and the rest of Gaul.

Beneath this veneer of prosperous Gallo-Roman aristocrats, however, lay political instability and an increasingly large number of disaffected rural peasants. In the third century Armorican coastal settlements proved vulnerable to North Sea pirates, like the Franks and the Saxons now raiding further south through the English Channel. This triggered a series of revolts in Gaul, the most serious of which led to the breakaway Gallic

10   Thompson, 1968, 203.
11   Wooding, 1996, 59.

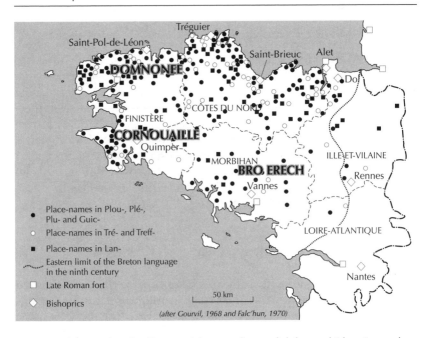

Map 7.2   Brittany showing Roman *civitates* and coastal defenses, bishoprics, and Brittonic placenames.

Empire of the Roman general Postumus in 260. Even though this revolt was suppressed by Aurelian in 274 and the Gallic provinces restored to the empire, bands of rural peasants called the Bacaudae terrorized the Armorican coast before being put down by regular troops. This coastal area, called the *Tractus Armoricanus et Nervicanus*, became heavily fortified during the reign of Diocletian, and Frankish *laeti* were seemingly brought in to bolster the defense of Armorica in the fourth century.[12]

But these measures did not bring stability to Armorica. The officer placed in charge of defending both sides of the Channel, Mausaeus Carausius, was rumored to be in collusion with the barbarians, and declared himself emperor in 287, seizing control of the British provinces. More usurpations followed – Magnentius in 350, Magnus Maximus in 382, Constantine III in 407 – and all involved rebel troops in Britain and Gaul, responding to the political instability of the western Roman administration and the increasing attacks, by land and sea, of the barbarians. In 410, according to

12   Galliou and Jones, 1991, 124.

Zosimus, the Armoricans and other Gauls followed the example of the Britons by finally expelling the Roman administration, abandoning Roman law and creating their own governments and militias.[13] In 417 imperial troops regained control of western Gaul, but the next 20 years witnessed a collapse of the social order capped off by a serious Bacaudae revolt in 435. From this point on, the 'Romans' who controlled Armorica and protected it from barbarian invaders would bear a different name: Britons.

The transition from Armorica to Brittany, that is, the establishment of Britons in the peninsula, remains a little understood process. Britons had of course traveled to Gaul throughout the Roman period – in military, ecclesiastical, and (we may assume) commercial capacities – but there is no indication of large distinct groups of Britons on the continent until the mid-fifth century. Sidonius Apollinaris, writing c.470, says that *Britanni* had settled north of the Loire, and that the *Britanni* answerable to the war-leader Riothamus were enticing slaves away from a Gallic estate.[14] Gildas was the first to describe the flight of Britons, in the wake of the Saxon invasions, 'for lands beyond the seas,' while Procopius was the first to apply the term *Britannia* to Armorica.[15] *Britannia* became the standard Latin term for the Armorican peninsula by the late sixth century, as seen in the writings of Gregory of Tours, Venantius Fortunatus, and Marius of Avenches. Although Bretons seem to have developed a vernacular name for themselves – *Letavii* (Old Breton *Letau*), from *Letavia*, a name probably brought over from Britain – Frankish writers did not differentiate between Bretons and insular Britons, calling them both *Brittones*.[16]

These sources, together with the Church documents discussed in the previous chapter, constitute the historical evidence for the British settlement in Armorica. There is also a legendary account, found in Geoffrey of Monmouth's *History of the Kings of Britain* as well as in the Welsh *Dream of Macsen Wledig*, which describes British soldiers who followed Magnus Maximus to Gaul staying behind, after his death in 388, and founding a kingdom in Brittany (after marrying local women) under Conan Meriadec.[17] Unfortunately there is no contemporary evidence for this, nor even for the existence of Conan, though he was a prominent royal figure in both Welsh and Breton traditions.[18]

---

13 Zosimus, 6.5.
14 Sidonius, *Epistulae*, 1.7.5 and 3.9.2. See the discussion below on Riothamus.
15 Gildas, *De Excidio*, 25.1; Procopius, *De Bello Gothico*, 8.20; Thompson, 1980.
16 Smith, 1992, 13. For *Letavia* in Welsh literature, see chapter 12 below.
17 See Matthews, 1983.
18 See Fleuriot, 1980, chs. 6 and 7.

Another way to look at the British settlement is through linguistic, toponymic, and archaeological evidence. Gallo-Roman settlement in Armorica had always been denser in the east, centered on the cities of Rennes, Nantes, and Vannes, while in the rural west the Gallo-Roman tongue was most quickly replaced by Breton. This east–west distinction may be reflected in early Church documents. In the previous chapter we saw that a bishop of Rennes, together with his colleagues in Angers and Tours, expressed his displeasure over the peculiar practices of the Breton priests Lovocat and Catihern, who were seemingly operating in rural parts of Armorica.[19] The proceedings of the Second Council of Tours in 567 strongly suggest that newcomer and native had not entirely fused in Brittany: 'In Armorica, neither *Brittanus* nor *Romanus* shall be consecrated bishop without the consent of the metropolitan and his provincial colleagues.'[20] Nora Chadwick interprets this distinction as a west–east linguistic divide, pointing out that the *Life of St. Samson* refers to western Armorica as *Britannia* and the eastern area as *Romania*.[21]

Léon Fleuriot has looked in detail at the placename evidence for early medieval western Gaul.[22] Placenames in Brittany and Normandy commemorate such peoples of the *Völkerwanderung* as the Burgundians, Sarmatians, Saxons, Alans, and Goths. The majority, however, recall the Britons, in forms like Brétigney, Brétagnolles, Bretagne, Bretenoux, Bretteville, Bretonvillers, Bertoncourt, Brettes, Breteuil, and Britten. Fleuriot classifies these names as sites where British troops were billeted in the Late Roman period, but many of these names may derive from much later French sources. Other toponymic studies have focused on such Brittonic elements as Plou- (from Latin *plebs*, 'people'), Gui- and Guic- (from Latin *vicus*), Lan- and Loc- (Latin *locus*, Welsh *llan*), Tré- and Treff- (Welsh *tref*), Lis- or Lez- (Welsh *llys*, 'court' or 'hall'), and Ker- (Welsh *caer*). These occur predominantly in the northwest, while names ending in -ac, -é, and -y (Vulgar Latin forms of *-acum* found in northern Gaul) occur overwhelmingly in the southeast (see map 7.2).[23] Again the general pattern is one of Latin-speaking communities surviving in eastern Brittany, where their Vulgar Latin would evolve into Old French, while Brittonic-speaking communities dominated the western half of the peninsula.

Another noticeable trend in Breton placenames is the large number of names borrowed directly from Devon and Cornwall. Dumnonia (Domnonée) in the north and Cornovia (Cornouaille) in the west are only

19 Howlett, 1995, 66–72.
20 *Concilium Turonense (A.D. 567)*, 179.91. See Thompson, 1980, 504.
21 Chadwick, 1969, 194–5.
22 Fleuriot, 1980, ch. 5.
23 See Chédeville and Guillotel, 1984, 89–112.

the most obvious examples. As we saw in the previous chapter, several British saints traveled from Cornwall to Brittany in the sixth century. Ceramic evidence also suggests that the revival of Mediterranean trade with Britain that began in the mid-fifth century also revived commercial ties between Brittany, Cornwall, and Wales.[24] The linguistic similarities between Cornish and Breton have led some to argue for a migration of Britons from specifically southern Wales and southwestern Britain to Brittany from the late fifth century. Since Saxon expansion had not reached these areas of Britain so early, Chadwick believes that these British refugees were fleeing from Irish rather than Saxon raids and settlement.[25] But the commercial and ecclesiastical links are sufficient to explain the linguistic evidence, and we need not postulate an Irish cause.

Riothamus and Sidonius

There is one British leader on the continent whom we do have good evidence for, but his ties to Brittany are tenuous. Around 470 the Gallic aristocrat Sidonius Apollinaris corresponded with a man named Riothamus, who was apparently well known in Gaul.[26] Sidonius praises the character of Riothamus, but complains that certain *Britanni* associated with him – 'a crowd of noisy, armed, disorderly men' – were enticing slaves away from the estate of one of his friends. In another letter, as we have seen, Sidonius locates these Britons north of the Loire.[27] The respect and familiarity that Sidonius shows Riothamus may indicate mutual friends or previous communications. In any case, Sidonius does not describe Riothamus' business in Gaul or his response to the letter.

More details about Riothamus' activities are provided by Jordanes, a Gothic cleric and *notarius* writing about 550 (but basing his account on an earlier work written by the Roman senator Cassiodorus):

> Now Euric, king of the Visigoths, perceived the frequent changes of Roman emperors and strove to hold Gaul in his own right. The [western] emperor Anthemius heard of it and asked the *Brittones* for aid. Their king Riotimus came with twelve thousand men into the state of the Bituriges [Aquitania] by the way of Ocean, and was received as he disembarked from his ships.[28]

24 Galliou et al, 1980.
25 Chadwick, 1965; idem, 1969.
26 Sidonius, *Epistolae*, 3.9. See also Adams, 1993.
27 Sidonius, *Epistulae*, 1.7.5.
28 Jordanes, *Getica*, 45.237–38.

Historians place this event around 468, the year of the treason of Arvandus. Arvandaus, then prefect of Gaul, betrayed his emperor by advising Euric to attack the Britons before they could join the anti-Goth coalition that Anthemius was forming. 'Euric . . . came against them with an innumerable army,' writes Jordanes, 'and after a long fight routed Riotimus, king of the Britons, before the Romans could join him.' It is not exactly clear what became of Riothamus after this battle in 470. Gregory of Tours confirms that *Brittani* were expelled from Bourges by the Goths and that many were killed near Déols, others fleeing to Lyons to seek refuge among the Burgundian federates.[29] Clovis is said to have defeated a British army on the Loire in 490, and as late as 530 a *legio Britannica* was stationed at Orléans, according to the *Life* of St. Dalmas, bishop of Rodez.[30]

What exactly should we make of Riothamus and these bands of British soldiers on the continent? First of all, Jordanes' statement that Riothamus' Britons came to Aquitania 'by way of Ocean' is unclear. Were these Britons coming from Britain, from Brittany, or simply from the sea (i.e. were they a naval patrol)? For a long time it was assumed that they were Bretons hired as federates to protect a prosperous part of 'Roman' Gaul. Riothamus, in this view, is regarded in the same way as Alaric, Childeric, or one of the many other barbarian kings given federate status. Maybe he could claim native Armorican royal blood, or perhaps he was a Roman *curialis* who had simply expanded his powers during the Armorican revolt of 409.

More recently opinion has swung toward Britain, with several scholars viewing Riothamus as an insular king whose authority reached across the Channel. Far from being an obscure Breton, there are now claims that Riothamus was really Ambrosius Aurelianus or even Arthur himself.[31] Still others have proposed a Late Roman military context. 'Riothamus crossed from Britain to the continent . . . with a considerable body of men,' writes Ian Wood. '[He] is perhaps best seen as a general who left Britain because he wanted to serve the imperial cause.'[32] It should be noted that Vortigern and the British council must have had a clear line of communication with northern Gaul in the mid-fifth century in order for the Britons to have arranged the hire of Germanic mercenaries fighting in the Rhine region.

29   Gregory, *History of the Franks*, 2.18.
30   Galliou and Jones, 1991, 132, 140.
31   Fleuriot, 1980; Ashe, 1981.
32   Wood, 1987, 261.

The Breton Church

In the sixth century our evidence is stronger for Church than State. Gregory of Tours mentions several Breton clerics, most memorably the priest Winnoch, who wore only sheepskins while making the pilgrimage to Jerusalem.[33] The hagiography is filled with accounts of British saints who traveled to Brittany, founding churches and monasteries and making an indelible impact on the landscape through dozens of placenames. The earliest account is, as we have seen, the *Vita Prima* of St. Samson, written by an anonymous monk of Dol, the abbey-bishopric founded by the saint in the mid-sixth century. Evidence of church dedications suggests that Samson's ministry extended over a wide area from the Trégor to the Seine valley.[34] As bishop he attended a Church council in Paris in 563 and was on good terms with King Childebert. According to his hagiography, Samson visited the Frankish king several times, once to obtain the release of the prince of Domnonia. In the ninth century Dol became the metropolis of an independent Breton Church, which, though disputed by Tours, served as a Breton archbishopric until the end of the twelfth century.[35]

The ninth-century *Vita Prima* of St. Tudual ascribes the foundation of Tréguier, the monastery from which the town and diocese grew, to the saint and nephew of Riwal, founder of the royal dynasty of Domnonia.[36] According to the *Life of St. Brioc*, the monastery of St. Brieuc was founded a bit earlier in the sixth century by another member of the Domnonian royal family.[37] The westernmost Breton bishopric, Saint Pol-de-Léon, was founded *c.*530 by the Welsh saint Paul Aurelian (Pol).[38] This is according to Wrmonoc, writing in 844, who states that Pol was given the land by a Breton count named Withur and his diocese was confirmed by King Childebert himself. This corpus of saints' lives, though much of it is admittedly late, suggests that the founders of the western Breton churches brought over from Britain such insular traditions as bishops attached to monasteries, rigorous asceticism, penitential literature, bells associated with Church leaders, and the 'Celtic' tonsure and dating of Easter. Chadwick has also pointed out that legislation against nature cults enacted at the Councils of Tours (567) and Nantes (658) may be evidence of lingering paganism in Brittany.[39]

33   Gregory of Tours, *HF*, 5.21 and 8.34. See also Gregory, *Liber in Gloria Confessorum*, 23.
34   Galliou and Jones, 1991, 142.
35   Chadwick, 1969, 255.
36   See La Borderie, *Les Trois Vies* (1887).
37   See Doble, *Saint Brioc* (1928).
38   See Doble, *Saint Paul of Léon* (1941), and discussion of Pol in the previous chapter.
39   Chadwick, 1969, 238 and 296.

While the monastic saints dominated western Brittany, in the east there were three long-established episcopal churches, in the cities of Rennes, Nantes, and Vannes. One Athenius, bishop of Rennes, was a signator at the Councils of Tours (461) and Vannes (465), while fifth-century bishops of Nantes and Vannes are attested in later sources. These three urban churches, as well as the newer western churches and monasteries, all fell under the jurisdiction of the metropolitan bishopric of Tours. But the Gallic clergy seem to have had little to do with western Brittany, and when Columbanus, ostracized by those same clerics, felt compelled to explain the practices of the *ecclesiae occidentis*, he may likely be referring to Irish and British clergy in Brittany as well as those in the Isles. The conservative and insular character of the Breton Church would last until the Carolingian reforms of the ninth century.

Bretons and Franks

One bishop of Tours did take note of the activities of Bretons: Gregory of Tours. In Gregory's *History of the Franks*, he describes a Brittany dominated by regional hereditary chieftains engaging in vicious feuds with one another and with the Merovingian Franks. He sees the activities of these Breton rulers, whose political status depended on raiding and distributing plundered wealth (including slaves), as threatening both political and ecclesiastical stability in western Gaul.[40] At the time of Gregory's writing, in the late sixth century, the expansionist Merovingians were trying to subject the Bretons to tributary status. Early attempts at establishing overlordship were made by Clovis, but his successor Childebert I (r.511–58) remained on good terms with all parties in Armorica.[41]

Around 560 the situation had changed. The flight of an exiled Merovingian prince to Brittany set off a series of disputes among Breton chieftains, vividly illustrated by Gregory's account of the feuding between the brothers Chanao and Macliaw.[42] The latter seized the bishopric of Vannes and was subsequently murdered, but his dynamic son Waroc led a force into the Vannetais in search of land and Gallo-Roman wealth. This move prompted Chilperic I (r.561–84) to send a force against the Bretons, and after three days of fighting in 578 he received the fealty of Waroc. Chilperic's successor Guntram (r.561–92) tried to renew the Frankish claim to overlordship in 587, but Waroc broke his oath and returned

40   See Smith, 1992.
41   Galliou and Jones, 1991, 140.
42   Gregory, *HF*, 4.4 and 4.20.

to his plundering ways (including seizing the vineyards of the Nantais).[43] In 635 the Breton king Judicael traveled to the Frankish court and paid tribute to Dagobert I (r.622–38), but refused to sit at table with the Frankish king and returned to Brittany laden with 'gifts.'[44] Other sources portray this relationship as an alliance rather than a submission, and in any case it is clear that such arrangements were short-lived throughout the Merovingian era. Gregory's statement that Breton rulers 'were called counts not kings' may or may not represent the Frankish perspective, but it certainly has nothing to do with the way the Breton princes saw themselves at this stage. Only under the Carolingians did the Bretons suffer from any real loss of political autonomy.

Gregory's picture is, for the most part, limited to southeastern Brittany; those Bretons to the north and west of Vannes were virtually unknown to Gallic authors until the ninth century. Most of Brittany was indeed isolated from the linguistic and cultural influence of its neighbors to the east. Its new villages and administrative districts took the names of migrant British saints and warriors, with most communities evolving from the original church parish or *plou*.[45] The land supported a mix of arable and pastoral farming, an idyllic (and persistent) picture contrasted with the political chaos described by Gregory of Tours. The Breton princes described by Gregory were established at rural stockades in which they accumulated a vast amount of wealth (indicated by the sums with which they were able to pay tribute to Frankish kings) and carried out trade, distribution of goods to retainers, and limited political administration. Unfortunately archaeology has revealed little of their strongholds, but later Frankish sources noted their command of both guerrilla forces and formidable cavalry expert at spear-throwing.[46]

Brittany and the Carolingian Empire

A note in the Annals of Metz under the year 691 states that the Bretons, who had once acknowledged Frankish supremacy, now enjoyed freedom.[47] This would be the state of affairs until the fall of the Merovingian kings and the ascendancy of the Carolingians.[48] Frankish chronicles speak frequently of raids by aggressive Carolingian rulers seeking plunder in Brittany, often

43   Gregory, *HF*, 9.18.
44   *Chronicle of Fredegar*, 4.78.
45   Galliou and Jones, 1991, 135–6.
46   See Smith, 1992, 17–18.
47   See Galliou and Jones, 1991, 143.
48   For Carolingian Brittany, in general, see Smith, 1992.

followed by Breton revolts. In 751 Pippin the Short, having seized the monarchy from the Merovingian Dagobert III, moved westward and took the city of Vannes. From that moment on the Carolingians began to construct the March of Brittany in the occupied counties of Rennes, Nantes, and Vannes. The most famous of the Frankish counts sent to control the Breton March was Roland, hero of the later *Chanson de Roland*. But despite many victories over the Bretons, not even Charlemagne could subjugate Brittany the way Saxony fell to his brutal expansionism. His son Louis the Pious acknowledged this failure by making the Breton Nomenoë his *missus imperatoris* (royal supervisor) in Brittany and sought a peaceful way to bring the Bretons into the Carolingian Empire. This also marked the first official recognition of Brittany as a single political unit.[49]

As Carolingian power began to grow weak in the west under Louis's son, Charles the Bald, Nomenoë's successors began steadily increasing their powers. His son Erispoë ruled as King of Brittany, though he promised fealty to Charles and remained loyal to the King of the West Franks for the rest of his reign. Such friendly relations were more or less maintained by the usurper Solomon (r.857–74), whom Charles eventually recognized as king. Frankish writers at the time frequently remarked on the martial abilities of the Breton light cavalry – 'warriors on war-horses' as the *Armes* poet called them – and indeed Breton personal names like Marrec ('horseman') and Guivarch ('worthy to have a horse') attest to the high status of these early Breton 'knights.'[50] The ninth century saw the beginning of the long-lasting trend of Breton warriors becoming vassals of French (and later Norman) lords.

Redon and Local Administration

At this time Breton society, and especially the clergy, were coming under the influence of the Carolingian Renaissance. Conservative liturgical practices were purged from Breton religious houses at the insistence of the emperor himself, beginning with the abbey of Landévennec in 818.[51] A surge in clerical literacy resulted in the production of many Breton manuscripts, displaying everything from musical notation to brilliant interlaced borders and illumination. (It should be noted that the earliest Breton manuscripts are written in insular script, and even those that adopted Carolingian minuscule continue to exhibit paleographical features that are character-

---

49   Galliou and Jones, 1991, 148–51.
50   *Armes Prydein*, line 154. See Galliou and Jones, 1991, 150; and Smith, 1992, 20.
51   See Guillotel, 1986.

istic of early Welsh manuscripts.)[52] Many contained polished and learned *Vitae* of Breton saints, like Wrmonoc's *Life of St. Paul Aurelian*, Wrdisten's *Life of St. Guénolé*, and Bili's *Life of St. Malo*. Others contained antiphonals with rare examples of *neumes*, the early medieval system of musical notation. Many are Breton copies of Latin 'classics' from Late Antiquity, from Augustine to Bede.

Recently historians have focused on a large group of Breton manuscripts containing legal works and charters. Most notable of the latter is the Redon Cartulary, a collection of 345 charters produced at the abbey of Saint-Sauveur de Redon between the years 801 and 924.[53] The abbey was founded by Conwoion in 832, and from the start its monks followed the (revised) Rule of St. Benedict, which was being promoted, for the sake of uniformity, by the Carolingians.[54] The Redon Cartulary gives us a rare glimpse of the workings of local administration in Brittany, including the important role of the *machtierns*, wealthy local rulers (of the *plou*) who presided over disputes and collected taxes (*mach tiern* = 'pledge chief'). Unlike the greater Breton nobles whom they represented, their power was totally local, evolving from the Late Roman town councils.[55] There is no true parallel to the machtiern elsewhere in medieval Europe.

A decrease in the power of the machtierns can be traced to growing royal bureaucracies, the advent of vassalage, and the increasingly serious threat of Viking invasions. Aided by riverine access, Vikings began to strike at the Breton interior in 843, when they slaughtered the bishop of Nantes, and continued their assaults for another century. Breton rulers and clerics fled, first inland and eventually overseas. The most famous of these exiles was Alain Barbetorte, count of Cornouaille, who returned to launch a campaign of reconquest in 936. But Alain and his son, Conan I, and their descendants until 1066, reigned not as kings but rather as *duces Britonum*. The political chaos caused by the Northmen, powerful enough to threaten the Carolingian dynasty, resulted in the disappearance of the kingdom of Brittany. What took its place was the duchy of Brittany, a feudal power of lesser stature that remained independent of the early Capetian monarchs but was often dominated by its aggressive neighbors, Normandy and Anjou.

Ducal Brittany

Louis IV d'Outremer (r.936–52) was the last Carolingian to receive homage from a Breton ruler, and no Breton duke performed homage to a

52 Smith, 1992, 14.
53 The most extensive discussion is in W. Davies, 1988.
54 See Brett, 1989.
55 Sheringham, 1981.

Capetian until 1199.[56] But the re-establishment of unity and autonomy in Brittany by Alain and his successors, particularly the counts of Rennes, followed French rather than Celtic political models.[57] The comital families of Rennes, Cornouaille, and Nantes are hard to distinguish from the other great castellan families of northern France in the eleventh century, while lesser Breton knights readily joined William of Normandy's adventure in 1066.

Not in politics, therefore, but in language and literature do we see Brittonic culture survive in Brittany in the eleventh and twelfth centuries. More than 500 years after the British migration to Armorica we can still see links to the insular Britons. For example, Old Breton in its earliest written form is insular in appearance and nearly identical to Old Welsh and Cornish. As Julia Smith points out, in the eleventh century at Llandaff Welsh and Bretons are described as 'of one language and one people, although geographically separate.'[58] It is not until this point that Old Breton and Cornish begin to evolve separately and no longer share a common orthography. Yet even in the twelfth and thirteenth centuries a common cultural icon – Arthur – could raise hopes and passions among the Cornish and the Bretons.[59]

56   Smitth, 1992, 189. For general discussion of Ducal Brittany, see Jones, 1988.
57   Jones, 1988, 3.
58   Smith, 1992, 13.
59   See discussion in chapter 13 below.

8
Cornwall and the Southwest

Cornwall and Brittany share many things in common. Both are rocky Atlantic peninsulas where fishing villages have nestled for centuries. Both lands were ruled by British kings in the early Middle Ages, and both were reduced by AD 1000 to the status of counties within much larger non-British kingdoms. The Cornish and Breton tongues were nearly indistinguishable in this period, and both Cornwall and Brittany were dotted with dedications to the same British saints. Cornwall's links to Brittany were in some ways even stronger than its ties to Wales and other parts of Brittonic-speaking Britain. Yet there is also much that is distinctive about Cornish culture, and much of what makes Cornwall unique can be traced to its rural seclusion in the post-Roman period. While Britons of the southwest gradually lost control of Avon, Dorset, Somerset, and Devon, they held on to Cornwall until the tenth century, long enough to preserve and secure Brittonic cultural identity in the peninsula.

The Southwest

The Durotriges of Somerset and Dorset were, as we have seen,[1] one of the Periphery tribes of the Late Iron Age. This meant that they were developing proto-towns, using coins, and consuming Mediterranean luxury goods on the eve of the Roman conquest. The Romans encouraged the growth of such towns as Dorchester (the *civitas* capital), Ilchester, Badbury, Wareham, and Shepton Mallet, and a group of about a dozen villas sprang up around Ilchester. Yet there is also evidence, in Somerset especially, of the continued occupation of hill-forts, some of which contained Romano-Celtic temples.

1 See chapter 2 above.

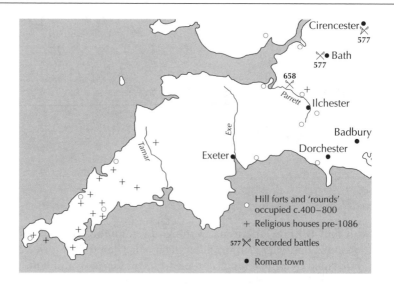

Map 8.1   British settlements in the southwest and recorded battles against the Saxons.

While the written sources are silent, there is archaeological evidence of dramatic change in the *civitas* at the beginning of the mid-fifth century.[2] Villas fell into disuse and the temples were demolished or dismantled, often to be replaced by modest Christian churches. Cemeteries like Brean Down and Poundbury saw increased use, including a return to pre-Roman slab-lined and cist burials along with apparent Christian inhumations. By the middle of the fifth century urban activity was in rapid decline, while intensive refortification occurred at hill-forts like Cadbury-Congresbury and South Cadbury. At Glastonbury, evidence of metal-working and Mediterranean imports may indicate the beginning of one of Britain's most famous monastic communities.

The historical evidence provides no details at all about British rulers and Church leaders from this period. Later English sources describe a gradual takeover of Durotrigan lands beginning in the second half of the sixth century by the Gewisse, a people who became the West Saxons. While the sixth-century conquests of the House of Cerdic described in the *Anglo-Saxon Chronicle* should not be taken as factual in detail, they may be a vague representation of the *process* of early Wessex expansion, beginning with victories by small Saxon war-bands and culminating in the

---

2   See Snyder, 1998, ch. 12.

establishment of a dynastic state. The following narrative, based on late literary evidence, should be compared with current placename and material evidence for early Saxon – and Jutish – westward settlement.[3]

Northwestern Saxon penetration from the Hampshire coast in the early sixth century is indicated by the battles attributed in the *Anglo-Saxon Chronicle* to Cerdic and Cynric. By the middle of the sixth century Cynric and his son Ceawlin have won victories over the Britons in Wiltshire, including Salisbury in 552 and Barbury Hill (near Swindon) in 556. After some years fighting Æthelberht of Kent, Ceawlin and his brother Cutha campaigned in the southwest against the Britons. The Chronicle records a victory in 571 at *Bedcanford*, after which Cutha took four villages: Limbury, Aylesbury, Benson, and Eynsham.

But the most important campaign came six years later:

> 577. In this year Cuthwine and Ceawlin fought against the Britons and slew three kings, Coinmail, Condidan, and Farinmail, at the place which is called Dyrham; and they captured three cities, Gloucester, Cirencester, and Bath.[4]

Traditionally historians have regarded the Battle of Dyrham as the key to the Saxon conquest of southwestern Britain. No other conflict between Saxon and Briton in the southwest is recorded in the Chronicle until the campaigns of Cenwalh and Centwine nearly a century later (see below). Victory at Dyrham gave the Saxons access to the west coast, and capturing these three cities would have effectively separated the British states of Wales from those in Devon and Cornwall. But is Dyrham an historical event? Dates of sixth-century battles taken from the *Anglo-Saxon Chronicle* are not reliable, and the Chronicle's depiction of a West Saxon state this early is surely an exaggeration. A multiplicity of smaller kingdoms and defended cities is probably closer to the truth.

Delineation of British- and Saxon-controlled lands may have been intended by the extensive network of dykes in Hampshire, Wiltshire, Somerset, and Dorset.[5] Though nearly impossible to date, many scholars have favored the explanation that such features as Bokerly Dyke, Grim's Bank, Selwood Forest, and East and West Wansdyke may have served as intentional boundaries, perhaps agreed upon by the kind of treaty described by Gildas (the 'unhappy partition with the barbarians'). These may have provided some protection for otherwise vulnerable British settlements like Silchester, Winchester, and South Cadbury, at least until the end of the sixth century. It should also be noted that both Cerdic and Ceawlin have

---

3   See discussion in chapter 5 above.
4   *The Anglo-Saxon Chronicle* (The Parker Chronicle), s.a. 577.
5   See Yorke, 1995, 22ff.

apparently *British* names (*Cerdic*, a form of *Ceretic* or *Caraticos*, was borne by a seventh-century British king of Elmet), while other members of their dynasty – most notably Caedwalla – have names that combine Brittonic and Old English elements.[6] Did lordship in Wessex derive from intermarriage between Saxon warlords and prominent Britons?

The southwest was, like other Periphery lands (the Midlands, Elmet, Bernicia), a hybrid zone where Britons and Saxons alternately fought against each other, traded with each other, formed alliances, and (by the seventh century) shared a common faith. Illustrative of this is the early history of Glastonbury. Philip Rahtz, the most recent excavator of Glastonbury Tor, is now inclined to see the Tor as the nucleus of an early (pre-Saxon) Christian settlement, perhaps a monastery, which continued to be supported by the Wessex kings who came to control Somerset in the seventh century.[7] These Saxon kings encouraged the expansion of the community to the site, at the foot of the Tor, where Glastonbury Abbey was later erected (perhaps in an effort to move away from the typically British eremitic monasticism practiced on the Tor).[8] While the new Saxon minster continued to thrive, especially through grants by King Ine (r.688–726) and under the reformer Abbot Dunstan (*c*.940), it remained connected with its Brittonic past. At least two early abbots bore British names (*Wealhstod* and *Cealdhun* or *Wealdhun*),[9] and the cults of the Britons Patrick and Arthur thrived there in the twelfth century. Similar to this but in a secular context is South Cadbury, the British hillfort which at some point fell to the West Saxons who eventually used it as a *burh* and royal mint; still, locals continued to associate it with Arthur into the sixteenth century.

The Cornovii and the Dumnonii

We get a different picture as we move from the Periphery to the Outer Zone, where Britons mixed less with Saxons and remained culturally conservative. Ninth-century Anglo-Saxon sources referred to these Britons as *Westwalas* and *Cornwalas*. The name Cornwall ultimately derives from a British tribe of the Iron Age, the Cornovii. There were three widely separated tribes in Britain noted by Roman writers bearing the name Cornovii.[10]

---

6   Yorke, 1995, 49.
7   Rahtz in Abrams and Carley, 1991, 34.
8   See Rahtz, 1993. However, Abrams, 1996, 2–7, reminds us of the limits of the evidence for Glastonbury's Christian origins.
9   See Sarah Foot in Abrams and Carley, 1991, 163–89.
10   See Webster, 1975, 17–18.

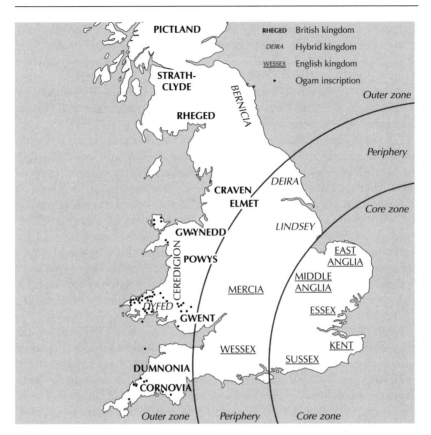

Map 8.2   The Core, Periphery, and Outer Zones in an early medieval context.

Inscriptions testify to the *civitas Cornoviorum* centered in Shropshire, Ptolemy locates the *Cornovioi* in Caithness, Scotland, and the Ravenna Cosmography records west of the river Tamar *Durocornavis*, 'the fortress of the Cornovii.' The Brittonic element *corn-*, like the Latin *cornu*, means 'horn', and may refer to the entire peninsula or to its many promontories. Alternately, it could refer to a horned animal or god (e.g. Cernunnos) from which the tribe derived its name. The latter may explain the appearance of Cornovii in non-peninsular parts of Britain.

If the Cornovii were indeed a people of southwestern Britain, they were likely a sub-group of the larger Dumnonii tribe. Like other Iron Age peoples in Britain's Outer Zone, the Dumnonii, whose lands (according to Ptolemy) stretched from Somerset to Lizard Point, lacked coinage and large tribal centers. Instead they are characterized by small univallate defended farmsteads – the conspicuous 'Cornish rounds' – and promontory forts, as well as hundreds of undefended homes and hamlets scattered along the sandy coasts.[11] These otherwise isolated people were connected to the wider world through the tin and lead trade, and indeed 'the Brettanic metal' (as tin was called by one Byzantine writer) made Cornwall famous throughout the ancient world.[12]

Tin mining in pre-Roman Cornwall was mostly a small-scale industry. Dumnonian families dug pits in streams and collected the ore from alluvial gravel, sorting, washing, and eventually smelting to produce pure ingots that could be bartered at local ports. The Romans had little interest in supporting new civilian settlement in Cornwall, and did not pay much attention to the area's mineral resources until the late third century. With Spanish tin production disturbed by civil unrest, and needing lead for water-pipes and pewter objects, Rome encouraged both new and extant production centers in southwestern Britain. The Mendip lead mines were exploited, for example, with a new settlement of pewterers appearing at Camerton, while Cornish tin from Carnanton and Treloy made its way to the Roman world.[13]

While these industries brought some Roman goods to Cornwall, for the most part the land west of Exeter (*Isca Dumnoniorum*) was left to its native ways. Devon itself differed little in this regard, while Durotrigan lands in Dorset and Somerset received new temples, villas, and small towns. In Late Roman times Cornwall was part of the province of Britannia Prima, whose capital was in far-off Cirencester (*Corinium*) and whose Channel coast had no formal land defenses. Presumably when the *classis Britannica* ceased to operate in the Channel, Britain's entire southern coast was vulnerable to sea raids. While Cerdic himself may be a legendary figure, the *Anglo-Saxon Chronicle's* depiction of Saxon boats landing in Southampton and raiding inland may not be far from the truth.

Of course the Irish Sea coast was also vulnerable, and there is evidence which some scholars have interpreted as indicative of new Irish settlements in the sixth century (if not earlier) in western Cornwall.[14] The written evidence is rather slight, consisting mainly of a statement in the 'Glossary of Cormac' (*c.*900). More persuasive is the large number of stone inscriptions in Cornwall with Ogam script and/or Irish names represented. Given that another concentration of such stones occurs in Demetia, where written records attest to a royal dynasty with Irish roots,

11   Thomas, 1997, 62–4.
12   See Penhallurick, 1986.
13   Thomas, 1997, 63.
14   See Olson, 1989, 31–3; Okasha, 1993, 39; and discussion in chapter 9 below.

it has been suggested that the Irish in Cornwall may have come from southwest Wales rather than directly from Ireland. Nicholas Higham reminds us, however, that we may be seeing evidence of trade and ecclesiastical intercourse across the Irish Sea rather than large-scale Irish migration.[15]

Despite these barbarian threats, there is, as we have seen, increasing evidence for the survival of many Romano-British settlements in Avon, Devon, Dorset, and Somerset after 410. [16] Most prominent, however, is the refortification and revived occupation of the hill forts throughout the southwest. It is at these rural sites that signs of vigorous trade and industrial activity are greatest. In addition to Tintagel, Cornwall possessed substantial defended settlements like Castle Dore, Chun Castle, Grambla, Killibury, and the Rumps. Most common, however, are the smaller 'rounds,' enclosed familial homesteads that had an agricultural focus.[17] There are in excess of 1,500 rounds in the southwest, most of them in western Cornwall. The more substantial, like Trethurgy, performed some of the functions of the hill forts, and the presence of imported pottery (see table 8.1) suggests that they may have belonged to dependents of the local Cornish lords.

Tintagel and Dumnonian Kingship

By the sixth century there is both written and epigraphic evidence for British kings in Dumnonia. Names of fourth- and fifth-century rulers are recorded, but only in later Welsh verse and genealogies (see table 8.2). Most prominent of these shadowy early figures is Cynan (Conan Meriadoc), who appears in the poems *Armes Prydein*, *Glaswawt Taliesin*, and the *Dream of Macsen Wledig*, as well as in the Welsh Triads, Geoffrey of Monmouth's *History of the Kings of Britain*, and the Breton *Lives* of Sts. Goeznovius and Gurthiern.[18] In most versions Cynan follows Macsen (Magnus Maximus) to the Continent to fight for the imperial throne, then remains in Gaul to found the kingdom of Brittany. Since his descendants were remembered as kings of Dumnonia, it seems that there was a strong memory – on both sides of the Channel – of Dumnonian immigration to Brittany.

The earliest historical source is Gildas, who writes that Dumnonia was

15 Higham, 1992, 88.
16 See chapter 5 above.
17 Todd, 1987, 223ff.
18 See Pearce, 1978, 139–42.

Table 8.1 Post-Roman imported pottery in the southwest.

	ARSW	PRSW	Bi	Bii	Biv	Bv	Bvi	Bmisc	D ware	E ware
Bantham				*				*		*
Bath					*					
Cadbury-Congresbury	*	*	*	*				*	*	
Cannington				*				*		
Castle Dore								?		
Chun Castle			*							
Dorchester (Poundbury)					*	*				
Exeter						?				
Glastonbury		*	*	*	*			*		
Grambla		*	*	*	*			*		
Gwithian	*	*	*	*				*		*
Ham Hill				?						
Hellesvean, St. Ives				*						
High Peak			*	*				*		*
The Kelsies, Cubert										*
Killibury			*							
Looe Island			*							
Lydford	*		*	*						
Mawgan Porth			*							
Mothecombe			*	*						
Perran Sands		*						*		
Phillack		*								
The Scillies				*	*					
(St. Mary's, St. Martin's,										*

	ARSW	PRSW	Bi	Bii	Biv	Bv	Bvi	Bmisc	D WARE	E WARE
Samson, and Tean)										
South Cadbury	*	*	*	*	*	*			*	*
Tintagel	*	*	*	*	*	*			*	*
Trethurgy										*

ARSW African Red Slip Ware: popular fine wares produced in North Africa (probably Carthage), late fifth to early sixth century;

PRSW Phocaean Red Slip Ware: fine wares produced in western Turkey (probably Phocaea), c.500;

Bi amphoras: wine jars produced in the eastern Aegean, mid-sixth century;

Bii amphoras: wine jars produced in the eastern Mediterranean (Nubia, Cyprus and Antioch have all been proposed), mid to late fifth century;

Biv handled jars: one- and two-handled water (?) jars produced in Asia Minor (probably Sardis), mid fifth to mid sixth century;

Bv Byzacena amphoras: large cylindrical oil containers produced in the Byzacena region of North Africa, late fifth century;

Bvi Gaza amphoras: large cylindrical wine(?) containers produced at Gaza, mid-fifth to mid-sixth century

Bmisc B miscellaneous amphoras;

D WARE Grey ware bowls produced in the Bordeaux region, sixth century;

E WARE Kitchenware (jars, pots, bowls, jugs, pitchers, and beakers), some pieces containing traces of purple dye. Produced in western Gaul, c.600–700.

Source: Thomas, 1981; Olson, 1989; and Snyder, 1996.

Table 8.2 Dumnonian king-lists derived from Jesus College, Oxford, MS 20 (*left*) and *Bonedd y Saint*, the 'Lineage of the Saints' (*right*), both probably composed in the twelfth century.

Eudaf Hen	
Cynan	
Gadeon	
Gwrwawr	
Tudwawl	
Kynwawr (Cynfawr)	Custennyn Gorneu
Erbin	Erbin
Gereint	Gereint
Cado	Selyf
Peredur	Kyby
Theudu	
daughter?	
Judhael	

ruled in the early sixth century by the *tyrannus* Constantine, 'whelp of the filthy lioness of Damnonia.'[19] Gildas accuses this Dumnonian ruler of adultery and of murdering two royal youths at the altar 'under the cloak of a holy abbot.'[20] This Constantine appears in later Welsh genealogies as Custennin, son of Cynfawr, and in Geoffrey of Monmouth's *History* as Constantine, son of Duke Cador of Cornwall. In this latter guise he survives in Arthurian romance as King Arthur's cousin and successor.

The most famous, and perhaps most historical, king of sixth-century Cornwall was Cynfawr, whose Latinized British form is Cunomorus, 'Hound of the Sea.' The earliest evidence for this figure is the inscription on the so-called 'Tristan stone,' found near Castle Dore in Fowey. It reads DRUSTANUS HIC IACIT CUNOMORI FILIUS, 'Here lies Drustanus son of Cunomorus.' *Drustan* is evidently the Cornish (some have argued Pictish) original of Tristan, and Wrmonoc in the *Life of St. Pol de Leon* mentions a 'King Mark (*Marcus*) who is called by another name Cunomorus.' This string of evidence has led many to conclude that Cynfawr/Cunomorus was the sixth-century lord of Castle Dore and the King Mark of the Tristan legends (and Arthur's nemesis March in the Welsh Triads). Complicating matters, however, are two earlier continental references to Cunomorus: Gregory of Tours describes him as a Breton count, and in the *Life of St. Samson* he is a minor Breton lord of Carhaix

---

19   Gildas, *De Excidio*, 28.
20   Gildas, *De Excidio*, 2.28.

who rebels against Judhael, King of Domnonée.[21] Either Cunomorus held authority in Britain and Brittany, or the genealogists are confusing two different rulers.

If Dumnonia was a single kingdom, what was its capital? Many have searched for the royal citadel of Dumnonia, but no obvious candidate has presented itself. Scholarly opinion now favors Tintagel, which would have been an obvious candidate but for the assumption, for most of the twentieth century, that Tintagel was a 'Celtic'-style monastery. This, Radford's explanation, has been critiqued by Ken Dark and Charles Thomas, among others. Thomas, and Tintagel's most recent excavator, Christopher Morris, prefer to see the site as a secular stronghold with significant commercial activity.[22] But due to its exposed position, Tintagel may have been occupied only seasonally, leading Thomas to postulate an itinerant lord who came to Tintagel to receive tribute and distribute luxury items to his vassals.

Thomas Charles-Edwards has shown that itinerant kingship was common throughout the medieval Celtic fringe. Great kings of the southwest would have been hosted by abbots and by lesser lords. The discovery of several stone inscriptions commemorating otherwise unknown princes of the southwest (described as *principi*, *cumregnus*, etc.) suggests a multitude of lesser rulers.[23] So too does the *kevran*, the Cornish equivalent of the English 'hundred' and the Welsh *cantref*, which was a district capable of raising 100 recruits for a war-band. At least six are known from Cornwall, and we can expect the same pattern in Devon.[24]

Our fullest evidence for a Dumnonian monarch is that of Geraint, who ruled from *c.*670 to *c.*710.[25] According to the *Anglo-Saxon Chronicle*, 'Geraint (*Gerente*), king of the Britons (*Wealas*),' fought against Inne and Nunna of Wessex in the year 710. This is probably (though not certainly) the same Geraint who granted land to the West Saxon abbey of Sherborne, in Dorset, and who corresponded with Aldhelm, abbot of Malmesbury and bishop of Sherborne. The grant identifies the benefactor as *Gerontius rex*, and the land as Maker (*Macuir*), beside the Tamar River. Aldhelm's letter, written shortly after the Council of Hertford in 672, is addressed to 'the most glorious King *Geruntius*, the lord who guides the scepter of the western kingdom.'[26]

Once again the issue is clouded by later references to a 'Geraint, son of Erbin' in Welsh poetry, who is clearly the figure remembered in the

---

21   See Pearce, 1978, 141.
22   See discussion in chapter 5 above.
23   See Okasha, 1993; and Yorke, 1995, 17–18.
24   Thomas, 1997, 67–8.
25   See Grimmer, 2001.
26   *Aldhelm: The Prose Works*, p. 155.

Dumnonian king-lists. In the poem *Geraint filius Erbin* contained in the Black Book of Carmarthen (*c.*1250), Geraint leads 'the brave men of the land of Devon' at the Battle of Llongborth along with Arthur 'the Emperor,' and he is named as a companion of Arthur in *Culhwch and Olwen*. In a Welsh triad Geraint is named as one of the 'Three Seafarers of the Island of Britain,' and he is the hero and husband of Enid in the romance *Geraint ab Erbin*. The much earlier *Gododdin* includes a *Gereint rac deheu* ('Geraint for the South') in the list of British heroes attacking Anglian Catraeth *c.*572. As with Mark/Cunomorus, it has been suggested that there was more than one British ruler named Geraint. It is perhaps more than coincidental that Marcus, Constantinus, and Gerontius are names borne by British imperial usurpers in the last years of Roman rule.

Æthelstan and West Saxon Expansion

In his poem *Carmen Rhythmicum*, Aldhelm writes: 'When I had set out for dire Dumnonia (*Domnonia*) and was proceeding through cheerless Cornwall (*Cornubia*).'[27] Was this just anti-British prejudice on the English bishop's part, or did Aldhelm really observe a decaying and war-torn landscape? As we have seen, there is very little evidence of Germanic goods and burials as far west as Devon until after 600.[28] The first mention of battles between West Saxons and Dumnonian Britons occurs in sources for the seventh century, when the growth of Mercia forced the kings of Wessex to look southward for territorial expansion. The *Anglo-Saxon Chronicle* attributes a victory in 614 to the West Saxon kings Cynegils and Cwichelm, who are said to have killed 2,000 Britons at *Beandun*; but the number of casualties seems a bit high, and the identification of the battle with Bindon in Dorset is probably too far west.[29] The next battle, according to the *Chronicle*, was at *Peonum* in 658, when Cenwalh drove the Britons to the Parrett River in Somerset. This opened the way for Saxon penetration into Devon, and in 682 the *Chronicle* records, baldly, 'Centwine drove the Britons as far as the sea.' In 693 King Ine of Wessex issued laws that mentioned his 'Welsh' subjects, but it is unclear how far his power reached into Devon.

In the eighth century kings of Wessex were granting Devonshire lands to the English churches of Sherborne and Glastonbury. But the *Chronicle* is silent regarding Saxon victories in Dumnonia, while the *Annales*

27   *Aldhelm: The Poetic Works*, p. 177.
28   Chapter 5 above.
29   See Todd, 1987, 271.

Cambriae record a British victory at *Hehil* in Cornwall in 722. Dumnonian rulers may have gained a respite, but it was to end in the early ninth century. According to the Chronicle, Egbert of Wessex 'harried Cornwall from east to west' in 814, and in 825 a British rebellion was put down by 'the men of Devon' at a place called *Gafulford*, just east of the Tamar.[30] In 838 a Viking host landed in Cornwall and joined the Britons in fighting against Egbert, but were defeated at Hingston Down. Egbert now felt free to grant land in Cornwall to Sherborne. This may have marked the end of an independent British kingdom in the southwest. The last British king of Dumnonia recorded in the *Annales Cambriae* is 'Dungarth, king of *Cerniu*,' who drowned in 875, but by then such British rulers were likely vassals of the kings of Wessex.

Complete conquest of Devon and Cornwall may have been delayed by Viking activity in the southwest. While Alfred's will (*c*.880) shows us that northeast Cornwall had been all but annexed by Wessex, control of the rest of Dumnonia would come during the reign of his grandson Æthelstan (r.924–39).[31] According to William of Malmesbury, Æthelstan

> attacked them [the Britons of Dumnonia] with great energy, compelling them to withdraw from Exeter, which until that time they had inhabited on a footing of legal equality with the English. He then fixed the left bank of the Tamar as the shire boundary, just as he had made the Wye the boundary for the North Britons. Having cleansed the city of its defilement by wiping out that filthy race, he fortified it with towers and surrounded it with a wall of square-hewn stone.[32]

While attributing a victory to him over the Welsh and Strathclyde Britons in 927, the *Anglo-Saxon Chronicle* is silent about Æthelstan's Cornish campaigns and this seeming ethnic cleansing of Exeter, which occurred *c*.936. Æthelstan did, however, hold several councils in Devon, including one at Exeter in 928 and another at Lifton in 931.[33] It seems clear that Æthelstan now expected the Britons of Cornwall to accept the Tamar River as their eastern border, and that the English kings formally recognized the six 'hundreds' within Cornwall. From his involvement in the politics of Brittany, Æthelstan also collected Breton relics that he sent to English churches (including Devon) and likely encouraged further ecclesiastical contacts between Cornwall and Brittany.

---

30   See Orme, 2000, 6.
31   Pearce, 1978, 168–9.
32   William of Malmesbury, *Gesta Regum Anglorum*, 2.134.
33   Pearce, 1978, 169.

The Cornish Saints

Christianity in southwestern Britain is characterized by a vigorous monastic spirit spread by British saints who wandered ceaselessly through Wales, Cornwall, and Brittany. While this is the consistent picture given in the hagiography, the origins of Dumnonian Christianity lie in a few scattered finds stretching from Shepton Mallet to the Scillies.[34] The Late Roman villas at Frampton and Hinton St. Mary, near Dorchester, contained mosaics bearing unmistakable Christian symbols. Early Christian cemeteries are likely at Brean Down, Cannington, Lundy, Phillack, Poundbury, and Shepton Mallet, while a fifth-century mausoleum has been identified beneath the cathedral at Wells. The transition from paganism to Christianity is represented by churches succeeding temples at West Hill Uley, Cannington, and possibly Maiden Castle, Lamyatt, and Pagan's Hill.

There is good evidence for both pagan and early Christian activity in the Scilly Isles. A Roman altar has been found on St. Mary's, and clay figurines representing Roman deities have been excavated at Nornour.[35] Charles Thomas has postulated that the Nornour votive objects belonged to a native shrine, visited by Roman shipmen, which may have included a sacred beacon-fire to guide mariners into a nearby harbor.[36] The Scillies may also have harbored fugitives. According to Sulpicius Severus, writing *c.*400, two Priscillianist bishops from Gaul were banished in 384 to the island of *Sylina*, which most agree is a reference to Scilly.[37] A few west–east cist graves in the Scillies may belong to early Christian cemeteries, while on St. Helen's excavations revealed an early Christian wooden church replaced by a stone chapel.[38]

One important source for early Christianity in Dumnonia is the epigraphic evidence, consisting of roughly 79 inscribed stones dating from the fifth to the eleventh centuries.[39] These are comparable to the more numerous Welsh stones (with various combinations of Brittonic and Irish names transcribed in Latin and, occasionally, Ogam), though they tend to be a bit less descriptive. A recently discovered example from Tintagel, the Arthnou Stone, grabbed headlines for its similarity to the name Arthur (see plate 8.1). While not proving the legendary king's existence, it does serve as evidence of literacy at Tintagel.

34   In general see Snyder, 1998, ch. 12.
35   See Snyder, 1996, 26.
36   Thomas, 1985, 172.
37   Severus, *Chronicle*, s.a. 384. See Thomas, 1985, 149.
38   See Thomas, 1985, 173ff.; and Snyder, 1996, 26.
39   In general see Okasha, 1993; and Thomas, 1994. Specific stones can be searched for using the Celtic Inscribed Stones Project <http://www.ucl.ac.uk/archaeology/cisp/database/>.

Plate 8.1   The 'Arthnou stone,' a lightly inscribed slate associated with fifth/sixth-century inhabitation of Tintagel. The inscription read PATER/COLIAVIFICIT/ARTOGNOU/COL/FICIT, which Charles Thomas has translated as 'Arthnou, father of a descendant of Coll, has had [this] made.' The slate also bears a small cross, and may be a broken practice piece rather than a formal inscription. (© English Heritage.)

Another important source for early Christianity, in Cornwall at least, is placenames. Most early Cornish churches are indicated in the topography by a placename formed by *lann-* plus a personal name. A *lan*, equivalent of the Welsh *llan*, signifies an 'enclosure,' and came to describe specifically a church enclosed by a cemetery, and often by an oval or sub-rectangular embankment as well. Similar placenames formed by *eglos-* (from *ecclesia*) plus a personal name may simply indicate a church, which may or may not be enclosed. The personal name in these toponyms is almost always that of the patron saint of the church.

The earliest written information about Cornish Christianity derives, once again, from the *Life of St. Samson* composed by a Breton monk *c.*700. The author of the *Life* states that Samson crossed in a ship from South Wales to Cornwall, and that he traveled first to the monastery of *Docco*, probably St. Kew.[40] The monks there refused to receive him, say-

40   *La Vie Ancienne de Saint Samson de Dol*, 1.45–7. See also Orme, 2000, 7–8.

ing that Samson's ascetic standards were too high for them, so the saint continued on through the *pagus Tricurius*, Trigg in northern Cornwall. Here a count (*comes*) named Vedianus asked Samson to confirm the baptisms of the villagers, and told the saint about a huge serpent lurking in a nearby cave. Samson destroyed the serpent and made the cave his hermitage, then founded a monastic community in the region that, before leaving for Brittany, he left in the charge of his father and cousin.

According to the *Life*, Samson acquired horses in Cornwall to draw a *currus* that he had brought with him from Ireland. Gildas refers to such vehicles in his writings, castigating those Britons who join religious communities without giving up such worldly pleasures. The author of the *Life* provides some information that he himself has confirmed on his own travels to Britain. For example, he says that he placed his own hands on a cross that Samson himself (reputedly) carved on a standing stone in Cornwall.[41] At Samson's monastery (tentatively identified as Golant) the author made use of written works, including earlier hagiography derived in part from material brought from Brittany.

Two other early *Vitae* concerning Cornwall were produced in Brittany, specifically at Landévennec in the ninth century. In the *Life of St. Winwaloe*, the father of the Breton saint Winwaloe (or Guenolé, first abbot of Landévennec) is said to have been a nobleman from Dumnonia.[42] The *Life of St. Paul of Léon* was written by a Breton monk named Wrmonoc in 884. In it St. Paul Aurelian, a disciple of Illtud who later became the first bishop of Léon in northern Brittany, left the court of King Marcus and came to the southeastern shore of Cornwall to obtain passage across the Channel. Paul and his disciples stayed there at a religious house belonging to his sister, a holy virgin named Sitofolla. This is about all the information about Cornwall in the *Life*, and Wrmonoc is unlikely to have traveled there himself. Though early, Wrmonoc's *Life* combines traditions relating to three Pauls – the founder of the see of Léon, Paulinus of Wales, and the eponym of Paul's Path in Cornwall – which may or may not have been the same person.[43]

Another body of written evidence comes from English ecclesiastical writers, who were not always on the best of terms with their British neighbors. In these sources the Dumnonian clergy seem to reflect the conservatism and separatism that characterized the British Church in general. Aldhelm's purpose in writing to Geraint, for example, is to encourage the Dumnonian king to use his influence over his recalcitrant clergy, as the

---

41 *La Vie Ancienne de Saint Samson de Dol*, 1.48.
42 See Orme, 2000, 257.
43 Olson, 1989, 28.

Northumbrian king Oswiu had done after Whitby.[44] Aldhelm was disturbed that certain Dumnonian 'bishops and clerics' were still refusing the Roman tonsure and the Roman dating of Easter, 'employing tyrannous obstinacy' and 'haughtily spurning' with 'swollen pride' the practices of the English Church.[45] He also compares the bishops of Dumnonia and Demetia with 'the heretics who liked to call themselves cathari,' and is dismissive of British contemplatives who 'retire away in some squalid wilderness.' Bede believed that Aldhelm's letter met with some success, leading 'many of those Britons who were subject to the West Saxons' to abandon their errors.[46]

By the ninth century the English Church was successfully asserting its authority over churches in Dumnonia. Kenstec, a Cornish bishop from the monastery of *Dinuurin*, made a profession of obedience to Canterbury sometime between 833 and 870.[47] Asser tells us that Alfred rewarded him with 'Exeter with all its parishes in the Saxon lands and Cornwall.' Asser's authority over Exeter came as bishop of Sherborne, but after his death in 909 the see of Sherborne was divided and the new see of Crediton was given authority over the Cornish churches.[48] In Canterbury a contemporary observed that the English bishop of Crediton visited the Cornish people regularly to 'repress their errors, for formerly, in as far as they could, they resisted the truth and did not obey the apostolic decrees.'[49]

According to Dunstan of Glastonbury, Æthelstan granted the bishopric of Cornwall *c.*930 to one Conan, who, along with his successors Daniel and Comoere, were probably Britons.[50] The independence of this Cornish see was short-lived, however, for in 1050 Cornwall was demoted to the status of an archdeaconry within the new diocese of Exeter. It would remain at this status until the creation of the see of Truro in 1877. But through the vigorous promotion of the cults of its native saints, Cornwall would retain a distinctive and influential – if minority – church throughout the Middle Ages.

Karen Jankulak has illustrated this point in her recent study of St. Petroc.[51] Perhaps the best-known Cornish saint of the Middle Ages, Petroc's cult was spread across Cornwall and Brittany and could also be found in Ireland and Wales. There is a considerable body of hagiographical writing associated with Petroc, though it derives mostly from the eleventh

44   Grimmer, 2001.
45   *Aldhelm: The Prose Works*, pp. 156–9.
46   Bede, *EH*, 5.18.
47   Canterbury Cathedral Library, Register A, fo 292. See Olson, 1989, 51ff.
48   Orme, 2000. 9.
49   Birch, *Cartularium Saxonicum*, 2.277.
50   Orme, 2000, 9–10.
51   Jankulak, 2000.

century and later. He is depicted as the son of a Welsh prince, and uncle of St. Cadog, who migrated to Cornwall in the sixth century. (In late Welsh sources he is even one of Arthur's knights, who, after escaping Camlann alive, enters religious life.) His principle foundation – a *monasterium* with a bishop – was at Padstow, though his relics were later transferred to Bodmin. Padstow became a rich foundation in the years before the Norman Conquest and had a very active scriptorium. The veneration of Petroc in Brittany is attested by the many towns whose name were formed with the saint's name, and by the fact that his relics were actually stolen – a *furtum sacrum* – in 1177 and taken to Brittany in a complicated plot that involved some of the most important nobles and prelates of the days of Henry II.

The saint cults of Cornwall commemorate an unusually high percentage of Brittonic figures. According to a recent study by Nicholas Orme, 140 saints bearing Brittonic names (100 men, 40 women) were venerated at 185 Cornish churches and chapels in medieval Cornwall.[52] Most of these pre-date the English conquest, and a great many survived the pressure of new religious fashions brought in the tenth and subsequent centuries. 'They helped sustain a Cornish sense of being different,' writes Orme. 'It is notable that fifteenth- and sixteenth-century folklore gives them a "Celtic" context (usually Irish), not an English one, indicating consciousness of a separate Cornish heritage.'[53]

52   Orme, 2000, 21.
53   Orme, 2000, 44.

9

Wales and the Isle of Man

While Cornwall and Brittany maintained some degree of distinctively Brittonic culture in the early Middle Ages, it was Wales that defined medieval 'Britishness.' Nowhere were the ties to the past stronger, a past which the Welsh remembered as a Golden Age of British heroes, bards, saints, and above all, political autonomy. This picture of the past grew grander as political independence dimmed. Cut off from the Britons of Cornwall and Cumbria by expanding Wessex and Northumbria, harried by Vikings who wrested control of the Isle of Man, the Welsh became increasingly isolated and conservative. On the eve of the Norman Conquest the Welsh were seen as a backward nation needing to be integrated into the feudal and ecclesiastical mainstream of Europe. Their contributions to the medieval mainstream – missionary saints, penitentials, Asser – were to be mostly overlooked by their neighbors, until, beginning in the middle of the twelfth century, these neighbors were swept up in the wave of Arthurian enthusiasm that drew attention to the history and legends of the Welsh.

Historical Narrative

The written evidence is such that an historical narrative for early medieval Wales is difficult, but possible, beginning in the seventh century. While a brief narrative at this point is necessary, this chapter is decidedly not a history of early medieval Wales. Others have produced such histories, occasionally integrating the archaeological evidence, and it is to these that the reader should turn for a more detailed and comprehensive narrative.[1]

If we take the end of the Brittonic Age to be about 600, the history of Wales proper could be said to begin with two important events recorded

1   See, especially, W. Davies, 1982; and Arnold and Davies, 2000.

by Bede. The first is the Conference at Augustine's Oak *c*.603, at which the Welsh bishops refused to cooperate with and accept the authority of archbishop Augustine of Canterbury.[2] The second, which Bede relates to the first, is the Battle of Chester *c*.615 in which Æthelfrith of Northumbria defeated the Welsh and slew 1,200 monks from Bangor. While Bede is obviously selecting incidents here according to his providential history scheme, these two events do nevertheless illustrate the conservative stance that the Welsh Church would take for the next three centuries and the price that they had to pay for this stance: increasing isolation.

That is not to say that the early medieval Welsh princes were isolationists. The growing strength of Northumbria led Gwynedd, quickly becoming the most powerful Welsh kingdom, into an unlikely alliance with the still pagan English kingdom of Mercia (see map 9.1). This may have been a result of the defeat at Chester, which likely hurt Gwynedd most but may also have included men from Powys. One year after the battle Æthelfrith died and his kingdom was seized by Edwin. According to Bede, Edwin of Northumbria exercised greater power than any previous Anglo-Saxon king, and his conquests certainly reached farther west than those of any other English monarch:

> Edwin had still greater power and ruled over all the inhabitants of Britain, English and Britons alike, except for Kent only. He even brought under English rule the Mevanian Islands [Anglesey and Man] which lie between Britain and Ireland and belong to the Britons.[3]

Later Welsh sources, notably the Triads, confirm that Edwin was active in Anglesey and the Llŷn peninsula. Bede is exaggerating in claiming lordship over 'all the inhabitants of Britain' for Edwin, and the conquests of Anglesey and Man were short-lived. Nevertheless, it would take a powerful coalition to stop the vigorous Edwin. Cadwallon, the Christian king of Gwynedd who may have been driven from Anglesey by Edwin in the early 630s, made an alliance with Penda, the pagan Saxon king of nearby Mercia, in 633. Together they invaded Edwin's lands, and defeated and killed the Northumbrian king at the Battle of Hatfield Chase.[4]

Bede's depiction of Cadwallon is unfortunately colored. He is a 'barbarian who was even more cruel than the heathen [Penda],' and 'meaning to wipe out the whole English nation from the land of Britain.' Cadwallon and Penda continued their campaigning into the heart of Northumbria in 634, eliminating nearly all claimants to the land by killing princes of both

2 Bede, *EH*, 2.2. See discussion in chapter 6 above.
3 Bede, *EH*, 2.5.
4 Bede, *EH*, 2.20; *Historia Brittonum*, s.a. 630.

Map 9.1   The major British kingdoms of early medieval Wales.

Æthelfrith's and Edwin's lines. Bede claims that Cadwallon established himself as ruler of the Northumbrian kingdoms (presumably both Deira and Bernicia) for an entire year, 'not ruling them like a victorious king but ravaging them like a savage tyrant.'[5] Kari Maund has suggested that Britons living in Northumbria may have aided Cadwallon in these campaigns.[6] However, in 635 Æthelfrith'a son Oswald led an army against Cadwallon at Heavenfield, near Hexham, and defeated and killed the British king.[7]

5   Bede, *EH*, 3.1.
6   Maund, 2000, 31.
7   Bede, *EH*, 3.1; Adomnán, *Life of St. Columba*, 1.1; *Annales Cambriae*, s.a. 631; *Historia Brittonum*, 64.

The rulers of Gwynedd, and possibly Powys, continued amicable relations with Penda after Cadwallon's death. The Mercian king killed Oswald
in battle in 642, and while fighting his successor Oswiu in 655 he is said
to have restored to the Welsh treasures which had been stolen from them.[8]
But Penda fell to Oswiu shortly after this, and Mercia spent the rest of the
seventh century and much of the eighth fighting against Powys. These
battles are recorded (sparsely) in the *Annales Cambriae*, and perhaps recalled in the ninth-century poems which lament the death of the Powysian
prince Cynddylan. Mercia expanded into the valleys of the Dee and the
Wye at the expense of Powys, and St. Beuno is said to have fled to Gwynedd when he heard English being spoken on the west bank of the Severn!
Placename evidence suggests English colonists in Shropshire during Penda's
time, and it is likely that Wroxeter was abandoned about then.[9]

By the beginning of the eighth century, Britons living in the hills of
Gwynedd and Powys seem to have made some attempts to win back the
plains to their east. This may have prompted Æthelbald of Mercia (r.716–
57) to reach an agreement with Glywysing and to construct Wat's Dyke,
an earthwork that extends from the Severn valley to the estuary of the
Dee and thus marks the boundary of the lowlands. The Welsh were unlikely to gain much against the powerful Æthelbald, but in the wake of
his murder they made some attempt. The *Annales Cambriae* record a battle between Britons and Saxons at Hereford in 760, and the Pillar of Eliseg
claims that Eliseg (fl.750) 'united the inheritance of Powys . . . from the
power of the Englishmen both with his own sword and with fire.'[10] It
appears, from this and frequent references to *vastatio* in the annals, that
such 'devastation' by sword and fire was used by both the English and the
Welsh as a political statement in a war that was more complex than just
raiding and land conquest.[11]

This war reached a climax with the campaigns of Offa (r.757–96) in
the late eighth century, which were aimed mostly at Powys, Dyfed, and
the smaller southern British kingdoms. His 'devastations' may have been
preparation for the construction of an even more impressive earthwork,
Offa's Dyke, which stretches some 150 miles (240 kilometers, 12 kilometers
longer than Hadrian's Wall) and influenced the modern border between
Wales and England. Utilizing some natural features, the Dyke required
the construction of an additional 81 miles (130 kilometers) of bank (22
feet or 7 meters high) and ditch (6 feet or 2 meters deep and up to 65 feet

8   *Historia Brittonum*, 65.
9   Maund, 2000, 32.
10   Trans. D. R. Howlett.
11   W. Davies, 1982, 113.

or 20 meters wide). Since it was not garrisoned, it is unlikely that Offa's Dyke served a military purpose. Scholarly opinion now favors the interpretation that the Dyke was a boundary, a means of political and economic control negotiated between Offa and the Welsh kings.[12] Though it did not prevent subsequent raiding from both parties, the Dyke would have made the transportation of stolen livestock more difficult, and it did serve as a legal boundary in later English laws.

In the ninth century, Offa's Dyke provided little assurance to Powys and the southern Welsh kingdoms that Mercia was satisfied with its western border. With the Danish raids in the east leading to the fall of Northumbria, Mercia and Wessex both flexed their muscles and threatened the Britons of Wales and the southwest. Both the *Anglo-Saxon Chronicle* and the *Annales Cambriae* record continuing deaths and devastations: Saxons strangled Caradog of Gwynedd in 798 and ravaged Snowdon and Rhufoniog in 816, Cœnwulf of Mercia raided Dyfed in 818, and Degannwy fell to Mercians in 822, giving them temporary control of Powys.[13] Seemingly the one Welsh prince who met a good end was Cyngen of Powys, who erected the Pillar of Eliseg in honor of his great-grandfather. Cyngen re-established Powysian independence after the Mercian invasion of 823, and withstood threats for 30 years, dying on a pilgrimage to Rome in 854.

Upon Cyngen's death Powys came to be ruled by his nephew Rhodri ap Merfyn, called by later chroniclers Rhodri Mawr ('the Great'). Rhodri had become ruler of Gwynedd in 844, added the small kingdom of Seisyllwg in 871, and a year later assumed power in Ceredigion, giving him control over a vast northern kingdom stretching from Anglesey to Gower.[14] This hegemony stands in contrast to a half-century of civil warfare in Wales. In Gwynedd, the brothers Cynan and Hywel had been in a prolonged struggle for the throne, while in Powys the king Elise ap Cyngen had to kill his brother Griffri in order to secure the throne.[15] Rhodri's father, Merfyn Frych, was not in the patrilineal descent of Gwynedd (though his mother may have been of the ruling house), but appears to have usurped the throne *c.*825 and ruled over a united Gwynedd until his death in 844. During this time he either married into or allied with the ruling dynasty of Powys.

Rhodri then began his reign under fortunate circumstances. But while internal clashes were diminishing in north Wales, external pressures mounted in the middle of the ninth century. The first recorded Viking

---

12   W. Davies, 1982, 110; J. Davies, 1993, 64–6; Arnold and Davies, 2000, 176–8.
13   For references see W. Davies, 1982, 113.
14   J. Davies, 1993, 81.
15   Maund, 2000, 38.

raids in Wales were in 850 and 853, the 'black gentiles' killing a Welsh king named Cynin and ravaging Anglesey.[16] Rhodri became an internationally famous warrior-king by defeating the Danes in 856 and killing their chieftain Ormr. Irish chroniclers and Sedulius Scottus, at the court of Charles the Bald, took notice. The Vikings returned in 871 and Rhodri was forced to flee to Ireland in 877, though he was reinstated in Gwynedd a year later. The English kings were also exerting pressure. Egbert of Wessex and Cœnwulf of Mercia raided Wales in the 820s, and Æthelwulf of Wessex penetrated Powys in 853. In 878 Rhodri was fighting unnamed Saxons when he was killed, along with his son Gwriad. His long reign brought stability to northern Wales and perhaps saved it from the fate of Man, the Scottish Isles, and most of England, which came under Viking domination in the second half of the ninth century.

Rhodri's vast kingdom was ruled jointly by his surviving sons, though only two – Cadell and Anarawd – made an impression in the written sources.[17] The aggression of Rhodri's sons sent the rulers of the southern kingdoms of Dyfed and Brycheiniog to seek assistance from Alfred the Great, who had already offered protection to the kings of Gwent and Glywysing from Æthelred of Mercia. The king of Wessex, after his defeat of the Danes in 878, had achieved hegemony over all of the Anglo-Saxon kingdoms. According to his Welsh biographer Asser, Alfred may have achieved this in Wales as well. It appears that Asser's *Life of Alfred* was in part an attempt to convince Welsh princes and prelates to submit to the leadership of the Christian King Alfred in his struggles against the heathen. At first the sons of Rhodri resisted Alfred's offer, preferring instead an alliance with the Danish kingdom of York, which had ties with Dublin. But in the end the princes of Gwynedd changed their minds, and around 892 Anarawd traveled to meet with Alfred himself, who accorded the Welsh prince the same rank as Æthelred.[18]

The Welsh princes stood with their ally Wessex in a campaign against a new Viking invasion, in the Severn–Wye area, around 893.[19] Though defeated, the Vikings were to return the next year to seize Chester, while another band from Dublin invaded Anglesey in 903 and killed Merfyn ap Rhodri. An alliance with the English, however, allowed the surviving sons of Rhodri to continue their expansion in southern Wales. In 895 Anarawd invaded Ceredigion with the help of an Anglo-Saxon force, and around 905 Anarawd and Cadell moved into Dyfed following the death of its

16   *Historia Brittonum.*
17   See Maund, 2000, 42ff.
18   Asser, *Life of Alfred the Great*, 80.
19   Maund, 2000, 44.

king Llywarch ap Hyfaidd. In 910 Cadell died and his lands in the south-west passed to his son Hywel, while the north went to the sons of Anarawd upon his death in 916. The *Annales Cambriae* honored Anarawd's achievements by calling him simply 'the king of the Britons.'

The line of Merfyn and Rhodri thus became split into a northern and a southern half. The southern half was at first preeminent, due to the achievements (and propaganda) of Hywel ap Cadell, later called Hywel Dda ('the Good'). Around 930 Hywel obtained Brycheiniog, and this new enlarged kingdom came to be known as Deheubarth. Continuing the tradition of alliance with the kings of Wessex, Hywel made submission to Edward in 921 and Æthelstan in 927.[20] He was a frequent visitor to the English court thereafter, appearing as witness to several charters (as *regulus* or *subregulus*). His cousin, Idwal ab Anarawd, who had also made submission to Edward, was not on friendly terms with Wessex. He fought intermittently against Æthelstan, and in 942 he led a revolt against the English and was killed along with his brother Elise. The opportunistic Hywel quickly invaded Gwynedd and expelled the sons of Idwal, adding Gwynedd and Powys to his dominions.

Hywel Dda was certainly 'good' at acquiring Welsh lands and adept at diplomacy with English monarchs. But this is not how he earned his epithet. In 929 Hywel went on a pilgrimage to Rome, perhaps modeling himself after Alfred the Great. Later tradition maintained that he took with him a copy of the Welsh laws, which he was responsible for codifying, in order for the pope to bless them.[21] The notion that Hywel convened a council of noblemen to formalize customary law, and that he was the first to promulgate the Welsh laws, was promoted by the southern Welsh in the thirteenth century. No tenth-century evidence exists for his involvement in legislation, though he may have been remembered as a king who made special recourse to customary law in order to bring some cohesion to his vast territory.

When Hywel died in 949 this cohesion vanished. He left his kingdom to his three sons, but their authority in the north was challenged by the sons of Idwal. The latter won decisive victories at Carno in 950 and Llanrwst in 954,[22] securing Gwynedd for their branch of the family and leaving the sons of Hywel with only Deheubarth. Owain ap Hywel, the only son to survive this period of civil warfare, turned his attention to the smaller southern kingdoms bordering Deheubarth. He and his sons, Einion and Maredudd, raided Morgannwg in 960 and Gower several times in

---

20   *The Anglo-Saxon Chronicle* (Laud Chronicle), 922 and 926.
21   J. Davies, 1993, 87.
22   *Annales Cambriae.*

the following decade, eventually bringing the latter under their control.[23] Owain enjoyed a long reign, during which time Deheubarth produced the A-text of the *Annales Cambriae* (at St. David's) and its associated genealogies, all of which favor the southern branch of Merfyn's family.

The years between 950 and 1050 witnessed incessant civil war between Gwynedd and Deheubarth, whose rulers often turned to English and Viking allies to gain the upper hand. Viking attacks on the Welsh coast were also constant in the last decades of the tenth century, with Anglesey suffering the worst. Within Gwynedd the sons and grandsons of Idwal struggled violently against one another for the throne. The more stable Deheubarth witnessed a period of expansion, and from 984 to 999 Maredudd ap Owain nearly succeeded in re-creating the kingdom of his grandfather Hywel.[24] He won control of Gwynedd in 986, and conquered Morgannwg in 992 with the aid of Viking mercenaries. A year later, however, his hegemony over the north ended in a battle against Meurig ab Idwal. Maredudd died in 999 as 'the most famous king of the Welsh,'[25] but his inability to transmit his kingdom to his children led to the decline and replacement of the house of Merfyn.

The beginning of the eleventh century saw the appearance of several new dynasties. A man named Llywelyn ap Seisyll displaced the sons of Meurig ab Idwal and became king of Gwynedd around 1010. Not much is known about Llywelyn, other than that he had married the daughter of Maredudd (which would not have made him heir to Maredudd's power). In 1022 Llywelyn came south to defeat a man who was claiming to be the son of Maredudd, and while there he plundered Deheubarth and asserted his control there. He died just a year later, leaving a very young son named Gruffydd. Control of Gwynedd reverted to Iago ab Idwal ap Meurig, of the northern branch of the house of Merfyn, while another new dynast named Rhydderch ab Iestyn, then king of Morgannwg, seized power in Deheubarth. Rhydderch was killed by the Irish in 1033, and Deheubarth reverted to the southern branch of the house of Merfyn.

This is the situation at the beginning of the ascent of Gruffydd ap Llywelyn. Now a young man, Gruffydd sought to win back the dominions of his father, and in 1039 he began by killing Iago and seizing control of Gwynedd. He then turned immediately south and drove out the king of Deheubarth, before moving against the English on the Severn and killing the earl of Mercia. In 1042 Gruffydd suffered his first setback, being captured by a Viking war-band in Gwynedd. He was free by 1044 and re-

23   Maund, 2000, 53.
24   J. Davies, 1993, 98; Maund, 2000, 57.
25   *Brut y Tywysogyon*, s.a. 998–9.

suming aggression against Hywel ap Edwin of Deheubarth, and Hywel hired a Viking fleet to harass Gruffydd, but was defeated and killed at the mouth of the River Tywi. Gruffydd was unable to hold Deheubarth, however, for the sons of Rhydderch moved in and held the land, once again with the help of Norsemen from Ireland. In 1052 Gruffydd resumed raiding the English border, and a year later the eldest son of Rhydderch died. This resulted in a showdown between Gruffydd and the surviving son (another Gruffydd) in 1056, and victory for Gruffydd ap Llywelyn gave him lasting control of the south.

Between 1056 and his death in 1064, Gruffydd ap Llywelyn ruled all of Wales, the only Welsh king to have ever accomplished this feat. He was also the first Welsh king since Cadwallon to play a major role in English politics.[26] Gruffydd sought alliance with powerful English nobles who could help him gain territory on the Anglo-Welsh border. His first alliance, with Swegen Godwinesson, eldest son of Earl Godwine of Wessex, ended quickly with Swegen's exile in 1047. By 1055 Gruffydd had made a new alliance with Ælfgar, the deposed earl of Anglia and son of the powerful Leofric, earl of Mercia. Ælfgar, with a band of Hiberno-Norse mercenaries, joined forces with Gruffydd to invade Herefordshire.[27] After sacking Hereford and resisting capture by Earl Harold Godwinesson, Ælfgar and Gruffydd were given concessions by King Edward the Confessor. A second campaign in 1058, this time with the added assistance of King Magnus of Norway, resulted in similar concessions for the allies, and Gruffydd made a token submission to Edward.[28] By this time Gruffydd had also married Ealdgyth, the daughter of his ally Ælfgar.[29]

In 1062 or 1063, Ælfgar died, and Gruffydd's fortunes immediately waned.[30] Harold Godwinesson brought an army into Wales seeking revenge. He burned Gruffydd's stronghold of Rhuddlan to the ground, and in 1064 joined forces with his brother Tostig to attack Gruffydd. While they failed to capture the Welsh king, they did force large numbers of Welsh to abandon their allegiance to Gruffydd, whose hegemony over all Wales was now broken. Finally members of his own household, perhaps bribed by the English, assassinated Gruffydd. Harold took Ealdgyth as his own wife, and imposed submission upon Gruffydd's successors in Gwynedd. The southern Welsh dynasts, releasing years of frustration and resentment, were only too happy to resume control in Deheubarth, Morgannwyg, and Powys.

---

26 See Maund, 2000, 65ff.
27 *The Anglo-Saxon Chronicle*, s.a. 1055.
28 *The Anglo-Saxon Chronicle*, s.a. 1058.
29 Orderic Vitalis, *Ecclesiastical History*.
30 See Maund, 2000, 68ff.

Welsh Kings and Kingdoms

Gruffydd ap Llywelyn's reign over a unified Wales, won through years of hard and ruthless conquests, was short-lived. It was also an anomaly. While England had emerged as a unified kingdom under Alfred in the ninth century, the Welsh preference for segmentation over primogeniture resulted in generation after generation of civil strife both within and among the many Welsh dynasties. And while the Welsh may have developed a sense of national identity long before the English, they were from the sixth century (if not earlier) marked by a tradition of petty kingdoms and local power.

The earliest written evidence for Welsh kingship is Gildas's *De Excidio Britanniae*. Gildas locates the return of native British kingship in the years following the Battle of Badon Hill, that is, at the end of the fifth century.[31] 'Britain has kings,' begins his memorable line, 'but they are tyrants.'[32] Gildas then goes on to name five of these tyrannical kings, and gives us geographic information about three of them. Constantine, as we have seen, is associated with Dumnonia.[33] Vortipor is called 'tyrant of the Demetae,' and Maglocunus 'dragon of the island.'[34] The Demetae occupied southwestern Wales in the LPRIA, a region that would come to form the kingdom of Dyfed, and Maglocunus is almost certainly Maelgwn of Gwynedd, whom later sources link with the 'island' of Anglesey. The remaining two kings of the *De Excidio* – Aurelius Caninus and Cuneglasus – are not associated specifically with Welsh locales, though some have theorized (through process of elimination) that they must be located in southeastern (Glywysing or Brycheiniog) and northeastern Wales (Powys or Ceredigion) respectively.

This is admittedly thin evidence to begin discussion of the origins of the Welsh kingdoms. A handful of early Christian monuments bear testimony to Welsh kings of the sixth to eighth centuries, and in a couple of instances they include a wealth of detail.[35] But these details are usually genealogical and associated with later dynastic claims, as is the Harleian collection of Welsh royal genealogies, which is riddled with contradictions and obvious propaganda.[36] Equally difficult is the evidence of the *Liber Landavensis* ('Book of Llandaff'), which includes several charters associated with named kings of the late fifth and sixth centuries.[37] None

31   *De Excidio*, 26.2.
32   *De Excidio*, 27.1.
33   Chapter 8 above.
34   *De Excidio*, 31.1; 33.1.
35   See Nash-Williams, 1950; and now *CISP: The Celtic Inscribed Stones Project*.
36   See Bartrum, 1966; and Dumville, 1977.
37   See W. Davies, 1978; and discussion below.

of these sources is contemporary with the kings they describe (though they may be based on earlier information), and thus the following discussion of the individual kingdoms and dynasties must be tentative until it reaches the seventh and eighth centuries, when the evidence is much more trustworthy (see chart 9.1).

Gwynedd (Latin *Venedotia*) may have been, from the very beginning of post-Roman kingship, the most powerful of the medieval Welsh kingdoms. The Ordovices had been the major Iron Age tribe in northwest Wales, but no *civitas* capital is recorded for this rural fortified region of Roman Britain. The story of Cunedda, a chieftain of the Votadini who allegedly moved from near Edinburgh to northwest Wales in order to expel Irish raiders, has been used to postulate a Votadini origin of the Venedotian dynasty.[38] The Cunedda story is now discredited, though there is slight evidence, written and material, for both northern British influence in Gwynedd and possible Irish settlement in the Llŷn peninsula.[39] It is most likely, however, that a local dynasty asserted its power in Late Roman Britain and seized control of both local forts and hill-forts after 410. Ken Dark has postulated that this nascent Ordivican kingdom was overthrown by Maelgwn, perhaps a sub-king controlling Anglesey who Gildas claims killed many kings – including his uncle – along his path to power.[40]

Once in power, Maelgwn is described by Gildas as 'higher than almost all the generals in Britain, in your kingdom as in your physique.'[41] Similarly, the *Historia Brittonum* calls Maelgwyn *magnus rex*, 'great king.'[42] Clearly the kings of Gwynedd were asserting their superiority among Welsh kings from an early date. Cadfan, the father of Cadwallon, is described on his Anglesey memorial stone as 'the wisest and most renowned of all kings.'[43] Bede calls Cadwallon 'the king of the Britons,' while Adomnán adds 'the most powerful king of the Britons.'[44] Cadwallon's son Cadwaladr, who died (according to the *Annales Cambriae*) of the plague in 682, is depicted in the *Armes Prydein* and by Geoffrey of Monmouth as the most powerful British king of his day. The title *rex Brittonum* is later given to both Rhodri Mawr and his son Cynan, while Merfyn Frych is called 'glorious king of the Britons' on the ninth-century Bamberg cryptogram.[45] Through conquest and propaganda, the dynasties of Maelgwn and Merfyn

---

38   *HB*, 62. See also Dumville, 1977; and discussion below.
39   See Maund, 2000, 24ff.
40   Dark, 1994, 77–8.
41   *De Excidio*, 33.2.
42   *HB*, 62.
43   *ECMW* no. 13.
44   Bede, *EH*, 3.1; Adomnán, *Life of St. Columba*, 1.1.
45   See W. Davies, 1982, 104.

THE EARLY KINGS OF GWYNEDD
AND THE HOUSE OF MERFYN FRYCH

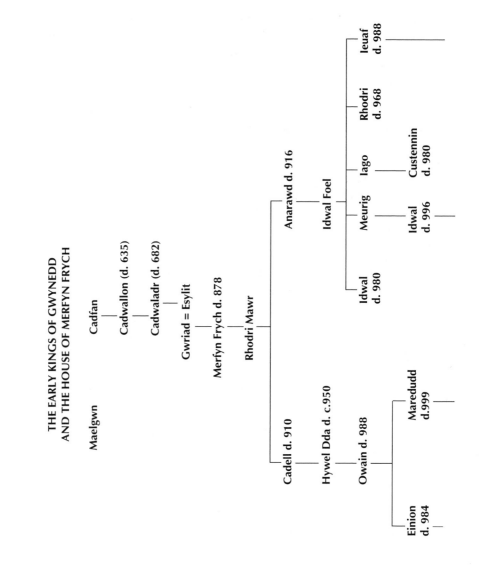

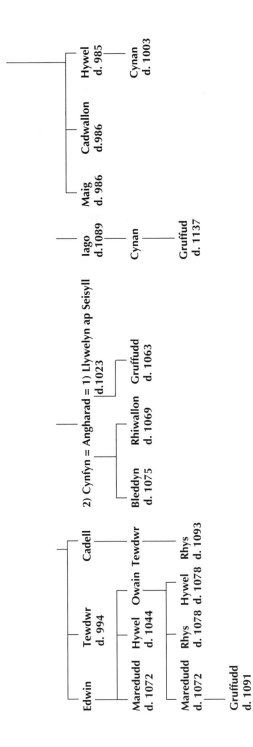

Figure 9.1 The known kings of early medieval Gwynedd, featuring the dynasty of Merfyn Frych.

made Gwynedd the preeminent kingdom of early medieval Wales, a position it would return to in the thirteenth century.

Gwynedd's chief rival early on seems to have been Powys. The name is thought to derive from *pagenses*, 'country people,' though this land of the Iron Age Cornovii did have a major urban capital, Wroxeter (*Viroconium*), as well as a legionary fortress at Chester (*Deva*). Whatever powerful magnate was responsible for the great timber complex built in late fifth-century Wroxeter may have relocated his power base in the sixth century to the nearby hill-fort of the Wrekin. Gildas describes Cuneglasus (Cinglas) as 'driver of the chariot of the Bear's Stronghold.'[46] This is almost certainly a reference to a hill-fort, perhaps Bryn Euryn in Denbighshire (where the medieval parish name *Dineirth* means 'fortress of the bear') which was a stronghold of the sub-kingdom of Rhos.[47] Cinglas and Maelgwn appear in a Harleian genealogy as great-grandsons of Cunedda, which likely reflects the claim of ninth-century kings of Gwynedd over Powys.

The *Annales Cambriae* record the death of Selyf ap Cynan at the Battle of Chester in 615, and Selyf appears in later Powysian pedigrees. After the battle Powys probably lost control of the city of Chester, with its defenses (still standing in 894) and active church and port. No king of Powys appears in contemporary sources, which simply describe frequent Mercian raids into Powys in the eighth and ninth centuries. The Cynddylan elegies (circa ninth century) provide only murky details, including the possibility that this Powysian prince was a pagan. The Pillar of Eliseg provides a pedigree for Cyngen's Powysian dynasty that stretches all the way back to Magnus Maximus and Vortigern.[48] Though Eliseg had driven the English out of his kingdom, after the death of his grandson Cyngen in 855 Powys fell permanently under the control of Gwynedd.

The kingdom of Dyfed has the most unusual origins. The *civitas* of the Demetae was fairly rural and un-Romanized, with a capital at Carmarthen (*Moridunum*) but no other urban settlements and only a few villas. Nor did the Romans bother to fortify its coasts against Irish raids, as they certainly did in the northwest.[49] This leads one to wonder if arrangements were made for protection of the southwest by settled *foederati*. According to *The Expulsion of the Déisi*, an Irish prose tale written in the ninth century, a tribe called the Déisi were driven from Meath to Leinster and then 'over the sea into the land of Dyfed.' Their king, Eochaid son of Artchorp, died there, but founded a dynasty whose members include one

---

46   *De Excidio*, 32.1.
47   See Edwards and Lane, 1988, 27.
48   See Bartrum, 1966.
49   Arnold and Davies, 2000, 143.

Gartbuir, an Irish spelling of Vortipor.[50] Gildas, who described Vortipor as 'tyrant of the Demetae' and 'bad son of a good king,' does not indicate that he is a member of an Irish ruling dynasty, but most scholars support this conclusion. The *Historia Brittonum* and the Welsh genealogy of the royal line of Dyfed both refer to Irish in southwest Wales, and more than 20 memorial stones in Dyfed bear Irish names and/or the Ogam script.

Cultural contacts between southwest Wales and Ireland likely date back to pre-Roman times, but we do have enough evidence to envision a movement of peoples from Ireland to Dyfed, perhaps in the fourth century. If the Déisi were accepted as Roman federates, and began intermarrying with the local Romano-British elite, Gildas may not have objected outright to their descendants, more than a century later, ruling Dyfed. One sixth-century man in Carmarthenshire was commemorated on a stone that bears the Irish, British, and provincial Latin versions of his name – *Votecorix*, *Voteporix*, and *Protector*, respectively – which means 'king of refuge.'[51] Ecclesiastical contacts between Dyfed and Ireland could also explain the bilingual memorial stones and Irish burial customs found in the peninsula. St. David's, Penally, and Caldey Island were important early medieval monastic sites noted for their itinerant saints.

Several rural settlements of the Demetae survived into the Roman and early medieval periods. Coygan Camp, Gateholm, and Longbury Bank have all revealed evidence of high-status occupation, and other defended sites like Castell Henllys and Tenby may also have served the princes of Dyfed. The later medieval kings of Dyfed occupied Dinefwr Castle, which may have succeeded an earlier hill-fort.[52] In any event, it seems clear that Dyfed had many sub-kingdoms (perhaps identical to the later *cantrefi*) and that some of these split off as early as the sixth century. One of these was Brycheiniog, which shared many cultural and political similarities with Dyfed. Meaning 'the kingdom of Brychan,' Brycheiniog had no Roman towns (though several forts lay along its Roman roads) and displayed its probable Irish origins in its pedigrees and numerous Ogam inscriptions. Its most prominent excavated settlement is a large crannog built in Llangorse lake by the kings of Brycheiniog in the ninth century (see plate 9.1). Though it fell under the influence of Dyfed in the eighth century, Brycheiniog still boasted a king in the ninth – Tewdwr ab Elise, who paid homage to Alfred the Great.

The minor kingdom of Ceredigion, on Cardigan Bay, also shared similarities with Dyfed. If it too was a splinter kingdom, its creation was later than

50   See Maund, 2000, 23.
51   *ECMW* no. 138; CDWYR/1/1 in *CISP*. See the note by Eric Hamp in *Studia Celtica*, 30 (1996): 293.
52   Dark, 2000, 190.

Plate 9.1 Reconstruction drawing of a large *crannog* built in Llangorse Lake by the kings of Brycheiniog in the ninth century. (Drawing by Tony Daly.)

that of Brycheiniog (probably in the seventh or eighth century) and unlike Brychan its eponymous founder, Ceredig, bears a British name (a form of Caratacus). It remained disputed land between Gwynedd, Dyfed, and the mid-Welsh kingdoms throughout the Middle Ages. Southeast Wales in the Brittonic Age saw the creation of several small kingdoms. Two of these – Gwent and Glywysing – were formed from the *civitas* of the Silures and continued to use Romano-British settlements like Caerwent (from which Gwent derives its name), Caerleon, Glan-y-Mor, Llandough, and Llantwit Major.[53] One Glywysing king or noble also fortified the hilltop at Dinas Powys and held court there, receiving tribute in the form of food renders and distributing imported luxury items from the fifth to the seventh centuries.[54]

In interpreting the evidence from Dinas Powys, its excavator Leslie Alcock followed the depiction of the Welsh prince (*teyrn*) and his court (*llys*) found in the Welsh laws and vernacular poetry.[55] While it is not

53 Dark, 1994, 84.
54 Alcock, 1963.
55 Alcock, 1987.

always advisable to combine written and material evidence, there is a substantial body of the former for Welsh kingship dating from the eighth to the eleventh centuries. Wendy Davies has done a good deal of work on this topic, looking at both Latin and vernacular evidence but especially the Llandaff Charters.[56] While the ecclesiastical authors obviously admire the Christian qualities of Welsh kings, and expect them to be good governors and statesmen, the poets constantly stress their military virtues. A praiseworthy king is bold, powerful, wealthy, generous, a good horseman, able to not just defend his subjects but to extend the boundaries of his kingdom. He often resides in a hall (*neuadd*) with his war-band (*teulu*), employs a bard (*bardd*) to sing his praises and craftsmen, witnesses charters and grants land to religious houses, and governs the subjects (*gens, clas, llwyth*) of his kingdom (*regnum, gwlad*).

In the ruling houses of early medieval Wales primogeniture was not strictly established, so all males of the royal line had the right to compete for the throne.[57] Only late did the Welsh adopt the concept of a designated heir, the *gwrthrych* or *edling* (borrowed from the English *aetheling*).[58] Clientship was clearly important at an early date, most likely developing from the *clientela* of the Late Roman aristocracy.[59] Welsh patron/client relationships were more flexible and less permanent than contemporary continental vassalage, but it would not have been a difficult transition to make for Welsh rulers in the twelfth century.

The Llandaff Charters and Roman Survival in Southern Wales

Our best evidence for clientage comes from the laws and the so-called Llandaff Charters, a collection of 158 grants made to the bishopric of Llandaff from the sixth to the eleventh centuries. Although the relevant material in the *Liber Llandavensis* dates from the twelfth century, when the Anglo-Norman bishop of Llandaff was making new claims to estates, Wendy Davies has argued that the manuscript contains charters which must derive from a much earlier date.[60] Due to textual corruption and the insertion of hagiographic material, some experts have cast recent doubts on the reliability of the charters for pre-800 historical details.[61] However,

56 See, for example, W. Davies, 1978; idem, 1982, 121ff; and idem, 1990.
57 Maund, 2000, 45.
58 W. Davies, 1982, 125.
59 W. Davies, 1978, 22–4.
60 W. Davies, 1978.
61 See, for example, the discussion in Dark, 1994, 140–8.

they remain a valuable source of information about estate management in southeastern Wales from at least the eighth to the eleventh centuries.

Davies suggests that a number of Late Roman villa estates in this area survived, mostly intact, after the Roman administrative and military withdrawal. These large land units, defined by Roman measurement terms and clustered along Roman roads, continued to exist until the eighth century, after which the land grants became smaller and defined by other means. Davies sees the earlier grants coming from local princes, while the later grants were made increasingly by the laity. The details of this land management will continue to be debated, but there is no reason to doubt the general picture of Roman cultural survival – and adaptation by new native rulers – in this the most Romanized part of Wales.

Hill-forts and Trade

Less controversial is the assertion that early medieval Wales was overwhelmingly rural, with a diversified agrarian economy – arable and pastoral – that was dependent on both a warrior aristocracy and a servile population.[62] While industrial activity was slight, trade flourished between the Welsh and the English, and luxury items were obtained by Welsh elites from Gaul and the eastern Mediterranean in the late fifth to seventh centuries. While there was a diversity of settlement types throughout early medieval Wales, showing much Iron Age and Roman continuity, the British elites here, as in Brittany and Cornwall, defined themselves by their hill-forts and other rural defended settlements.

A number of extensively excavated hill-forts give us some idea of high-status settlement in pre-Viking Wales.[63] Dinorben, Degannwy, Dinas Emrys, Breiddin, Capel Maelog, Coygan Camp, Longbury Bank, Dinas Powys, Hen Gastell, Carew, Drim Camp, Gateholm, and Rhuddlan (which became an English *burh* in 921) have all yielded evidence of early medieval occupation and were chosen for their natural defenses. The Late Roman defenses at Caerleon, Caernarvon, and Caerwent were likely used through the fifth century at least, while at the royal citadel of Aberffraw, on Anglesey, it has been suggested that the kings of Gwynedd rebuilt the stone rampart of a Late Roman auxiliary fort. The Llangorse crannog was built specifically for defense by the rulers of Byrcheiniog, and the lower-status hut groups of Graeanog and Ty Mawr are similarly remote and enclosed. That many of these sites were occupied in the Late Roman

---

62   W. Davies, 1978, 25.
63   See Edwards and Lane, 1988; and Snyder, 1997.

period suggests that the Welsh aristocracy was reasserting its powers and privileges even before the formation of the Welsh kingdoms.

Most of these sites have been identified as high-status settlements due to the presence of imported glass and pottery and fine metalwork (weapon finds are extremely rare). The imported pottery is of the same range as that found in the southwest, with fine table wares and amphoras manufactured in North Africa and the eastern Mediterranean and bowls and other kitchenware originating in Bordeaux and northwestern Gaul (see table 9.1). Often associated with the continental pottery are glass vessels, especially cone beakers made in Bordeaux.[64] A few other items, most notably glass beads, indicate trade with Anglo-Saxon settlements as far east as Sutton Hoo.

Once broken, pieces of imported glass were probably used in making fine jewelry. Both enameling and *millefiori* were known in early medieval Wales. Lidded crucibles with traces of gold and bronze ingots have been found at several Welsh sites, where craftsmen would have melted the metals in hearths and poured them into clay molds to make pins and brooches. While a few pieces are Irish in inspiration, most distinctive are the Welsh penannular brooches. Shale was also used to make bracelets, and bone and antler for making composite combs.

The Irish in Wales and Man

Irish interest in northern Wales and the Isle of Man grew steadily from the Late Roman period to the Viking advent. Caer Gybi and other fortifications on Holyhead and Anglesey were constructed by Roman authorities to guard Irish Sea commerce from Irish piracy.[65] We have seen that, despite this, Irish settlement is almost certain in Dyfed and the Llŷn peninsula. Ogam stones must at the very least mean that there were Irish speakers within British communities in these areas, some of whom were undoubtedly itinerant Irish ecclesiasts and scholars. Irish military adventurers should also be added to this list, while the Irish names glimpsed in the royal genealogies of Gwynedd, Dyfed, and Brycheiniog suggest a degree of intermarriage among the Irish and British aristocracies.

The Isle of Man became an outpost of Irish culture long before the Viking invasions. Little is known about pre-Viking Man, though physical evidence suggests persistent trade with Ireland dating back at least to the Bronze Age. Roundhouses and promontory forts appear on Man in the Iron Age,

---

64 Arnold and Davies, 2000, 172.
65 Arnold and Davies, 2000, 143.

Table 9.1 Post-Roman imported pottery in Man, Wales and along the Anglo-Welsh border.

	ARSW	PRSW	Bi	Bii	Biv	Bv	Bvi	Bmisc	D ware	E ware
Caerleon						*				
Caldey Island	*	*								*
Chester		*			*				*	*
Coygan Camp			*							
Degannwy			*					*		
Dinas Emrys					*					*
Dinas Powys		*	*	*					*	*
Gloucester						*				
Kiondroghad										*
Lesser Garth Cave										*
Longbury Bank		*	*	*	*			*	*	*
Hen Gastell			*	*					*	*
Wroxeter							*			

ARSW	African Red Slip Ware: Popular fine wares produced in North Africa (probably Carthage), late fifth to early sixth century;
PRSW	Phocaean Red Slip Ware: fine wares produced in western Turkey (probably Phocaea), c.500;
Bi	Bi amphoras: wine jars produced in the eastern Aegean, mid sixth century;
Bii	Bii amphoras: wine jars produced in the eastern Mediterranean (Nubia, Cyprus and Antioch have all been proposed), mid to late fifth century;
Biv	Biv handled jars: one- and two-handled water (?) jars produced in Asia Minor (probably Sardis), mid fifth to mid sixth century;
Bv	Byzacena amphoras: large cylindrical oil containers produced in the Byzacena region of North Africa, late fifth century;
Bvi	Gaza amphoras: large cylindrical wine(?) containers produced at Gaza, mid fifth to mid sixth century;
Bmisc	B miscellaneous amphoras;
D WARE	Grey ware bowls produced in the Bordeaux region, sixth century;
E WARE	Kitchenware (jars, pots, bowls, jugs, pitchers, and beakers), some pieces containing traces of purple dye. Produced in western Gaul, c.600–700.

Source: Thomas, 1981; and Snyder, 1996.

with broad affinities to both British and Irish examples. The Romans certainly had knowledge of *Manavia Insula*, but a mere five Roman coins are all that remain of the island's ties to Roman Britain.[66] The lack of defenses associated with roundhouses from the Roman period perhaps suggests security on the island as a result of the presence of Roman ships in the Irish Sea.[67] The Isle of Man was part of the Irish Sea 'Ogam zone' by the fifth century. Personal names in Ogam inscriptions prove that Man was originally Brittonic-speaking, but by about the seventh century Irish immigrants were becoming dominant. Presumably most of these Irish immigrants were clerics, who founded the many *keeills* (simple rectangular churches) that dot the island. A piece of seventh-century Gaulish pottery found at Kiondroghad shows that Man was part of the Atlantic trade network that connected ecclesiastical sites like Iona and Whithorn with Gaul.[68]

While the Manx Church became dominated by Irishmen, the island may have remained under British political control until the sixth century or later. According to the Red Book of Hergest, Merfyn Frych was 'from the land of *Manaw*,' and the name of Merfyn's father – Guriad – is found on an early cross from the Isle of Man.[69] This has led John MacQueen to argue that the British king Tudwal, who opposed the missionary activity of St. Ninian (according to Ailred), ruled over Man as part of a fifth-century *regnum* which extended from Galloway to Anglesey.[70] That Ninian himself may have brought Christianity to Man is supported by the dedication of St. Trinian's church in Marown.

The Welsh Church

The testimony of Gildas and the early Welsh inscriptions make it clear that Christianity was well established in Wales by the end of the fifth century. Paganism, on the other hand, is not indicated by the written and epigraphic evidence. If Welsh Christianity was established in the Late Roman period, it would have been based in urban bishoprics. Since only the towns along the Severn (Caerwent, Gloucester, Worcester, Wroxeter) survived much after 500, the bishoprics in the rest of Wales likely became territorial and coterminous with the Welsh kingdoms.[71] By the beginning of the sixth century there were already numerous religious communities

66   Kinvig, 1975, 32.
67   Kinvig, 1975, 35.
68   Thomas, 1981, 21.
69   See MacQueen, 1990, 13; and the Harleian Genealogy IV of Hywel Dda.
70   MacQueen, 1990, 16, 87.
71   Pryce, 1992, 47.

designated *monasteria*; some of these were aristocratic and hereditary foundations (Llandough, Llantwit Major), others were rigorously eremitic and isolated (Caldey, Penally). Most were mixed communities (laity, regular and secular clergy) under the authority of an abbot, though some monasteries (e.g. St. David's) were ruled by bishops.

Pastoral duties were shared by all members of the clergy, from deacons to bishops. Huw Pryce has studied the evidence for pastoral care in the early medieval Welsh Church.[72] Baptism (*bedydd*) and adult confirmation were performed from at least the sixth century, and the laity were given communion, according to the vernacular poetry. Two early penitentials also prescribe penances for laity as well as clergy. Welsh kings donated land to the Church as a form of penance, and gave alms as well, while the Church in return was expected to look after orphans, widows, and the infirm. Welsh saints are depicted delivering public Mass. Intensely localized lay devotion is indicated by a high percentage of church and holy well dedications to local saints, a pattern we observed for Brittany and Cornwall as well.[73]

Burial customs in Wales, like elsewhere in the Brittonic Outer Zone, were conservative, preserving both Iron Age and Roman practices. Welsh Christians also reused prehistoric burial sites, some in close proximity to Bronze Age barrows and henges. Inhumation was practiced almost exclusively in early medieval Wales, and the grave is a constant feature of early Welsh poetry. From both written and material evidence we see the use of wood coffins, stone-lined graves ('long cist' burials), and burial beneath earthen mounds and stone cairns.[74] Persons of high status were often buried with a stone marker. Literary references indicate burial in isolated places, while Roman extramural cemeteries at Caerwent and possibly Carmarthen continued in use well past the sixth century. At first, burial within a church was solely for saints and martyrs, and the churchyard was reserved for members of the religious community. By the eleventh century high-ranking laity, especially kings and donors, could be buried in churches and churchyards.[75]

Toward the end of the millennium we see the emergence in Wales of the *clas*, a large mother-church whose parishes coincided with the cantrefs or commotes. The *clas* community (*claswyr*) was ruled by an abbot and consisted of both regular and secular clergy, who often married and transmitted property rights hereditarily.[76] Hereditary succession was also practiced

72   Pryce, 1992.
73   See Pryce, 1992, 60; and discussion in chapters 7 and 8 above.
74   W. Davies, 1982, 185–91.
75   Pryce, 1992, 44.
76   W. Davies, 1982, 149; Walker, 1990, 11.

by the bishops of St. David's, which had by Asser's day become the wealthiest and most powerful religious center in Wales. The fact that Alfred turned to Asser to stimulate his educational reforms, and the literary sophistication of Asser's biography of the English king, speaks to the quality of scholarship to be found at St. David's in the ninth century. A large corpus of texts dating to the ninth and tenth centuries and consisting of vernacular glosses, grammars, and calendar computations gives us some idea of the intellectual preoccupations of Welsh clerics.[77]

While the early Welsh Church was clearly producing scholars, it did so for the most part in isolation. The Welsh Church began to conform to the decision of Whitby only in 768, and by that time the English Church was fully oriented toward the continent (witness Alcuin's career). Welsh ecclesiastical reform is attributed to Elfoddw, patron of Nennius, who was probably based in Bangor. Elfoddw is called 'the archbishop of Gwynedd,' a title which Asser's kinsman Nobis held at St. David's. With its two intellectual centers in the extreme northwest and southwest, both areas vulnerable to Viking raids, it is not surprising that the Welsh Church never fully joined in English reforms. We have seen that Asser's *Life of Alfred* was in part an attempt to convince Welsh princes and prelates of the need to cooperate with the Christian English king at a time when many Welsh were tempted into alliances with the pagan Norse. That such an argument needed to be made speaks volumes for the character of English–Welsh relations at the end of the first millennium.

77   W. Davies, 1982, 213.

10

Northern Britons

The links between the Welsh and the northern Britons were extensive. When Cadwallon brought his army from Gwynedd to Northumbria in 634, he was not traversing a cultural divide. The cults of Kentigern and Ninian traveled south just as easily as those of Patrick and David traveled to Scotland. Stories about the prophet Myrddin, perhaps an historical figure who lived in southern Scotland in the sixth century, were relocated to Carmarthen in southern Wales, while the folkloric Arthur is commemorated in the Scottish landscape as much as that of Cornwall and Wales. When 'the Britons rise again,' predicts the author of the *Armes Prydein*, 'the Men of the North (*Gwyr Gogled*) will be in the place of honor about them.'[1]

Cultural unity, however, does not mandate political unity. Nick Higham describes the period 350–685 in the north as 'the return to tribalism.'[2] While there is a danger that such statements will engender notions of devolution and primitivism – reviving the Dark Age myth – it is true that we see a revival of tribal government in the north by the fifth century. Provincial administration fades after 410 and is replaced by dynastic kingship. Should we be surprised? 'The indigenous people of northern Britain,' observes Higham, 'were little affected by romanization as far as their culture, language, and economy were concerned.'[3] There are exceptions to this rule – e.g. Christianity, the continued use of Roman forts, lingering Roman titles – but overall cultural continuity from the Iron Age may be more important in understanding the northern Britons than the Roman interlude.

The northern Britons were scattered and divided, and thus their fate in the wake of the barbarian invasions was varied. We will look first at the northern British tribes as they existed in the Roman period, and then survey

1 *Armes Prydein Vawr*, ll. 12–15.
2 Higham, 1986, title to ch. 6.
3 Higham, 1993, 42.

the various British kingdoms which emerged in the post-Roman centuries. As with reconstructing the early history of the Welsh kingdoms, we must here be aware that much of the written evidence comes not from contemporary histories and annals, but from pedigrees and bardic poetry which are both hard to date and prone to corruption. This is the case, for example, in dealing with the Coelings – the dynasty founded by Coel Hen ('Ole King Cole') – who tend to dominate discussion of most of the northern kingdoms, even though they may never have had legitimate contemporary claims to some of the lands with which they are associated.[4]

The Parisii

The Parisii occupied Humberside/East Yorkshire, according to Ptolemy. The name *Parisii* is obviously paralleled in Gaul, and this tribe's ties with the continent are most clearly seen in the 'Arras culture' burials of south Yorkshire.[5] The *civitas* capital of the Parisii was probably Brough-on-Humber (*Petuaria*), an important commercial (a mosaic workshop flourished there) and administrative center whose exact status is uncertain. By the fourth century Brough may have had a naval base that served the *classis Britannica*, the Roman fleet in the Channel, in similar fashion to the Saxon Shore forts of the south.[6]

Evidence of fifth-century activity in Parisii territory is varied. Beadlam villa yielded chip-carved ornaments and coins showing prosperity at the beginning of the fifth century.[7] The Langton villa survived a possible attack in *c*.367, after which its economy flourished well into the fifth century. Several native farmsteads in Humberside show evidence of occupation into the sixth century.[8] The kingdom of Deira is the most likely successor to the *civitas Parisiorum*, but it seems to have been controlled only briefly by Britons before Angles made it their own.

The Brigantes

Brigantia was the largest *civitas* in Roman Britain. *Brigantes* (the plural of *Brigans*) may derive from a Celtic root meaning 'high ones' or 'hill-dwellers.' Ptolemy locates the *Brigantes* in Wexford, Ireland, as well as in

---

4   See Miller, 1975a.
5   See chapter 2 above.
6   Johnson, 1980, 130.
7   Ramm, 1978, 131–2.
8   Ramm, 1978, 136.

Map 10.1 The kingdoms of northern Britain in the early Middle Ages.

northern Britain, and Bregenz in western Austria may also preserve the name. Most scholars believe the Brigantes were a tribal confederation, perhaps formed by one of Cartimandua's immediate ancestors.[9] The settlement pattern in Iron Age Brigantia was overwhelmingly rural and dispersed, with abandoned hill-forts and no apparent *oppidum*.[10] The principal tribal center, and Cartimandua's court, was Stanwick, in North Yorkshire, whose massive earthworks may have enclosed *oppidum*-like activity in the LPRIA.

Brigantian agriculture was mostly pastoral, and the leading industry in the Roman period was mining (lead, copper, and iron).[11] There were less than 20 villas in Brigantia, and nearly all were clustered around York (*Eburacum*), a legionary fortress and veterans' colony, and Aldborough

9   Hartley and Fitts, 1988, 1–2.
10   Hartley and Fitts, 1988, 68.
11   Hartley and Fitts, 1988, 88.

(*Isirium Brigantum*), the *civitas* capital.[12] Most of these villas were built in the third or early fourth century, more that ten generations after the Roman conquest of Brigantia.[13] Not one Roman inscription in the north shows a native Briton involved in commerce.

Constantine the Great strengthened the defenses at York, which may have been the headquarters of the *dux Britanniarum*. There is not much evidence of destruction in Brigantia around the time of the 'barbarian conspiracy' of 367, but soon after this a series of signal stations were built along the Yorkshire coast. These undoubtedly worked with the *classis Britannica*, and may have been part of the command of the *dux*. Spears, javelins, and spurs found at Catterick indicate the presence of a late Roman mounted unit.[14] But the presence of women and children in the Wall forts at this time suggests a general depletion of regular army forces in the north.[15]

Cist burials (e.g. at Crambeck and Wetherby) and placenames show the survival of British communities into the fifth century.[16] There is also evidence of urban survival at Aldborough, Catterick, Malton, and York.[17] We have already seen the evidence for industrial activity and the construction of buildings and defenses at York in the Brittonic Age.[18] New timber buildings were being constructed within the walls of Catterick in the fifth century, and finds of early Saxon graves and goods near the Roman amphitheater may indicate the settlement of Germanic mercenaries by British authorities.[19] If these mercenaries had wrested control of the fort from the British community, this provides a reasonable context for the *Gododdin*'s Battle of Catraeth, usually identified with Catterick: a British war-band from the north trying to retake a southern fort, perhaps under the context of freeing the Britons who still occupied the *vicus*.

Ken Dark has suggested that York survived as the political center of Brigantia for much of the fifth and sixth centuries.[20] He points out that not only do much of its defenses survive, but also that it is the only Romano-British town north of the Humber to yield imported Mediterranean amphoras (see table 10.1). The road connecting York to the Wall forts was maintained after 410, and many of the forts themselves show signs of fifth- and sixth-century occupation.[21] Should we see fifth-century York as

12   Hartley and Fitts, 1988, 72.
13   Higham, 1993, 40.
14   Hartley and Fitts, 1988, 114.
15   Hartley and Fitts, 1988, 111.
16   Faull, 1984, 49; Hartley and Fitts, 1988, 116.
17   Dark, 1992, 113.
18   See chapter 5 above; and Dark, 1994, 74.
19   Cramp, 1999, 4.
20   Dark, 1994, 74.
21   See Dark, 1992; and discussion below.

Table 10.1 Post-Roman imported pottery in northern Britain and Scotland.

	ARSW	PRSW	Bi	Bii	Biv	Bv	Bvi	Bmisc	D ware	E ware
Dumbarton			*	*						*
Lincoln				*						
Mote of Mark	*		*		*	*		*	*	*
Whithorn			*	*	*			*	*	*
York				*	*					*

ARSW	African Red Slip Ware: popular fine wares produced in North Africa (probably Carthage), late fifth to early sixth century;
PRSW	Phocaean Red Slip Ware: fine wares produced in western Turkey (probably Phocaea), c.500;
Bi	Bi amphoras: wine jars produced in the eastern Aegean, mid sixth century;
Bii	Bii amphoras: wine jars produced in the eastern Mediterranean (Nubia, Cyprus and Antioch have all been proposed), mid to late fifth century;
Biv	Biv handled jars: one- and two-handled water (?) jars produced in Asia Minor (probably Sardis), mid fifth to mid sixth century;
Bv	Byzacena amphoras: large cylindrical oil containers produced in the Byzacena region of North Africa, late fifth century;
Bvi	Gaza amphoras: large cylindrical wine(?) containers produced at Gaza, mid fifth to mid sixth century;
Bmisc	B miscellaneous amphoras;
D WARE	Grey ware bowls produced in the Bordeaux region, sixth century;
E WARE	Kitchenware (jars, pots, bowls, jugs, pitchers, and beakers), some pieces containing traces of purple dye. Produced in western Gaul, c.600–700.

Source: Thomas, 1981; and Snyder, 1996.

the seat of a lingering Roman military commander, or is it rather the administrative center of a revived Brigantian dynasty? Peter Field has suggested that York, not Caerleon, is Gildas's *urbs legionem* – 'the city of the legions' – and the site of one of Arthur's battles in the *Historia Brittonum*.[22] Gildas decries the fact that Britons can no longer travel safely to the shrines of Sts. Aaron and Julian in the *urbs legionem* because of 'the unhappy partition with the barbarians,' suggesting that the city (or lands surrounding it) had recently fallen to the English.[23] However, York (*Ebrauc*) survives in Welsh verse and pedigrees as a British royal center associated with sixth-century princes like Peredur.

Nick Higham has argued that both York and Aldborough were in a state of decline in the Late Roman period, and that Catterick became the true center of Brigantia.[24] But while archaeological evidence verifies fifth- and sixth-century activity there, the character of that activity is tied up with our understanding of the Battle of Catraeth, currently a matter of much debate (see below). Brigantia, then, has several candidates for fifth-century political centers, but no British kingdom survived long enough for us to be certain about royal capitals.

The Carvetii

The Carvetii occupied a much smaller territory and may have been subservient to the Brigantes. The name *Carvetii* means 'deer people.' The *civitas Carvetiorum* has been identified from two local Roman inscriptions, one of which commemorates a decurion. Early Roman inscriptions from Brougham and Old Penrith show a native aristocracy bearing mostly Celtic names, though in some cases the sons of these aristocrats have adopted Greco-Roman names.[25] Although the identity of the pre-Roman tribal center is uncertain, Carlisle (*Luguvalium*) was the major Roman settlement and was elevated to the status of *civitas* capital rather late, perhaps in the third century. By the fourth century Carlisle may have been the headquarters for the command of Hadrian's Wall, under the *dux Britanniarum*, but this is still debated.[26]

Archaeological evidence indicates tremendous cultural conservatism among the Carvetii. Native habitation types dating back to the Bronze Age, such as round huts and enclosures, continue to be dominant in the Late

22 Field, 1999.
23 *De Excidio*, 10.2.
24 Higham, 1993, 90.
25 Higham and Jones, 1991, 13–14.
26 Dark, 1994, 70.

Iron Age and the early Roman period.[27] There were no villas in the *civitas*, and Cumbrian industrial activity in the Roman period included stone-quarrying and lead-mining, similar to the pattern we observed in Cornwall.

The second half of the fourth century was a time of instability in the *civitas*. The emperor Constans came to Britain in 343 and is credited with a victory over the barbarians in the north, which Ammianus Marcellinus indicates were Picts, Scots, and Attacotti. In 367 the *dux Britanniarum* was captured (at Carlisle?), part of Bewcastle was destroyed, and Rudchester, Haltonchesters, South Shields, and Wallsend show some signs of abandonment.[28] Ravenglass, possibly a fleet base, also shows signs of destruction *c*.367.[29] There is archaeological evidence that some of the Cumbrian coastal forts were rebuilt at this time to protect against raids coming from across the Irish Sea. Lancaster, listed in the *Notitia Dignitarum*, was a Saxon Shore type coastal fort built, according to coin evidence, during the reign of Constans.[30] The *civitas Carvetii* may have been included in the province of Valentia, created by Theodosius *c*.370 during his strengthening and reorganization of British defenses.

It is uncertain whether continental *foederati* were settled this far west. An irregular unit of Frisian cavalry was stationed at Housesteads in the late Roman period. Coin sequences and ceramic dating end in the early fifth century, and as yet no imported pottery – Gallic or Mediterranean – has been found in sub-Roman Cumbria. Birdoswald and Ravenglass are candidates for Bannavem Taburniae, St. Patrick's enigmatic hometown,[31] and at Ravenglass a bath-house wall still stands at a height of 10 feet. Early British monasteries may be indicated by churches within elliptical enclosures at Hoddom (associated with St. Kentigern), Ruthwell, and Ninkirk ('Ninian's church').[32] Numerous church dedications to Kentigern found in Carvetian lands may date to the sixth century, but are just as likely a result of Strathclyde influence in the tenth century.[33]

The strongest evidence of British activity in the sub-Roman period comes from Carlisle (*Caer Luel*, from the British name *Luguvalos*). At Blackfriars Street two Roman masonry buildings were reconstructed in timber in the early fifth century, replaced after a time by a large hall-like building.[34] A large town-house on Scotch Street also showed signs of continued use and

---

27   Higham and Jones, 1991, 8.
28   Higham and Jones, 1991, 124–5.
29   Higham, 1986, 236.
30   Higham and Jones, 1991, 123–4.
31   See chapter 6 above.
32   Higham and Jones, 1991, 130–1.
33   See Higham and Jones, 1991, 132; and discussion below.
34   Snyder, 1996, 45.

wear in the fifth century. Most remarkable, however, is the continuity of the British Christian community at Carlisle. When St. Cuthbert visited Carlisle in the seventh century, he was greeted by a man described as *praepositus civitatis*, and was able to walk along the town walls and see a working fountain (implying that there was a still-functioning aqueduct).[35] The British church at Carlisle was formally granted in 685 to Cuthbert, who grew up among Britons in the Tweed basin and may have been bilingual.[36] Another grant to Cuthbert's church 'included the estate of Cartmel [south Cumbria] with all the Britons belonging to it.'[37]

'On the whole,' remark Higham and Jones, 'evidence supports the survival of a [British] peasantry and aristocracy into the sub-Roman period, capable of forming the basis of a strong successor state as late as the last quarter of the sixth century.'[38] That successor state was Rheged, a vast but short-lived northern kingdom of which Cumbria likely comprised a southern district.

Britons beyond the Wall: the Novantae, the Selgovae, the Damnonii, and the Votadini

The tribes between the walls formed a buffer zone between the unconquered Picts and the Roman province to the south. Because Roman roads and military installations continued to be used in this area, it is presumed that Rome had established treaties with these British tribes, none of whom are named as raiders even in the tumultuous years of the third and fourth centuries. Contact with the south is confirmed by the large number of Roman coins and other small objects found in native settlements between the walls.

Unfortunately, we have almost no contemporary written records describing the fate of these inter-wall tribes. Identifying them geographically means relying upon Ptolemy's map of the province, an occasional placename, and the claims of early medieval dynasts. The Novantae are to be located in Galloway and Dumfries. Later kings of Galloway traced their ancestry back to Magnus Maximus, recalling ties (perhaps military) with Late Roman Britain.[39] The Selgovae seem to have been based in the Tweed River basin. Their name means 'the Hunters.'[40] Almost nothing is known of them during the Roman period, but they may have resurfaced in the composition of the post-Roman British kingdom of Bernicia. The

---

35 *Vita Sancti Cuthberti*, 4, written by an anonymous monk of Lindisfarne *c*.700.
36 See Phythian-Adams, 1996, 87.
37 Higham, 1986, 292.
38 Higham and Jones, 1991, 137.
39 Higham and Jones, 1991, 126.
40 Thomas, 1997, 86.

Damnonii were based in the Clyde River basin. They seem to be the basis from which the kingdom of Strathclyde sprang.

We are on slightly better ground in discussing the Votadini, due to some significant archaeological finds. The Votadini are without dispute the basis of the early medieval British kingdom known as Gododdin. In the Roman period the Votadini were in control of territory extending throughout Lothian and just north of the Firth of Forth. Most people have assumed that the tribal center of the Votadini was Traprain Law. Excavations in the early twentieth century revealed Neolithic and Iron Age artifacts, intense domestic and industrial activity in the early Bronze Age, and a Late Roman rampart and house under whose floor was buried a substantial hoard of Roman silver datable to the reign of Honorius (AD 395–423). Current excavation of the summit has produced a single early Christian burial, and Peter Hill has suggested that the silver hoard and burials indicate a religious rather than a royal use of the hill during the Iron Age and Roman periods.[41]

A religious function has also been proposed for the post-Roman occupation of Cramond, on the River Almond near Edinburgh.[42] Cramond was an important military base during the Antonine occupation of Scotland and the early third-century Severan campaigns. Though the fort was likely evacuated in AD 211 or 212, sporadic finds indicate use from the fourth to the tenth centuries. The earliest form of the name, *Caramonde*, preserves the Brythonic element *cair/caer* ('fort') plus the river name Amon, and therefore means 'fort on the river Almond'; the name must have originated prior to the conquest of this area by Anglo-Saxon Northumbria in the middle of the seventh century. While Cramond's Roman defenses were apparently not reused after the Severan campaigns, activity did continue at the fort's administrative center, where the medieval church and churchyard were later established. Craig Cessford has postulated that ownership of the fort passed into the hands of the native dynasty of the Votadini after its abandonment by Roman forces, and that the Votadini prized Cramond for its location (on a Roman road and with access to the sea) and quarry. At some point, whether by British or English clerics, a church was established within the walls of the fort, maintaining Cramond's importance long after its Roman functions had ceased.

British Survival along Hadrian's Wall

Before examining the successor kingdoms, it is worth noting that not every British polity in the north in the fifth century developed from Iron Age

41   See *British Archaeology*, 57 (Feb. 2001).
42   See Cessford, 2001.

tribal roots. It is now becoming clear that activity continued along Hadrian's Wall throughout the fifth century and perhaps into the sixth. Ken Dark was the first to direct our attention to the increasing amount of material evidence being uncovered at the Wall forts.[43] This need not, however, have much to do with the continuity of Roman military commands. Rather, the new halls and strengthened walls of these forts may have been the work of *tyranni* who, like their southern contemporaries, derived their power from a mixture of military abilities, dynastic claims, and clientage.

The most complex and intriguing activity went on at Birdoswald, on the western section of the Wall.[44] A depleted but still active garrison dismantled the fort's large stone granaries, installing a hearth in one to use it as an assembly hall. Sometime after *c*.420, new lean-to structures appeared utilizing both existing Roman masonry and new timber (see plate 10.1). After this phase, probably in the late fifth century, a defensive bank was revetted and extensive timber structures were built, including a hall-type building on the rubble-platform of a granary and a reconstructed gateway. This occupation continued until about 520, according to the most recent excavator, Tony Wilmott. Wilmott sees the Birdoswald *limitanei* as having local roots and, by the fourth century, integrated into the local community, perhaps as landowners.[45] Such soldiers would have stayed put after 410, supported by food from the local community in exchange for defense.

Elmet

Starting below the Wall and moving northward, the first British kingdom we encounter is Elmet. Though attested in early written sources, Elmet is not easy to define in terms of territorial limits and population.[46] It appears from placename evidence that Elmet at first covered much of west and south Yorkshire, with a western boundary near Craven, itself a possible minor British kingdom. Elmet's northeastern and southern boundaries may have been marked by a series of linear earthworks, the Aberford Dykes complex and the Roman Ridge, which separated Elmet from Deira and Mercia respectively.[47] These dykes, though difficult to date, not only marked British territory but may also (along with possible reoccupied

43 Dark, 1992.
44 See Wilmott, 1997.
45 Wilmott, 1997, 225.
46 See Taylor, 1992.
47 Hartley and Fitts, 1988, 116; Higham, 1993, 61, 87; Wood, 1996.

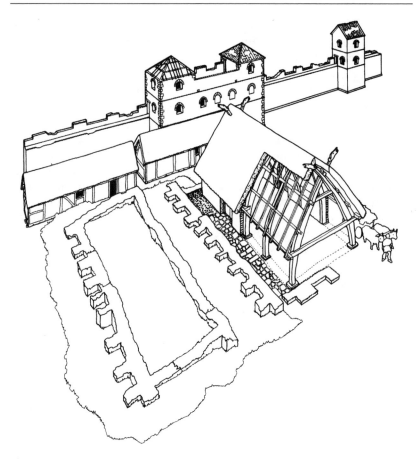

Plate 10.1   Reconstruction drawing of the post-Roman timber hall at Birdoswald, along Hadrian's Wall. (© English Heritage.)

hill-forts in the area) have protected Elmet from its English neighbors. Bede links Leeds with Elmet, stating, for instance, that the region of *Loidis* (Leeds) is within 'the forest of Elmet.'[48] There are also ties with Wales. An early Christian inscription from Caernarvonshire reads ALIORTVS ELMETIACOS HIC IACET, 'Aliortus the Elmetian lies here.'[49] The Welsh equivalent of Elmet, Elfed, is the name of a *cantref* of Dyfed. With Deiran expansion, some Britons would have naturally fled Elmet and headed to any number of western kingdoms.

48   Bede, *EH*, 2.14.
49   *ECMW*, no. 87.

Poetic sources mention the names of two early kings of Elmet, Gwallawc and Madog. Madog fell at the Battle of Catraeth, while Gwallawc fought against the Deirans *c.585* and is described in the Taliesin poetry as 'judge over Elmet.' The last British king of Elmet was Cerdic, or Ceredig, possibly the son of Gwallawc, who reigned in the early seventh century. According to British sources, Cerdic was defeated by Edwin of Deira and expelled from Elmet in 617.[50] It may have been an act of vengeance, for during Æthelfrith's last years one Hereric, nephew of Edwin and father of the abbess Hilda, was poisoned while in exile at the court of Elmet.[51] The English takeover of British Elmet was perhaps the inevitable result of Deiran expansion. While Gildas tells us that the Saxons were settled 'on the east side of the island' to protect against Pictish raids, cemetery evidence tells us that there were actually very few Anglo-Saxons in the northeast in the fifth century. The English in Lindsey and the East Riding of Yorkshire did not, apparently, expand far beyond the settlements established by the Britons for defense before the late fifth century.[52] By the second half of the sixth century, however, the vigorous dynasty of Ida and Æthelfrith put the freedom of Elmet and surrounding British communities into serious jeopardy as it began to construct Northumbria.

Elmet (*Elmetsæte*) appears in the late seventh-century Tribal Hidage, where it is characterized as a minor kingdom (only 600 hides). But Mercia and Deira may have split Elmet territory between them, and thus the 600 hides could be just the Mercian portion of Elmet.[53] Dark believes that Elmet was a sub-kingdom of the Brigantes in the fifth and sixth centuries, and that it continued to be recognized as a British enclave by the Northumbrian kings.[54] The survival of British communities within Elmet after it passed into English control may be implied by the numerous *Ecles-* placenames in west Yorkshire and Lancashire, and *Wal-* placenames in these areas as well as in Durham.[55] In Lancashire, the British system of rights to cattle pastures survived centuries later as the *horngeld*.[56] A proliferation of St. Helen holy wells in the Yorkshire region may indicate the survival of a British cult of Constantine's mother.

---

50   *AC*, s.a. 616; *HB*, 63. Kirby, 2000, 60, suggests that this date is too early.
51   Bede, *EH*, 4.23. See Kirby, 2000, 60–1.
52   Eagles, 1980, 287.
53   M. Ziegler, pers. com.
54   Dark, 1994, 151–2.
55   Taylor, 1992; Higham, 1993, 101.
56   Higham, 1993, 102–3.

Deira and Bernicia

Northumbria was constructed by uniting two large kingdoms, Deira and Bernicia, both of which had British roots. To begin with, the names *Deira* and *Bernicia* are of British origin, the former being an Anglicization of *Deru* ('oak') and the latter of *Bernech* or *Bernaccia*.[57] Deira approximates the territory of the Parisii, where both the River Derwent and Malton (*Derventio*) are located. Bernicia, perhaps the post-Roman kingdom of the Selgovae, was separated from its northern neighbor Gododdin by the Lammermuir Hills.

The royal seat of Bernicia may have been Bamburgh. This fort, which Bede describes as a royal *urbs*, was originally held by British kings, judging by linguistic evidence and the presence of native pottery.[58] Ida, the reputed first king of Anglian Bernicia, may have seized Bamburgh from the Britons after defeating their king Outigern (Euderyn) in the mid-sixth century. According to the *Historia Brittonum*, Æthelfrith (r.592–616) renamed Bamburgh, which bore the British name *Din-Guaïroï*, 'Bebbanburg' in honor of his queen, Bebba.[59] Recent excavation of the cemetery at the base of the fortress has revealed signs of a transition between British and Anglian inhabitants at Bamburgh.[60] The cemetery, in use from about the late fifth century through the eighth century (and perhaps beyond), contained several unaccompanied long-cist graves oriented west–east, typical of British Christian burial (see plate 10.2 and figure 10.1). Isotope analysis of teeth from other, simple dug graves (dating to the seventh century), revealed individuals of non-local origin, including a male from Iona or the Lake District.

Æthelfrith ruled over both Deira and Bernicia and received tribute from the British king of Elmet. After the latter died in 616, Edwin absorbed Elmet. Higham has frequently discussed his notion of a developing Northumbrian over-kingship, in which several British kings – from Wales and the north – came to Yeavering to pay tribute to Æthelfrith.[61] A similar power is attributed to Edwin, who held Cadwallon 'personally responsible' for collecting tribute from the Welsh kings. This is surely an exaggeration of the situation, based on too literal an interpretation of Bede's biased evaluation of the Northumbrian kings.[62] In any case, such tribute

57   Higham, 1993, 59, 81.
58   Faull, 1984, 52.
59   *HB*, 63. See also Bede, *EH*, 3.6.
60   Pending publication of the excavations, see the following web sites: <http://www.bamburghresearchproject.co.uk/> and <http://www.mun.ca/mst/heroicage/issues/4/Bamburgh.html>.
61   See Higham, 1993, 111, 116.
62   See Kirby, 2000, 70.

Plate 10.2   A long-cist burial from the early medieval cemetery at Bamburgh. The style and orientation suggest that this was a Christian Briton. (Photo courtesy of Bamburgh Research Project.)

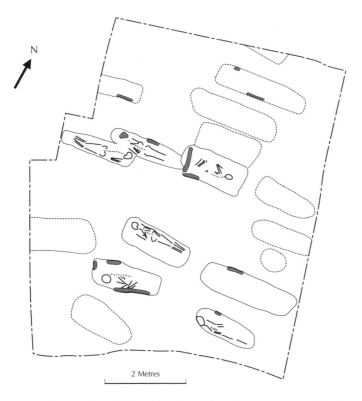

Figure 10.1   A long-cist burial from the early medieval cemetery at Bamburgh.

paying was short-lived, for the alliance of Cadwallon and Penda brought down Edwin and temporarily reversed the situation. Cadwallon ravaged Northumbria in 634 and controlled both Deira and Bernicia, perhaps with the aid of northern Britons. A year later, Æthelfrith's son Oswald killed Cadwallon at the Battle of Heavenfield and retook control of Northumbria, whose northern border was extended into Lothian by 638.

Cadwallon's actions in Northumbria are unclear. Kirby suggests that, if Cadwallon believed himself to be descended from the Votadini chieftain Cunedda, he may well have wished to support Gododdin in its continuing war with the northern Angles.[63] Higham sees Cadwallon's actions as an attempt to resuscitate British kingship and the British Church in the north, in essence to reverse the previous fifty years of Anglian gains.[64] The successes of Ida, Æthelfrith, Edwin, and bishop Paulinus had come at the expense of the Britons. But Oswald and his successors may have sought a rapprochement with their British neighbors. According to the *Historia Brittonum*, Oswald's brother Oswiu married Rieinmellt, daughter of Royth, son of Rhun of Rheged.[65] Oswald may have married a niece or other kinswoman of King Beli of Strathclyde, though Alex Wolf has suggested that Beli married a daughter of Edwin of Deira by his first wife Coenburgh.[66] In any case, Mercians had replaced Britons as the most serious threat to the Northumbrian kings. The next burst of expansionist energy came in the person of Ecgfrith, who sought to expand Northumbrian control beyond the Forth in 685. His disastrous defeat by the Picts at the Battle of Nechtanesmere (Dunichen Moss) signaled to the northern Britons, as well as the Picts and Scots, that Northumbria would no longer be a serious threat in Scotland.

Bede gives testimony to the role that Iona monks played in the creation of a Christian Northumbria, but he is silent on the northern British clergy. Both Oswald and Oswiu were baptized as refugees on Iona, most likely by the half-British abbot Fergna (*c*.616). Melrose, which lay on the route from Iona to Lindisfarne, was a Bernician abbey with a British name and perhaps a partially surviving British community. But as the English acquired more and more British lands, the British clergy in the north were not wont to cooperate with them. From Ripon *c*.670 Wilfrid observed all the surrounding lands to which the British clergy had fled during the English conquests, suggesting to the Northumbrian kings that these lands should be given rightfully to their new bishop (i.e. himself).[67] While the

---

63   Kirby, 2000, 72.
64   Higham, 1993, 124–6.
65   See Ziegler, 2001.
66   Wolfe, 1998, 162.
67   Eddius Stephanus, *Life of Wilfrid*, 17.

British kings and clergy fled, presumably the British parishioners remained behind and were granted to Wilfrid, like those Britons in Carlisle who were granted to Cuthbert just a few years later.[68]

Rheged

In the eyes of the Welsh, the most illustrious of the northern British kingdoms was certainly Rheged. Urien, famed king of Rheged in the later sixth century, was the subject of a large body of praise-poetry associated with the greatest of the early Welsh bards, Taliesin. Yet we know little for certain about the home of Urien and Taliesin. Because it apparently straddled the western portion of Hadrian's Wall, Rheged must have included lands of both the Carvetii and the Novantae. Dunragit in Wigtonshire may preserve the name of the kingdom (*Dun-Recet*, 'the fort of Rheged'), but few other clues exist. Its northern border likely extended up to Ayrshire, where the minor British kingdom of Aeron was eventually absorbed by either Rheged or Strathclyde.

An early center of some import was the Mote of Mark, a craggy hillock rising above a side estuary of the Solway Firth. Its summit is enclosed by a timber-reinforced stone wall, built in the mid to late fifth century and destroyed by fire a century or so later.[69] Excavations revealed imported Gaulish pottery, Germanic glass, and an assemblage of pins, brooches, and jewelry-making equipment (including molds for producing interlace metalwork). Though not founded on the site of an Iron Age hill-fort, the Mote of Mark appears to be a princely *llys* (court) with attendant jeweler, comparable to several reoccupied hill-forts in Wales and the southwest. Alternatively, the Mote may have been a purely industrial site, a metalworking center protected by wooden ramparts which served British and later English aristocrats.

Rheged may have formed gradually from the unification of smaller northern polities, including Carlisle and native forts. We may glimpse some of these petty kings at the Battle of Arderydd (Arthuret, in Cumbria) in 573.[70] According to the *Annales Cambriae*, it was a battle between Gwenddolau ab Ceidio and 'the sons of Eliffer,' in which 'Gwenddolau fell and Myrddin went mad.'[71] Gwenddolau's power base was probably Carwinley (*Caer-Wenddoleu*), about 10 miles north of Car-

68   Higham, 1993, 99–100.
69   Longley, 1982.
70   See Miller, 1975b.
71   On Myrddin, see discussion below and in chapter 12.

NORTHERN BRITISH DYNASTIES

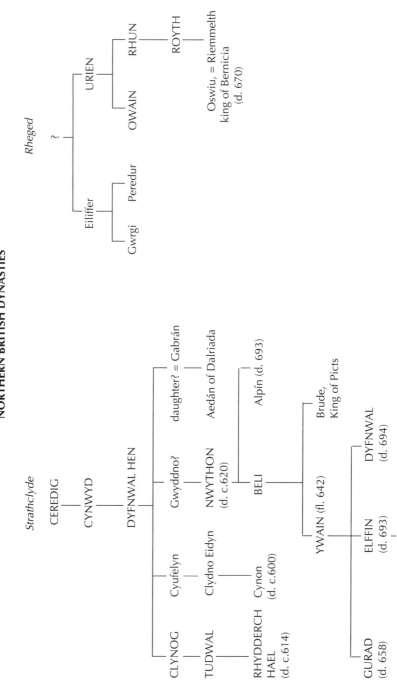

Rheged

?

Eiliffer

Gwrgi   Peredur

URIEN

OWAIN   RHUN

ROYTH

Oswiu, = Riemmelth
king of Bernicia
(d. 670)

Strathclyde

CEREDIG

CYNWYD

DYFNWAL HEN

CLYNOG   Cyufelyn   Clydno Eidyn   Cynon (d. c.600)   Gwyddno?   NWYTHON (d. c.620)   daughter? = Gabrán

TUDWAL

RHYDDERCH HAEL (d. c.614)

Aedán of Dalriada

BELI

Alpín (d. 693)

YWAIN (fl. 642)

Brude, King of Picts

GURAD (d. 658)   ELFFIN (d. 693)   DYFNWAL (d. 694)

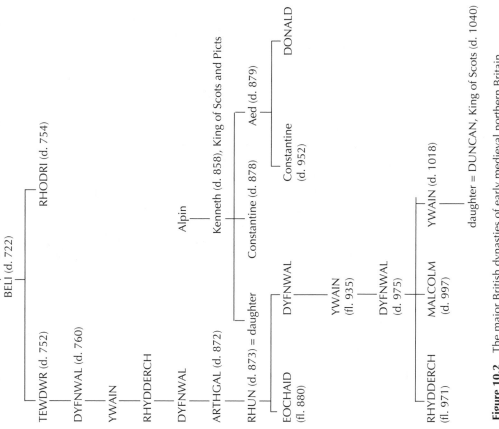

Figure 10.2 The major British dynasties of early medieval northern Britain.

lisle. The sons of Eliffer (Gwenddolau's uncle in the pedigrees) include Peredur and Gwrgi, both killed at the battle of *Caer Greu* in 580. In the Myrddin poems, however, the chief opponent of Gwenddolau was Rhydderch of Strathclyde (see below). The scattered geography points to the difficulty in using non-contemporary annals, poetry, and pedigrees to reconstruct a presumably historical battle. Gwenddolau would appear to have been a minor northern chieftain involved in an intra-dynastic dispute, though one Welsh elegy describes him as *pen teernet goglet*, 'the chief of the kings of the North.' Another Cumbrian dynasty may have been established at the Roman fort of *Derventio* (Papcastle) by Pabo, whose son Dunod died in 595, according to the *Annales Cambriae*.

Dunod ap Pabo, who was also present at Arthuret, was, according to the poets, the enemy of Owain ap Urien. Urien's dynasty may have ruled over the lands of the Novantae, the Carvetii, and the Brigantes. Urien's court is located in the Taliesin poems at *Llwyfenyd*, Lyvennet in Cumbria. There is an undated hut-group in this area (Burwens), and a banked enclosure (the Park Pale), but no hill-fort presents itself as an obvious candidate.[72] Higham and Jones believe this is because royal authority in Rheged was decentralized, with itinerant kings moving from estate to estate, while Dark prefers to see Rheged's royalty as based in Carlisle.[73] *Canu Taliesin* regards Urien as the ruler of Catraeth, and Rosemary Cramp has suggested that Anglian leaders took over control of Catraeth after Urien's death.[74] Catterick is a bit far to the southeast of Rheged's center, and if Urien controlled it this speaks of an extraordinarily widespread authority. 'The stark truth,' warns Tim Clarkson, 'is that we still cannot define with confidence the heartland of Rheged, still less its frontier provinces, and we cannot therefore weave with unchecked enthusiasm our hypotheses concerning the kingdom's foreign policy.'[75]

According to the *Historia Brittonum*, Urien was murdered by his ally Morcant, a prince of Gododdin, while he was besieging the Bernician king Theodoric (r.572–9) at Lindisfarne.[76] Urien 'possessed so much superiority over all the kings in military science,' wrote the chronicler, perhaps explaining the volume of praise-poetry that survives. Higham sees the assassination of Urien Rheged as marking the end of the northern Britons' ability to resist Northumbrian expansion.[77] It may also have signaled the beginning of the end for the kingdom of Rheged, which suf-

72   Higham and Jones, 1991, 133.
73   Higham and Jones, 1991, 133; Dark, 1994, 72.
74   Cramp, 1999, 4.
75   Clarkson, 1999a.
76   *HB*, 63.
77   Higham, 1993, 99.

fered from the expansion of Northumbria and Mercia as well as northern British kingdoms like Strathclyde. Arthuret may, indeed, represent an effort by lesser British kings to seize pieces of Urien's hegemony upon his death. Riemmelth (d.642), great-granddaughter of Urien and perhaps the last of the royal British line of Rheged, was married to the Northumbrian prince Oswiu around 635, but the ultimate fate of Rheged still remains a mystery.

Both placename evidence and early work on blood-group distribution (showing a similarity between the modern Cumbrian population and that of central Wales) indicate continuity of the local British population after 600 with little influx of English peasants from Northumbria.[78] The rugged terrain of Cumbria makes it likely that Anglian influence there was gradual rather than the result of a sudden and decisive conquest.[79] British placenames dominate particularly in north Cumbria, near the minor headwater tributaries of the major river-systems.[80] The kings of Rheged may have departed, but a Brittonic-speaking population remained, continuing to name local fortified places (*caers*) after British kings and folk-heroes. Those who called themselves 'Cumbrians' in this period, writes the local historian Charles Phythian-Adams, 'never ceased to feel in some sense British despite their semi-Anglian context.'[81]

Gododdin

The most dramatic collapse of a northern British kingdom belongs to Gododdin. Linguistically, the Votadini become *Guotodin*, the kingdom of Gododdin. By the sixth century the royal seat was certainly in Edinburgh (*Din Eidyn*), probably at Castle Rock, beneath the medieval castle where excavators have proposed aristocratic residence on the summit dating from the Late Roman period.[82] A region or sub-kingdom called Manau or Manaw was centered around Stirling Castle, Bede's *urbs Giudi*.[83] Other forts are scattered throughout Lothian, like Dunbar, whose great timber hall likely belonged to a sixth-century British prince. Similar halls were uncovered at Doon Hill and Yeavering, both of which were probably British strongholds taken over by the English in the sixth century.

In the poem *Y Gododdin*, Din Eidyn is the fortress where the British

---

78 See Higham and Jones, 1991, 138.
79 Phythian-Adams, 1996, 51.
80 See Phythian-Adams, 1996, 83.
81 Phythian-Adams, 1996, 109.
82 Driscoll and Yeoman, 1997, 226–9.
83 Thomas, 1997, 88.

king Mynyddog Mwynvawr feasts his assembled war-band before their disastrous raid on the Deirans at Catraeth, witnessed by the bard Aneirin. While the *Historia Brittonum* depicts Aneirin as a contemporary of Maelgwn Gwynedd (d.547) and Ida of Northumbria (r.547–59), most scholars have tended to date the battle toward the end of the sixth century and, as we have seen, identified Catterick as the site of the battle. Historians have long realized the difficulty in trying to reconstruct the exact details of this campaign, based on an elegiac and grandiose poem. Nevertheless, other details about British culture can be culled from these lines. Jenny Rowland, for example, has read the references to warfare and weapons in the poem as indicating that the British war-band consisted of light cavalry wielding swords and javelins.[84]

John Koch has recently published a new edition of *Y Gododdin* with a radical reinterpretation of both its textual history and its historical context.[85] Koch argues that the oral *Gododdin* tradition passed from Lothian to Strathclyde before the mid-seventh century, where the Ur-text then split into two versions: one (A) traveled to Wales in the late seventh century, the other (B) stayed in Strathclyde for another two centuries. Koch doubts that the 'first poet' (not Aneirin) made any claims to be at the battle of Catraeth, which he redates to c.570, and also doubts that the Gododdin army was wiped out at the battle. Mynyddog Mwynvawr was not the name of the Gododdin's lord – it was a description meaning 'mountain feast' or 'mountain chief' – who could be either Ureui of Eiddin or Gwlyget Gododdin.[86] Using evidence from *Canu Taliesin* and other Welsh verse, Koch argues that Urien of Rheged was the true victor of Catraeth; that he and Rhydderch of Strathclyde, backing the Coeling claimant to Elmet, Gwallawc, cut down the Gododdin army, which was traveling south to support the other Elmet claimant, Madauc; that Deirans aided Urien at Catraeth while Bernicians fought with the Gododdin war-band; and that Urien remained overlord of Catraeth by tolerating the Anglo-Saxons settled there and by allying himself with the predominantly Anglian polity of Deira. Such intra-British strife, recorded by the 'first poet,' was suppressed by later Welsh and Strathclyde poets for nationalist purposes, and the English became the one and only enemy of the British.

Oliver Padel and Tim Clarkson have pointed out the weaknesses in this reconstruction.[87] It rests on Koch's equation of *Canu Taliesin*'s Battle of Gwen Ystrat with the Battle of Catraeth. While the former battle is de-

---

84   Rowland, 1995.
85   Koch, 1997.
86   On Mynyddog, see also Isaac, 1990.
87   Padel, 1998; Clarkson, 1999.

picted as a victory by Urien Rheged leading the men of Catraeth, it is not placed at Catraeth in the poem and seems rather to have occurred at a place called Llech Wen in the valley of Gwen. Furthermore, no Gododdin warriors appear in Taliesin's poem on Gwen Ystrat. Other British elite sites in Gododdin, like Coldingham, Abercorn, and Dunbar (all coastal sites), were seized by the English in the late sixth and early seventh centuries.

The Annals of Ulster record the *obsesio Etin* in 638, which has been interpreted as the destruction of Din Eidyn and the absorption of Gododdin by the Northumbrian king Oswald.[88] As Cessford has pointed out, this is only an interpretation, for the annal entry identifies neither who was involved in the siege nor the outcome.[89] After Oswald's death, when Penda and the Welsh kings harassed his brother Oswiu c.642–55, they chased him to the northern extremes of Northumbrian territory, to Iüdeu (Stirling), beyond Edinburgh.[90] English kings would rule over Lothian for several centuries, though again we should expect little true demographic change in the indigenous British population.

Strathclyde

Strathclyde was the last surviving British kingdom in the north. It seems to derive from the territory of the Damnonii (or Dumnonii), and its royal citadel, Dumbarton Rock, preserves the root *Dum-*. Bede knew Dumbarton as *Alcluith* (*Alt Clut*), 'the Rock of the Clyde,' and described it as *civitas Brettonum munitissima*, 'a most fortified place of the Britons.'[91] Its twin craggy summits are indeed still imposing. Excavations have revealed a dry-stone terrace or fighting platform, laced and revetted with timber beams, built in the sixth century AD and repaired in the seventh.[92] Dumbarton has also yielded Merovingian glass and both imported Mediterranean amphoras and Gaulish pottery, suggesting to Alcock 'a family wealthy enough to acquire wine from the eastern Mediterranean [and perhaps] a resident jeweler.'[93]

The first recorded king of Strathclyde is one Ceredig, whom many have equated with the British tyrant Coroticus castigated by Patrick in the late fifth century.[94] But our information about Ceredig and his descendants

88 See Higham, 1986, 262.
89 Cessford, 1999, 152.
90 See Koch, 1997, liv.
91 *EH*, 1.12.
92 Alcock, 1983, 2.
93 Alcock, 1983, 4.
94 MacQuarrie, 1998, 2–6.

derives mostly from the problematic Harleian genealogies, which date to the ninth century. Adomnán writes that, in the time of St. Columba (d.597), Rhydderch ap Tudwal was 'King of Dumbarton.'[95] This is the man referred to in Welsh sources as Rhydderch Hael ('the Generous'), and may be one of the four British kings (*Ryderthen*) in the *Historia Brittonum* who fought against Theodoric of Bernicia. In the twelfth-century *Life of St. Kentigern* he appears as King Rederech, patron and friend of the saint, and in the Welsh poem *Yr Afallennau* ('The Appletrees') he is depicted as the victor of the Battle of Arderydd and tormentor of the mad prophet Myrddin.[96] While Rhydderch's historicity is secure, further details of his life come only from these late poetic and hagiographic sources.[97]

Adomnán portrays the kings of both British Strathclyde and Scottish Dalriada as being close to Columba, implying a friendship between the two kingdoms.[98] Bede and other sources similarly lump Britons, Scots, and Picts together as allies against Northumbria. The Pictish king Bridei was the son of Bili, a king of Strathclyde. But the career of Áedán mac Gabráin, King of the Dalriada Scots, shows that the situation was more complicated. According to the *Annals of Ulster*, Áedán led an expedition against the Picts in the Orkneys in 580 or 581, and two years later he was victorious in a campaign against *Manu*, which could be either Manaw in Gododdin or the Isle of Man. One Welsh Triad has him attacking Dumbarton. In 603, however, he led a great force through the British kingdoms to attack Æthelfrith at *Degsastan*, somewhere in the Scottish lowlands. It seems probable in this case that he had the assistance of Strathclyde and perhaps Rheged.

This campaign was a failure, and the British kingdoms were perhaps made to suffer for it. Strathclyde was, during the latter half of the seventh century, subject to some degree to the Northumbrian kings Oswald, Oswiu, and Ecgfrith. Eadberht of Northumbria laid siege to Dumbarton (with Pictish aid) in 756, but then lost nearly his entire army in a battle against the Britons at Newburgh on the Tyne. With Northumbria's decline in the eighth century, however, Strathclyde and Dalriada seem to have reached a peaceful equilibrium. And while Dalriada channeled its energies into Pictish affairs, Strathclyde was able to expand southward. But Viking incursions in the ninth century devastated Strathclyde, and the union of Dalriada and Pictland by Kenneth MacAlpin in 843 meant that a new and more powerful kingdom of Scotland could overwhelm the remaining Britons in the north. Irish Sea Vikings sacked Dumbarton in 870, and accord-

95 Adomnán, *Life of Columba*, 1.15.
96 See Tolstoy, 1985, 26ff.
97 See Clarkson, 1999b.
98 See Sharpe, in Admomnán, *Life of Columba*, note 97.

ing to the chronicles the death of Eochaid map Rhun, a grandson of Kenneth's, in 889 meant the extinction of the British kings of Strathclyde. The land was effectively annexed by the Scottish king Donald II, and the next year many of the surviving British nobles fled to Gwynedd.

While both Strathclyde and Rheged now ceased to exist as British kingdoms, a new entity – Cumberland – came into being in the tenth century with ties to both. It has been assumed that the revival of British power in the area around the Solway was the result of an extension of the kingdom of Stratchlyde.[99] Brittonic placenames in northeast Cumbria, along with the county name 'Cumbra-land,' have been used as evidence of Strathclyde influence. More recently, however, it has been argued that the new 'king of the Cumbrians' was chosen, by the Scottish monarchy, from among the surviving British aristocracy of Cumbria to rule both Cumbria and Stratchlyde under the suzerainty of Scotland.[100] It is also likely that these tenth-century kings of Cumberland had kinship ties to the old royal house of Strathclyde. They showed a renewed hostility toward the English, allowing further Irish–Norse settlement in the region (noticeable in placenames like Glenamara and Briscoe, 'wood of the Britons') and allying with Viking and Scottish leaders in rebellion against the English.

The English kings reacted by launching several northern expeditions. Æthelstan defeated a coalition of Britons, Scots, and Hiberno-Norse at *Brunaburh* in 937, and in 945 Edmund defeated the Cumbrian king Dunmail map Owain and tried to destroy his claims to the throne by blinding two of his sons. Edmund granted Cumbria to Malcolm I of Scotland, but British kings related to the Scottish royal house continued to rule Cumberland. Æthelred ravaged the region again in 1000, and the death of Owen the Bald *c.*1018 signaled the end of British royalty in the north. Duncan, grandson of the Scottish king Malcolm II, assumed the kingship of Strathclyde, and the Solway basin was incorporated within the Scottish kingdom.

The 'Heroic Society' of the North

The four centuries between the end of Roman Britain and the advent of the Vikings has been viewed, especially in northern Britain, as the Heroic Age. The exploits of the northern British kings, as sung by the great Welsh bards enjoying their own Golden Age, seem to echo the deeds of heroes in Celtic mythology, whose stage was a pre-Christian, Iron Age (or even

---

99   See, for example, Higham, 1986, 318.
100   Phythian-Adams, 1996, 109ff.

Bronze Age) society. Fighting is individualistic, gold torcs and swift chariots return, alcohol (especially mead) is consumed in large quantities by boastful warriors on couches in large feast-halls. Saints found churches and work miracles while bards entertain courts and mad prophets run with the animals.

The minimalist references to northern events in the annals almost force one to view the age through the eyes of the bard. Caution is advised. And yet, archaeological finds often support this picture. Extensive evidence of metalworking has been found on such northern British sites as the Mote of Mark, Buston crannog, Dalmahoy, and Whithorn.[101] Imported glass drinking vessels, penannular brooches, and silver chains have also come from such sites. It even works in the negative: Higham points out, for example, that neither the *Gododdin* nor Anglo-Saxon inhumations in the north suggest that helmets were commonly worn by either British or English warriors.[102]

If this was a Heroic Age, how did it become so? Ken Dark believes that the roots of the British heroic society lay in the Roman world of Late Antiquity, with its aristocratic clientage, elaborate feasts, and sung panegyrics.[103] In Late Roman Britain this may have been syncretistic, with local elites who were drawing on Iron Age custom and applying it in a new, Christian idiom. But north of the Wall it can hardly be anything but the perpetuation of Iron Age lifestyles, by both the elite and the peasantry who supported them.

'Taxation in kind,' remarks Higham, 'dominated by the estate owner . . . became the customary system of food rents by which Celtic (and eventually English) kings were maintained.'[104] The maintenance of the professional war-band required a farming peasantry, who in turn needed the warriors' protection. It was slaves, however, that provided the northern British kings with an entrée to the international markets, where they could acquire prestige items for their own households and for their retainers.[105] Patrick and Gildas testify that slave-raiding was endemic throughout Britain and Ireland, and warn Britons that they should not be engaging in slave transactions – especially Christian slaves – with the pagan Scots and Picts. Northern Britain seems to have been particularly active in the slave trade.

Much effort has been made lately by scholars to de-emphasize the differences between Britons and Saxons, especially in the north.[106] They point

---

101   See Cessford, 1999, 153.
102   Higham, 1993, 93.
103   Dark, 1994.
104   Higham, 1993, 61.
105   Higham, 1986, 252.
106   See, for example, Koch, 1997; and Clarkson, 1999.

to numerous cases of Anglo-British alliances as well as the constant inter-
necine strife between the British kingdoms. But let us not mistake the
politics of a few British kings with the sentiment of the average British
warrior. As Higham rightly points out, there is absolutely no evidence
that British warriors took service with English kings, nor vice versa.[107]
And, according to the written sources, there was little if any cooperation
between British and English clergy in the north. In addition to the hostile
words which Bede attributes to Wilfrid at the Synod of Whitby, Eddius
Stephanus describes the British clergy as 'fleeing from our own hostile
sword.'[108] There is even some evidence that northern British elites avoided
trade with their English neighbors, instead obtaining Germanic glassware,
for example, from continental wine merchants.[109]

From Bede we have inherited the tendency to view the early history of
Scotland from a Northumbrian perspective.[110] The British component of
Scottish history has never been fully examined. In southern Scotland, early
inscribed stones bearing British names are found in Galloway, in Lothian,
and in the Borders.[111] Craig Cessford has even suggested that some of the
alleged Pictish symbols carved on objects found in southern Scotland may
have been made by northern Britons.[112] Charles Thomas has emphasized
the persistence of the linguistic links between the Brittonic north and the
Brittonic south.[113] This can be seen in placenames, for example: Scotland's Terregles, Penpont, and Tranent are closely paralleled by Cornwall's Treveglos, Penpons, and Trenance. Here again we are seeing the
culturally conservative nature of Outer Zone Britons. Lloyd Laing has
pointed out that every single category of LPRIA settlement in the north
reappears in the early medieval period. 'The settlement types of Early
Christian Scotland,' he writes, 'are those of the Iron Age,' just as the British kingdoms of the north so frequently reflect the tribal structure of the
LPRIA.[114]

Ultimately, the Britons of the north were absorbed by the emerging
states of England and Scotland. The Norman Conquest of 1066 certainly
did not reverse this process. But the new Norman lords of England entered into a complicated love–hate relationship with the Britons. While

107   Higham, 1993, 97.
108   Eddius Staphanus, *Life of Wilfrid*, 17.
109   Cessford, 1999, 157.
110   See Cessford, 1999.
111   Redknap, 1995, 754.
112   Cessford, 1999, 155.
113   Thomas, 1997, 90.
114   Laing, 1975, 33–5.

they did have aspirations of acquiring land in the surviving British king-doms – Brittany and Wales – the Normans also developed, under French influence, a love for British tales about Arthur and Merlin. These legendary Britons, with their connections to the Heroic Age of North Britain, would come to dominate the next chapter of Brittonic history.

Part IV

Conquest, Survival, and Revival

11

Normans and Britons

By the year 1000 both Brittany and Cornwall had been reduced to the status of counties within, respectively, the kingdoms of France and England. In 1063 Gruffydd ap Llywelyn, the only Welsh king to rule all of Wales, was assassinated and his widow was soon after betrothed to Gruffydd's foe, Harold Godwinsson. Also dead by the end of the eleventh century was Owen, the last British king of Strathclyde–Cumbria, and his people were absorbed by the Scottish kingdom. The Brittonic speaking peoples, who had been gradually pushed to Europe's Atlantic fringe, were now almost entirely subject to alien polities. The Red Dragon had, apparently, been conquered.

The story of the Britons arguably ends here, with the Norman Conquest of England and the creation of new nation states in England and France that were enormously successful in including minority populations. But the twelfth century saw a renewed interest in the British past, including the truly international craze for the Arthurian legends, and Britons everywhere took a new pride in their heritage. Their king had returned to them, and the prophecies of Merlin that were also now circulating widely in Britain promised yet another national redeemer who would restore sovereignty to the Britons, or at least to the Welsh. The banner of the Red Dragon was passed to a succession of Welsh princes, who, surrounded by poets and prophets, attempted to fulfill the role of redeemer. Their pride in their past, in their laws and legends, solidified Welsh national identity in the thirteenth century and remained even after the English seized the title Prince of Wales.

In the final chapters of this book, we turn to examine this process, moving increasingly away from political narrative and looking more closely at the sentiments which formed Brittonic identity at the end of the Middle Ages.

'I am born of the famous race of Britons,' exclaimed the Welsh poet Ieuan ap Sulien at the end of the eleventh century.[1] Were the Britons really famous around the year 1100? How are we to understand this proud assertion? The author of the *Life of Edward the Confessor* described the Welsh as 'an untamed people' (*gens indomita*), and the Norman barons recently established along the Welsh border saw conquest as the way to tame these latter-day barbarians.[2] By the eleventh century the Britons of Cornwall, Wales, and Brittany were prevented from any meaningful political or military connections which might restore Brittonic sovereignty; many Bretons had, in fact, become part of the Norman Conquest of Britain. Ironically, at the low point of Brittonic political prestige arose the sleeping hero, King Arthur, to defeat the Saxons by winning the hearts and minds of *their* conquerors, the Norman and Angevin kings. The 'mainstreaming' of Arthur and British myths in the twelfth century led to a renewed pride among the Welsh, who began developing a distinct national identity, based on the past but with the present hope that one of their princes would restore native sovereignty in Wales.

Bretons and the Norman Conquest

The fortunes of Brittany and Normandy became tied during the concurrent minorities of Conan II, who became Duke of Brittany in 1040, and William the Conqueror, who had assumed his ducal title five years earlier.[3] As William came of age and grew his military reputation, he began attracting into his service Breton lords from the northeastern parts of the duchy. In 1064 he fought in Brittany against Conan while supporting Rivallon of Combour. Conan died two years later without a male heir, and his title passed to Hoël, count of Cornouaille and Nantes, who had married Conan's sister and whose son Alain would later marry a daughter of William's. The figure of Count Hoël of Brittany, cousin of King Arthur in Geoffrey of Monmouth's *History of the Kings of Britain*, is an obvious reference to this powerful Duke of Brittany.

Yet it was another branch of the family that would reap the benefits of association with William the Conqueror. In 1066 William took with him to Britain several sons of the Breton count Eudes, uncle of Conan II. Eudes's family was rewarded after the Conquest with the earldom of Richmond, one of the most valuable benefices in England. Other Breton knights ac-

1   See Michael Lapidge, 'Welsh Latin Poetry of Sulien's Family,' *Studia Celtica*, 8–9 (1973–4), 83.
2   *Vita*, 9.57–8. See Gillingham, 1990, 106.
3   Galliou and Jones, 1991, 187ff.

companying William were granted land in Cornwall and Wales because the Normans felt that cultural affinity would insure successful colonization. Notable among the Bretons along the Welsh border were Wethenoc of Monmouth, his nephew William fitz Baderon, and Alan fitz Flaad, who came to Oswestry shortly after the battle of Hastings. Another Breton noble, named Hervé, became bishop of Gwynedd c.1090.

This partnership between Norman and Breton could also turn sour. Such was the case with Raoul of Gaël, the Breton earl of East Anglia, who revolted against William in 1075. William crushed the revolt, and was able to rid his kingdom of 'the vomit of the Bretons' as Archbishop Lanfranc put it, but it forced the king into campaigns against Raoul and his allies in Brittany. One of these allies, Philip I of France, helped the Bretons lift William's siege of Dol in 1076. Nevertheless the Normans were able to maintain their strong ties with Brittany for another generation. William and his successors repeatedly recruited troops in Brittany and, in 1113, Louis VI of France formally recognized Norman suzerainty over Brittany in the Treaty of Gisors.

The Marcher Lords and the First Welsh Rebellions

The Norman presence along the Welsh border dates to c.1047, when Edward the Confessor established his nephew, Ralph of Mantes, in Herefordshire. Other Normans followed prior to 1066, and by 1071 William had created three Norman earldoms – Hereford, Shrewsbury, and Chester – entrusting these entry points into Wales to Norman lords experienced in border defense and giving them much autonomy. Thus began the creation of the *Marchia Wallie*, the 'March of Wales', at once both a defensive system for England and an opportunity for ambitious Norman nobles to expand Anglo-Norman influence in Wales.

After his victory at Hastings, William does not appear to have been interested in conquering Scotland and Wales outright. In 1072 Malcolm III of Scotland submitted to the Conqueror, but no Welsh ruler followed suit. On the contrary, the Welsh harbored English rebels from 1067 to 1069 and it may have been this that encouraged William to create the border earldoms.[4] In 1072 the *Brut y Tywysogyon* records that some Normans insinuated themselves into Welsh civil strife, and a few years later the Marcher Lords were building castles to the west of the border towns. The presence of Scandinavian mercenaries in south Wales led William to march with an army to St. David's in 1081, where he received the submission of Rhys ap Tewdwr, prince of Deheubarth. Homage for north Wales was paid by Robert of Rhuddlan, a Norman lord who had laid claim to Gwynedd at about the

4 Carr, 1995, 31.

same time. With the death of Rhys in 1093, other Marcher Lords followed Robert's example by seizing Brycheiniog and Deheubarth and building castles in Pembroke and at Cardiff.

Historians have written frequently about the emergence of a Marcher society in Wales following these events. The military activities of the Marcher Lords, including private wars and castle-building, was conducted without royal interference. Rural manors and chartered towns developed in the March, attracting both English and Welsh settlers (later known, respectively, as the Englishry and the Welshry) whose lifestyles changed but little. The author of the *Deeds of King Stephen* believed that the Normans 'perseveringly civilized' Wales, 'imposed law and made the land productive.'[5]

Nevertheless, most contemporary writers – Norman and Welsh – commented on the relentless militancy and ruthlessness of the Marcher Lords. The Norman Orderic Vitalis described the arrogance of men like Hugh of Chester, Roger de Montgomery, Warin the Bald, and Robert of Rhuddlan, 'who harried the Welsh mercilessly for fifteen years.'[6] In his poem *Sanctus* (*c*.1094), Rhigyfarch, son of Bishop Sulien of St. David's, laments the devastation wrought by the Normans upon every facet of Welsh culture.[7] The castle served as the most visible sign of Norman dominance. In the *History of Gruffydd ap Cynan*, a thirteenth-century vernacular work based on an earlier Latin original, the clerical author views the Normans as weak and unfair because of their reliance upon castles.[8]

This antipathy extended to the Anglo-Norman kings as well. The Welsh chroniclers resented the kings for denying them their own laws, and feared the rapid expansion of the Anglo-Norman kingdom.[9] These Welsh fears are expressed in the entry under the year 1114 in the *Brut y Tywysogyon*, in the context of a major royal expedition: '[the Normans sought] to exterminate all the Britons completely, so that the Britannic name should never more be remembered.'[10]

The Welsh nobility, however, did not suffer these Norman outrages quietly. Large-scale revolts broke out in both north and south Wales in 1094, resulting in the restoration of Gruffydd ap Cynan in Gwynedd and Cadwgan ap Bleddyn in Powys. Cadwgan's son Owain succeeded him and was knighted (perhaps the first Welshman to receive a knighthood) while traveling with Henry I to Normandy in 1115.[11] A year earlier Henry

5   *Gesta Stephani*, 14–17. See Gillingham, 1990, 111.
6   Orderic Vitalis, *Historia Ecclesiastica*, 5.24.
7   See McCann, 1991, 40ff.
8   *Historia Gruffud vab Kenan*, p. 20. See McCann, 1991, 57.
9   See McCann, 1991, 50.
10 *Brut y Tywysogyon*, 78–81.
11 *Brut y Tywysogyon* (Penairth 20 version),

had invaded Gwynedd as a warning to Gruffydd and Owain, and he was to return to warn Powys similarly in 1121. This did not stop Gruffydd ap Rhys from revolting in Deheubarth in 1115, and a year later several of his young followers were moved to rebel against Henry I by 'an urge to restore and renew the Britannic kingdom.'[12]

Following Henry's death in 1135 with its resultant succession crisis, the Welsh princes were able to regain much of their lands. Both Gruffydd ap Cynan and Gruffydd ap Rhys died in the year 1137, and they were succeeded by their sons Owain, known as Owain Gwynedd, and Rhys ap Gruffydd, known as the Lord Rhys. These two vigorous princes were to launch several eastward advances beginning in 1157, but each advance was checked by the young Angevin king, Henry II Plantagenet. In 1164 Henry launched the first full-scale military invasion of Wales, backed by continental mercenaries and a fleet from Dublin. The Welsh united to resist his advance, under the leadership of Owain Gwynedd, but the English army was driven back across the mountains by summer storms. Henry abandoned attempts to invade Wales, and instead built a close friendship with the Lord Rhys.

The era of Rhys and Owain Gwynedd was one of unusual stability in Wales, and of a cultural revival capped by the rise of the *Gogynfeirdd*, the 'Poets of the Princes.'[13] Rhys built churches, shepherded a revival of native law, and held the first recorded *eisteddfod* in 1176 at Cardigan Castle.[14] Yet for all his achievements, Rhys was still just one of many barons in Wales and the border who paid homage to the King of England. Even in the Welsh chronicles, Welsh princes cease to be called 'king' after *c.*1150, and the Welsh are themselves no longer called Britons (*Britones/Brytanyeit*) but rather *Wallenses* and *Kymry*. This was a surrendering by the Welsh to the way others saw them, and an abandonment, in the face of the development of the Anglo-Norman state, of the old hope that the Britons would regain the Sovereignty of the Island.[15] However, it was not, as we will see, an abandonment of the desire of the Welsh princes to restore native control of Wales, nor of the Welsh to see themselves as a single nation.

Geoffrey of Monmouth

The Sovereignty of Britain, a theme seen as early as the time of Gildas, becomes the dominant theme in the most popular 'historical' work of the twelfth century, Geoffrey of Monmouth's *History of the Kings of Britain*.

---

12 *Brut y Tywysogyon*, 86–7.
13 See discussion in chapter 12 below.
14 Carr, 1995, 46–8.
15 See McCann, 1991, 47–8; and R. Davies, 1991, 19.

WELSH ROYAL DYNASTIES

Gwynedd

GRUFFYDD AP CYNAN (d. 1137)

OWAIN GWYNEDD (d. 1170)

- DAFYDD (d. 1203)
- Rhodri (d. 1195)
- Iorwerth
  - LLYWELYN (d. 1240)
    - Gruffydd (d. 1244)
      - Owain
      - LLYWELYN (d. 1282)
        - Gwenllian (d. 1337)
      - DAFYDD (d. 1283)
        - Rhodri (d. 1315)
          - Thomas (d. 1363)
            - Owain (d. 1378)
    - DAFYDD (d. 1246)

Powys

BLEDDYN AP CYNFYN (d. 1075)

- CADWGAN (d. 1111)
- MAREDUDD (d. 1132)
- Iorwerth (d. 1111)

OWAIN (d. 1116)

- MADOG (d. 1160)
  - Llywelyn (d. 1160)
  - GRUFFYDD MAELOR (d. 1191)
    - MADOG (d. 1236)
      - GRUFFYDD (d. 1269)
        - Gruffydd Fychan (d. 1289)
- Gruffydd (d. 1128)
  - OWAIN CYFEILIOG (d. 1197)
    - GWENWYNWYN (d. 1216)
      - GRUFFYDD (d. 1286)
        - Owain (d. 1293)

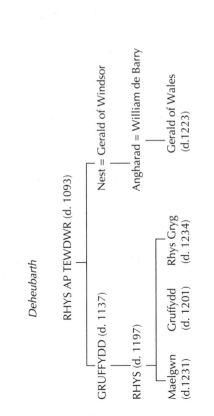

Figure 11.1 The princely families of Gwynedd, and Powys, c.1066–c.1300.

Geoffrey's work became extremely popular in Wales, where it was seen as an exaltation of national history. But, of course, the *History* was much more than that. It launched the reputation of Arthur as a globally recognized and idolized Christian king, and gave British national myth an international audience and real import.

Despite his fame, Geoffrey of Monmouth remains a shadowy and little understood figure for modern scholars. Various scholarly theories have made Geoffrey Welsh, Cornish, Breton, or Anglo-Norman. From his writings it is evident that Geoffrey knew southeast Wales better than any other region, and was familiar with the Welsh language but not Breton.[16] The traditional date for the composition of the *History* is 1136. Henry of Huntingdon read a copy of the *History* at the monastery of Bec in January 1139, and there is reason to believe that Geoffrey had finished the work only shortly before this.[17]

While some have claimed Geoffrey's *History* is pure parody – or 'mockery and mischief,' to use Christopher Brooke's alliteration – others have suggested that Geoffrey had serious political aims. Stephen Knight, for example, has interpreted the *History* as political allegory, with the acts of Arthur and the British kings reflecting the deeds and ambitions of the early Anglo-Norman monarchs.[18] There are dedications in early manuscripts to Robert of Gloucester, to Robert and Waleran of Beaumont, and to Robert and King Stephen (one version has no dedication at all).[19] Neil Wright has shown, however, that the *History* was originally and primarily dedicated to Robert, half-brother and ally of Matilda in her civil war against Stephen. Robert of Gloucester is the key to understanding the political environment in which Geoffrey wrote.

Geoffrey himself claims that he wrote the *History* as a response to the English historians William of Malmesbury and Henry of Huntingdon, who slighted the Britons in their recent works. John Gillingham argues that the contemptuous attitude toward the Welsh, all but dormant since the days of Bede and Eddius Stephanus, was revived in literary circles by William.[20] As news of Welsh and Scottish savagery during the wars against King Stephen reached Anglo-Norman authors, writers like William adopted old Roman attitudes toward barbarians and applied them to their own Christian but less cultured neighbors, the Irish, the Scots, and the Welsh. From an English perspective the Welsh were poor (even, comparatively, their nobles) and pastoral, had no real towns, and continued to practice –

---

16   Gillingham, 1990, 104.
17   See Gillingham, 1990, 100.
18   Knight, 1983, 52ff.
19   See Tatlock, 436–7.
20   Gillingham, 1990, 106ff.

like the Scots – war as an opportunity for slave-hunting. After William's influential *Deeds of the Kings of England* was 'published' in 1125, it became commonplace for Anglo-Norman authors to view the Welsh as barbarians. This attitude would be echoed by some French writers (Chrétien de Troyes repeats, in his *Perceval*, that 'Welshmen are more stupid than beasts') and even come to influence the way Gerald of Wales viewed his fellow countrymen.

In writing the *History*, however, Geoffrey of Monmouth asserts that the Britons not only had a long and distinguished history but also that they had long been both civilized and Christian. The Britons are portrayed as a noble and distinct race – he uses the terms *gens* and *natio*, used later by Gerald of the Welsh – descended from a Trojan hero and led later by Christian kings. Thus the *History* was at least in part an answer – or antidote – to William of Malmesbury and his followers. But it was also, argues Gillingham, an attempt to persuade Robert of Gloucester to make an alliance with the Welsh princes Morgan and Iowerth ap Owain who had launched a successful rebellion against Stephen in 1136. Morgan had recently captured Caerleon and it was no coincidence, says Gillingham, that Geoffrey chose that city for Arthur's court in the *History*. At around this time the Anglo-Norman *Description of England* was composed, with references to these Welsh revolts:

> Well have the Welsh revenged themselves . . .
> Some of our castles they have taken,
> Fiercely they threaten us,
> Openly they go about saying,
> That in the end they will have all,
> By means of Arthur they will have it back . . .
> They will call it Britain again.[21]

Geoffrey of Monmouth calls the *History* his *gesta Britonum* in another work, the enigmatic poem *Vita Merlini* ('The Life of Merlin'). Visited by the bard Taliesin, Merlin makes the following prediction of the Britons' future deliverance from the Saxons:

> The British shall be without their kingdom for many years and remain weak, until Conan in his chariot arrives from Brittany, and that revered leader of the Welsh, Cadwaladr, and there be formed together in a strong confederation the Scots and the men of Strathclyde, the men of Cornwall and those of Brittany, and the crown that they had lost they shall restore to their people, after driving the enemy forth and renewing the days of Brutus.[22]

21   Gillingham, 1995, 53–4.
22   *Vita Merlini*, ll.965–8.

In both works, Geoffrey utilizes an historical myth that was common to Britons in Wales, Cornwall, and Brittany.[23] 'In the twelfth century British history belonged to the Britons,' writes John Gillingham, 'not to the kings of England, for whom the possibility of Arthur's return fighting-fit from the Isle of Avalon would have been an uncomfortable prospect.'[24] By the end of the century, however, Geoffrey's early history of Britain was making its way into *English* histories. 'The Matter of Britain,' observed Rees Davies, was effectively 'hijacked and put into the service of England.'[25] Furthermore, royal patronage of the Arthurian romances and the alleged discovery of Arthur's body at Glastonbury meant that, from the Plantagenets to the Tudors, British history would continue to be expropriated and made politically useful by the kings of England.

Arthur and the Plantagenets

'At that time,' commented Alfred of Beverley in the middle of the twelfth century, 'tales of British history were being produced by so many mouths, that whoever did not have knowledge of such tales risked being branded an ignorant clod.'[26] When Gerald of Wales refers to 'our own famous Arthur,' he is testifying to the Welsh, Cornish, and Breton pride in *their* famous king. Yet it was not only the descendants of the Britons who laid claim to Arthur in the twelfth century. Arthur, as Robert Bartlett has observed, 'conquered not only Saxons and Romans but also the fashion-conscious aristocracy of Norman England.'[27] The latter included particularly the house of Plantagenet. Henry, Eleanor, and their sons all showed enthusiasm for the Arthurian legends, from patronizing poets to collecting Arthurian memorabilia. Whether or not Arthur served as a military role model for Henry II or Eleanor as the inspiration for literary Guineveres, it is hard to doubt the appeal of the legendary history of the Britons among the Plantagenets.

It is still a matter of debate how the first Arthurian tales reached the French-speaking courts of the Plantagenets. They may have been brought by Breton singers, or via Welsh bards in the March, or perhaps both.[28] Henry may have become attracted to the exploits of Arthur and the Britons

23   See Roberts, 1976, 40.
24   Gillingham, 1990, 103.
25   R. R. Davies, 1996, 17. Roger of Howden, for example, transformed Arthur from *rex Britonum* to *rex Anglie*.
26   Alfred of Beverley, *Historia*.
27   Bartlett, 2000, 250.
28   See Radiker, 1995, 7ff.

as a youth in the guardianship of his uncle, Robert of Gloucester, who was the patron of William of Malmesbury, Henry of Huntingdon, and Geoffrey of Monmouth.[29] Later, Marie de France was to dedicate her Tristan lay *Chevrefueil* ('Honeysuckle') to the 'noble king,' and the Anglo-Norman poet Thomas gave the hero of his *Tristan* the gold lion shield device favored by Henry. The poet Wace, later commissioned by Henry to write a Norman history, presented a copy of his *Roman de Brut* (inspired by Geoffrey's *History*) to Queen Eleanor. Just before the king's death, a British bard allegedly disclosed to Henry the location of Arthur's grave. Richard, Henry's son and successor, sponsored an excavation at Glastonbury Abbey in 1190 to uncover the bones of both Arthur and Guinevere, which were subsequently re-interred in a sumptuous marble tomb that received royal visits from later Plantagenets including Edward I (see plate 11.1).

Now that they possessed the body of Arthur, the Plantagenet kings could borrow more than just his reputation. Richard claimed to possess Arthur's sword *Caliburne*, which he gave as a gift to his fellow crusader Tancred of Sicily. The dragon banner that Richard carried at the battle of Arsuf in 1191 may have been inspired by the prophecies of Merlin.[30] One of the Anglo-Norman lords who served as a hostage in Germany in 1194 for Richard I's ransom possessed a copy of a French Lancelot poem, which he lent to the Swiss cleric Ulrich von Zatzikhoven, who used it as the basis for the German romance *Lanzelet*. A royal letter patent states that Tristan's sword was among King John's regalia.

Perhaps the culmination of this Arthurian enthusiasm was the christening, in 1187, of Henry II's grandson Arthur. The son of Geoffrey Plantagenet and Constance of Brittany, this Arthur became the Duke of Brittany upon his father's untimely death that year, and, for a while, was even proclaimed the heir of his uncle, Richard I. The beleaguered Conan IV had handed over the duchy to Henry in 1166, and Henry, waiting for his son to come into his inheritance, imposed Angevin political institutions on Brittany, to the growing displeasure of the Bretons. Breton grievances against the Plantagenets are satirized by Etienne de Rouen in his *Draco Normannicus* (c.1170). In the poem, King Arthur writes an angry letter to 'the young Henry' in which he recounts his world conquests in order to scare Henry away from oppressing the Bretons. Henry, 'smiling to his companions,' pens his response, declaring that he holds Brittany legitimately as the descendant of Rollo, but, out of respect for Arthur, he agrees to hold Brittany as the king's vassal!

Some have seen the christening of Arthur of Brittany as an act of

29   Snyder, 2000, 128ff.
30   See Bartlett, 2000, 251.

Plate 11.1   An artist's rendering of the excavation of Arthur's grave at Glastonbury, 1190. (Illustration by Judith Dobie, © English Heritage.)

defiance by the Duchess Constance, who was disliked and mistreated by Henry, Richard, Eleanor, and John.[31] On the other hand, it may have simply been a fashionable choice of name, given the Arthurian interests of the Plantagenets. In any case, this Arthur was an enigmatic and ultimately tragic figure, murdered by his uncle John at the age of 16 after allying with the Capetians. Contemporary writers called him 'the hope of the Bretons,' who saw in him the possible return of their famous king and national redeemer. Even his death in 1203 did not deter the Bretons and the Cornish from their fervent belief that *the* Arthur was not dead, only sleeping somewhere waiting for the right moment to return, as the monk Robert of Gloucester most elegantly describes:

31   See William of Newburgh, *Historia Rerum Anglicarum*, 3.7.

[Arthur] deid as the best knigt that me wuste euere yfounde
And natheles the Brutons and the Cornwalisse of is kunde
Weneth he be aliue yut and abbeth him in munde
That he be to comene yut to winne agen this lond.[32]

While the military exploits of Arthur and his knights were captivating
audiences in English and French courts, the supposed prophecies of Merlin were also becoming quite popular. According to Gerald of Wales, Henry
II was aware of a prophecy of Merlin's which stated that the king who
would conquer Ireland would die once he crossed a certain bridge in Wales:
Henry safely crossed it and announced 'Merlin is a liar. Who will trust
him now?'[33] Another prophecy, in the Black Book of Carmarthen, refers
to the defeat of the Saxons and to the Britons playing football with their
enemies' heads![34] McCann has shown that the Welsh vaticinatory poems
in general are consistently hostile toward the Normans, with the poets
viewing Norman military successes as both the cause and the result of
their moral decadence.[35] They would also prove to be politically useful to
later Welsh princes as they sought justification for their rebellion.

Gerald of Wales

There is no more prominent Welsh voice in medieval historical writing
than Gerald of Wales. Born in 1146, Gerald was the son of William de
Barri, lord of Manorbier, and Anghard, great-granddaughter of Rhys
ap Tewdwr. Thus Gerald had connections to the royal dynasty of south
Wales, but he was most directly related to a Norman Marcher clan.
French was his native tongue, Latin his language of schooling, and though
he had an interest in Welsh words he could not speak fluent Welsh, nor
did he know much English. His immediate family were landowners and
knights, but Gerald chose a career in the Church, becoming a secular
cleric and scholar (he studied for ten years at the schools of Paris). In
1175 he was appointed archdeacon of Brecon, and from 1184 to 1194
he served as a royal clerk furthering the aims of the Angevin monarchs
in Wales. His most stormy years were spent as a candidate for the episcopal seat of St. David's, from 1198 to 1203. This unsuccessful candi-

---

32   *The Metrical Chronicle of Robert of Gloucester.* Vivid testimony to this hope is given
by Herman of Laon, Alain de Lille, and Gerald of Wales, among others.
33   Gerald, *The Conquest of Ireland*, 1.33. Cf. William, *Historia Rerum Anglicarum*, 1.166.
See Gillingham, 1990, 102; and Crick, 1992, 360–1.
34   *Black Book of Carmarthen*, 16.9–10. See McCann, 1991, 60.
35   McCann, 1991, 62.

dacy turned his last years into a bitter resentment of the Angevins, and he died in 1223, praising the Capetians and utterly disillusioned by the Welsh.

The mature Gerald produced many substantive works that incorporate elements of history, etymology, ethnography, political commentary, and travel literature. For our purposes it is essential to look at those works in which Gerald commented on Wales and the Welsh, and to address the issue of how Gerald saw himself in this context. Gerald identifies himself in his writings as *Giraldus Cambrensis*, purposely avoiding the identifier *Wallia* because of its pejorative connotations.[36] But how should we translate *Giraldus Cambrensis*? 'Gerald of Wales,' or 'Gerald the Briton'? The former implies merely an accident of geography, while the latter puts him in the camp of writers like 'Nennius' and Geoffrey of Monmouth, whose self-identity and sympathies are with the Britons.

In his early writings, Gerald makes it clear that he is serving his king by offering advice on the conquest and containment of the Welsh. The king could 'make Wales a colony,' suggests Gerald, 'after he has expelled the old inhabitants and deported them to other kingdoms,' or else he could simply 'make a forest of it.'[37] The Welsh, writes Gerald, are an unruly, backward, and barbarous nation ('barbarous' is a term he uses frequently to describe the Welsh as well as the Irish and the Scots), and he reinforces this judgment by citing several examples of medieval Welsh customs that closely resemble those of the ancient Britons described by Caesar and other Roman writers (e.g. fosterage, cultivating long mustaches, polygamy, and even head-hunting).[38] Gerald reinforces prevailing Anglo-Norman attitudes toward Welsh warriors, who were seen as barefoot, animal-like guerrillas who were fierce but faithless.[39]

Gerald's literary assaults on the Welsh, Irish, and Scots are clearly intended to play to the prejudices of his Angevin patrons and scholarly readers. He makes use of the classical barbarian stereotype revived by William of Malmesbury and uses it to justify Plantagenet military policy in Ireland and Wales, taking a shot or two at Geoffrey of Monmouth along the way (perhaps because Geoffrey's more popular literary works had translated him into an episcopal appointment). But during his campaign for the bishopric of St. David's, Gerald reverses his attitude toward Wales, showing pride in his Welsh heritage while condemning the English:

---

36   R. Davies, 1991, 4.
37   Gerald, *Description of Wales*.
38   Gerald, *Description of Wales*, 1.10–11, 2.6, 2.9; idem, *Conquest of Ireland*, 2.36. See Jones, 1971; and Snyder, 1996.
39   See Suppe, 1994, 7ff.

How does Andrew [an English canon at St. David's] have the effrontery to set the English nation above our British nation or even to compare them! Of all nations the English are regarded as the most worthless . . . In their own land the English are slaves of the Normans and the most worthless of slaves. In our land there are none but Englishmen in the jobs of ploughman, shepherd, cobbler, skinner, artisan and cleaner of the sewers too . . . But our British nation, now called by the false name Welsh, is descended from the lineage of Troy as were the Romans, and so it defends its freedom against the Normans and the Saxons with continuous rebellion.[40]

This strategy, attacking Canterbury's appointment of English clerics in Wales, failed to win Gerald the bishopric.[41] The archbishop, Hubert Walter, wanted 'no Welshman or even anyone born in Wales' to be promoted; the Norman Church, like the Norman knights, was fighting to restrain 'the barbarism of that wicked and unbridled race' of Britons, who 'boast that all of Britain is theirs by right.'[42] Accused by his opponents of inciting the Welsh to rebellion, Gerald sadly returns in his last works to a hostile attitude toward the Welsh, blaming his Welsh blood for his defeat.

Robert Bartlett has pointed out that Gerald saw himself as a man of mixed descent who was often rejected by both Norman and Welsh society.[43] The Welsh, understandably, held him in suspicion, while his Norman colleagues mocked him with phrases like 'A typical Welsh error!' and 'Can anything good come from Wales?' (a medieval version of Ausonius' fourth-century slur against the Briton Silvius 'the Good': 'No good man is a Briton').[44] His failure to win proper rewards from the Angevin kings, and especially his failed attempt to become bishop of St. David's, could all be conveniently blamed on 'that suspect, dangerous, hateful name – Wales.' And yet it is that epithet, *Cambrensis*, which has distinguished him, and his vivid prose, for the last eight centuries.

Welsh Nationalism and the Two Llywelyns

Ironically, the advice given by Gerald regarding the conquest of Wales – e.g. the necessity of long campaigns, castle-building, and use of light-armed troops – bears resemblance to the actual tactics employed a century later by Edward I.[45] Edward's Welsh campaigns, which resulted in the near total loss of native political autonomy, followed on the heels of Welsh

40 Gerald, *Invectiones*, p.93.
41 See Richter, 1976; and Johnson, 2000, 18ff.
42 Gerald, *De Jure*, 120, 201; idem, *De Invectionibus*, 84–5.
43 Bartlett, 1982, 17ff.
44 Gerald, *De Principis Instructione*, preface. On Ausonius, see chapter 4 above .
45 Bartlett, 1982, 15–16.

military successes and a great burst of national sentiment in Wales. The Welsh political revival of the thirteenth century was largely the work, well chronicled, of two great princes of Gwynedd: Llywelyn ap Iowerth and Llywelyn ap Gruffydd. But the emergence of Welsh nationalism is a broader and more complex phenomenon.

By the year 1200, Llywelyn ap Iowerth, a grandson of Owain Gwynedd, had fought his way to the top in north Wales and was on his way to becoming the most dominant prince of Wales. Llywelyn completed a treaty with King John the following year, married the king's illegitimate daughter Joan, and invaded southern Powys. But in 1211 John turned against Llywelyn, invading Gwynedd and forcing the Welsh princes into an alliance with the French. John's subsequent defeat in France, and his concessions in Magna Carta, restored power to Gwynedd, which became the conduit between Welsh nobles and the English monarchy.[46] In 1230 Llywelyn adopted a new title, 'prince of Aberffraw and lord of Snowdon,' and spent his last years working tirelessly for a treaty recognizing the supremacy of Gwynedd in Wales. After his death in 1240 he was remembered, even by the English, as Llywelyn Fawr, Llywelyn the Great.

Llywelyn's son and successor, Dafydd, was unable to secure the kind of treaty that his father craved. Nor was even able to secure his father's territorial gains, which were seized by Henry III. Though he styled himself Prince of Wales, Dafydd accomplished little before his death in 1246. After a decade of succession strife Llywelyn ap Gruffydd, Dafydd's nephew, succeeded in Gwynedd and began reconquering the lands seized by Henry III. Now with the support of the other Welsh princes, Llywelyn moved into the March and made an alliance with Simon de Montfort, leader of the Baronial War of 1264, who promised to secure the royal treaty that would recognize Llywelyn as Prince of Wales. Despite Simon's defeat and death at the hands of Henry's son Edward, Llywelyn was now in a strong enough position to demand a treaty from the king. In 1267 Henry signed the Treaty of Montgomery, formally acknowledging the right of the prince of Gwynedd (and his heirs) to the title Prince of Wales and granting the prince authority over 'all the Welsh barons of Wales.'

This important step toward political unification in Wales was complemented by a new and widespread sense of Welsh national identity. Rees Davies points out that while Wales lacked the centralized governance of such developing nation-states as England and France, it nevertheless possessed many key ingredients of national identity.[47] Even when divided politically, the Welsh recognized a common history and mythology, one language and distinct literary traditions, and one law. Their shared his-

---

46 See Carr, 1995, 57.
47 See, for example, R. Davies, 1984; idem, 1991.

torical vision, as we have seen, was of descent from heroic Britons like Brutus and Arthur, famous conquerors who established British sovereignty on the island that bears their name. Their language distinguished the Welsh from the Normans and the English, 'foreign, alien-tongued people,' and the thirteenth century saw a flowering of Welsh vernacular literature. [48]

Welsh law formalized this distinction between the *Cymro* and the *alltud* (alien), and more than one war was fought to preserve native law, which they attributed to one of their great princes, Hywel Dda. Bernard, the first Norman bishop of St. David's, identified law as one thing that distinguished the Welsh from other peoples in Britain.[49] In 1201 King John formally recognized *lex Wallie* as legitimate and distinct from *lex Anglie*.[50]

The sporadic expressions of Welsh nationalism that we have traced were followed by a torrent in the late twelfth and thirteenth centuries:

> 1198: Gwenwynyn of Powys planned to restore to the *Cymry* their ancient liberty and their ancient proprietary rights and their borders [together with] all the princes of Wales.[51]

> c.1265: The Welsh, who are used to slaying the Saxons, salute their relations the Bretons and Cornishmen; they require them to come with their sharp swords to conquer their Saxons enemies . . . The soothsayer Merlin . . . foretold that the mad people should be expelled . . . If our valiant predecessor, King Arthur, had been now alive, I am sure not one of the Saxon walls would have resisted him. May the Omnipotent procure him a successor only similar to him . . . who may deliver the Britons from their old grievances, and restore to them their country and their country's glory.[52]

> 1282: The prince and his predecessors have had pure authority [in Wales] since the time of Camber son of Brutus . . . Likewise, for that reason the prince should not renounce his hereditary possessions . . . and receive land in England, of whose language, way of life, laws and customs he is ignorant; where . . . also he will be subject to malicious intentions born out of old, established hatred . . . Likewise, the nation of Snowdon declares, that even if their prince permitted the king to take up seisin of the people, nevertheless they would refuse to do homage to any one who is a foreigner, of whose language, customs, and laws they are utterly ignorant.[53]

---

48   *Llawysgrif Hendregadredd*, trans. John Morris-Jones and T. H. Parry-Williams (Cardiff, 1933), p. 218. See chapter 12 below for discussion of Welsh language and literature.
49   Gerald of Wales, 'De Invectionibus,' ed. W. S. Davies, *Y Cymmrodor* 30 (1920), 142.
50   See R. Davies, 1984, 58.
51   *Brut y Tywysogyon* (Red Book of Hergest Version), s.a. 1198.
52   From *The Song of the Welsh*, a Latin poem written during the time of the Baronial War, found in *The Political Songs of England, from King John to Edward II*, ed. and trans. T. Wright (London, 1839), 56–8.
53   C. T. Martin (ed), *Registrum Epistolarum fratris Johannis Peckham*, Rolls Series 1882–5, 2.469–71 (trans. in Johnson, 2000, 147).

Remarkably similar to the Scottish Declaration of Arbroath, this last statement was issued by Llywelyn ap Gruffudd just days before the prince's death. Llywelyn was also the deliverer of the Britons and successor to Arthur described above by the poet of *The Song of the Welsh*. Yet not ten years after the Treaty of Montgomery was signed, Llywelyn's fortunes had begun to wane, and with them those of Wales itself.

Edward I and Wales

The new king of England, Edward I, was harboring two Welsh nobles who had plotted the death of Llywelyn and who were now raiding his lands. Llywelyn withheld payments he owed Edward and refused on several occasions to do homage to the king until the fugitives were handed over. The stalemate was broken when Edward declared war in 1276, bringing three armies into Wales to seize Llywelyn's eastern lands while a royal fleet captured Anglesey. With the passivity of the remaining Welsh princes, Edward was able to build a series of magnificent castles to control Gwynedd and forced Llywelyn to do homage and accept humiliating terms. War broke out again in 1282 when royal officials in the *cantrefs* controlled by Llywelyn's brother Dafydd flouted Welsh laws and customs. Dafydd attacked one of Edward's castles and a Welsh 'parliament' at Denbigh declared war against England. The archbishop of Canterbury met with Dafydd and Llywelyn to negotiate a peace settlement, and heard without interest Welsh complaints of English oppression. The Welsh princes refused the terms (in the passage cited above), defeated an English force at the Menai Straits, and Llywelyn moved his army into mid Wales. There, in December 1282, the Prince of Wales was killed, his head cut off and paraded by the English troops before being displayed, with that of Dafydd's, on the Tower of London.

    With this victory, Edward I subsumed the principality of Wales and bestowed its title upon his son and heir. Less than a year after his first Welsh campaign, Edward and his queen visited Glastonbury and exhumed the bones of Arthur; in 1283, while holding court in Llywelyn's Welsh castles, Edward displayed to the locals an object which he claimed was Arthur's crown; the following year, he held a Round Table tournament at Nefyn specifically to celebrate his conquest of Wales.[54] Edward became a noted Arthurian enthusiast, but, as his pangyricists made explicit, he wanted to show the Welsh in particular that *he* was the true heir to Arthur, and indeed had surpassed the British king's legendary achievements.[55]

54   See Radiker, 1995, 45–6, 123.
55   See, for example, Pierre de Langtoft, *Edward I*; and *The Chronicles of the Reigns of Edward I and Edward II* (ed. Stubbs), Rolls Series.

Welsh hopes for a restoration of political autonomy, however, did not end with the death of Llywelyn. Rhys ap Maredudd, a prince of Deheubarth whom the poets described as 'defender of Wales . . . shield-shorn like Arthur,' launched a short-lived and unsuccessful revolt against Edward in 1287.[56] Even with most of the native royalty now gone, Welsh poets and diplomats concocted an even grander scheme: to drive the English out of Britain altogether with the help of the resurgent Scots. In 1307, the year Robert the Bruce returned to Scotland, a prophecy that was circulating in Wales was brought to the attention of the dying Edward:

> The people believe that Bruce will carry all before him, exhorted by false preachers from Bruce's army . . . For these preachers have told the people that they have found a prophecy of Merlin, that after the death of *le roy coveytous* [Edward I] the people of Scotland and the Welsh shall band together and have full lordship and live in peace together to the end of the world.[57]

This prophecy is mentioned again in 1315, the year after Edward II lost to Robert the Bruce at Bannockburn, in the context of the rebellion of Llywelyn Bren in Glamorgan:

> The Welsh, formerly called the Britons, were once noble and owned the whole realm of England, but they were expelled by the on-coming Saxons and lost both name and kingdom. The fertile plains went to the Saxons; the sterile mountainous districts remained to the Welsh. Moreover, from the sayings of the prophet Merlin they still hope to recover England. Hence it is that the Welsh frequently rebel, hoping to give effect to the prophecy.[58]

Both Robert and Edward Bruce sought Irish and Welsh support during their wars against Edward II. Late in the year 1316 Edward Bruce sent out a general plea to Wales, offering to help lift 'the English yoke' from the Welsh, who, according to Edward, 'come from one original stock, kin and nation' as the Scots, and thus should be reunited as one sovereign people.[59] The plea was answered by Sir Gruffydd Llwyd, a Welshman who had been a loyal servant of Edward II's in North Wales but who, around 1315, was having trouble with the Mortimers. Llwyd sent a letter to Edward Bruce suggesting that the Welsh *nobiles* would support a Scottish invasion of Wales and, once the English were defeated, would divide *Britannia* with the Scots.[60] This letter, which echoes the Merlinic

---

56 See R. Davies, 1991, 380–1; and Radiker, 1995, 23.
57 See Barrow, 1988, 172–3; and Snyder, forthcoming.
58 *Vita Edwardi Secundi*, s.a. 1315 (trans. J. Beverly Smith in Pugh, 1971, 77).
59 See Smith, 1976, 478; and Snyder, 1996, 168ff.
60 See Smith, 471–2, 477–8.

prophecy of 1307 and which resulted in Llwyd's imprisonment, refers also to Brutus' conquest of Britain, and it is clear that Llwyd and the Bruces were using Geoffrey of Monmouth's vision of a once united Britain for their own political aspirations.

Owain Glyn Dŵr

It is in the context of these political prophecies that we will examine the last, and most successful, of the medieval Welsh revolts. In the fourteenth century there were attempts to restore the princely House of Gwynedd, most colorfully by Owain ap Thomas, known as Owain Lawgoch ('Red Hand'), and Yvain de Galles, great-nephew of Llywelyn ap Gruffydd, whom the French sent to invade Britain on two unsuccessful naval expeditions in 1369 and 1372.[61] With his death campaigning in France in 1378, the direct male line of the Gwynedd dynasty came to an end, but the poets and barons of Wales continued to look for a national redeemer whose name was Owain and who, like King Arthur, was said to be sleeping in a cave until the moment of delivery arrived.

This moment appeared to have arrived on September 16, in the year 1400, when Owain Glyn Dŵr was proclaimed Prince of Wales at his manor Glyndyfrdwy.[62] The wealthiest of the surviving native Welsh aristocracy, Glyn Dŵr was a descendant of the royal houses of Powys and Deheubarth, with ties to the Lestranges Marcher family as well. He performed military service for Richard II in Scotland in 1385 and in the English Channel two years later, though he had not received a knighthood. A series of events transformed Owain Glyn Dŵr from loyal squire to rebel prince. Roger Mortimer, earl of March, died in 1398, and a year later Richard II was deposed. Owain, then in a border dispute with his neighbor Reginald de Grey, was proclaimed in what must have been a premeditated act following years of Welsh grievances. With the wealth, bloodline, and auspicious name of Owain, Glyn Dŵr was the perfect choice to lead the revolt.

The proclaimed Prince of Wales was joined by the brothers Gwilym and Rhys ap Tudur, who led an uprising in Anglesey while other Glyn Dŵr supporters attacked several English towns in northeast Wales. This brought the new king of England, Henry IV, into north Wales, where many of the rebels submitted. Owain briefly disappeared, and Parliament enacted a series of penal statutes against the Welsh. 'What care we for barefoot rascals?' was Parliament's answer to Welsh complaints.

---

61   See Carr, 1995, 103–4.
62   See Carr, 1995, 108–17, for a concise account of the revolt.

On Good Friday 1401 Gwilym and Rhys seized Conwy Castle, and Owain defeated a royal force in Cardiganshire. Henry returned to Wales but was frustrated by Glyn Dŵr, who avoided battle with the king. In 1402 Owain captured Reginald de Grey and Edmund Mortimer, and another English invasion was foiled by bad weather. The next year an unlikely partner joined the Welsh in revolt: Henry Percy, Shakespeare's Hotspur, son of the Earl of Northumberland who was then justiciar of north Wales. Hotspur was defeated and killed by Henry at Shrewsbury, but Glyn Dŵr took advantage by capturing some English castles and burning Cardiff, utilizing the speed and mobility for which his army became renowned.

In 1404 Owain summoned a Welsh parliament at Machynlleth in Powys. Here he was joined by several prominent Welsh clerics, who began helping the Prince to create an administrative infrastructure. He also engaged in diplomatic relations with France, Castile, Scotland, and Ireland. In 1405 Owain joined a French force that marched from Carmarthen across the English border to near Worcester. But later that year the revolt began to fizzle, with an English army from Dublin restoring order in Anglesey. In 1408 Owain's family was captured by the English, and after a raid on the English border in 1410 Glyn Dŵr completely disappears from view. Offered a pardon by Henry V, he may have died around the year 1415.

Although his revolt was ultimately unsuccessful, Owain Glyn Dŵr does not simply disappear from the folk conscience in Wales. Recently, scholars have stressed the importance of political prophecy during the Glyn Dŵr rebellion, and the nature of this Welsh prophecy led to the establishment of Owain Glyn Dŵr as a folk hero, a national redeemer in the tradition of another British king whose end was shrouded in mystery: Arthur.[63] Even before his proclamation in 1400, Glyn Dŵr seems to have surrounded himself with professional poets and soothsayers. They spoke to him often of *y mab darogan*, 'the Son of Deliverance,' and, since 'Owain' was already a recognized name for the expected deliverer, he clearly came to see himself in this role. 'Owain's thought-world was one of mythology and prophecy,' writes Rees Davies, 'of bitter tales of oppressions of the Island of Britain, and of the fervent expectation of the deliverance of the Britons.'[64]

It is not so surprising that Glyn Dŵr would eventually adopt as his standard the dragon, the symbol of the ancient Britons and of Arthur. What is surprising is that his obsessions with mythology and prophecy would help shape his diplomatic strategy. In 1401 and 1402, Glyn Dŵr sent letters to King Robert III of Scotland and to various Irish leaders,

63 See especially R. Davies, 1995; and Henken, 1996.
64 R. Davies, 1995, 160.

seeking their aid. The letter to Robert begins with Glyn Dŵr mentioning 'Brutus, your most noble ancestor and mine,' and his sons Albanactus, Locrinus, and Kamber.[65] 'You are descended in a direct line from Albanactus,' he tells the Scottish king, '[while] the descendants of Kamber reigned as kings until Cadwaladr . . . I, dear cousin, am descended directly from Cadwaladr.' 'The prophecy,' Glyn Dŵr writes, 'says that I will be delivered from the oppressions and bondages [of the English] by your aid.'

The British princes mentioned by Glyn Dŵr in his letter to the Scots are all central figures in Geoffrey of Monmouth's *History*, from Brutus the first sovereign British ruler to Cadwaladr the last. Glyn Dŵr also appeals to British prophecy in his letter to the Irish lords. 'Seeing that it is commonly reported by the prophecy that, before we can have the upper hand [against the English], you and yours, our well-beloved cousins (*consanguinei*) in Ireland, must stretch forth hereto a helping hand.'[66] Glyn Dŵr's soothsayers were blamed, by later writers, for 'putting in his head . . . Merlin's prophecies,' 'construed very advantageously . . . swelling the mind of Glyn Dŵr' and giving him 'hopes of restoring the Island back to the Britons.' Even Shakespeare knew of Glyn Dŵr's recourse to such prophecies, having Hotspur complain that 'Sometimes [Glendower] angers me / with telling me . . . / Of the dreamer Merlin and his prophecies.'[67]

In these remarkable letters to the Scottish and Irish rulers, Glyn Dŵr recalls the nationalist tone of the *Historia Brittonum*, the *Armes Prydein*, and Geoffrey's *History*, reminding his fellow Celtic rulers of Merlin's prophecy that the Red Dragon – that is the Britons – will one day defeat the White Dragon of the Saxons and expel them from the island.

Like the pan-Celtic coalitions of the *Armes* and the *Vita Merlini*, these alliances were mostly wishful thinking, brought on by necessity and English military pressure. They were also schemes concocted by elites, members of the courtly culture of medieval Europe, rarely an accurate barometer of widespread societal beliefs. But this is not sufficient reason to dismiss them. As Elissa Henken has pointed out, the vatic poetry, though aristocratic, 'must nevertheless have relied on commonly held lore and beliefs because it served as part of the structure which bound the people and the ruler together.'[68]

The great princes of medieval Wales chronicled in this chapter had this in common. They called upon British history and mythology to gain the

65   Adam of Usk, *Chronicle*, 72–3 (trans. in R. Davies, 1995, 158).
66   See Henken, 1996, 60–1.
67   *Henry IV*, Part I.
68   Henken, 1996, 9. Cf. R. Davies, 1995, 159.

support of their people and to focus aggression on the traditional enemy, the kings of England. While this seldom paid off in terms of political and territorial gains, it did nonetheless provide a catalyst for the growth of Welsh nationalism, which would replace older, vaguer notions of Brittonic sovereignty and which would long outlive the Middle Ages.

12
Language and Literature

We saw in the previous chapter the importance of language and literary tradition in the growth of national identity in Wales. Indeed, these had been two important factors in the very first manifestations of Brittonic identity. 'The roots of a sense of nationality among the *Cymry*,' writes Thomas Charles-Edwards, 'were largely linguistic and cultural and depended on a contrast between "us" and the Romans.'[1] This contrast was continued by Britons in the early Middle Ages as 'us versus the English,' 'us versus the French,' and 'us versus the Normans.' With the overwhelming influences of the Church and feudalism, which tended to internationalize European peoples, the Britons clung to their language and their myths as the remaining factors of distinction. Rather than disappearing along with the political autonomy of the Britons, however, the Brittonic languages and myths enjoyed a flowering from the eleventh to the fourteenth centuries. It proved to be the twilight of the Britons, before the onset of distinctly Welsh, Cornish, and Breton identities.

The Development of the Brittonic Languages

In the early eighteenth century, following the pioneering studies of such scholars as Edward Lhuyd, linguists adopted the theory that the language spoken by ancient Gauls was related to contemporary Irish, Scots Gaelic, and Welsh. The term 'Celtic' was resurrected and applied to this group of languages, which also came to include Breton, Cornish, and Manx, as well some identifiable ancient tongues (see chart 12.1). After the 'discovery' of an Indo-European family of languages in 1786, the so-called Celtic languages took their place next to Greek, Italic, Germanic, and other related branches. The Celtic branch became further divided into groups based

1   Charles-Edwards, 1995, 714.

on early linguistic divergences. For example, Goidelic (Gaelic) is known as Q-Celtic because it retained the Indo-European *kw* sound, writing it as *q* and later *c*, while Gallo-Brittonic is called P-Celtic because the *kw* sound developed into *p*. The words *mac* and *map*, meaning 'son of' in Gaelic and Welsh respectively, illustrate this principle.

We are, of course, interested in the P-Celtic or Brittonic group of languages, which includes Breton, Cornish, and Welsh. The classic study of the Brittonic languages is Kenneth Jackson's *Language and History in Early Britain*, published originally in 1953 but still being reprinted and used by scholars of the early Middle Ages. Here, in addition to providing detailed technical discussion of the linguistic elements of Brittonic, Jackson attempted to write a history of a language that has survived only in a very small number of early texts. What he and subsequent linguists have written about Brittonic has, therefore, relied upon much epigraphic and placename evidence and follows historical and archaeological models.

The evidence for what Jackson has termed Early British comes entirely from Classical sources (including Romano-British inscriptions and placenames in Greek and Roman geographies), apart from a few coins issued by LPRIA British kings. For Late British (fifth and sixth centuries AD), evidence comes from the early Christian inscriptions and British words used by contemporary Latin writers like Patrick and Gildas, as well as a few slightly later Latin sources like Bede and the earliest saints' lives, which derive some of their British material from earlier written sources. Textual evidence is also slight for the period from the seventh to the twelfth centuries, which saw the emergence of Old Welsh, Old Cornish, and Old Breton. For this period we have British words and glosses in Latin texts; a few grammars and *computi*; some British material in the *Historia Brittonum* and the *Annales Cambriae* and in Asser's *Life of Alfred*; a few short poems in the Juvencus Manuscript; the Welsh genealogies; and more inscriptions. The bulk of British literary material, including the great works of vernacular literature in Middle Welsh and Middle Breton, springs from the eleventh and twelfth centuries and will be discussed in the chapter sections that follow.

From this early material a few general observations can be made regarding the Britons, before we look at the development of the individual Brittonic tongues. First, there is orthographic uniformity throughout the Brittonic texts from the earliest period of divergence (i.e. Old Welsh, Old Cornish, and Old Breton).[2] Changes in spelling do not occur until about the eleventh century, under the influence of English, French, and Anglo-Norman. Secondly, lenition is rarely recognized in the spelling of Brittonic

---

2 Jackson, 1994, 67–8.

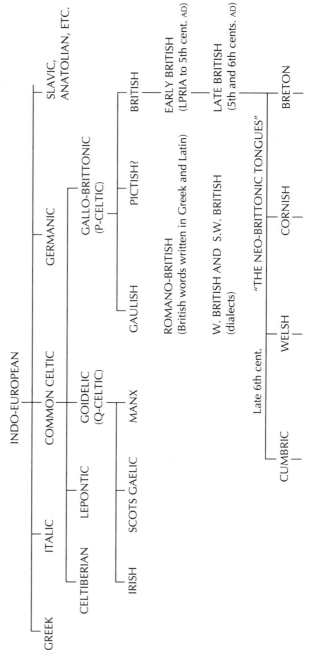

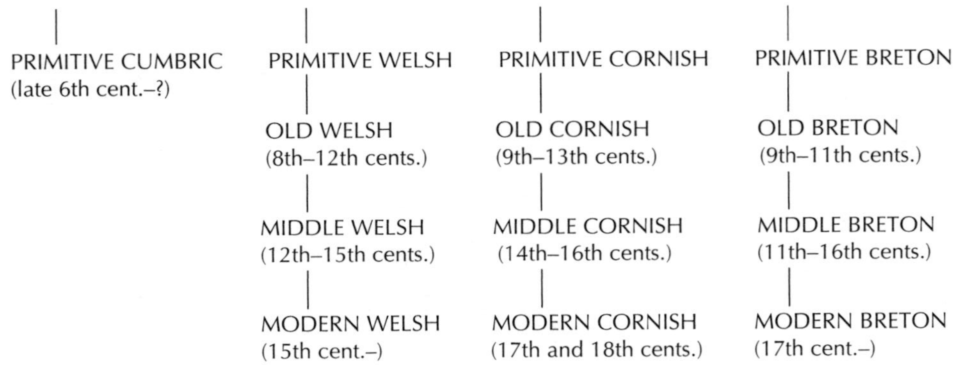

PRIMITIVE CUMBRIC
(late 6th cent.–?)

PRIMITIVE WELSH

OLD WELSH
(8th–12th cents.)

MIDDLE WELSH
(12th–15th cents.)

MODERN WELSH
(15th cent.–)

PRIMITIVE CORNISH

OLD CORNISH
(9th–13th cents.)

MIDDLE CORNISH
(14th–16th cents.)

MODERN CORNISH
(17th and 18th cents.)

PRIMITIVE BRETON

OLD BRETON
(9th–11th cents.)

MIDDLE BRETON
(11th–16th cents.)

MODERN BRETON
(17th cent.–)

Figure 12.1 The Celtic language tree, with the Brittonic languages given in detail.

words. Lastly, the Brittonic languages include many loan words, but also in turn lent words to neighboring tongues. A large number of Latin words were borrowed by Brittonic speakers. These tend to be words for Roman things unknown to Britons before the Roman conquest, later joined by Latin biblical and ecclesiastical terms. We have seen that there were probably large communities of Irish speakers – lay and ecclesiastical – in western Wales in the fifth and sixth centuries, and thus there are some Irish loan words in Welsh, for example. But mostly the Irish left their mark in placenames in Wales and, to a lesser extent, the southwest. British placenames and geographical terms entered both Latin and Old English, while British Latin ecclesiastical terms entered Irish, beginning with the missionary activity of the fifth century.

Since Brittonic was a synthetic language and Welsh an analytic one, we should be able to date the emergence of Welsh by tracing the transition from word-endings to prepositions and word order. However, no full written sentence of Brittonic has survived, so we can only look at clues like the disappearance of the last syllable of certain Brittonic nouns, which occurs around 600. Only three words of Cumbric have survived – *galnes* (blood-fine), *mercheta* (daughter), and *kelchyn* (circuit) – all three legal terms preserved in an eleventh-century text known as the *Leges inter Brettos et Scotos*. The rest of our information comes from a handful of Cumbric placenames borrowed into English. Jackson believes that Cumbric agreed closely with Welsh.[3] Strathclyde likely remained Cumbric-speaking until the kingdom's collapse in the eleventh century. A handful of medieval Cornish texts are extant (most notably liturgical drama written in Middle Cornish), and spoken Cornish survived in Devon until around 950 and in Cornwall until the eighteenth century. Cornish exists today only as a language revived by scholars, though with a growing following. Of all the Brittonic tongues, only Welsh and Breton survive today as both spoken and written languages. They are languages of beauty and creativity, though predictions concerning their long-term survival are mostly pessimistic.

As Gerald of Wales pointed out in the twelfth century, the Breton and Cornish languages were especially close. 'There is little doubt,' writes Jackson, 'that a Cornishman and a Breton could have understood one another without great difficulty as long as Cornish was a living language.'[4] We have seen that this linguistic evidence has led to the belief that Brittany was settled primarily by British emigrants from Devon and Cornwall in the late fifth and sixth centuries.[5] An especially large migration of Brit-

---

3   Jackson, 1994, 10.
4   Jackson, 1994, 12.
5   See chapter 7 above.

ons from the southwest to Brittany in the second half of the sixth century may explain why Breton and Cornish diverge much later than the divergence of Welsh and Cornish.[6] Continued intercourse by sea between Brittany and Cornwall, noticeable especially in the hagiography, may have helped to preserve the unity of Breton and Cornish for several centuries, as was certainly the case for Irish and Scots Gaelic.

Lastly, comment should be made on the failure of Brittonic to remain the *lingua franca* of Britain. It was certainly the language of the majority throughout the Iron Age and probably the Roman period as well. Unlike the other western provinces of the empire, Britain did not emerge in the post-Roman centuries speaking a Romance language; but neither did native Brittonic become the dominant language in Britain in the Middle Ages. Old English, the language spoken by a relatively small number of immigrants in the fifth and sixth centuries, became the dominant language in Lowland Britain in only a few centuries, and was so strongly rooted that it remained dominant despite linguistic incursions from Danish and French. The Brittonic languages, meanwhile, began their steady recession, which continues to this day.

Neither historians nor linguists have adequately explained this phenomenon. Taking their cue from archaeology and placename studies, however, most scholars now believe that Brittonic speakers remained in very large numbers within the Anglo-Saxon kingdoms for several centuries. Undoubtedly famine, war, and dislocation, all of which are described vividly in the contemporary sources, did take their toll on many British communities. As we have seen,[7] towns and regions where Britons still dominated demographically within England were designated as such by English speakers through the use of the roots *Cumbre-* and *Walh-*. Gradually, however, even these communities gave in linguistically to the pressures of an English-speaking minority who held the political, economic, and eventually ecclesiastical advantages. That the Brittonic languages survived at all may be due to the Danish and Norman disruptions of Anglo-Saxon and Frankish expansion and to the political fragmentation of feudalism. After a hiatus of several centuries, which witnessed the flowering of Brittonic vernacular literature, new enemies – Tudor and Valois centralism, the Protestant Reformation, railroads and factories – would appear and spread through the Brittonic lands, resulting in the death of Cornish and the rapid decline of Breton and Welsh.[8] It remains to be seen whether two new forces, the European Community and political devolution within Britain, will prevent the demise of these last two Brittonic tongues.

6   See Jackson, 1994, 26–7.
7   Chapter 5 above.
8   See chapter 13 below.

British Latin Writers

Before we look at British vernacular literature, it is worth recalling that the earliest writings we have from British hands are works in Latin. A list of such writings, spanning a thousand years, includes some of the most famous authors of the Middle Ages.[9] Pelagius, Patrick, Gildas, 'Nennius,' Asser, Caradoc of Llancarfan, Geoffrey of Monmouth, Peter Abelard, John of Cornwall, Peter of Cornwall, and Gerald of Wales were all Britons by birth, though each became part of something else, namely the international brotherhood of ecclesiastical intelligentsia.

As David Howlett has remarked, most scholars have viewed this as 'the emergence of able men from a Celtic ghetto.'[10] While I hope that this study has shown that early medieval Britons were hardly ghettoized, it is fair to ask whether this group of British Latin writers reflects British culture. The answer varies according to the circumstances of the individual writer. The Briton Patrick, for example, spent most of his lifetime in Ireland, his adopted home, and Abelard eagerly fled Brittany and had few good words to say about his homeland. Gildas has sympathies for the Britons, but praising them would have undermined the purpose of his epistle. Asser and Gerald were writing for non-British patrons. So too was Geoffrey, but the greatness of his achievement was that he was able to tell the old native tales (along with a few he invented) in a manner appealing to a broad audience. These are individuals who can, to varying degrees, move between two worlds: that of the Catholic Church and that of the local prince with his war-band and bards.

The Bard in the Early Middle Ages

To understand British vernacular literature, as it emerged from oral performance to written form in the tenth and eleventh centuries, one must comprehend the shadowy world of the early medieval bard. Classical and medieval writers consistently define the bard as a storyteller and musical performer with priestly powers. For example, Strabo wrote that, in ancient Gaul, bards (βάρδοι) were 'singers and poets.' They were, in pre-Christian society, related to the Druids, whom Caesar claimed could 'commit to memory immense amounts of poetry.' Posidonius may have been the first Classical author to identify, among Celtic speakers, men

---

9   These works are identified in Michael Lapidge and Richard Sharpe, *A Bibliography of Celtic-Latin Literature, 400–1200* (Dublin, 1985).
10   Howlett, 1995, 389.

who recite praise-poetry for their chieftains, using the term *parasitoi* (parasites).[11] Gildas employs this same term (in Latin *parasiti*) to describe flatterers at the court of Maelgwn in sixth-century Gwynedd.[12] These men are most likely court bards, and elsewhere Gildas implies that even the British clergy enjoyed hearing their 'foolish stories.'[13]

The Italian poet Venantius Fortunatus wrote, in 566, about barbarous songs which 'the British harp (*crotta Britanna*) sings.'[14] Venantius contrasts the *crotta* (Middle Welsh *crwth* and *croth*) with a continental lyre, but implies that the Britons, like the Franks, had poets who celebrated the heroic deeds of their royal patrons to the accompaniment of a stringed instrument.[15] Welsh law texts refer to two classes of bard: the *pencerdd*, 'chief of song,' and the *bard teylu*, 'poet of the war-band.' When the *bard teylu* came into his profession, he was given a harp which he was always to have with him.[16] As we saw earlier, it was the Lord Rhys who, in 1176, hosted at Cardigan the first *eisteddfod*. It was, according to the chronicler, an international competition of bards, poets, pipers, and players of 'various classes of string music,' and the victors were from Deheubarth and Gwynedd.[17]

Cerdd dafod, 'the craft of the tongue,' is honored alongside *cerdd dant*, 'the craft of the string,' in Welsh poetry. In the fourth branch of the *Mabonogi* Gwydion assumes the role of the *pencerdd* at the court of Pryderi, while the *Dream of Rhonabwy* makes a distinction between bard (*bardd*) and storyteller (*cyfarwydd*). Gerald of Wales and later Welsh sources ascribe three functions to the bard: to recite the deeds of British kings and princes, to be the custodians of the Welsh language, and to know the genealogies and heraldry of the Welsh nobility.[18] In Gerald's days the Welsh bards, though capable of reciting from memory, were keeping 'copies of the genealogies of these princes in their old manuscripts . . . written in Welsh.' Gerald also described the ability of contemporary Welsh poets (*awenyddion*) to go into a shaman-like trance, their bodies taken over by the *awen*.[19] In Wales *awen* was a type of muse or poetic inspiration which the early bards literally inhaled (it derives from an Indo-European root meaning 'to breathe') from the gods.[20] The songs of the

11   See Tierney, 1959–60.
12   Gildas, *De Excidio*, 35.3. See J. E. C. Williams, 1984.
13   Gildas, *De Excidio*, 66.4. See also Richter, 1994.
14   *MGH, AA*, vol. 4 (1891), 7.8.
15   Moisl, 1980–2, 273.
16   Richter, 1994, 219.
17   *Brut y Tywysogyon*, Red Book Version, s.a. 1176.
18   Gerald, *Description of Wales*, 1.3. See Richter, 1994, 216.
19   Gerald, *Description of Wales*, pp.194–5. See Ford, 1974, 58.
20   J. E. C. Williams, 1984, 24.

early bards would, in turn, not just praise their patrons but would inspire
heroic qualities within them.

The *Cynfeirdd*

'The bards of the world judge the men of valor,' runs the line from the
Gododdin. This guaranteed the privileged position of the bard at medieval British courts. Welsh literary tradition honors especially a group of
men known as the *cynfeirdd*, 'early poets.' In the *Historia Brittonum* there
is a list of the most famous of these early poets: Talhaearn ('the father of
poetry'), Neirin, Taliessin, Bluchbardd, and Cian ('who is called "wheat
of song"'). Of these poets only Aneirin and Taliesin have left their names
on extant poems. Their verses, as well those of the *cynfeirdd* Myrddin
Wyllt and Llywarch Hen, survive in much later manuscripts, the most
important of which are the Black Book of Carmarthen (*c*.1250), the Book
of Aneirin (late thirteenth century), the Book of Taliesin (early fourteenth
century), the White Book of Rhydderch (*c*.1325), and the Red Book of
Hergest (*c*.1400).

Aneirin was a court bard in the northern British kingdom of Gododdin,
which was centered on the modern city of Edinburgh.[21] Traditionally he
has been viewed as the author of the poem *Y Gododdin*, a collection of
stanzas describing the raid on Catraeth (Catterick) *c*.572.[22] Aneirin apparently witnessed the ensuing battle in which the Gododdin's war-band
was wiped out, and later composed an elegy to the fallen British soldiers.
The poem is generally considered the oldest extent verse from Scotland,
the earliest poem in Welsh, and may contain the first mention of both
Arthur and Merlin:

> *Gochore brein du ar uur*
> *Caer ceni bei ef arthur*

> He [Gwawrddur] fed black ravens on the rampart
> Of a fortress, though he was no Arthur.

> *Amuc moryen gwenwawd mirdyn*
> *A chyvrannv penn prif eg weryt*

> Morien defended the fair song of Myrddin
> And laid the head of a chief in the earth.[23]

---

21   See discussion in chapter 10 above.
22   See, however, Koch, 1997.
23   *Y Gododdin*, stanzas 38 and 43. See Snyder, 2000, 92–8.

Taliesin was probably the most revered of the *cynfeirdd*. Like Aneirin, Taliesin was believed to be a sixth-century bard from the north, associated especially with the British kingdom of Rheged and its king Urien. Both Urien and his son Owain are praised in poems bearing Taliesin's name. Not all of the poems in the Book of Taliesin attributed to the bard are genuinely early, however. Many clearly employ the name of Taliesin as a tribute to the legendary bard.

There are several references to Arthur in the Taliesin poems, but the king plays a substantial role only in *Preiddeu Annwn* ('The Spoils of Annwfn'). This is an adventure tale describing a raid by Arthur and his men on Annwfn, the Welsh pre-Christian Otherworld (described in the poem as 'the fairy fort' and 'the fortress of glass'). Arthur's warriors sail in several ships to Annwfn in an attempt to seize its treasures, the most important of which is a magical cauldron. There are other Welsh tales analogous to this adventure in *The Spoils*, including a similar episode in *Culhwch and Olwen*, where the cauldron rests in Ireland. All of these stories may derive from a common Celtic theme of 'raid on the Otherworld,' and they most certainly contributed to the development of the Grail tradition and its association with Glastonbury, 'The Fort of Glass.' In the poem Taliesin boasts of his own role in Arthur's voyage to Annwfn, thus implying that the two were contemporaries. But although the narrator of the poem assumes the persona of Taliesin, the work itself dates from the period *c*.850–1150.

The third of these venerated British bards, and perhaps their contemporary, is Myrddin, better known by his Latinized name Merlin. Myrddin may be less 'historical' than Aneirin and Taliesin, and like the latter his name was attached to many works of many different periods. Some have even suggested that Taliesin and Myrddin were names given interchangeably to accomplished Welsh bards, serving as an archetype for 'the poet.' The name Myrddin may derive from *Moridunon*, Latinized as *Maridunum*, which Roman sources record as the original name of Carmarthen in southwest Wales. In modern Welsh Carmarthen is Caer-fyrddin, 'the Myrddin-town' (*m* having mutated to *f*), and Geoffrey of Monmouth states that Merlin was indeed born there and that the town was later renamed after him. Others have claimed that Myrddin was an entirely mythical figure invented to explain the name of the town.

The name Myrddin appears in two early works, the *Gododdin* and *Armes Prydein*. In the first case the context is ambiguous and the line may be a later interpolation. In the second, Myrddin is clearly viewed as a famous British prophet: 'Myrdin foretells that they will meet in Aber Peryddon, the stewards of the Great King.'[24] The earliest poems attrib-

---

24 *Armes Prydein*, ll.17–18.

uted to Myrddin seem to place him in sixth-century northwestern Britain, thus making him a contemporary and neighbor of Taliesin. But these poems exist only in later manuscripts like the Black Book of Carmarthen. The oldest of them may be *Yr Afallennau* ('The Apple-trees'), an ode to a magical apple-tree 'hidden in the forest of Celyddon.' In the poem, the narrator Myrddin tells his audience that he has been living in hardship for the past 50 years in the Caledonian woods, hiding from Rhydderch Hael (Roderick the Generous), king of Strathclyde. Before coming to Celyddon, Merlin had served the Cumbrian prince Gwenddolau and the two had fought together (Myrddin had worn a torc of gold, in the style of the ancient Celtic warriors) at the Battle of Arderydd (AD 573). Gwynddolau fell in the battle, and in witnessing the carnage (which included the death of his sister Gwynddydd's son) Myrddin lost his wits, running wild into the forest, uttering prophecies and keeping fellowship with animals.

Other Welsh poems trace these strange adventures, describing a deeply grieving Myrddin who has somehow acquired the gift of prophecy. Scholars have pointed to a similar 'wild man in the forest' tradition in Scottish literature, where the tragic figure is named Laloecen or Lailoken (the Welsh form of this name, *Llallogan*, is ascribed to Myrddin in another poem). In both traditions the wild man is blest, ironically, with the ability to prophesy, and this made Myrddin an attractive figure to politically minded writers from the twelfth century onward.[25] Geoffrey of Monmouth took the figure of Myrddin and combined him with the prophetic boy Ambrosius culled from the *Historia Brittonum*, thus creating the composite figure Merlin (*Merlinus*) from the town of Carmarthen (*Kaermerdin*). An early *Life of St. Kentigern* made a similar connection between Lailoken and '*Merlynus*, an extraordinary prophet of the British.' Geoffrey was also the first to link the figures of Arthur and Merlin, though admittedly there is only a slight relationship in his *History*, which was elaborated by later writers of romance.

Little remains from the other *cynfeirdd*. In the Red Book of Hergest there is a collection of poems attributed to one Llywarch Hen. Some of these poems are in the earlier Black Book of Carmarthern and were, most likely, also to be found in the fragmentary White Book of Rhydderch. The medieval Welsh believed Llywarch to be a warrior and poet of the Heroic Age, and associated him with Arthur's court, with Urien Rheged (Llywarch's first cousin in the genealogies), and with Cynddylan of Powys (seventh century). This would make Llywarch 'the Old' very old, so an historical Llywarch remains a shadowy figure whose name – and reputation – were apparently appended to these poems by a ninth- or tenth-

25 See discussion in chapter 11 above.

century court poet.[26] Nevertheless, the poetry is 'of the highest professional caliber,' writes Patrick Ford, and 'worthy of comparison with the works of Aneirin and Taliesin.'[27]

It is clear that Llywarch Hen is more a character in the poems than their author. The Red Book contains a large number of related stanzas (of both *englyn* and *awdl* meters), some of which refer to Llywarch and his sons, others to Cynddylan, Cadwallon, and Geraint.[28] The stanzas are lyric in style, with narrative that preserves the names of heroic individuals and places where battles were fought or heroes fell. The elegiac stanzas are quite similar to those in the *Gododdin*, and perhaps more moving. Here Llywarch is the old warrior bewailing the loss of sons and friends and his own old age:

> I am not nimble, I hold no host,
>   Nor can I freely roam.
> Let the cuckoo sing as long as it likes.
>
> I listened to a cuckoo on an ivy-covered branch.
>   My shield-strap has slackened;
> Grief for what I loved grows.
>
> Before I was decrepit, I was bold.
> They welcomed me in the taverns of
> Powys, paradise of the Cymry.
>
> Crutch of wood, constant branch,
> May you support an old man full of longing –
> Llywarch, the steadfast talker.
>
> I had, though they were generous,
> It will be sad being without them,
> Many fair and merry children;
> But tonight, I am alone.[29]

These elegies and other somber saga *englynion* may have been originally inspired by the dire political situation in Wales in the eighth and ninth centuries. But they also explore broader themes, such as the limitations of the heroic ethos, the tensions between familial and political ties, and the conflicts between religious and secular values.[30]

26 Ford, 1974, 4. Cf. Rowland, 1990, 7ff.
27 Ford, 1974, 11.
28 See Rowland, 1990.
29 *The Poetry of Llywarch Hen*, stanzas 3, 8, 34, 40, 230.
30 Rowland, 1990, 2.

'The Great Prophecy of Britain'

The *Awen* foretells, [Cynan and Cadwaladr] will hasten:
We shall have wealth and property and peace,
And wide dominion, and ready leaders;
   . . . .
The warriors will scatter the foreigners . . .
And there will be reconciliation between the Cymry and the men of Dublin,
The Irish of Ireland and Anglesey and Scotland,
The men of Cornwall and of Strathclyde will be made welcome among us.
The Britons will rise again [and] prevail,
For long was prophesied the time when [Cynan and Cadwaladr] will come,
As rulers whose possession is by [the right of] descent.[31]

Thus begins the *Armes Prydein Vawr*, 'The Great Prophecy of Britain.' The
Armes was composed between 935 and 950 by a poet from south Wales.[32]
It may be a product of St. David's, for the poet says that the Britons will
rally the Irish to their cause under the standard of St. David. In the poem
the Welsh are called *Kymry* (it is the first appearance of the term) and are
part of the larger group, the *Brython*, which includes the Cornish, the Men
of the North, and the Bretons. In contrast the English are called *allmyn*, a
half-Welsh half-English word meaning 'foreigners' (and perhaps a commentary on *wealsc*, the English term for the Britons), as well as *granwynyon*,
which is similar to the nickname 'palefaces' used by Native Americans.[33]

 David Dumville warns us not to see this as a pan-Celtic coalition, but
rather as an alliance of all the Britons (from Wales, Strathclyde, Cornwall, and Brittany) with other Insular peoples threatened by the consolidation of English power.[34] Gwynedd had allied with Northumbrian Vikings
between 878 and 893, and an Irish Sea coalition of Dublin Vikings, Scots,
and Britons from Strathclyde challenged Æthelstan in 937 and again in
939 or 940. But the Bretons were not then likely to join an alliance against
Æthelstan, who gave refuge to Alain Barbetorte and other Breton exiles,
so the poet must have had something in mind other than political expedi-
ency.[35] The *Armes* 'derives its strength not merely from a reading of political possibilities and options,' comments Brynley Roberts, 'but from an
emotional appeal to an accepted myth.'[36]

 This myth, of the old Brittonic unity, would appear again in its most

31 *Armes*, ll.1–14.
32 See I. Williams, 1972, xiv–xx; and Dumville, 1983, 147–8.
33 I. Williams, 1972, 20, 41.
34 Dumville, 1983, 147.
35 I. Williams, 1972, xxii.
36 Roberts, 1976, 36.

powerful and influential expression in Geoffrey of Monmouth's *History of the Kings of Britain*. In his restatement of the prophecy (*Vita Merlini*, lines 965–8) Geoffrey does not mention the Dublin Danes, perhaps to strengthen his vision of the Britons' sovereignty on the island.

The Welsh Triads

We do not know the identity of the author of the *Armes*. Most early Welsh poetry remains anonymous, collected and added to over the years by countless unremembered bards. Such is a large collection of Welsh verses called *Trioedd Ynys Prydein* ('The Triads of the Island of Britain'), commonly referred to as the Welsh Triads. These poems were grouped in threes (a sacred number but also a mnemonic device for the bards) according to a common theme, sometimes comical. For example, there are the 'The Three Fair Princes of the Island of Britain,' 'The Three Frivolous Bards,' and 'The Three Powerful Swineherds.' The Triads survive in several manuscripts, the oldest dating from the thirteenth and fourteenth centuries, which are based on a collection put together in the eleventh or twelfth century. Though relatively late in date, the Triads include tales that must derive from an earlier period of oral performance, for they appear (in altered form) in such early works as *Culhwch and Olwen*. Other poems in the collection are entirely late and influenced by such written texts as Geoffrey's *History*.

The Triads comprise a heterogeneous collection, with the growing popularity of Arthur reflected mostly in late additions where Arthur has sometimes ousted other ancient heroes. There are over two dozen Arthurian references in the Triads, with Arthur either appearing as one of the three figures in the list or else added as a fourth and exceptional example (e.g. 'and Arthur himself was more generous than the three').[37] In the Triads Arthur is Chief Prince (*Pen Teyrnedd*) of the Island, ruling over Wales, Cornwall, and northern Britain from his court of *Celliwig*, in Cornwall. Praised as a great warrior and hunter, he is served by such men as Cai and Bedwyr and is the rival of King March (Mark of Cornwall). Five of the Triads also refer to 'Camlan,' Arthur's last and fatal battle.

The *Mabinogi*

Rachel Bromwich cites many parallels in the Triads with motifs from early Irish literature.[38] Many of the figures in the Triads appear in the tales of

---

37   *Trioedd Ynys Prydein*, no. 2. See Roberts, 1991.
38   Bromwich, 1978, lxvi.

the *Mabinogi*, which also have several close parallels in Irish myths. In the early nineteenth century Lady Charlotte Guest collected 11 Welsh prose tales from the Red Book of Hergest and the Book of Taliesin and published her translations. She named this collection *The Mabinogion*, and it was assumed that all the tales were linked by the theme of youth (*mab* meaning 'boy, son'). *Mabinigion*, however, is actually a scribal error for *mabinogi*, the term now preferred by most scholars, who believe that this word means something like 'the collective material pertaining to the god *Maponos* ("the divine youth," an ancient Brittonic deity).'[39] The earliest versions of these tales can be found in the White Book of Rhydderch and in four Peniarth manuscripts (in the National Library of Wales, Aberystwyth).

The *Mabinogi* proper includes only the first four tales or 'branches' – of Pwyll, Branwen, Manawydan, and Math – which probably date from the middle of the eleventh century. Their characters and themes, however, are very ancient. The first branch, *Pwyll, Prince of Dyfed*, relates the adventures of the mortal Pwyll in the Otherworld, his marriage to the strong and assertive Rhiannon, and the birth of their son Pryderi. *Branwen Daughter of Llŷr*, the second branch, is the tragic tale of the war between Ireland and Wales which results from the ill-fated marriage of Branwen and the Irish king Matholwch. The third branch, *Manawydan Son of Llŷr*, brings the first two together, when Pryderi and Manawydan escape the war in Ireland and go on several adventures together in an enchanted England (*Lloegyr*). The final branch, *Math Son of Mathonwy*, is a strange collection of tales concerning various members of the family of the goddess Dôn, including her brother Math and son Gwydion, both powerful magicians, and her daughter Aranrhod and her son Lleu. Gwydion's tricking Pryderi into giving him the swine he had obtained in the Otherworld brings the branches together in a cohesive cycle.

These tales, often wonderful and compelling, weave together strands of myth and folklore that would have been available to British bards and poets for centuries. They are unique in the Welsh canon in focusing on the adventures of divinities and magic rather than figures like Arthur whom medieval audiences would have regarded as securely historical. Modern editors, however, see the four branches as related to other early compositions and often include the latter in their editions and translations of the *Mabinogi*. *Culhwch ac Olwen* ('Culhwch and Olwen') is the earliest of these related tales, and likely dates from the beginning of the eleventh century. Surviving in both the White Book and the Red Book, it is the story of Arthur's cousin Culhwch ('pig pen'), who is fated to love only

---

39 See Hamp, 1974–5; and Ford, 1977, 2–3.

one woman, Olwen ('white track'), daughter of the giant Ysbaddaden. Arriving at Celliwig to seek the king's advice, Culhwch is given seven of Arthur's men to help him win Olwen. Her father, however, imposes a series of seemingly impossible tasks on Culhwch before he will consent to the marriage. With the help of Arthur and his warriors, Culhwch eventually completes the tasks, Ysbaddaden is killed, and the young lovers are united.

Despite the plot and title, this tale is not so much about Culhwch and Olwen as it is about the spectacular adventures accomplished by Arthur's company. Here we find Cei, Bedwyr, Glewlwyd Gafaelfawr (Arthur's porter), and mythological personages like Mabon son of Modron and Gwyn son of Nudd. Arthur himself joins the adventure, sailing off on his ship Prydwen, and is described as 'chief of the princes (*pen teyrnedd*) of this island.' Stephen Knight has argued that this Arthur was modeled after historical 'over-kings' of Wales, especially Rhodri Mawr and Hywel Dda.[40] It is true that while other British heroes are identified with a particular tribe or kingdom in the Welsh vernacular tradition, Arthur never is; rather, he is a roaming king associated with Britain at large. This makes him a particularly attractive figure for later Welsh political prophecy.

In *Culhwch and Olwen*, Arthur appears more the hero from a wonder tale than the great feudal lord of the French romances. This, along with spelling and other linguistic features of *Culhwch*, have convinced scholars that the work was composed much earlier than the romances, making it the oldest full Arthurian story in the Welsh canon. The Red and White Books contain another group of three related Arthurian tales which were included in Guest's *Mabinogion* collection: *Geraint ab Erbin* ('Geraint son of Erbin'), *Owain: Chwedl Iarlles Y Ffynnon* ('Owain: Or the Tale of the Lady of the Fountain'), and *Ystoria Peredur ab Efrawg* ('The History of Peredur son of Efrawg'). Written in the thirteenth century and labeled by scholars the 'three Welsh romances,' these prose tales are basically analogues of three French romances written in the late twelfth century by Chrétien de Troyes, namely *Erec et Enide, Yvain,* and *Perceval. Geraint,* sometimes called *Geraint and Enid,* is the closest to the French version, but commemorates the historical Dumnonian king.[41] *Owain* is the tale (*chwedl*) or story (*ystori*) of Owain ab Urien, who is here depicted as one of Arthur's knights. So too is *Peredur,* which perhaps preserves a tradition concerning the sixth-century British lord of Eburacum (York).[42]

Another Arthurian tale often associated with the *Mabinogi* is *Breuddwyd Rhonabwy* ('The Dream of Rhonabwy'), though it survives only in the

40   Knight, 1983, 32–4.
41   See chapter 8 above.
42   See chapter 10 above.

Red Book and appears to be the product of only one, probably thirteenth-century, author. *The Dream of Rhonabwy* opens with the fictional character Rhonabwy, who sets off to seek the brother of Madog ap Maredudd, the historical ruler of Powys *c.*1130–60. Lodging for the night on this journey, Rhonabwy is granted a *drych* (vision or dream) that transports him back to the days of Arthur. In this dream he comes upon Arthur and his men encamped and awaiting the Battle of Badon. Arthur himself is occupied playing a board-game with Owain ab Urien, from which he can't tear himself away despite messages that his own men are attacking and in turn being slain by Owain's ravens! A truce is finally called – without the actual battle happening – and Arthur leaves to gather his forces in Cornwall. With that Rhonabwy awakens (having slept three days and three nights), and the story ends with no explanation given for the strange dream.

As modern commentators have pointed out, *The Dream of Rhonabwy* shows us an Arthurian world turned upside down. The Battle of Camlan precedes that of Badon, Arthur is abused by minor characters, and the great king is so distracted by a competition against one of his own supporters that he allows his men to die and neglects to face his real enemy at Badon. The dream journey motif and geographical precision of *The Dream of Rhonabwy* have only one clear parallel in the Welsh tradition, *Breuddwyd Macsen Wledig* ('The Dream of Emperor Maximus'), which gives a Welsh explanation for Magnus Maximus coming to Britain (and Caernarvon in particular). As we have seen, British traditions claimed Maximus as the founder of Brittany as well as the dynasty of the kings of Dyfed.[43] In the Triads, Maximus' title is *gwledic*, which, like its Breton counterpart *gloedic*, was usually applied to the leader of a local militia.[44] Thus *The Dream of Maximus* apparently preserves a quite old tradition that saw Maximus as a local hero, a British emperor. It is a marvelous adventure tale, synthesizing this tradition with British legends concerning Constantine the Great and St. Helena.[45]

The Breton *Lais*

The Magnus Maximus story is only one of many literary links between early Wales and early Brittany. The Britons who came to Brittany in the fifth and sixth centuries brought their myths with them and, presumably, their bards. Brittany, as we have seen, maintained ties with both Wales and especially Cornwall during the first few centuries after the migra-

---

43   See chapters 7 and 9 above.
44   Bromwich, 1978, 454.
45   See Bromwich, 1978, 454; Matthews, 1983; and Snyder, forthcoming.

tions. Both the *Historia Brittonum* and *The Dream of Maximus* preserve, from the Welsh perspective, old stories about the British diaspora. While the Bretons retained their own language, most medieval Breton writing was done in Latin and, later, Old French. Of the Latin works there are several lives of British saints, and two of these – the *Life of St. Efflam* and the *Legend of St. Goeznovius* – include adventures of Arthur.

From the twelfth to the sixteenth centuries several Breton tales about Arthur and other British heroes were written in the form of *lais* (lays). English and Anglo-Norman writers of the twelfth century, like Henry of Huntingdon and Wace, describe Brittany as the origin point of several Arthurian traditions, including the Round Table, the enchanted Forest of Brocéliande, and the belief in Arthur's return. Medieval Brittany, like much of Europe, enjoyed a thriving oral culture where bards, minstrels, and *jongleurs* entertained crowds and patrons with their vernacular tales. By the twelfth century the French-speaking nobility of Normandy, France, and England apparently became quite attracted to these Breton tales, especially those having to do with Arthur and his knights. A genre known as the Breton *lai* swept through the French-speaking world, and soon writers of chronicles and romances were incorporating themes and characters from the oral Breton *lais* into their own written compositions.

The word *lai* is a common Celtic term, which, in a Breton context, came to describe a short song played on a harp or other string instrument, usually accompanying the telling of a tale. In some Arthurian stories the characters themselves perform lays. Some Breton bards or minstrels learned to perform lays in French and traveled throughout the vast French-speaking world, where they could perform at markets, fairs, and, if they were lucky, at the courts of the great nobles. These courts often had resident poets called *trouvères* who were learned men – and women – composing works of literature to suit the tastes of their aristocratic patrons. For secular compositions they often drew from material that would come to be called the *matière de Bretagne* ('Matter of Britain'), predominantly stories of Arthur and his knights. The most famous 'composer' of Breton *lais* was Marie de France, a resident of England in the late twelfth century, who composed poems at the Anglo-Norman courts of the Angevins. Marie wrote twelve *lais* as well as a collection of fables (*Ysopet*) and a legend of St. Patrick's Purgatory.

Two of Marie's lays were overtly Arthurian: *Chevrefueil* ('Honeysuckle') and *Lanval*. The first poem recounts a brief but passionate encounter between Tristan and Isolde in the forest. Their dependent but doomed love is likened, in the poem, to the intertwining of the honeysuckle and the hazel, where one cannot live without the other. More narrative is *Lanval*, the tale of a young knight whose fairy lover requires him to keep their love a secret. At Arthur's court he is seduced by Guinevere, but in repelling her advances he reveals his secret and is accused of insulting and lying to the Queen. Despite breaking his oath, Lanval is saved at the last minute when his otherworldly lady arrives and reveals the truth. The plot is very similar to that of *Graelent*, a non-Arthurian *lai* about a werewolf.

Marie was one of the first writers to explore the conflicts between romantic and chivalric ideals. Subsequent *lais* parodied these themes (and Arthur), such as Robert Biket's *Lai du Cor* ('Lay of the Horn') and the *Lai du Cort Mantel* ('Lay of the Short Mantle'). Other Breton lays clearly draw on older, pre-courtly themes, such as the now-lost *Merlin le Sauvage* ('Merlin the Wild Man') and *An Dialog Etre Arzur Roe D'an Bretounet Ha Guynglaff* ('A Dialogue between Arthur, King of Britain, and Guynglaff'), a rare Breton-language composition featuring the wild man and magician Guynglaff, who prophesies to Arthur about political events which will occur in Britain down to the 1580s.

Welsh Chronicles and Histories

The figure of Arthur dominates medieval British historiography from his first appearance in the *Annales Cambriae* to the late medieval Welsh prophecies and chronicles. Gildas is often called by medieval writers 'the historian of the Britons.' Though composing a lengthy sermon in the form of an epistle, Gildas does (following Augustine) include a brief providential history of his people. The *Historia Brittonum* follows Gildas's view of history, though here history is employed more to celebrate the achievements of Britons in their struggle with the English. Geoffrey of Monmouth carries this celebration of British heroes to great heights in his *History of the Kings of Britain*. While not employing sound historical methodology, Geoffrey nonetheless achieved a moving and ultimately tragic history of the rise and fall of a noble race.

British historical writing in the vernacular appears rather late, and most works are inspired by Geoffrey's *History*. The most significant medieval Welsh historical tradition is that of the *Brut*. Isidore of Seville wrote that *Britto*, the preferred medieval term for 'Briton,' derived from *brutus*. At a time when the Franks and other European peoples were tracing their ethnic origins to the fall of Troy, the British author of the *Historia Brittonum* (or more likely his source) stated that the Britons are the descendants of a Trojan refugee named Brutus. This foundation legend is more fully explored by Geoffrey of Monmouth. So popular was Geoffrey's history of Brutus and his royal descendants that *Brut* became the generic term for 'British histories,' whether they be bare-bones chronicles or romantic fables, in both Welsh and Anglo-Norman literature.

There are several works written in Middle Welsh with the title *Brut* or in the *Brut* traditon. The *Brut y Brenhinedd* ('Chronicle of the Kings') is a straightforward Welsh translation of Geoffrey's *History*. The *Brut y Tywysogyon* ('Chronicle of the Princes') is based on a now lost Latin chronicle (related to the *Annales Cambriae* and the *Cronica de Wallia*) compiled at the end of the thirteenth century at the Cistercian abbey of Strata Florida. Three independent Welsh translations of this chronicle are extant, known respectively as the 'Peniarth MS. 20 version,' the 'Red Book of Hergest version,' and the '*Brenhinedd y Saesson* version.' The *Brenhinedd y Saesson* ('Kings of the Saxons') is a composite of the Strata Florida chronicle and the *Annals of Winchester*. Taken as a whole, these texts show that written Welsh had finally taken its place beside Latin as a language of both learning and culture.

Of greatest interest to historians is the *Brut y Tywysogyon*. The Red Book and Peniarth versions of the *Brut* are chronicles in the form of brief annals running from 680 to 1282 and 1332 respectively. The first entry in the *Brut* records the death in Rome of 'Cadwaldr the Blessed, son of Cadwallon ap Cadfan, king of the Britons . . . as Myrddin had before prophesied.'[46] 'And from that time forth,' continues the entry, 'the Britons lost the crown of the kingdom; and the Saxons gained it.' The *Brut* thus establishes itself as a continuation of Geoffrey's *History*, which had ended with Cadwaladr and the Britons' loss of the Sovereignty. It also emerges as a distinctively Welsh national history, with references to Britons (*Brytanyeit*) giving way to *Kymry*. Still, all the later medieval Welsh chroniclers, including the author of the *Brut y Tywysogyon*, are concerned with the past unity of the island of Britain, a unity which, in the words of W. J. McCann, 'the Welsh are constantly harking back and to which it is hoped that they will eventually return, with the Welsh, as the rightful heirs to this historical inheritance, as rulers.'[47]

The Last of the Royal Bards

The Welsh chroniclers were, despite these sentiments, quicker to come to terms with the political realities of the later Middle Ages than were the Welsh court bards and authors of the political prophecies. We saw in the previous chapter that Welsh political prophecy was extremely popular in the twelfth and thirteenth centuries, despite the losses suffered by the Welsh princes. The name of Merlin (or Myrddin) was often attached to these prophecies, which cast Arthur, Cadwaladr, and other British princes in

---

46   *Brut y Tywysogyon*, Red Book Version, s.a. 680–2.
47   McCann, 1991, 47.

the role of national messiah. Owain Glyn Dŵr, encouraged by the poets he kept in his entourage, attempted to fulfill the messianic role himself, using the ancient historical myths to rally support both within Wales and from Ireland and Scotland.

Like the Irish and Scottish kings, the Welsh princes kept bards at court for as long as their dynasties continued to exercise power. These poets, though highly skilled professionals, were committed to continuing the functions of the ancient British bards that we discussed earlier: praise their patrons, recite history and genealogy, and preserve the Welsh language. 'The poet's art,' observes McCann,

> was both conservative to the point of archaism (rather like his view of society) and complex to the point of obscurity . . . There is a consciousness of a greater whole of which the kingdoms are part, but rather than being a united Wales, this is a harking back to an undivided Britain . . . They seem to live in a world where, in spite of English hegemony in Britain, there is a continuity between the tribal warfare of the past . . . and the endemic border warfare between English and Welsh which will go on for ever in the traditional way: the Normans are seen as just one more element in the old pattern.[48]

In the 1280s the Welsh court poets were robbed of their princely patronage. They continued on, however, until about 1600 under new patrons: the Welsh and Anglo-Welsh gentry. The works of about 150 of these *beirdd y uchelwyr* ('poets of the gentry') have survived, mostly praise-poems utilizing the traditional *awdl* meter or, more commonly, the new metrical form of the *cywydd*, a rhyming couplet of seven-syllabled lines. This complex and enigmatic verse was both perfected and popularized in the hands of the last, and perhaps greatest, of the medieval Welsh poets, Dafydd ap Gwilym.

Dafydd ap Gwilym

Where the Welsh court poets perpetuated the 'culture wars' between England and Wales, Dafydd ap Gwilym sought to synthesize the two literary traditions, drawing inspiration from both bardic poetry and Anglo-Norman verse. Born near Aberystwyth around 1320, Dafydd describes himself as a member of the *clêr*, or 'wanderers.'[49] Though without a formal occupation, he nevertheless was of sufficient wealth to support this lifestyle of traveling throughout Wales and the border shires entertaining

48 McCann, 1991, 64–6.
49 See the introduction by Rachel Bromwich in *Dafydd ap Gwyilym* (1982).

audiences with his *cywyddau*. Dafydd accompanied his *cywyddau* with a harp, and he shows considerable technical knowledge of harp-playing. He also occasionally turned to the panegyric genre, composing praise-poems and elegies (using both *awdl* and *englyn* metres) for his patrons. Dafydd's rich vocabulary was the result of an extensive knowledge of the language of Welsh poetry as well as words of French origin, and he is responsible for introducing *fabliaux* and self-deprecating irony into Welsh verse, partly inspired by his contemporary, Geoffrey Chaucer.

Most of Dafydd's poems celebrate, above all, Love and Nature. The two themes are often intermingled, as when he longs for a tryst with his lover in a wooded oasis. The poems are very personal, with Dafydd singing of his own travels and his own misadventures in love. In 'Journeying for Love,' for example, he asks

> Did ever anybody, tyrannized by love,
> travel as I have done, for a girl's sake,
> through frost and snow . . .
> through rain and wind for her dazzling form?

The object of his quest, we learn, is the unobtainable 'Morfudd Like the Sun':

> I woo a softly-spoken girl,
> pale as fine snow on the field's edge;
> God sees that she is radiant . . .
> She knows the way to win a love-song from my lips . . .
> The people's princess, in cloak of fine fur,
> she knows how to deride her ugly husband.
> Lovely Morfudd, woe to the weak idle poet
> who loves her. . . .

With Dafydd ap Gwilym we come full circle. Arthur, king of the Britons, inspired the British bards of the early Middle Ages to sing the deeds of his court of heroes. These tales reached the French-speaking courts of the eleventh and twelfth centuries, where they became the subject matter of troubadours and court poets, working to refine the ideals of courtly love. A century later these tales returned in chivalric form to Wales, inspiring Dafydd to wander like a troubadour, singing and suffering for his love.

But the land through which Dafydd wandered in the fourteenth century was a land bereft of native princes and heroes. *Britannia* had become *Cymru*, and Dafydd was, like Dante in Italy and Chaucer in England, about to receive from his nation the laurel wreath (metaphorically speaking) as the first great distinctively Welsh poet, recognized both at home and abroad for his significant literary achievements.

13
Conclusion

The great popularity of Celtic literature and Celtic themes in the high Middle Ages had spent its strength by the beginning of the sixteenth century. The Renaissance, with its emphasis on Greco-Roman rationality and naturalism, seemed incompatible with the fantastic and otherworldly tales of Brittany and Wales, despite the courtly sophistication of late medieval writers like Dafydd ap Gwilym. This decline was brought on in part by the loss of political autonomy in Brittany and Wales, which reached its completion in the early years of the sixteenth century. But due to a renewed interest in the ancient history of Britain and France, and yet another wave of Arthurian enthusiasm, there was a British revival in the seventeenth century that continues to this day. While the Sovereignty of the Island did not return to the Britons, the Cornish and Welsh could at least take some pride in the fact that it was a *British* Empire declared in the 1707 Act of Union.

The Loss of Sovereignty

Cornwall and Cumbria, as we have seen, lost their political autonomy by the eleventh century. Britons in the north were quickly Anglicized, though they were split by the border competition between England and Scotland. Cornish isolation meant that Anglicization there was slower, but in Cornwall too British culture was rapidly receding in the Early Modern period. The most serious impediment to this recession came in 1497. In response to the heavy taxation campaign of Henry VII, some 10,000 Cornishmen killed a Taunton tax-collector and marched on London. Led by Michel Joseph An Gof ('the smith'), the Bodmin lawyer Thomas Flamank, and James Touchet, seventh Baron Audley, they were met by the king's army at Blackheath and defeated. Some 2,000 Cornish rebels were slaughtered and their leaders were all executed.

Just three months after the suppression of the An Gof Rebellion, the royal pretender Perkin Warbeck sailed from Ireland to Cornwall and was supported by some 2,000 men from Penwith and Kerrier Hundreds. Warbeck's defeat at Taunton did not completely quiet the Cornish. The 1549 Act of Uniformity, which required all clergymen in the realm to use the new Book of Common Prayer, ignited a rebellion of a different sort in Devonshire and Cornwall. Devonshire villagers forced their priest to celebrate the Mass in the old style, and the Cornish complained that the English of the Book of Common Prayer was incomprehensible to most of them. In August the Privy Council sent mercenaries to aid the local landowners in annihilating the rebels; some 4,000 were killed, and many of the Cornishmen were left hanging from the gallows as a warning against future rebellion.

Brittany had, like Cornwall, been reduced to the status of a duchy by this time, with a feudalized and French-speaking aristocracy at the reins. Similarly, popes in the eleventh and twelfth centuries had ordered reform in the Breton Church to bring it in line with the rest of France, and required the archbishop of Dol to relinquish his primacy in Brittany in favor of the see of Tours. Before the outbreak of the Hundred Years War between England and France, Brittany suffered a succession crisis that plunged the duchy into a civil war.[1] From 1341 to 1365, noble factions disputed the ducal succession in an interesting precursor to the more famous Valois royal succession. One result of the crisis was that the Valois decision on Brittany drove the failed claimant, Jean de Montfort, into the open arms of Edward III of England, who was looking for an excuse to invade France and make good his own claim to the French succession. Edward himself led an expedition to Vannes in 1342, and though a treaty was arranged between Edward and the Valois monarch Philip IV, the Breton succession crisis became a permanent part of the continuing struggle between the two great powers.

For the course of the war and beyond, Brittany was the possession of the Montfort dukes. They continued their alliance with England and Burgundy until the Treaty of Arras in 1435, whence they tried to plot a neutral course. But beginning with Louis XI (r.1461–83), the Valois monarchs sought to return Brittany to its former dependency on the French crown. Breton nobles and officials fought bitterly over how to oppose the Valois, while other European potentates came into the picture at the end of the fifteenth century, when Brittany seemed about to be left without a male heir and France stood poised to gobble up the duchy. In 1491 the last Montfort duke, François II, died leaving only unmarried

1   See Galliou and Jones, 215–29.

daughters. Many of Europe's nobles sought the hand of the eldest daughter and heiress, Anne, and in 1490 the Habsburg emperor Maximilian had wedded her by proxy. But aid sent by both Maximilian and Henry Tudor failed to support her cause against the French. Nantes and Rennes were delivered to the Valois monarch, Charles VIII, and since neither Anne nor Maximilian seemed eager to be united, the Bretons advised ending war with France through a new marriage.

In December 1491 Charles and Anne were married, and the Duchess of Brittany now became the Queen of France. Anne outlived Charles only to be passed along to the next King of France, Louis XII (r.1498–1515). Louis allowed a Breton council to run the daily governing of Brittany, but Anne's daughter Claude turned her ducal rights over to her husband, Francis I (r.1515–47). In 1532 Francis had their son, the dauphin François III, crowned Duke of Brittany, confirmation of a formal act of union between France and Brittany. Like its cousin Wales, Brittany struggled throughout the Middle Ages for political autonomy, but, through a bloodless coup, entered the Modern period as an appendage of a more powerful nation state. Its once close ties with Cornwall were also severed in the sixteenth century when, during the height of the English Reformation, Breton priests were no longer welcomed in Cornwall.

Owain Glyn Dŵr's revolt, which collapsed in 1405, was the last serious attempt by a Welsh magnate to wrest political control from the English. Penal laws enforced in 1431, 1433, and 1447 excluded Welshmen from both bishoprics and the chief secular offices in the Principality.[2] 'Woe unto us,' wrote the contemporary Welsh poet Guto'r Glyn, 'born into slavery.' Yet in the fifteenth century the Welsh gentry continued to prosper (leaving the memory of Glyn Dŵr to the commoners), and Welsh merchant communities sprang up in Bristol and London. Gentry and barons alike were caught up in the second half of the century in the Wars of the Roses, where both the Yorkists and the Lancastrians relied heavily upon their territories in Wales for troops. During these wars, both Edward IV and Henry VII used the symbols of Arthur and the Red Dragon to legitimize their victories.

But it was Henry Tudor who was to be most closely associated with Arthur and the Welsh. Henry's grandfather Owain ap Maredudd, a distant cousin of Owain Glyn Dŵr (after whom he was named), had secretly married Henry V's widow Catherine in 1431. He took as his surname the name of his grandfather, Tudur ap Goronwy (*tudur* means 'territorial king'), and his two sons, Edmund and Jasper, became staunch Lancastrian supporters. Edmund married Margaret Beaufort and was made Earl

2   See J. Davies, 1993, 203–23.

of Richmond, while Jasper became Earl of Pembroke and virtually ruled Wales and the March for Henry VI. Jasper also worked tirelessly to raise support for his nephew, Henry Tudor, who became the champion of the Lancastrian cause following the death of Henry VI and his son. In 1471 Jasper and Henry sailed to France to raise support, and were detained for 13 years in Brittany. The Welsh poets described the young prince beyond the sea as a second Arthur, who would return to Britain to rescue the Welsh from Saxon thralldom.

Finally, in the summer of 1485, Henry landed in Wales and began his march for the throne. On August 21, 1485, fighting under the banner of the Red Dragon, Henry Tudor defeated the Yorkist Richard III at Bosworth Field and began the Tudor dynasty. The new king commissioned Owen Poole and John King to research his Welsh ancestry, and a year after Bosworth the burgesses of York presented Henry with a history of the king's descent from Arthur and Brutus.[3] By then Henry's new bride, Elizabeth of York, was pregnant, and the king decided to take his wife to Winchester, then believed to be Arthur's Camelot. Elizabeth was delivered of a baby boy, christened Arthur, in the shadow of the great Round Table that still hangs in Winchester Castle.

Arthur Tudor was born during an Indian summer of chivalry sparked by the publication, in 1485, of Sir Thomas Malory's Arthurian masterpiece, *Morte d'Arthur*. The book was published posthumously by William Caxton, England's first printer and a Yorkist supporter, who had published an edition of the Prose *Brut* in 1480. Two of Caxton's associates, Petrus Carmelianus and Johannes de Gigliis, composed nativity poems which predicted the return of the once and future king in the person of Arthur Tudor. Caxton himself presented the young Prince Arthur with a medieval translation of Virgil in 1490 and became a Tudor propagandist. On November 29, 1489 Arthur Tudor was installed as Prince of Wales, and a few years later Henry VII negotiated a marriage for his son to Catherine of Aragon. The marriage took place on November 14, 1501, but within six months Arthur was dead. Britain was, yet again, denied a second King Arthur.

Tudor connections with Arthurian myth did not necessarily translate into favorable treatment of the Welsh. Jasper Tudor had obtained most of the offices of the Principality and the March, and when he died in 1495 his lordships passed to the crown. In 1496, however, there was a surge of Welshmen holding lay and ecclesiastical offices in Wales, and opportunities for the Welsh in England also multiplied. But Henry VIII, who succeeded his father in 1509, developed a more drastic solution to bringing

3   See Levy, 1967, 66.

Wales fully under crown control. The Marcher lordships had all but disappeared by his succession and the crown directly controlled these once troublesome territories. Henry executed the Duke of Buckingham in 1521 to add the lordships of Brecon and Newport to his possessions, and in 1531 Rhys ap Gruffudd met the same fate. Rhys was accused of plotting with the King of Scotland to make himself ruler of Wales, and used as evidence against him was the accusation that he was flaunting his descent from ancient British kings by adopting the name Fitzurien.[4]

But the most devastating blow came in 1536, when the English Parliament (which had no Welsh members) passed legislation uniting the Principality and the March and stating that Wales 'is and ever hath bene incorporated . . . and subject to' the English crown. Wales was divided into counties and given 26 seats in Parliament, but Welsh laws were abolished and the Welsh language was forbidden in court and by those holding public office. Though the English government was most likely seeking a more efficient administration of Welsh lands, denying the Welsh their laws and their language was to deny them their ancient British heritage and remove what made them a distinct people.

Antiquarian Revival

The Tudors, despite their Welsh ancestry, could also feel justified in usurping Arthur and the British national myth. It was, after all, a practice of English monarchs going back to Henry II.[5] In 1511 Henry VIII spent over 4,000 pounds on a tournament in Winchester celebrating the birth of yet another Prince Arthur, and in 1522 he showed the visiting emperor Charles V the Winchester Round Table, complete with a newly painted Arthur bearing an uncanny resemblance to Henry! Following skepticism over Arthur's historicity voiced by Polydore Vergil in 1534, there was a torrent of Tudor chronicles celebrating the dynasty's descent from the legendary kings of the Britons. Arthur Kelton, Richard Robinson, William Warner, Thomas Churchyard, Raphael Holinshed, and John Leland continued this tradition into the reign of Elizabeth, who was herself fond of Arthurian pageants. Edmund Spenser's *The Faerie Queene* (1590), dedicated to Elizabeth, makes explicit the blood connections between Arthur, the Welsh kings, and the Tudors.

It was at this time that humanist scholars were studying the languages of ancient Europe, concluding that the languages then spoken by the Welsh, the Cornish, and the Bretons were related to the language of the ancient

4   J. Davies, 1993, 223.
5   See chapter 11 above.

Gauls.[6] Eventually the term *Celts* came to be applied to the various ancient and medieval peoples – Gauls, Britons, Irish, Welsh, Scots, Bretons – who spoke these related languages. Sixteenth-century curiosity about the ancient Celts became mixed with the general European fascination with primitives – 'noble savages' – discovered during recent journeys across the Atlantic. Writers and artists began to transfer traits associated with these Native Americans and Eskimos to the ancient Britons and Picts (see plate 13.1). Eskimo women, commented William Camden, paint their faces 'with a blue colour like the ancient Britons,' who, added Theodor de Bry, were just 'as savage' as the Indians encountered in Virginia.[7]

For early modern Europeans, the most savage and exotic of the ancient Britons were the Druids. Revival of interest in the ancient Druids dates back to French nationalist writings of the 1530s, and by the early seventeenth century English and German writers were weighing in.[8] The British antiquarian John Aubrey (c.1680) was the first to link the Druids and Stonehenge. William Stukeley (1687–1765), a Lincolnshire doctor who studied Britain's Neolithic and Bronze Age burial mounds, attempted to reconcile Christianity with Druidism and eventually adopted for himself the Druidic name Chyndonax. In 1717 John Toland of Londonderry formed the modern Druidic Order on Primrose Hill, and in 1781 Henry Hurle inaugurated the Ancient Order of Druids, also in London. These eighteenth-century British antiquarians continually emphasized the links between the Druids and Britain's ancient megaliths, and were followed by French writers who made similar claims for Brittany's ancient stone monuments.

The alleged mysticism and tragic fate of the Druids appealed to many of the great writers of the Romantic period, including Thomas Gray, William Wordsworth, and William Blake. The Scottish writer James Macpherson was so swept up in this Celtic nostalgia that he created one of the great forgeries of European literature, *Poems of Ossian* (1765), which Napoleon made use of in his attempted Gallic revival. This European fascination with Druids and bards sparked a revival of interest in Welsh poetry and songs. In 1771 the Society of Gwyneddigion was founded for the scholarly study of Welsh literature. Despite its links with Celtic revivalism, it did serve as an important tool for preserving the Welsh language. The Honorable Society of Cymmrodorion, founded in London by Lewis and Richard Morris in 1751, continues to this day to promote Welsh literature, sciences, and the arts.

Somewhat less scholarly were the activities of Edward Williams of Gla-

6   See chapter 12 above.
7   See Piggott, 1989, 74–6.
8   See Green, 1997, 139–57.

Plate 13.1   Ancient Britons, as imagined by sixteenth-century artists who were influenced by Europe's recent encounters with the 'noble savages' of North America. (From John Speede's *Historie*, 1611, © British Library, London.)

morgan (1746–1826), who assumed the Bardic name of Iolo Morgannwg. Iolo forged documents to prove the links between ancient Druids and the medieval Welsh, then single-handedly revived the medieval Welsh *eisteddfod* ('assembly') in 1819. The ceremonies associated with the modern National Eisteddfod were utterly invented by Iolo, including his 'Circle of

Bards,' which became the inspiration for the Gorsedd y Beirdd, honoring writers and musicians who have made a significant contribution to modern Welsh culture.

Macpherson's pseudo-bardic odes also inspired the romanticism of Francois-René de Chateaubriand, who was born in Saint-Malo and spent his first 18 years in Brittany. The eighteenth century saw a politically tinged revival of interest in the Breton language, aided by Ar Gonideg (Le Gonidec) who compiled a Breton dictionary and set down the basics of modern Breton orthography in 1830. One of his acquaintances, Hersart de la Villemarqué, produced the cornerstone of modern Breton literature, the Barzaz-Breiz. This was presented as a collection of ballads from folk tradition, and was largely accepted as such by La Villemarqué's contemporaries. In fact, irked by the loss of all medieval Breton literature, La Villemarqué had set about reinventing it, and most of the mythological and historical ballads in his collection were his own work. In 1843, inspired by the efforts of the Society of Gwyneddigion, Le Gonidec and La Villemarqué founded the Association Bretonne to work for the establishment of Breton-language education in Breton schools. It was not until the Vichy Government in 1941 that this language campaign met with success, but this was overturned in 1947.

While attempts to integrate Celtic language instruction at the primary and secondary education levels were failing, interest in the Celtic languages and literatures was growing at many universities. In 1865 and 1866 the English writer Matthew Arnold, inspired by the recent studies of the Frenchman Ernest Renan, delivered a series of lectures on 'The Study of Celtic Literature' at Oxford.[9] After setting up an opposition between Celt and Teuton, Arnold called for a bridging of the gulf through public (specifically English) support of the study of Celtic literature and languages. The founding of the Celtic chair at Oxford was one example, said Arnold, of proper reparation. Arnold's writings would play a part in inspiring W. B. Yeats and other writers of the Celtic Twilight in turn-of-the-century Ireland. Closer to home, they would be answered by a man with a particular interest in the ancient Britons. When Charles James O'Donnell of Camberwell died in 1935, he bequeathed a sum of money to be spent on a Celtic lecture series to be held, alternately, at the National University of Ireland and the Universities of Oxford, Wales, Edinburgh, and Dublin. The lectures at the three British universities were to adhere to a specific theme: the Celtic element in the English language and population.

Several of the most accomplished scholars in Celtic studies have delivered O'Donnell Lectures since 1957, and their scholarship has added greatly

---

9 See Sims-Williams, 1986.

to our knowledge of the Celtic-speaking peoples in the Middle Ages in particular.[10] However, many of the O'Donnell lecturers have strayed from, and in some cases rejected, the required topic. The O'Donnell mandate has been called 'Celtic Philistinism,' based on a faulty opposition of 'Celtic' and 'Germanic' and leading to the 'ill-informed Celtomania' plaguing modern books, films, and art.[11] From the very departments of Celtic studies created by the nineteenth-century Celtic revival a backlash from academics has created a trendy skepticism in the academy of the public interest in things Celtic.

Academic skepticism and specialization have worked together to marginalize the Britons and exclude them from general studies of the Middle Ages. In his *Select Charters of English Constitutional History* (*c.*1900), Bishop Stubbs described the English race as 'strictly careful of the distinction between themselves and the tolerated remnant of their predecessors.' This attitude, from one of the founding fathers of British historiography, dismissed the contributions of the Britons and, according to Rees Davies, put them firmly in their place – 'on the margins of academic history.'[12] Celtic scholars have cooperated in this ghettoization, believes Davies, preferring the isolation and purity of their discipline to the chance to engage the public and scholars in other fields in broader conversation.[13]

There are some signs that this marginalization of the Britons might be coming to an end. Rees Davies, beginning with his inaugural address as President of the Royal Historical Society, has led the call for inclusion in British history, whereby the Welsh, along with the Scots and the Irish, are removed from the 'Celtic fringe' to be full partners with the English in broader perspectives of the history of the isles. American scholars, such as the members of the North American Conference on British Studies, have answered this challenge and are both revising traditional English history survey courses and implementing new courses on Ireland, Scotland, and Wales. This new attitude of inclusion is also reflected in recent conference papers and textbooks, and in America there is new-found public interest in studying the Cornish, Welsh, and Breton languages.

While a broad public in both Britain and America are drawn to the myths and material culture of the Britons, it is encouraging to see a significant minority who have committed to serious study of the historical sources and the languages. Both enthusiasts and scholars are, in fact, needed to reverse a process that has been going on for centuries.

---

10   See, for example, Lewis, 1963.
11   Evans, 1980–2, 230, 237. On Celtomania and Celto-skepticism, see chapter 1 above.
12   R. Davies, 1979, 24–5.
13   This issue is addressed in Hale and Payton, 2000.

Nationalism, Separatists, and Devolution

Linda Colley has demonstrated that it was a century of wars against Catholic France that encouraged Britain's Protestant inhabitants in the eighteenth century – be they from Cornwall, Wales, England, or Scotland – to accept the terms of the 1707 Act of Union and begin defining themselves collectively as 'Britons.'[14] Of course, the economic benefits of industrialization and the British Empire did not hurt either. 'Britishness,' argues Colley, 'was superimposed over an array of internal differences in response to contact [and conflict] with the Other,' and when the French 'Other' disappears as a political and religious threat, this artificial sense of Britishness erodes, leaving Welsh, Scottish, and even English nationalism to take its place.[15]

It was Irish nationalism, however, that was to pave the way for other 'Celtic' separatist groups in the nineteenth century. The Irish model, which combined nationalism with political protest, armed rebellion, and cultural pride, proved to be the inspiration for many early separatist groups in Wales and Brittany. Inspired by Fenian efforts, David Lloyd George, Michael Jones, and Thomas E. Ellis formed the first Welsh independence movement in 1888, Cymru Fydd ('Future Wales'), followed soon after by the Young Wales party.[16] But as Lloyd George and other Welsh Liberal Party Members of Parliament rose to cabinet-level positions at Westminster, political devolution in general and Welsh independence in particular both took a back seat to other issues.

While new Prime Minister Lloyd George was fighting *against* Irish nationalists in 1918, the Labour Party sought support in Wales by portraying itself as the self-government party. When it too failed to move forward on Welsh independence, despite gaining many Welsh seats, the playwright John Saunders Lewis led a group of scholars and clerics in forming Plaid Cymru ('The Party of Wales') in 1925. Three party leaders turned to violent protests in 1936, and in 1939 Plaid Cymru took the unpopular stance of neutrality during World War II. In the 1950s Plaid Cymru was re-energized by Gwynfor Evans, who obtained some success in gaining support for a Welsh Parliament. A Conservative government created the first Minister for Welsh Affairs in 1951, and in 1958 Evans argued the case for Welsh independence to the United Nations. 1964 saw the creation of the Welsh Office at Westminster and the first Secretary of State for Wales. Anti-Welsh economic

14   Colley, 1992.
15   Ibid., 6–7.
16   See Ellis, 1985.

policies in the late fifties and sixties, however, revived militant republicanism in Wales, which manifested itself mostly in environmental terrorism.

Protesting less violently in the 1960s were several Welsh language preservation groups, including the new Welsh Language Society. Gwynfor Evans's election to Parliament in 1966 was not followed by many Plaid Cymru electoral victories in the 1970s. Neither Prince Charles speaking Welsh during his investiture at Caernarfon Castle in 1969 nor the popularity of Diana, Princess of Wales, was translated into Welsh political gains in the seventies and eighties, and the militant groups continued their violent protests. A national referendum proposing an Assembly for Wales in 1979 failed miserably. But the Labour Party national victory in 1997 carried with it a huge victory for both Scotland and Wales. The Conservatives, the only anti-devolution party, won no Welsh seats in the general election, and a new referendum on Wales passed, albeit by a narrow margin. A new Welsh National Assembly was created, holding its first sessions in Cardiff in 1999.

Unlike the Scottish Parliament, the 60-member Welsh Assembly was granted neither legislative powers nor the right to vary taxation levels. It was, however, given the task of supervising the Welsh Office, and it could also adapt secondary legislation to suit the needs of Wales. The 1999 elections gave a slight edge to the Labour Party, who quickly formed a coalition with the Liberal Party. Currently, Plaid Cymru members hold 4 seats in Westminster, 17 in the Welsh National Assembly, and 2 in the European Parliament.

Political devolution has not been extended to the Bretons and other nationalist groups within France. Reaction against the long neglect of Brittany by the central government of France manifested itself in political parties, separatist groups, and cultural advocates as early as the eighteenth century.[17] The first formal party was the Union Régionaliste Bretonne (URB), founded in 1898 in Morlaix by a group of intellectuals to promote the Breton language, administrative decentralization, and a Breton regional constitution. The URB was succeeded shortly thereafter by the Fédération Régionaliste de Bretagne, which added economic demands to the URB platform. Bleuñ-Brug ('Flower of Heather'), founded in 1905 by a Breton priest to defend the Breton language and Roman Catholic religion, spawned the youth movement Urz Goanag Breiz ('Order of the Breton Hope') in 1943, built on the model of the Order of the Welsh Hope. The Parti National Breton (PNB), created in 1932 to establish an independent Brittany, took its case to the Nazis following the

---

17   See Galliou and Jones, 1991, 285ff.

defeat of France in 1940. The PNB went so far as to launch a youth paramilitary group in 1941, Bagadoù Stourm ('Battle Groups'), as well as Bezen Perrot, who fought locally under German uniform and command as the Bretonische Waffenverband der SS. More recently the Front pour la Libération de la Bretagne (FLB) has worked through the university for Breton language preservation, while the militant Le Poing dans la Gueule (PDG: 'A Fist in the Mouth') has developed close links with the Irish Republican Army.

Finally, there are some international organizations that have linked the nationalist agendas of the Celtic lands with preservation of Celtic languages and culture. The Celtic Congress, which held its first meeting in 1917, had early links with the National Eisteddfod, the Gorsedd of Bards, and Welsh language societies. It now has national branches in Scotland, Brittany, Wales, Ireland, Cornwall, and the Isle of Man which in turn meet in an annual International Congress in order 'to promote the knowledge, use, and appreciation of the languages and cultures of the six Celtic countries.' The Celtic League, formed in 1961 with the aid of Gwynfor Evans and Plaid Cymru, has grown to attract many Breton and Irish nationalists. Its non-violent campaigns 'for the social, political and cultural rights of the Celtic nations' are conducted through a quarterly magazine and, of course, the World Wide Web. It is on this new frontier that the contemporary Hope of the Britons has been most widely disseminated.

The Britons in Perspective

Throughout this work I have drawn from historical, linguistic, and archaeological studies to provide an outline of Brittonic history and delve into some areas of Brittonic culture. In examining the Britons from the Bronze Age to the late Middle Ages it surprised me to see how closely they fit, throughout their history, into the Core–Periphery paradigm proposed by Barry Cunliffe and other archaeologists for Iron Age Britain (see map 8.2 and table 13.1).[18] Innovations (political, economic, cultural) in the Core gradually reached the Periphery and Outer Zone, where they remained after the Core was subsequently conquered by the Romans, the English, and the Normans. While successive waves of Romanization and Anglicization slowly filtered through the Periphery, the Outer Zone remained mostly untouched until the late Middle Ages. This resulted in continued contacts and cultural affinities between the peoples of the Outer

18   See discussion in chapter 2 above.

Table 13.1 Characteristics of Britain's Core, Periphery, and Outer Zone, from the Iron Age to the high Middle Ages.

Characteristics of the Core	Characteristics of the Periphery	Characteristics of the Outer Zone
Bronze and Iron Age trade with central Gaul and Italy.	Become middlemen in trade, exchanging slaves from the Outer Zone for prestige goods acquired from the Core.	Bronze and Iron Age trade with Scandinavia, Atlantic fringe (Brittany, northwest Spain), and Mediterranean.
British elites establish cultural and kinship ties with Belgae and northern Gauls in the Iron Age.	Establish many hillforts and a few *oppida*, but states remain decentralized and without coinage in the LPRIA.	Slow adoption of continental cultural innovations, including Celtic languages.
British elites adopt weapons, religious rites, burial customs from La Tène Gauls in LPRIA.	Native aristocracy cooperates with Romans during the conquest in order to preserve some autonomy.	Characteristic Iron Age settlements include hillforts, brochs and duns, and crannogs.
British tribes import coinage and wine from Italy via Gallic merchants, begun building centralized states around numerous proto-towns (*oppida*).	Fewer Roman towns are established, mainly just tribal capitals.	No oppida and no state formation in the LPRIA.
Roman conquest of the Core states, whose aristocracy became the first to be Romanized (with the help of native allies like Cogidubnus).	Not provided with Germanic federates in the Late Roman period.	War mostly for the acquisition of livestock and slaves. Slaves become chief export.
Native uprisings (Caratacus and Boudica) put down most severely by the Romans. British aristocracy decimated in the battle against Suetonius Paulinus, who follows up with a campaign of genocide against natives of the Core.	Periphery towns no evacuated, hold out longer against federate rebels.	Some trade with Periphery for elite acquisition of prestige items.

Core	Periphery	Outer Zone
Urbanization accelerated during the period of Roman occupation, which also saw a transformation of native agricultural economy by the importation of villa estates.	Fierce resistance against Saxon expansion in the late fifth and sixth centuries. Battle of Badon Hill probably fought in the Periphery, which agreed to subsequent treaty defining border between free Britons and new Saxon states.	Not at first affected by the Roman conquest. Served as refuge for Druids and rebels.
Core settlements most vulnerable to North Sea pirates, especially Saxons.	Slow Anglo-Saxon conquest of Periphery states and settlements.	Welsh tribes aided in the guerilla resistance of Caratacus against the Romans.
Germanic federates settled in Core river valleys to protect Core towns and villas.	Slow adoption of Old English, with many placenames retaining their British names or with English names describing a predominantly British settlement.	Mountain tribes in Wales and Scotland fought longest against Roman expansion.
Rebellion of the federates, fall of the Core towns, and settlement of Anglo-Saxons.	Intermarriage between British and Anglo-Saxons elites and English takeover of British states (e.g. Elmet).	Rome established forts in the Outer Zone but almost no towns or villas.
Withdrawal/expulsion of Roman administration from the Core, evacuation of Romano-British elites and bishops from Core towns.	Trade and ecclesiastical contacts between Britons and Saxons in the Periphery.	Continuity of many Iron Age settlements throughout the Roman period.
Formation of the first Germanic states in Britain, who establish dynastic and trade ties with Merovingians across the Channel.	Fiercest Anglo-Saxon resistance to both Danish and Norman conquests.	Native aristocracy returns to hillforts by the fourth century.
New ecclesiastical ties with Rome through Italian and Gallic missionaries.	Establishment of aggressive continental barons (e.g. Marcher Lords).	Outer Zone lands in Roman Briton most vulnerable to Irish and Pictish raids.
Rapid adoption of a new language, Old English, which has almost no borrowings from preceding Brittonic tongue.	Slow adoption of the new language, Middle English, with much regional dialects remaining (e.g. Yorkshire, Midlands, Somerset).	Irish and Pictish settlement, beginning in the fourth century, leads to intermarriage with native Britons and reinforcement of conservative Iron Age or 'Celtic' cultural traits from other Outer Zone peoples.

Table 13.1 *cont'd*

Characteristics of the Core	Characteristics of the Periphery	Characteristics of the Outer Zone
Edward the Confessor establishes ties between England and Normandy.		Late adoption of Christianity, lingering paganism.
The Norman Conquest of England brings the Core into closer political and cultural relationship with France.		Not affected by rebellion of Germanic federates, and very little intrusion by Anglo-Saxon kings until the seventh century.
Core sees influx of Norman bishops and other continental elites, who bring feudalism and the French language to the Core aristocracy.		Very little adoption of English until the twelfth century.
New language of the Core, Middle English, is mix of English and French.		Formation of small kingdoms by native, Celtic-speaking dynasts.
		Christian churches in Outer Zone remain conservative. British clerics maintain contacts with Ireland, Brittany, and Galicia but remain isolated from English church and its continental innovations.
		Outer Zone returns to pre-Roman trade networks with Scandinavia, Atlantic fringe, and the Mediterranean.
		Iron Age warrior ethos, slave and cattle raids, and bardic poetry remain important cultural traits.
		Outer Zone suffers early and much from Viking raids, but absorbs Scandinavian elements in Scottish Isles, Isle of Man, and

Ireland. British states less affected.

Outer Zone is not at first affected by Norman conquest of England.

Some intrusion of Norman barons in Cornwall, Scotland, and Wales by the late eleventh century, not until the mid twelfth century in Ireland.

Brittonic and Goidelic languages remain the dominant languages until the end of the Middle Ages.

Zone, especially the Bretons with the Cornish, the Welsh with the northern Britons, and the Scots with the Irish and the Picts. Of these peoples the Britons, and especially the Welsh, remained amazingly conservative, while other Outer Zone peoples absorbed Scandinavian elements. This conservatism can be seen in their religion, burial practices, architecture, settlement types, and mythology.

Of all their cultural traits, the Britons clung most tightly to their language and myth-history, two things that made them both distinct from their neighbors and, through the Arthurian legends, somewhat famous in the high Middle Ages. But despite the surge of antiquarian interest in the eighteenth and nineteenth centuries, this fame has not endured to the present day. Like the old woman in *Monty Python and the Holy Grail*, my first-year college students frequently ask 'Who are the Britons?' It is not a question they ask of the Romans, the English, or the Irish, though they may carry many misconceptions of these peoples. For my students, just as for French and Anglo-Norman audiences in the twelfth century, the Britons are a fascinating enigma, but an enigma nonetheless.

One way to answer their question, however, is to echo the words of Graham Chapman's King Arthur, as he informs the old woman that 'We are all Britons.' For if our current theories about the Anglo-Saxon advent are correct, most of the indigenous people who inhabited ancient Britain, whom the classical writers called 'Britons,' were not annihilated and replaced by English-speaking invaders. The Britons remained, many adopting the new language and contributing in countless ways to the new English state that emerged in the Middle Ages, just as both Gauls and Bretons contributed to the development of France. The artificial creation of a 'British' state in 1707, then, may not be so artificial after all.

Chronology of Events

197/213	Britain divided into two provinces.
208–11	Campaigns of Septimius Severus in Scotland.
259/60–74	Britain part of the Gallic Empire.
277/9	Burgundian and Vandal troops settled in Britain.
282–5	Britain under the rule of Carinus.
287	Carausius seizes Britain.
296	Britain recaptured by Constantius I.
306	Campaign of Constantius in Scotland; Constantine proclaimed emperor at York.
314	British bishops at Council of Arles.
350–3	Britain under the rule of Magnentius.
358/9	Julian ships grain from Britain.
359	British bishops at Council of Rimini.
360	Picts and Scots attack frontier region of Britain.
367–9	The 'barbarian conspiracy' in Britain, subsequent recovery by Count Theodosius.
383–8	Britain under the rule of Magnus Maximus.
c.396	Victricius, bishop of Rouen, visits Britain.
398/400	Victories over Picts, Scots, and Saxons.
c.402	Stilicho withdraws troops from Britain.
406–7	Marcus, Gratian, and Constantine proclaimed in Britain.
407–11	Constantine III rules the western provinces from Gaul.
409–10	The Britons revolt from Rome; the Rescript of Honorius.
429	First visit of St. Germanus to Britain.
c.443–c.450	Plague infects Britain and much of Europe.
c.445	St. Germanus makes a second visit to Britain.
c.455–c.485	Britons convene a council and decide to hire Saxon mercenaries. The *superbus tyrannus* settles the Saxons in northeastern Britain, from whence they rebel. The British survivors turn to Ambrosius Aurelianus, who leads them to a series of victories over the Saxons.
460s	Britons recorded in Brittany.
c.470	Britons are settled north of the Loire. Riothamus, their king, fights the Visigoths in Aquitania.
c.485	The Battle of Mount Badon and slaughter of the Saxons. The birth of Gildas.
490	Clovis defeats a British army on the Loire.
518	Entry for the Battle of Badon in the *Annales Cambriae*.
c.529	Gildas writes the *De Excidio Britanniae*.

539	Entry for the Battle of Camlann in the *Annales Cambriae*.
c.540–70	Gildas corresponds with Uinniau (or Finnio), possibly a teacher of St. Columba, and writes a monastic penitential.
542–9	Bubonic plague devastates Constantinople, eventually reaching Britain and Ireland.
c.547	The death of Maelgwn, king of Gwynedd.
563	St. Samson, bishop of Dol, attends a Church council in Paris.
563–5	St. Columba establishes a monastery on Iona, and begins his mission among the Picts.
567	The Council of Lugo, from which comes the first mention of Britons in Galicia.
c.570	The death of Gildas *sapiens*, according to the *Annales Cambriae*.
c.570–612	*Floruit* of St. Kentigern (Mungo) of Glasgow.
572	A British bishop called Mailoc, probably from Bretoña, attends the Second Council of Braga.
c.572	The Battle of Catraeth. British war-band from Din Eidyn wiped out by the Saxons. Urien of Rheged assassinated while besieging Lindisfarne.
573	According to the *Annales Cambriae*, the Battle of Arfderydd in which Gwenddolau fell and Myrddin went mad.
577	According to the *Anglo-Saxon Chronicle*, the Battle of Dyrham in which the British towns of Gloucester, Cirencester, and Bath fall to the Saxons.
578	The Merovingian king Chilperic I defeats a Breton force and receives the fealty of their prince, Waroc.
c.580	*Floruit* of Rhydderch Hen, king of the Strathclyde Britons.
597	Papal missionaries led by St. Augustine arrive at Canterbury. The death of St. Columba at Iona.
c.600	St. Kentigern (Mungo) a British missionary in Strathclyde, founds the first church in Glasgow.
601	The death of St. David, according to the *Annales Cambriae*.
c.603	The Conference at Augustine's Oak, at which the Welsh bishops refuse to cooperate with and accept the authority of Archbishop Augustine of Canterbury.
614	According to the *Anglo-Saxon Chronicle*, the Battle of *Beandun*, in which the West Saxon kings Cynegils and Cwichelm are said to have killed 2,000 Britons.
c.615	The Battle of Chester, in which Æthelfrith of Northumbria defeated the Britons and slew 1,200 monks from Bangor.
617	Edwin of Deira defeats the last British king of Elmet and annexes his territory.

*c.*625	The death of Cadfan, king of Gwynedd.
633	The Battle of Hatfield Chase, in which Edwin is killed by Cadwallon of Gwynedd and Penda of Mercia.
635	The Breton king Judicael travels to the Frankish court and pays tribute to Dagobert I. Oswald of Northumbria kills Cadwallon in battle near Hexham.
638	The *Annals of Ulster* record a 'siege of Edinburgh.'
642	Domnall Brecc, king of Scots, slain by Strathclyde Britons in battle of Strathcarron. Cynyddylan is king of Powys.
655	Cadafael, king of Gwynedd, withdraws on the eve of the Battle of Winwæd in which Penda of Mercia is slain.
658	According to the *Anglo-Saxon Chronicle*, the Battle of *Peonum*, when Cenwalh of Wessex drove the Britons to the Parrett River in Somerset.
660–80	Anglian conquest of Cumbria.
664	The Synod of Whitby.
*c.*670–*c.*710	The reign of the Dumnonian monarch Geraint.
682	Death of Cadwaladr, king of Gwynedd.
685	The Battle of Nechtanesmere, where Ecgfrith of Northumbria is killed fighting against the Picts.
710	The *Anglo-Saxon Chronicle* records that Ine and Nunna of Wessex fought against Geraint, king of the Britons.
722	The *Annales Cambriae* record a British victory at *Hehil* in Cornwall.
*c.*730	Whithorn becomes a Northumbrian see.
731	Bede completes his *Ecclesiastical History of the English People*.
750–2	Tewdwr ap Bili, king of the Strathclyde Britons, becomes overlord of the Picts.
751	Pippin the Short, the new Frankish king, takes the city of Vannes and begins to construct the March of Brittany in the occupied counties of Rennes, Nantes, and Vannes.
756	Eadberht of Northumbria, in conjunction with the Picts under Oengus mac Fergus, assaults Dumbarton and forces Dyfnwal ap Tewdwr to accept terms.
760	The *Annales Cambriae* record a battle between Britons and Saxons at Hereford.
768	Elbodugus, archbishop of Gwynedd, induces the British Church to accept the Roman dating of Easter.
778 and 784	The *Annales Cambriae* record the devastation of the Britons by Offa, king of Mercia.

*c.*786	First Viking raids on Britain.
798	Caradog, king of Gwynedd, is murdered by Saxons.
809	Death of Archbishop Elbodugus.
818	Cœnwulf of Mercia raids Dyfed.
822	Degannwy falls to Mercians in 822, giving them temporary control of Powys.
825	Merfyn Frych establishes the Second Dynasty of Gwynedd.
*c.*830	Composition of the *Historia Brittonum.*
838	The Battle of Hingston Down, where Ecgberht of Wessex defeats the Britons of Dumnonia and their Viking allies.
843	Vikings began to strike at the Breton interior, and slaughter the bishop of Nantes.
843–50	Kenneth mac Alpin unites the Scottish and Pictish thrones, becoming the first king of Scotland.
844	The death of Merfyn, king of Gwynedd, and beginning of the reign of his son, Rhodri Mawr.
850 and 853	The first recorded Viking raids in Wales.
853	Joint Mercian and West Saxon attack on Wales.
854	Death of Cyngen, king of Powys, in Rome.
856	Rhodri the Great, king of Gwynedd, slays the Viking leader Horm.
857–74	Reign of the Breton king Solomon.
870–1	Olaf the White and Ivarr sack Dumbarton.
872	Artgal, king of the Strathclyde Britons, slain at the instigation of Constantine I of Scotland.
874–5	Hafdan, king of the Northumbrian Danes, attacks the Picts and the Strathclyde Britons.
875	The last British king of Dumnonia, 'Dungarth, king of *Cerniu,*' drowns, according to the *Annales Cambriae.*
877	Rhodri of Gwynedd driven out of his kingdom by Vikings.
878	Rhodri and his son Gwriad are killed while fighting Saxons.
884	The Breton monk Wrmonoc writes the *Life of St. Paul of Léon.*
*c.*885	Asser leaves the monastery of St. David's and enters the service of Alfred the Great.
*c.*885–93	The kings of South Wales submit to Alfred.
892	Anarawd ap Rhodri, king of Gwynedd, travels to the English court and submits to Alfred. Asser completes his *Life of King Alfred.*
900	Scots annex Strathclyde. Migration of the Strathclyde British aristocracy to North Wales.

903	Vikings from Dublin invade Anglesey and kill Merfyn ap Rhodri.
910	The death of Cadell ap Rhodri and succession of his son, Hywel Dda.
916	Death of Anarawd of Gwynedd.
920	The Strathclyde Britons sign a treaty with Edward the Elder.
927	Morgan, king of Gwent and Glywsying, and Hywel Dda, king of Deheubarth, submit to Æthelstan at Hereford.
929	Hywel Dda goes on a pilgrimage to Rome.
c.935–50	Composition of the *Armes Prydein Vawr*.
936	Æthelstan attacks the Britons of Dumnonia and compels them to withdraw from Exeter. Alain Barbetorte, count of Cornouaille, returns from exile in Britain to launch a campaign of reconquest.
937	The Battle of Brunanburh, in which Æthelstan defeats an alliance of Scots, Dublin Danes, and Strathclyde Britons.
942	Idwal ab Anarawd, king of Gwynedd, leads a revolt against Æthelstan and is killed along with his brother Elise.
945	Edmund ravages Cumbria and Strathclyde, and grants conquered British territory to Malcolm, king of the Scots.
949	The death of Hywel Dda.
952 and 954	The sons of Idwal defeat the sons of Hywel and ravage Dyfed and Ceridigion.
973	Edgar receives the submission of Kenneth II of Scotland, Malcolm, king of Strathclyde and Cumbria, and Iago and Hywel of Gwynedd.
974	Death of Morgan, king of Gwent and Glywysing.
983	Death of Hywel of Gwynedd.
988	Death of Owain, king of Deheubarth.
999	Death of Maredudd, king of Deheubarth. Death of Morgenau, bishop of St. David's.
1018	The Battle of Carham, in which Malcolm II of Scotland and Owen the Bald of Strathclyde defeat the English of Bernicia. Llywelyn ap Seisyll slays Aeddan ap Blegywryd.
1023	Death of Llwelyn ap Seisyll, king of Gwynedd.
1033	Death of Rhydderch ab Iestyn, king of Deheubarth.
1039	Death of Iago ab Idwal, king of Gwynedd, and the succession of Gruffudd ap Llwelyn ap Seisyll.
1044	Gruffudd ap Llwelyn kills Hywel ab Edwin, king of Deheubarth.
c.1050	The four branches of the *Mabinogi* are collected. Cornwall is

	demoted to the status of an archdeaconry within the new diocese of Exeter.
1055	Gruffudd ap Llywelyn kills Gruffudd ap Rhydderch, king of Deheubarth.
1055–c.1060	Gruffudd ap Llywelyn establishes himself in Morgannwg, becomes ruler of all Wales.
1056	Gruffudd ap Llywelyn swears an oath to Edward the Confessor.
1063	Harold of Wessex invades Wales. The assassination of Gruffudd ap Llywelyn.
1066	Death of Edward the Confessor and crowning of Harold. Norman invasion of England and the Battle of Hastings.
c.1090	The *Life of St. Cadog* by Lifris of Llancarfan.
c.1100	The date of the manuscript in BM Harley 3859 which contains the *Historia Brittonum* and the *Annales Cambriae*. The final version of *Culhwch ac Olwen* appears in writing.
c.1136–8	Geoffrey of Monmouth completes his *History of the Kings of Britain*, incorporating an earlier work, *The Prophecies of Merlin*.
1137	Death of Gruffudd ap Cynan, king of Gwynedd. Succeeded by Owain Gwynedd.
1146	Birth of Gerald of Wales.
1176	The Lord Rhys hosts the first *eisteddfod* at Cardigan.
c.1190	Glastonbury monks excavate the grave of Arthur and Guinevere. Layamon publishes his *Brut*.
Late 12th cent.	The *lais* of Marie de France.
13th cent.	Oldest manuscripts containing the Welsh Triads.
1240	Death of Llywelyn the Great.
c.1250	Date of the Black Book of Carmarthen.
1267	Henry III signs the Treaty of Montgomery, recognizing the right of the House of Gwynedd to the title Prince of Wales.
1276–1282	Edward I's campaigns in Wales.
Late 13th cent.	Date of the Book of Aneirin.
Early 14th cent.	Date of the Book of Taliesin.
1320	The birth of Dafydd ap Gwilym.
c.1325	Date of the White Book of Rhydderch.
1400	Owain Glyn Dŵr is proclaimed prince of Wales.
c.1400	Date of the Red Book of Hergest.
1410	Owain Glyn Dŵr disappears after a raid on the English border.
1485	Henry Tudor defeats Richard III at Bosworth Field. Publica-

	tion of Sir Thomas Malory's *Morte Darthur*.
1491	Anne, Duchess of Brittany, becomes Queen of France.
1532	Francis I crowns his son Duke of Brittany, the confirmation of a formal act of union between France and Brittany.
1536	Parliamentary legislation declaring the union of the Principality of Wales and the Welsh March with England.
1707	The Act of Union creating the United Kingdom of Great Britain.
1819	Iolo Morgannwg revives the medieval Welsh *Eisteddfod*.

Feast Days of the British Saints

January 13	St. Kentigern (St. Mungo)
January 29	St. Gildas
February 7	St. Illtud (Iltyd, Iltut)
February 9	St. Teilo
March 1	St. David (Dewi Sant)
March 3	St. Nonn (Nonnita)
March 5	St. Piran
March 17	St. Patrick
May 1	St. Asaph
May 16	St. Carantoc
June 4	St. Petroc
July 28	St. Samson
September 16	St. Ninian (Nynia)
October 10	St. Paul Aurelian (St. Pol)
November 8	St. Cybi (Cuby)
November 14	St. Dubricius (Dyfrig, Dubric)

Principal Sources:

The Anglo-Saxon Chronicle.
Annales Cambriae.
Bede, *Ecclesiastical History of the English People.*
Brut y Tywysogion.
Historia Brittonum.
Orme, Nicholas, *The Saints of Cornwall* (Oxford, 2000).
Salway, Peter, *The Oxford Illustrated History of Roman Britain* (Oxford, 1993).
Snyder, Christopher A., *An Age of Tyrants: Britain and the Britons*, AD 400–600 (University Park, PA, 1998).
—— *The World of King Arthur* (New York, 2000).
Williams, Ann, Alfred P. Smyth, and D. P. Kirby, *A Biographical Dictionary of Dark Age Britain: England, Scotland and Wales c.500–c.1050* (London, 1991).

Bibliography

Primary Sources (individual works and collections)

The Anglo-Saxon Chronicle, ed. and trans. G. N. Garmonsway (London, 1994).

Aldhelm: The Prose Works, ed. and trans. Michael Lapidge and Michael Herren (Cambridge, 1979).

Aldhelm: The Poetic Works, ed. and trans. Michael Lapidge and James Rosier (Cambridge, 1985).

Armes Prydein ('The Great Prophecy of Britain') from the Book of Taliesin, ed. Ifor Williams, trans. Rachel Bromwich (Dublin, 1972).

Ausonius, trans. Hugh G. Evelyn White, Loeb edition, 2 vols. (Cambridge, 1919).

Bartrum, P. C., *Early Welsh Genealogical Tracts* (Cardiff, 1996).

Bede, *The Ecclesiastical History of the English People*, trans. Bertram Colgrave (Oxford, 1994).

Bieler, Ludwig (ed). *The Irish Penitentials*, Scriptores Latini Hiberniae (Dublin, 1963).

Birch, W. de Gray, *Cartularium Saxonicum: A Collection of Charters Relating to Anglo-Saxon History*, 4 vols. (London, 1885–99).

Brett, Caroline (ed. and trans.), *The Monks of Redon* (Woodbridge, 1989).

Brut y Tywysogyon, or 'The Chronicle of the Princes', Peniarth MS 20 Version, trans. Thomas Jones (Cardiff, 1952).

Brut y Tywysogyon, or 'The Chronicle of the Princes', Red Book of Hergest Version, trans. Thomas Jones (Cardiff, 1955).

Caesar, *The Gallic War*, trans. Carolyn Hammond (Oxford, 1996).

CISP: The Celtic Inscribed Stones Project <http://www.ucl.ac.uk/archaeology/cisp/database/>.

Claudian, ed. and trans. Maurice Platnauer, Loeb edition, 2 vols. (Cambridge, MA, 1922).

Constance de Lyon: Vie de Saint Germain d'Auxerre, ed. and trans. Rene Borius (Paris, 1965).

Culhwch and Olwen: An Edition and Study of the Oldest Arthurian Tale, ed. Rachel Bromwich and D. Simon Evans (Cardiff, 1992).

Dafydd ap Gwilym: A Selection of Poems, ed. Thomas Parry and trans. Rachel Bromwich (Llandysul, 1982).

Davies, Oliver, and Thomas O'Loughlin, *Celtic Spirituality* (New York. 1999).

Davies, Wendy (ed). 1979, *The Llandaff Charters* (Aberystwyth, 1979).

Doble, G. H, *Saint Brioc* (Exeter, 1928).

—— *Saint Paul of Léon* (Lampeter, 1941).

—— *Lives of the Welsh Saints*, ed. D. Simon Evans (Cardiff, 1971).

Evans, D. Simon, *A Medieval Prince of Wales: The Life of Gruffudd ap Cynan* (Lampeter, 1990).

Finberg, H. P. R., *The Early Charters of Devon and Cornwall* (Leicester, 1963).

Flobert, Pierre (ed. and trans.), *La Vie Ancienne de Saint Samson de Dol* (Paris,1997).

Ford, Patrick K. (ed. and trans.), *The Poetry of Llywarch Hen* (Berkeley, CA, 1974).

Gildas. *'The Ruin of Britain' and Other Works*, ed. and trans. Michael Winterbottom (London and Chichester, 1978).

Gregory of Tours. *The History of the Franks*, trans. Lewis Thorpe (London, 1974).

Haddan, Arthur West, and William Stubbs (eds.), *Councils and Ecclesiastical Documents Relating to Great Britain and Ireland*, 3 vols. (Oxford, 1964).

The Historical Works of Giraldus Cambrensis, ed. and trans. Thomas Forester, Richard Colt Hoare, and Thomas Wright (London, 1894).

Ireland, Stanley, *Roman Britain: A Sourcebook*, 2nd edn. (London and New York, 1996).

Koch, John T. (ed.), *The Celtic Heroic Age: Literary Sources*, 2nd edn. (Malden, MA, 1995).

La Borderie, A. de (ed.), *Les Trois Vies anciennes de Saint Tudual* (Paris, 1887).

The Mabinogion, trans. and introd. Gwyn Jones and Thomas Jones (London, 1961).

Monumenta Germaniae Historica, ed. Theodor Mommsen, et al. (Berlin, 1826–   ).

Nash-Williams, V. E., *The Early Christian Monuments of Wales* (Cardiff, 1950).

Orosius, *Seven Books of History Against the Pagans*, trans. I. W. Raymond (New York, 1936).

Patrick, Saint, *His Writings and Muirchu's 'Life,'* ed. and trans. A. B. E. Hood (London and Chichester, 1978).

Procopius. *History of the Wars*, trans. H. B. Dewing, Loeb Edition (Cambridge, MA, 1919)

Rowland, Jenny, *Early Welsh Saga Poetry: A Study and Edition of the* Englynion (Woodbridge, 1990).

Salvian. *The Writings of Salvian*, trans. J. F. O'Sullivan (Washington, 1962).

Sidonius Apollinaris: Poems and Letters, ed. and trans. W. B. Anderson, Loeb Edition, 2 vols. (Cambridge, MA, 1936), 2 vols.

Sozomen, *The Ecclesiastical History*, trans. Edward Walford (London, 1855).

Strabo, *Geography*.

Tacitus. *Agricola*, trans. Herbert W. Benario (Norman, OK and London, 1991).

Trioedd Ynys Prydein: The Welsh Triads, ed. and trans. Rachel Bromwich (Cardiff, 1978).

XII Panegyrici Latini, ed. R. A. B. Mynors (Oxford, 1964).

Wade-Evans, A. W., *Vitae Sanctorum Britanniae et Genealogiae* (Cardiff, 1944).

Wright, Neil (ed.), *The 'Historia Regum Britannae' of Geoffrey of Monmouth I: The Bern MS* (Cambridge, 1984).
Zosimus: New History, trans. Ronald T. Ridley (Sydney, 1982).

Chapter 1: Who are the Britons?

Brown, Terence (ed.), 1996, *Celticism*, Studia Imagologica: Amsterdam Studies on Cultural Identity 8 (Amsterdam and Atlanta, GA).
Chapman, Malcolm, 1992, *The Celts: The Construction of a Myth* (New York).
Collis, John, 1996, 'The Origin and Spread of the Celts,' *Studia Celtica*, 30: 17–34.
—— 1997, 'Celtic Myths,' *Antiquity*, 71, no. 271: 195–201.
Cunliffe, Barry, 1997, *The Ancient Celts* (Oxford and New York).
Graves-Brown, Paul, Siân Jones, and Clive Gamble (eds.), 1996, *Cultural Identity and Archaeology: The Construction of European Communities* (London and New York).
Hill, J. D., 1993, 'Can we recognize a different European past? A contrastive archaeology of later prehistoric settlements in Southern England,' *Journal of European Archaeology*, 1: 57–75.
—— 1996, 'Weaving the Strands of a New Iron Age,' *British Archaeology*, 17 (September).
James, Simon, 1998, 'Celts, Politics and Motivation in Archaeology,' *Antiquity*, 72, no. 275: 200–9.
—— 1999, *The Atlantic Celts: Ancient People or Modern Invention?* (London and Madison, WI).
James, Simon, and Valery Rigby. 1997, *Britain and the Celtic Iron Age* (London).
Megaw, J. V. S. and M. R. 1996, 'Ancient Celts and Modern Ethnicity,' *Antiquity*, 70, no. 267: 175–81.
—— 1998, 'The Mechanism of (Celtic) Dreams?: A Partial Response to Our Critics,' *Antiquity*, 72, no. 276: 432–5.
Merriman, Nick. 1987, 'Value and motivation in prehistory: The evidence for "Celtic spirit,"' in I. Hodder (ed.), *The Archaeology of Contextual Meanings* (Cambridge), 111–16.
Pittock, Murray G. H. 1999, *Celtic Identity and the British Image* (Manchester and New York).
Sims-Williams, Patrick, 1986, 'The Visionary Celt: The Construction of an Ethnic Preconception,' *CMCS* 11: 71–96.
Snyder, Christopher A. 1996, 'Celtic Continuity in the Middle Ages,' *Medieval Perspectives* 11, 164–78.
Tolkien, J. R. R. 1963, 'English and Welsh,' in Tolkien et al., *Angles and Britons* (Cardiff), 1–41.

Chapter 2: The Late Pre-Roman Iron Age

Arnold, Bettina, and D. Blair Gibson (eds.), 1995, *Celtic Chiefdom, Celtic State* (Cambridge).

Chadwick, Nora, 1966, *The Druids* (Cardiff).

—— 1970, *The Celts* (London).

Champion, T. C. and J. R. Collis (eds.), 1996, *The Iron Age in Britain and Ireland: Recent Trends* (Sheffield).

Collis, John R. 1984, *Oppida: Earliest Towns North of the Alps* (Sheffield).

—— 1997, *The European Iron Age* (London and New York).

Collis, John R. (ed.), 1977, *The Iron Age in Britain – A Review* (Sheffield).

Creighton, John, 2000, 'Understanding the British Iron Age: An Agenda for Action' <http://www.rdg.ac.uk/~lascretn/IAAgenda.htm>

Cunliffe, Barry, 1978, *Hengistbury Head* (London).

—— 1983, *Danebury: Anatomy of an Iron Age Hillfort* (London).

—— 1984, *Danebury: An Iron Age Hillfort in Hampshire*, CBA Research Report 52, 2 vols. (London).

—— 1991, *Iron Age Communities in Britain* (London and New York). [First published in 1974.]

—— 1995 *English Heritage Book of Iron Age Britain* (London).

—— 1997, *The Ancient Celts* (Oxford and New York).

Cunliffe, Barry (ed.), 1998, *Prehistoric Europe: An Illustrated History* (Oxford).

Cunliffe, Barry, and David Miles (eds.), 1984, *Aspects of the Iron Age in Central Southern Britain* (Oxford).

Green, Miranda J., 1997, *Exploring the World of the Druids* (London and New York).

Harding, D. W., 1974, *The Iron Age in Lowland Britain* (London and Boston).

Hawkes, C. F. C., 1977, *Pytheas: Europe and the Greek Explorers*, Eighth J. L. Myres Memorial Lecture (Oxford).

James, Simon, and Valery Rigby, 1997, *Britain and the Celtic Iron Age* (London).

Kruta, Venceslas, et al. (eds.), 1999, *The Celts* (New York).

MacReady, Sarah, and F. H. Thompson (eds.), 1984, *Cross-Channel Trade Between Gaul and Britain in the Pre-Roman Iron Age*, Society of Antiquaries Occasional Paper NS 4 (London).

Matthews, Keith J., 1999, '*Britannus/Britto*: Roman Ethnographies, Native Identities, Labels and Folk Devils,' in Alan Leslie (ed), *Theoretical Roman Archaeology and Architecture: The Third Conference Proceedings* (Glasgow), 14–32.

Nash, Daphne, 1976, 'Reconstructing Poseidonios' Celtic Ethnography,' *Britannia*, 7, 11–26.

Piggott, Stuart, 1985, *The Druids* (London and New York). [First published in 1968.]

Rankin, H. D., 1987, *Celts and the Classical World* (London).

Rivet, A. L. F., and Colin Smith, 1979, *The Place-Names of Roman Britain* (Princeton, NJ).

Ross, Anne, 1996, *Pagan Celtic Britain* (Chicago). [First published in 1967].

Salway, Peter, 1993, *The Oxford Illustrated History of Roman Britain* (Oxford and New York).

Sharples, Niall M., 1991, *English Heritage Book of Maiden Castle* (London).

Stead, I. M. et al., 1986, *Lindow Man: The Body in the Bog* (London).

Tierney, J. J., 1960, 'The Celtic Ethnography of Posidonius,' *Proceedings of the Royal Irish Academy*, 60C: 189–275.

Turner, R. C. and R. G. Scaife (eds.), 1995, *Bog Bodies: New Discoveries and New Perspectives* (London).

Wait, G. 1985, *Religion and Ritual in Iron Age Britain*, British Archaeological Reports British Series 149 (Oxford).

Webster, Graham A., 1980, *The Roman Invasion of Britain* (London).

Wheeler, R. E. M., 1943, *Maiden Castle, Dorset* (Oxford).

Chapter 3: The Roman Period

Allason-Jones, Lindsay, 1989, *Women in Roman Britain* (London).

Birley, Anthony, 1980, *The People of Roman Britain* (Berkeley and Los Angeles).

Birley, Robin, 1990, *The Roman Documents from Vindolanda* (Carvoran).

Blagg, T. F. C., and A. C. King (eds.), 1984, *Military and Civilian in Roman Britain*, British Archaeological Reports, British Series 136 (Oxford).

Bowman, Alan K., 1983, *The Roman Writing Tablets from Vindolanda* (London).

Bowman, Alan K., and J. D. Thomas. 1983, *Vindolanda: The Latin Writing Tablets*, Britannia Monograph Series no. 4 (London).

Branigan, Keith, 1991, 'Images – or Mirages – of Empire? An Archaeological Approach to the Problem,' in Loveday Alexander (ed.), *Images of Empire* (Sheffield), 91–105.

Braund, David, 1984, *Rome and the Friendly King* (London and New York).

Burnham, B. C., and H. B. Johnson (eds.), 1979, *Invasion and Response: The Case of Roman Britain*, British Archaeological Reports, British Series 73 (Oxford).

Clayton, Peter (ed.), 1980, *A Companion to Roman Britain* (London).

Cunliffe, Barry, 1973, *The Regni*, Peoples of Roman Britain (London).

Dunnett, Rosalind, 1975, *The Trinovantes*, Peoples of Roman Britain (London).

Eagles, Bruce, 1980, 'Anglo-Saxons in Lindsey and the East Riding of Yorkshire in the Fifth Century,' in Philip Rahtz et al. (eds.), *Anglo-Saxon Cemeteries 1979*, British Archaeological Reports, British Series 82 (Oxford), 285–7.

Esmonde Cleary, A. S., 1987, *Extra-Mural Areas of Romano-British Towns*, British Archaeological Reports, British Series 169 (Oxford).

Frere, S. S., 1987, *Britannia: A History of Roman Britain*, 3rd edn. (London).

Fulford, Michael, 1982, 'Town and Country in Roman Britain – A Parasitical Relationship?' in Miles, 403–19.

Green, Miranda J., 1976, *A Corpus of Religious Material from the Civilian Areas of Roman Britain*, British Archaeological Reports 24 (Oxford).

Hall, Jenny, and Ralph Merrifield, 1986, *Roman London* (London).

Hanson, W. S., 1987, *Agricola and the Conquest of the North* (Totowa, NJ).

Henig, Martin, 1984, *Religion in Roman Britain* (London).

Hingley, Richard, 1989, *Rural Settlement in Roman Britain* (London).

Holder, P. A., 1982, *The Roman Army in Britain* (New York).

Johns, Catherine, 1996, *The Jewellery of Roman Britain: Celtic and Classical Traditions* (Ann Arbor, MI).

Jones, Barri, and David Mattingly, 1990, *An Atlas of Roman Britain* (Oxford).

Miles, David (ed.), 1982, *The Romano-British Countryside*, British Archaeological Reports British Series 103, 2 vols. (Oxford).

Millett, Martin, 1990, *The Romanization of Britain* (Cambridge).

—— 1995, *Roman Britain* (London).

Rivet, A. L. F. and Colin Smith, 1979, *The Place-Names of Roman Britain* (Princeton, NJ).

Salway, Peter, 1967, *The Frontier People of Roman Britain*, 2nd edn. (Cambridge).

—— 1981, *Roman Britain* (Oxford).

—— 1993, *The Oxford Illustrated History of Roman Britain* (Oxford and New York).

Todd, Malcolm, 1973, *The Coritani*, Peoples of Roman Britain (London).

—— 1981, *Roman Britain 55 bc –ad 400* (London).

Wacher, J. S., 1978, *Roman Britain* (London).

—— 1979, *The Coming of Rome* (London).

Webster, Graham, 1975, *The Cornovii*, Peoples of Roman Britain (London).

—— 1978, *Boudica: The British Revolt Against Rome* (Totowa, NJ).

—— 1981, *Rome Against Caratacus: The Roman Campaigns in Britain, ad 48–58* (Totowa, NJ).

—— 1986, *The British Celts and their Gods under Rome* (London).

—— 1993, *The Roman Invasion of Britain*, rev. edn. (London and New York).

Chapter 4: Late Roman Britain

Bartholemew, Philip, 1984, 'Fourth-Century Saxons,' *Britannia*, 15: 169–85.

Birley, Anthony, 1980, *The People of Roman Britain* (Berkeley and Los Angeles).

Burrow, Ian, 1981, *Hillfort and Hill-Top Settlement in Somerset in the First to Eighth Centuries AD*, British Archaelogical Reports, British Series 91 (Oxford).

Carver, Martin, 1995, 'Roman to Norman at York Minster,' in Derek Phillips and Brenda Heywood, *Excavations at York Minster*, Vol. I (London), 177–95.

Casey, P. J., 1978, 'Constantine the Great in Britain – the evidence of the coinage at the London mint,' in J. Bird, H. Chapman, and J. Clark (eds.), *Collectanea Londiniensia*, London and Middlesex Archaeological Society Special Paper no. 2 (London), 181–93.

—— 1994, *Carausius and Allectus: The British Usurpers* (London)

Dark, K. R., 1993, *Civitas to Kingdom: British Political Continuity, 300–800* (Leicester).

—— 1994, *Discovery by Design: The Identification of Secular Elite Settlements in Western Britain AD 400–700*, British Archaelogical Reports, British Series 237 (Oxford).

—— 1996, 'Proto-industrialisation and the End of the Roman Economy,' in K. R. Dark (ed.), *External Contacts and the Economy of Late-Roman and Post-Roman Britain* (Woodbridge), 1–22.

Davies, J. L., and D. P. Kirby. 1995, Review of *Civitas to Kingdom* by K. R. Dark, *CMCS* 29: 70–2.

De la Bédoyère, Guy, 1999, *The Golden Age of Roman Britain* (Stroud).

Dixon, Philip. 1992, ' "The Cities are not populated as once they were," ' in John Rich (ed.), *The City in Late Antiquity* (London), 145–60.

Esmonde Cleary, A. S., 1989, *The Ending of Roman Britain* (London).

Evans, Jeremy, 1990, 'From the End of Roman Britain to the Celtic West,' *Oxford Journal of Archaeology*, 9: 91–103.

Faulkner, Neil, 2000, *The Decline and Fall of Roman Britain* (Stroud).

Frere, Sheperd, 1978, *Britannia: A History of Roman Britain*, 2nd edn. (London).

Garner, Andrew, 1999, 'Military Identities in Late Roman Britain,' *Oxford Journal of Archaeology*, 18: 403–15.

Hunter-Mann, Kurt. 1993, 'When (and What) Was the End of Roman Britain?' in Eleanor Scott (ed.), *Theoretical Roman Archaeology: First Conference Proceedings* (Aldershot), 67–78.

Johnson, Stephen, 1976, *The Roman Forts of the Saxon Shore* (London).

—— 1980, *Later Roman Britain* (London).

Jones, Michael E., 1987, 'The Failure of Romanization in Celtic Britain,' *Harvard Celtic Colloquium*, 7: 126–45.

—— 1996a, *The End of Roman Britain* (Ithaca, NY, and London).

—— 1996b, 'Geographical-Psychological Frontiers in Sub-Roman Britain,' in Ralph Mathisen and Hagith Sivan (eds.), *Shifting Frontiers in Late Antiquity* (Aldershot), 45–58.

Matthews, J. F., 1975, *Western Aristocracies and Imperial Court* AD *364–425* (Oxford).

—— 1983, 'Macsen, Maximus and Constantine,' *Welsh Historical Review*, 11: 431–48.

Miller, Mollie, 1975, 'Stilicho's Pictish War,' *Britannia*, 6: 141–5.

Millet, Martin, 1990, *The Romanization of Britain* (Cambridge).

Reece, Richard M., 1980, 'Town and Country: The End of Roman Britain,' *World Archaeology*, 12: 77–92.

Salway, Peter, 1981, *Roman Britain* (Oxford).

—— 1993, *The Oxford Illustrated History of Roman Britain* (Oxford and New York).

Snyder, Christopher A., 1998, *An Age of Tyrants: Britain and the Britons,* AD *400–600* (University Park, PA, and Gloucester).

Todd, Malcolm, 1977, '*Famosa Pestis* and Britain in the Fifth Century.' *Britannia*, 8: 319–25

Watts, Dorothy, 1998, *Religion in Late Roman Britain: Forces of Change* (New York and London).

Welch, Martin, 1994, 'The Archaeological Evidence for Federate Settlements in Britain Within the Fifth Century,' in Françoise Vallet and Michel Kazanski, *L'armée romaine et les barbares du IIIe au VIIe siècle* (Rouen), 269–77.

Wood, Ian, 1990, 'The Channel from the Fourth to the Seventh Centuries AD,' in Sean McGrail (ed.), *Maritime Celts, Frisians and Saxons*, CBA Report no. 71 (London), 93–7.

Chapter 5: Britons and Saxons

Alcock, Leslie, 1971, *Arthur's Britain* (New York).

—— 1987, *Economy, Society, and Warfare Among the Britons and Saxons* (Cardiff).

—— 1995, *Cadbury Castle, Somerset: The Early Medieval Archaeology* (Cardiff).

Arnold, C. J., 1997, *An Archaeology of the Early Anglo-Saxon Kingdoms*, 2nd edn. (New York and London).

Barker, Philip, et al. 1997, *The Baths Basilica, Wroxeter: Excavations 1966–90*, English Heritage Archaeological Report 8 (London).

Bartholemew, Philip, 1982, 'Fifth-Century Facts,' *Britannia* 13: 261-70.

—— 1984, 'Fourth-Century Saxons,' *Britannia*, 15: 169–85.

Bassett, Steven (ed.), 1989, *The Origins of Anglo-Saxon Kingdoms* (Leicester).

Biddle, Martin., 1976, 'Towns,' in David M. Wilson (ed.), *The Archaeology of Anglo-Saxon England* (London), 99–150.

Böhme, Horst Wolfgang, 1986, 'Das Ende der Römerherrschaft in Britannien und die Anglesächsische Besiedlung Englands im 5. Jahrhundert,' *Jahrbuch des Romisch-Germanischen Zentralmuseums Mainz*, 33: 469–574.

Bremmer, Rolf H., Jr., 1990, 'The Nature of the Evidence for a Frisian Participation in the *Adventus Saxonum*,' in Alfred Bammesberger and Alfred Wollmann (eds.), *Britain 400–600: Language and History* (Heidelberg), 353–71.

Burgess, R. W., 1990, 'The Dark Ages Return to Fifth-Century Britain: The 'Restored' Gallic Chronicle Exploded,' *Britannia*, 21: 185–95.

Dark, K. R., 1992, 'A Sub-Roman Re-Defense of Hadrian's Wall?' *Britannia*, 23: 111–20.

—— 1993, *Civitas to Kingdom: British Political Continuity, 300–800* (Leicester).

—— 2000, *Britain and the End of the Roman Empire* (Stroud).

Dark, K. R. (ed.), 1996, *External Contacts and the Economy of Late Roman and Post-Roman ritain* (Woodbridge).

Dark, S. P., 1996, 'Paleoecological Evidence for Landscape Continuity and Change in Britain *c.*AD 400–800,' in K. R. Dark (ed.), *External Contacts* (Woodbridge), 23–52.

Dixon, Philip, 1982, 'How Saxon is the Saxon House?' in P. J. Drury (ed.), *Structural Reconstruction*, British Archaeological Reports, British Series 110 (Oxford), 275–87.

Dumville, David N., 1977, 'Sub-Roman Britain: History and Legend,' *History*, 62: 173–92.

—— 1984. 'The Chronology of *De Excidio Britanniae*, Book I,' in M. Lapidge and D. Dumville (eds.), *Gildas: New Approaches* (Woodbridge), 61–84.

—— 1989, 'The Origins of Northumbria: Some Aspects of the British Background,' in S. Bassett (ed.), *The Origins of Anglo-Saxon Kingdoms* (Leicester), 213–22.

—— 1995, 'The Idea of Government in Sub-Roman Britain,' in Giorgio Ausenda (ed.), *After Empire: Towards and Ethnology of Europe's Barbarians* (Woodbridge), 177–216.

Charles-Edwards, Thomas. 1991, 'The Arthur of History,' in Rachel Bromwich et al. (eds.), *The Arthur of the Welsh* (Cardiff), 15–32.

Cunliffe, Barry, and Peter Davenport, 1985, *The Temple of Sulis Minerva at Bath. Vol. 1. The Site* (Oxford).

Dumville, David N., et al. 1993, *St. Patrick, AD 493–1993* (Woodbridge).

Eagles, Bruce. 1989, 'Lindsey' in S. Bassett (ed), *The Origins of Anglo-Saxon Kingdoms* (Leicester), 202–12.

Esmonde Cleary, Simon. 1995, 'Changing Constraints on the Landscape AD 400–600,' in Della Hooke and Simon Burnell (eds.), *Landscape and Settlement in Britain, AD 400–600* (Exeter), 11–26.

Evison, Vera I. (ed.). 1981, *Angles, Saxons, and Jutes: Essays Presented to J. N. L. Myres* (Oxford).

Frere, Sheppard. 1983, *Verulamium Excavations (1972–84)*, 3 vols. (London).

Fulford, Michael G., 1985, *Guide to the Silchester Excavations: The Forum Basilica, 1982–84* (Reading).

—— 1989, 'Byzantium and Britain,' *Medieval Archaeology*, 33: 1–5.

Gilmour, B., 1979, 'The Anglo-Saxon Church at St. Paul-in-the-Bail, Lincoln,' *Medieval Archaeology*, 23: 214–18.

Härke, Heinrich, 1989, 'Early Saxon Weapon Burials: Frequencies, Distributions and Weapon Combinations,' in Sonia Chadwick Hawkes (ed.), *Weapons and Warfare in Anglo-Saxon England* (Oxford), 49–61.

—— 1997, 'Early Anglo-Saxon Social Structure,' in John Hines (ed), *The Anglo-Saxons from the Migration Period to the Eighth Century: An Ethnographic Perspective* (Woodbridge), 125–70.

Higham, Nicholas, 1992, *Rome, Britain and the Anglo-Saxons* (London).

—— 1994, *The English Conquest: Gildas and Britain in the Fifth Century* (Manchester).

Hines, John, 1990, 'Philology, Archaeology and the *adventus Saxonum vel Anglorum*,' in Alfred Bammesberger and Alfred Wollmann (eds.), *Britain 400–600: Language and History* (Heidelberg), 17–36.

—— 1994, 'The Becoming of the English: Identity, Material Culture and Language in Early Anglo-Saxon England,' *Anglo-Saxon Studies in Archaeology and History*, 7: 49–59.

Hodges, Richard, 1989, *The Anglo-Saxon Achievement* (Ithaca, NY).

Hooke, Della, 1998, *The Landscape of Anglo-Saxon England* (London and Washington, DC).

James, Simon, 1999, *The Atlantic Celts: Ancient People or Modern Invention?* (London and Madison, WI).

Jones, Michael E., 1996a, *The End of Roman Britain* (Ithaca, NY, and London).

—— 1996b, 'Geographical-Psychological Frontiers in Sub-Roman Britain,' in Ralph Mathisen and Hagith Sivan (eds.), *Shifting Frontiers in Late Antiquity* (Aldershot), 45–58.

Jones, Michael E., and John Casey, 1988, 'The Gallic Chronicle Restored: A Chronology of the Anglo-Saxon Invasions and the End of Roman Britain,' *Britannia*, 19: 367–97.

—— 1991, 'The Gallic Chronicle Exploded?' *Britannia*, 22: 212–15.

Knight, Jeremy, 1996, 'Seasoned with Salt: Insular-Gallic Contacts in the Early Memorial Stones and Cross Slabs,' in K. R. Dark (ed.), *External Contacts* (Woodbridge), 109–20.

Lapidge, Michael, and David N. Dumville (eds.), 1984, *Gildas: New Approaches* (Woodbridge).

Matthews, Keith J. 1999, '*Britannus/Britto*: Roman Ethnographies, Native Identities, Labels and Folk Devils,' in Alan Leslie (ed.), *Theoretical Roman Archaeology and Architecture: The Third Conference Proceedings* (Glasgow), 14–32.

Morris, John, 1965, 'Pelagian Literature,' *Journal of Theological Studies*, NS 16: 26–60.

—— 1973, *The Age of Arthur: A History of the British Isles from 350 to 650* (London).

Muhlberger, Steven, 1983, 'The Gallic Chronicle of 452 and its Authority for British Events,' *Britannia*, 14: 23–33.

Myres, J. N. L. 1960, 'Pelagius and the End of Roman Rule in Britain,' *Journal of Roman Studies*, 50: 21–36.

O'Brien, Elizabeth. 1999, *Post-Roman Britain to Anglo-Saxon England: Burial Practices Reviewed*, British Archaeological Reports, British Series 289 (Oxford).

Okasha, Elisabeth, 1993, *Corpus of Early Christian Inscribed Stones of Southwestern Britain* (Leicester).

Phillips, Derek, and Brenda Haywood, 1995, *Excavations at York Minster. Vol. I: From Roman Fortress to Norman Cathedral* (London).

Richards, Julian D. 1995, 'An Archaeology of Anglo-Saxon England,' in Giorgio Ausenda (ed.), *After Empire: Towards an Ethnology of Europe's Barbarians* (Woodbridge), 51–74.

Roskams, Steve, 1996, 'Urban Transition in Early Medieval Britain: The Case of York,' in Neil Christie and S. T. Loseby (eds.), *Towns in Transition: Urban Evolution in Late Antiquity and the Early Middle Ages* (Brookfield, VT), 262–88.

Russo, Daniel G., 1998, *Town Origins and Development in Early England, c.400–950 AD* (Westport, CT).

Snyder, Christopher A. 1996, *Sub-Roman Britain (AD 400-600): A Gazetteer of Sites*, British Archaeological Reports, British Series 247 (Oxford).

—— 1997, 'A Gazetteer of Sub-Roman Britain (AD 400–600): The British Sites,' *Internet Archaeology*, 3 <http://intarch.ac.uk/journal/issue3/snyder_index.html>.

—— 1998, *An Age of Tyrants: Britain and the Britons, AD 400–600* (University Park, PA, and Gloucester).

—— 2000, *Exploring the World of King Arthur* (London).

—— Forthcoming, 'Urban or Rural? Church and Churchmen in Sub-Roman Britain.'

Thomas, Charles, 1981a, *Christianity in Roman Britain to AD 500* (Berkeley and Los Angeles).

—— 1981b, *A Provisional List of Imported Pottery in Post-Roman Western Britain and Ireland* (Truro).

—— 1993, *Tintagel: Arthur and Archaeology* (London).

—— 1994, *And Shall These Mute Stones Speak? Post-Roman Inscriptions in Western Britain* (Cardiff).

Thompson, E. A. 1977, 'Britain, AD 406–410,' *Britannia* 8: 303–18.

—— 1982, 'Zosimus 6.10.2 and the Letters of Honorius,' *Classical Quarterly*, 32: 445–62.

—— 1983, 'Fifth-Century Facts?' *Britannia*, 14: 272–4.

—— 1984, *St. Germanus of Auxerre and the End of Roman Britain* (Woodbridge).

Welch, Martin, 1994, 'The Archaeological Evidence for Federate Settlements in Britain Within the Fifth Century,' in Françoise Vallet and Michel Kazanski, *L'armée romaine et les barbares du IIIe au VIIe siècle* (Rouen), 269–77.

Wiseman, Howard. 2000, 'The Derivation of the Date of the Badon Entry in the *Annales Cambriae* from Bede and Gildas,' *Parergon* NS, 17, no. 2: 1–10.

Wood, Ian, 1984, 'The End of Roman Britain: Continental Evidence and Parallels,' in M. Lapidge and D. N. Dumville (eds.), *Gildas: New Approaches* (Woodbridge), 1–25.

—— 1987, 'The Fall of the Western Empire and the End of Roman Britain,' *Britannia* 18: 251-62.

—— 1990, 'The Channel from the Fourth to the Seventh Centuries AD,' in Seán McGrail (ed.), *Maritime Celts, Frisians and Saxons*, CBA Research Report 71 (London), 93–7.

Yorke, Barbara, 1992, *Kings and Kingdoms of Early Anglo-Saxon England* (London).

Chapter 6: The British Church

Barley, M. W. and R. P. C. Hanson (eds.). 1968, *Christianity in Britain, 300–700* (Leicester).

Bassett, Steven, 1989, 'Churches in Worcester Before and After the Conversion of the Anglo-Saxons,' *Antiquaries Journal*, 69: 225–56.

—— 1992, 'Church and Diocese in the West Midlands: The Transition from British to Anglo-Saxon Control,' in J. Blair and R. Sharpe (eds.), *Pastoral Care Before the Parish* (Leicester), 13–40.

Birley, Anthony. 1980, *The People of Roman Britain* (Berkeley and Los Angeles).

Blair, John, and Richard Sharpe (eds.), 1992, *Pastoral Care Before the Parish* (Leicester).

Bradley, Ian, 1999, *Celtic Christianity: Making Myths and Chasing Dreams* (New York).

Brook, Diane, 1992, 'The Early Christian Church East and West of Offa's Dyke,' in N. Edwards and A. Lane (eds.), *The Early Church in Wales and the West* (Oxford), 77–89.

Carney, James, 1973, *The Problem of St Patrick* (Dublin).

Clancy, Thomas Owen, and Gilbert Márkus, 1998, *Iona: The Earliest Poetry of a Celtic Monastery* (Edinburgh).

Conneely, Daniel, 1993, *St Patrick's Letters: A Study of their Theological Dimension* (Maynooth).

Davies, Oliver, 1996, *Celtic Christianity in Early Medieval Wales* (Cardiff).

Davies, Oliver, and Thomas O'Loughlin. 1999, *Celtic Spirituality* (New York).

Davies, Wendy, 1992, 'The Myth of the Celtic Church,' in N. Edwards and A. Lane (eds.), *The Early Church in Wales and the West* (Oxford), 12–21.

—— 1998, *Whithorn and the World*, Sixth Whithorn Lecture (Stranraer).

Doble, G. H. 1971, *Lives of the Welsh Saints*, ed. D. Simon Evans (Cardiff).

Dronke, Peter, 1981, 'St Patrick's Reading,' *CMCS* 1: 21–38.

Dumville, David N., 1984, 'Gildas and Maelgwn: Problems of Dating,' in M. Lapidge and D. N. Dumville (eds.), *Gildas: New Approaches* (Woodbridge), 51–9.

—— 1985, 'Late-Seventh- or Eighth-Century Evidence for the British Transmission of Pelagianism,' *CMCS* 10: 39–52.

Dumville, David N. et al., 1993, *Saint Patrick, AD 493-1993* (Woodbridge).

Edwards, Nancy, and Alan Lane (eds.), 1992, *The Early Church in Wales and the West*, Oxbow Monograph 16 (Oxford).

Ferguson, John, 1956, *Pelagius* (Cambridge).

Flobert, Pierre (ed. and trans.). 1997, *La Vie ancienne de Saint Samson de Dol* (Paris).

Gardner, Rex, 1995, 'Gildas' New Testament Models,' *CMCS* 30: 1–12.

Hanson, R. P. C. 1968, *St. Patrick: His Origins and Career* (Oxford).

Henken, Elissa R., 1987, *The Traditions of the Welsh Saints* (Woodbridge).

—— 1991, *The Welsh Saints: A Study in Patterned Lives* (Woodbridge).

Herren, Michael W., 1989, 'Mission and Monasticism in the *Confessio* of Patrick,' in Donnchadh Ó Corráin et al. (eds.), *Sages, Saints and Storytellers: Celtic Studies in Honour of Professor James Carney* (Maynooth), 76–85.

——1990, 'Gildas and Early British Monasticism,' in A. Bammesberger and A. Wollmann (eds.), *Britain 400–600* (Heidelberg), 65–78.

Higham, Nicholas, 1992, *Rome, Britain and the Anglo-Saxons* (London).

Hill, Peter, 1997, *Whithorn and St Ninian: The Excavation of a Monastic Town* (Stroud).

Howlett, David R, 1994, *'Liber Epistolarum Sancti Patricii Episcopi': The Book of Letters of Saint Patrick the Bishop* (Dublin).

—— 1995, *The Celtic Latin Tradition of Biblical Style* (Portland, OR).

Hughes, Kathleen, 1981, 'The Celtic Church – Is This a Valid Concept?' *CMCS* 1: 1–20.

Jones, Barri, and David Mattingly, 1990, *An Atlas of Roman Britain* (Oxford).

Jones, Michael E., 1986, 'The Historicity of the Alleluja Victory,' *Albion*, 18: 363–73.

—— 1987, 'The Failure of Romanization in Celtic Britain,' *Harvard Celtic Colloquium*, 7: 126–45.

Kerlouégan, François, 1987, *Le 'De excidio Britanniae' de Gildas: Les destinées de la culture latine dans l'île de Bretagne au VIe siècle* (Paris).

Knight, Jeremy, 1996, 'Seasoned with Salt: Insular-Gallic Contacts in the Early Memorial Stones and Cross Slabs,' in K. R. Dark (ed.), *External Contacts*, 109–20.

Koch, John. 1990, '*Cothairche*, Esposito's Theory and Neo-Celtic Lenition,' in A. Bammesberger and A. Wollmann (eds.), *Britain 400–600* (Heidelberg), 179–202.

Lapidge, Michael, 1984, 'Gildas's Education and the Latin Culture of Sub-Roman Britain,' in M. Lapidge and D. N. Dumville (eds.), *Gildas: New Approaches* (Woodbridge), 27–50.

Lapidge, Michael, and David N. Dumville (eds.). 1984, *Gildas: New Approaches* (Woodbridge).

MacQueen, John, 1990, *St Nynia* (Edinburgh).

Miller, Mollie, 1974–76, 'Relative and Absolute Publication Dates of Gildas's *De Excidio* in Medieval Scholarship,' *BBCS* 26: 169–74.

Mohrmann, Christine, 1961, *The Latin of St. Patrick* (Dublin).

Morris, John, 1965, 'Pelagian Literature,' *Journal of Theological Studies*, NS 17: 342–91.

O'Donoghue, Noel Dermot, 1987, *Aristocracy of Soul: Patrick of Ireland* (Wilmington, DE).

O'Loughlin, Thomas, 1999, *Saint Patrick: The Man and His Works* (London).

—— 2000, *Celtic Theology* (London and New York).

O'Rahilly, T. F., 1957, *The Two Patricks* (Dublin).

Pearce, Susan, 1982, 'Estates and Church Sites in Dorset and Gloucestershire: The Emergence of a Christian Society,' in Susan M. Pearce (ed.), *The Early Church in Western Britain and Ireland*, British Archaeological Reports, British Series 102 (Oxford), 117–38.

Pryce, Huw, 1992, 'Pastoral Care in Early Medieval Wales,' in J. Blair and R. Sharpe (eds.), *Pastoral Care Before the Parish* (Leicester), 41–62.

Redknap, Mark, 1995, 'Early Christianity and its Monuments,' in Miranda J. Green (ed.), *The Celtic World* (London and New York), 737–78.

Sharpe, Richard. 'Gildas as a Father of the Church,' in M. Lapidge and D. N. Dumville (eds.), *Gildas: New Approaches* (Woodbridge), 191–206.

—— 1987, Review of *Who was St. Patrick?* By E. A. Thompson, *Journal of Ecclesiastical History* 38: 114–15.

Smith, Ian, 1996, 'The Origins and Development of Christianity in North Britain and Southern Pictland,' in J. Blair and M. Pyrah (eds.), *Church Archaeology* (York), 19–37.

Snyder, Christopher A., 1996a, 'Celtic Continuity in the Middle Ages,' *Medieval Perspectives*, 11: 164–78.

—— 1996b, Review of *The Celtic Latin Tradition of Biblical Style* by David Howlett, *Arthuriana*, 6, no. 3: 78–80.

—— 1998, *An Age of Tyrants: Britain and the Britons*, AD 400–600 (University Park, PA and Stroud).

Thomas, Charles, 1981, *Christianity in Roman Britain to* AD 500 (Berkeley and Los Angeles).

—— 1998, *Christian Celts: Messages and Images* (Stroud).

Thompson, E. A. 1999, *Who was St. Patrick?* 2nd edn.(Woodbridge).

Wilmott, Tony, et al., 1997, *Birdoswald: Excavations of a Roman Fort on Hadrian's Wall and Its Successor Settlement: 1987–92* (London).

Wood, Ian, 1988, 'Forgery in Merovingian Hagiography,' in *Fälschungen im Mittelalter* (Hannover), 369–84.

Wright, Neil, 1984, 'Gildas's Prose Style and its Origins,' in M. Lapidge and D. N. Dumville (eds.), *Gildas: New Approaches* (Woodbridge), 107–28.

Chapter 7: Brittany and Galicia

Adams, Jeremy DuQuesnay, 1993, 'Sidonius and Riothamus,' *Arthurian Literature*, 12: 157–64.

Arias Vilas, Felipe. 1992, *A Romanización de Galicia* (Vigo).

Ashe, Geoffrey, 1981, 'A Certain Very Ancient Book,' *Speculum*, 56: 301–23.

Balcou, Jean, and Yves Le Gallo (eds.). 1997, *Histoire littéraire et culturelle de la Bretagne* (Paris).

Brett, Caroline (ed. and trans.), 1989, *The Monks of Redon* (Woodbridge).

Briard, Jacques, et al., 1970, *Histoire de la Bretagne des origines à1341* (Morlaix).

Chadwick, Nora K, 1965, 'The Colonization of Brittany from Celtic Britain,' *Proceedings of the British Academy*, 51: 235–99.

—— 1969, *Early Brittany* (Cardiff).

Chédeville, André, and Hubert Guillotel. 1984, *La Bretagne des saints et des rois Ve-Xe siècles* (Rennes).

Cunliffe, Barry, 2001, *Facing the Ocean: The Atlantic and its Peoples, 8000 BC–AD 1500* (Oxford).

David, Pierre, 1947, *Études historiques sur la Galice et le Portugal du Vie au XIIe siècle* (Paris).

Davies, Wendy, 1988, *Small Worlds: The Village Community in Early Medieval Brittany* (Berkeley and Los Angeles).

Fleuriot, Léon, 1980, *Les origines de la Bretagne* (Paris).

Fleuriot, Léon, and Claude Evans, 1985, *A Dictionary of Old Breton*, 2 vols. (Toronto).

Fleuriot, Léon, and Pierre-Roland Giot, 1977, 'Early Brittany,' *Antiquity*, 51: 106–16.

Galliou, Patrick, and Michael Jones, 1991, *The Bretons* (Oxford).

Galliou, Patrick, et al. 1980 'La diffusion de la céramique "à l'éponge" dans le nord-ouest de l'empire romain,' *Gallia*, 38: 265–78.

Guillotel, Hubert, 1986, 'Les origines de Landévennec,' in Marc Simon (ed.), *Landévennec et le monachisme Breton dans le haut Moyen Age* (Landévennec), 97–114.

Jones, Michael, 1981, 'The Defence of Medieval Brittany,' *Archaeological Journal*, 138: 149–204.

—— 1988, *The Creation of Brittany, A Late Medieval State* (London and Ronceverte).

Matthews, John F., 1983, 'Macsen, Maximus, and Constantine,' *Welsh History Review*,11: 431–48.

Simon, Marc (ed.), 1986, *Landévennec et le monachisme Breton dans le haut Moyen Age* (Landévennec).

Sheringham, J. G. T., 1981, 'Les machtierns: Quelques témoignages gallois et cornouaillais,' *Memoires de la Société d'Histoire et d'Archéologie de Bretagne*, 58: 61–72.

Smith, Julia M. H., 1992, *Province and Empire: Brittany and the Carolingians* (Cambridge).

Thompson, E. A. 1968, 'Britonia,' in M. W. Barley and R. P. C. Hanson (eds.), *Christianity in Britain, 300–700* (Leicester), 201–5.

—— 1980, 'Procopius on Brittia and Britannia,' *Classical Quarterly*, 30: 498–507.

Torres Rodríguez, Casimiro, 1977, *El Reino de los Suevos* (La Caruña).

Wood, Ian, 1987, 'The Fall of the Western Empire and the End of Roman Britain,' *Britannia*, 18: 251–62.

Wooding, Jonathan, 1996, *Communication and Commerce along the Western Sealanes, AD 400–800*, British Archaeological Reports, International Series 654 (Oxford).

Chapter 8: Cornwall and the Southwest

Abrams, Lesley, 1996, *Anglo-Saxon Glastonbury: Church and Endowment* (Woodbridge).

Abrams, Lesley, and James P. Carley (eds.), 1991, *The Archaeology and History of Glastonbury Abbey* (Woodbridge).

Conner, Patrick W., 1993, *Anglo-Saxon Exeter: A Tenth-century Cultural History* (Woodbridge).

Elliott-Binns, L. E., 1955, *Medieval Cornwall* (London).

Filbee, Marjorie, 1996, *Celtic Cornwall* (London).

Grimmer, Martin, 2001, 'Saxon Bishop and Celtic King: Interactions between Aldhelm of Wessex and Geraint of Dumnonia,' *The Heroic Age*, 4 <http://www.mun.ca/mst/heroicage/issues/4/Grimmer.html>.

Jankulak, Karen, 2000, *The Medieval Cult of St. Petroc* (Woodbridge).

Okasha, Elisabeth, 1993, *Corpus of Early Christian Inscribed Stones of Southwestern Britain* (Leicester).

Olson, Lynette, 1989, *Early Monasteries in Cornwall* (Woodbridge).

Orme, Nicholas, 2000, *The Saints of Cornwall* (Oxford).

Padel, O. J. 1985, *Cornish Place-Name Elements* (Nottingham).

—— 1988, *A Popular Dictionary of Cornish Place-Names* (Penzance).

Payton, Philip, 1992, *The Making of Modern Cornwall* (Redruth).

Pearce, Susan, 1978, *The Kingdom of Dumnonia* (Padstow).

Penhallurick, Roger D., 1986, *Tin in Antiquity* (London).

Preston-Jones, Ann, 1992, 'Decoding Cornish Churchyards,' in N. Edwards and A. Lane (eds.), *The Early Church in Wales and the West* (Oxford), 104–24.

Thomas, Charles, 1981, *A Provisional List of Imported Pottery in Post-Roman Western Britain and Ireland* (Truro).

—— 1985, *Exploration of a Drowned Landscape* (London).

—— 1994, *And Shall These Mute Stones Speak? Post-Roman Inscriptions in Western Britain* (Cardiff).

—— 1997, *Celtic Britain* (London).

Todd, Malcolm, 1987, *The South West to AD 1000* (London and New York).

Webster, Graham, 1975, *The Cornovii*, Peoples of Roman Britain (London).

Yorke, Barbara, 1995, *Wessex in the Early Middle Ages* (Leicester).

Chapter 9: Wales and the Isle of Man

Alcock, Leslie, 1963, *Dinas Powys: An Iron Age, Dark Age and Early Medieval Settlement in Glamorgan* (Cardiff).
—— 1987, *Economy, Society, and Warfare Among the Britons and Saxons* (Cardiff).
Arnold, Christopher J., and Jeffrey L. Davies, 2000, *Roman and Early Medieval Wales* (Stroud).
Charles-Edwards, T. M., et al. (eds.), 2000, *The Welsh King and His Court* (Cardiff).
Dark, K. R., 1994, *Civitas to Kingdom: British Political Continuity, 300–800* (Leicester).
Davies, John, 1993, *A History of Wales* (London).
Davies, Oliver, 1996, *Celtic Christianity in Early Medieval Wales* (Cardiff).
Davies, Wendy, 1978, *An Early Welsh Microcosm: Studies in the Llandaff Charters* (London).
—— 1982, *Wales in the Early Middle Ages* (Leicester).
—— 1990, *Patterns of Power in Early Wales* (Oxford).
Dumville, David N., 1977, 'Sub-Roman Britain: History and Legend,' *History*, 62: 173–92.
Edwards, Nancy, and Alan Lane (eds.), 1988, *Early Medieval Settlements in Wales AD 400–1100* (Cardiff).
—— 1992, *The Early Church in Wales and the West*, Oxbow Monograph 16 (Oxford).
Higham, N. J., 1992, 'Medieval "Overkingship" in Wales: The Earliest Evidence,' *Welsh History Review*, 16: 145–59.
James, Heather, 1992, 'Early Medieval Cemeteries in Wales,' in N. Edwards and A. Lane (eds.), *The Early Church in Wales and the West* (Oxford).
Kinvig, R. H., 1975, *The Isle of Man: A Social, Cultural, and Political History*, 3rd edn. (Liverpool).
Loyn, H. R., 1984, 'The Conversion of the English to Christianity: Some Comments on the Celtic Contribution,' in R. R. Davies et al. (eds.), *Welsh Society and Nationhood* (Cardiff), 5–18.
Maund, Kari, 2000, *The Welsh Kings* (Stroud).
Ó Cathasaigh, Thomás, 1984, 'The Déisi and Dyfed,' *Éigse*, 20: 1–33.
Pryce, Huw, 1992, 'Pastoral Care in Early Medieval Wales,' in J. Blair and R. Sharpe (eds.), *Pastoral Care Before the Parish* (Leicester), 41–62.
—— 1993, *Native Law and the Church in Medieval Wales* (Oxford).
Walker, David, 1990, *Medieval Wales* (Cambridge).

Chapter 10: Northern Britons

Alcock, Leslie, 1984, 'Gwyr y Gogledd: An Archaeological Appraisal,' *Archaeologia Cambrensis*, 132: 1–18.
Cessford, Craig, 1999, 'Relations Between the Britons of Southern Scotland and

Anglo-Saxon Northumbria,' in Jane Hawkes and Susan Mills (eds.), *Northumbria's Golden Age* (Stroud), 150–60.

—— 2001, 'Post-Severan Cramond: A Late Roman and Early Historic British and Anglo-Saxon Religious Centre?' *The Heroic Age*, 4 <http://www.mun.ca/mst/heroicage/issues/4/Cessford.html>.

Clarkson, Tim, 1999a, 'The *Gododdin* Revisited,' *The Heroic Age*, 1 <http://www.mun.ca/mst/heroicage/issues/1/hatf.htm#gododdin>.

—— 1999b, "Rhydderch Hael," *The Heroic Age*, 2 <http://www.mun.ca/mst/heroicage/issues/2/ha2rh.htm>.

Cramp, Rosemary, 1999, 'The Northumbrian Identity,' in Jane Hawkes and Susan Mills (eds.), *Northumbria's Golden Age* (Stroud), 1–11.

Dark, K. R., 1992, 'A Sub-Roman Re-Defense of Hadrian's Wall?' *Britannia*, 23: 111–20.

Driscoll, Stephen T., and Peter A. Yeoman, 1997, *Excavations Within Edinburgh Castle in 1988–91* (Edinburgh).

Eagles, Bruce, 1980, 'Anglo-Saxons in Lindsey and the East Riding of Yorkshire in the Fifth Century,' In Philip Rahtz et al. (eds.), *Anglo-Saxon Cemeteries 1979*, British Archaeological Reports, British Series 82 (Oxford), 285–7.

Faull, Margaret L. 1984, 'Settlement and Society in North-East England in the Fifth Century,' in P. R. Wilson et al. (eds.), *Settlement and Society in the Roman North* (Bradford), 49–52.

Field, P. J. C., 1999, 'Gildas and the City of the Legions.' *The Heroic Age*, 1 <http://www.mun.ca/mst/heroicage/issues/1/hagcl.htm>.

Hartley, B. R., and R. Leon Fitts, 1988, *The Brigantes* (Gloucester).

Higham, N. J., 1986, *The Northern Counties to AD 1000* (London).

—— 1987, 'Brigantia Revisited,' *Northern History*, 22: 1–19.

—— 1993, *The Kingdom of Northumbria AD 350–1100* (Stroud).

Higham, Nicholas, and Barri Jones, 1991, *The Carvetii* (Stroud).

Hill, Peter, 1997, *Whithorn and St. Ninian: The Excavation of a Monastic Town, 1984–91* (Stroud).

Isaac, Graham, 1990, 'Mynyddawg Mwynfawr,' *BBCS* 37: 111–13.

Kirby, D. P., 2000, *The Earliest English Kings*, rev. edn. (London).

Koch, John T., 1997, *The Gododdin of Aneirin: Text and Context from Dark-Age North Britain* (Cardiff).

Laing, Lloyd R., 1975, *Settlement Types in Post-Roman Scotland*, British Archaeological Reports, 13 (Oxford).

Longley, David, 1982, 'The Date of the Mote of Mark,' *Antiquity*, 56: 132–4.

MacQuarrie, Alan, 1998, 'The Kings of Strathclyde, *c*.400–1018,' in Alexander Grant and Keith J. Stringer (eds.), *Medieval Scotland: Crown, Lordship and Community* (Edinburgh), 1–19.

Miller, Molly, 1975a, 'Historicity and Pedigrees of the Northcountrymen,' *BBCS* 26, no. 3: 255–80.

—— 1975b, 'The Commanders at Arthuret,' *Transactions of the Cumberland and Westmorland Antiquarian and Archaeological Society*, 75: 96–118.

—— 1978–80, 'Hiberni Reversuri,' *Proceedings of the Society of Antiquaries of Scotland*, 110: 305–27.

Padel, Oliver, 1998. "A New Study of the Gododdin". *Cambrian Medieval Celtic*

Studies, 35 (Summer): 45–55.

Phythian-Adams, Charles, 1996, *Land of the Cumbrians: A Study of British Provincial Origins ad 400–1120* (Aldershot).

Ramm, Herman, 1978, *The Parisii* (London).

Rowland, Jenny, 1995, 'Warfare and Horses in the *Gododdin* and the Problem of Catraeth.' *CMCS* 30: 13–40.

Smyth, Alfred P., 1984, *Warlords and Holy Men: Scotland AD 80–1000* (Edinburgh).

Taylor, C. M., 1992, 'Elmet: Boundaries and Celtic Survival in the Post-Roman Period,' *Medieval History*, 2: 111–29.

Thomas, Charles, 1997, *Celtic Britain* (New York).

Tolstoy, Nikolai, 1985, *The Quest for Merlin* (Boston).

Wilmott, Tony, et al., 1997, *Birdoswald: Excavations of a Roman Fort on Hadrian's Wall and Its Successor Settlements, 1987–92* (London).

Wood, P. N., 1996, 'On the Little British Kingdom of Craven,' *Northern History*, 32: 1–20.

Woolf, Alex, 1998, 'Pictish Matriliny Reconsidered,' *Innes Review*, 49: 147–67.

Ziegler, Michelle. 2001, 'Oswald and the Irish.' *The Heroic Age*, 4 <http://www.mun.ca/mst/heroicage/issues/4/ziegler.html>.

Chapter 11: Normans and Britons

Barrow, G. W. S., 1988, *Robert the Bruce and the Community of the Realm of Scotland*, 3rd edn. (Edinburgh).

Bartlett, Robert. 1982, *Gerald of Wales 1146–1223* (Oxford).

—— 2000, *England Under the Norman and Angevin Kings 1075–1225* (Oxford).

Carr, A. D., 1995, *Medieval Wales* (New York).

Crick, Julia, 1992, 'Geoffrey of Monmouth, Prophecy and History,' *Journal of Medieval History*, 18: 357–71.

Davies, R. R., 1984, 'Law and National Identity in Thirteenth-Century Wales,' in R. R. Davies et al. (eds.), *Welsh Society and Nationhood* (Cardiff), 51–69.

—— 1991, *The Age of Conquest: Wales 1063–1415* (Oxford).

—— 1995, *The Revolt of Owain Glyn Dŵr* (Oxford).

—— 1996, *The Matter of Britain and the Matter of England* (Oxford).

Davies, R. R. et al. (eds.). 1984, *Welsh Society and Nationhood* (Cardiff).

Edwards, J. G., 1956, 'The Normans and the Welsh March,' The Raleigh Lecture on History, *Proceedings of the British Academy* 42: 155–78

Gillingham, John, 1990, 'The Context and Purpose of Geoffrey of Monmouth's *History of the Kings of Britain*,' *Anglo-Norman Studies*, 13: 99–118.

—— 1995, 'Foundations of a Disunited Kingdom,' in Alexander Grant and Keith J. Stringer (eds.), *Uniting the Kingdom? The Making of British History* (London), 48–64.

Griffiths, Ralph, 1994, *Conquerors and Conquered in Medieval Wales* (New York).

Henken, Elissa, 1996, *National Redeemer: Owain Glyndŵr in Welsh Tradition* (Ithaca, NY).

Johnson, Lizabeth J., 2000, *Welsh Nationalism in the Period 1188–1282*, MA thesis, the University of New Mexico (Albuquerque, NM).

Jones, W. R., 1971, 'The Image of the Barbarian in Medieval Europe,' *Comparative Studies in Society and History*, 13: 376–407.

Knight, Stephen, 1983, *Arthurian Literature and Society* (New York).

McCann, W. J., 1991, 'The Welsh View of the Normans in the Eleventh and Twelfth Centuries,' *Transactions of the Honorable Society of Cymmrodorion*, 39–67.

Maund, Kari, 2000, *The Welsh Kings* (Stroud).

Pugh, T. B. (ed.), 1971, *Glamorgan County History. Vol. III: The Middle Ages* (Cardiff).

Radiker, Laura J., 1995, 'The Politics of Arthurian Legend in the Plantagenet Empire: A Study of Literary and Historical Sources from the Time of Henry II to Edward I,' MA thesis, Western Michigan University (Kalamazoo, MI).

Reeves, A. C., 1983, *The Marcher Lords* (Llandybïe).

Richter, Michael, 1976, *Giraldus Cambrensis: The Growth of the Welsh Nation* (Aberystwyth).

Roberts, B. F., 1976, 'Geoffrey of Monmouth and the Welsh Historical Tradition,' *Nottingham Medieval Studies*, 20: 29–40.

Smith, J. Beverly, 1976, 'Gruffydd Llwyd and the Celtic Alliance, 1315–18,' *BBCS* 26: 463–78.

Snyder, Christopher A., 1996, 'Celtic Continuity in the Middle Ages,' *Medieval Perspectives*, 11, 164–78.

—— 2000, *Exploring the World of King Arthur* (London).

—— Forthcoming, 'The Once and Future Kings: Political Prophecy in the Medieval Celtic Fringe.'

Suppe, Frederick C., 1994, *Military Institutions on the Welsh Marches: Shropshire, AD 1066–1300* (Woodbridge).

Tatlock, J. S. P., 1950, *The Legendary History of Britain* (Berkeley. CA).

Walker, David, 1984, 'Cultural Survival in an Age of Conquest,' in R. R. Davies et al. (eds.), *Welsh Society and Nationhood* (Cardiff), 35–50.

Chapter 12: Language and Literature

Balcou, Jean, and Yves le Gallo (eds). 1997, *Histoire littéraire et culturelle de la Bretagne* (Paris).

Bammesberger, Alfred, and Alfred Wollmann (eds.). 1990, *Britain 400–600: Language and History* (Heidelberg).

Bromwich, Rachel (ed. and trans.). 1978, *Trioedd Ynys Prydein: The Welsh Triads* (Cardiff).

Bromwich, Rachel, et al. (eds.). 1991, *The Arthur of the Welsh: The Arthurian Legend on Medieval Welsh Literature* (Cardiff).

Charles-Edwards, Thomas, 1995, 'Language and Society among the Insular Celts, AD 400–1000,' in Miranda J. Green (ed.), *The Celtic World* (London and New York), 703–36.

Dumville, David, 1983, 'Brittany and *Armes Prydein Vawr*,' *Etudes Celtiques*, 20: 145–59.

Evans, Stephen S., 1997, *The Lords of Battle: Image and Reality of the* Comitatus *in Dark-Age Britain* (Woodbridge).

Ford, Patrick K., 1974, *The Poetry of Llywarch Hen* (Berkeley, CA).

——(trans. and ed. with introd.). 1977, *'The Mabinogi' and Other Medieval Welsh Tales* (Berkeley, CA).

Hamp, Eric, 1974–5, 'Mabonogi,' *Transactions of the Honorable Society of Cymmrodorion*, 243–9.

Howlett, D. R,. 1995, *The Celtic Latin Tradition of Biblical Style* (Dublin).

Jackson, Kenneth, 1994, *Language and History in Early Britain* (Dublin).

Jarman, A. O. H., 1978, 'Early Stages in the Development of the Myrddin Legend,' in R. Bromwich and R. Jones (eds.), *Astudiaethau ar yr Hengerdd* (Cardiff), 326–49.

Knight, Stephen, 1983, *Arthurian Literature and Society* (New York).

Koch, John T., 1997, *The* Gododdin *of Aneirin: Text and Context from Dark-Age North Britain* (Cardiff).

McCann, W. J., 1991, 'The Welsh View of the Normans in the Eleventh and Twelfth Centuries,' *Transactions of the Honorable Society of Cymmrodorion*, 39–67.

Matthews, J. F., 1983, 'Macsen, Maximus and Constantine,' *Welsh History Review* 11: 431–48.

Moisl, Hermann, 1980–2, 'A Sixth-Century Reference to the British *bardd*,' *BBCS* 29: 269–73.

Padel, O. J., 2000, *Arthur in Medieval Welsh Literature* (Cardiff).

The Poets of the Nobility (1282–1526), 21+ vols. (Aberystwyth, 1994–   ).

The Poets of the Princes, 7 vols. (Cardiff, 1989–96).

Richter, Michael, 1994, *The Formation of the Medieval West: Studies in the Oral Culture of the Barbarians* (New York).

Roberts, Brynley, 1991, '*Culhwch ac Olwen*, the Triads, and the Saints' Lives,' in R. Bromwich et al. (eds.), *The Arthur of the Welsh* (Cardiff), 73-95.

Rowland, Jenny, *Early Welsh Saga Poetry: A Study and Edition of the* Englynion (Woodbridge, 1990).

Sims-Williams, Patrick, 1990, 'Dating the transition to Neo-Brittonic: Phonology and History, 400–600,' in A. Bammesberger and A. Wollman (eds.), *Britain 400–600: Language and History* (Heidelberg), 217–61.

— 1991, 'The Emergence of Old Welsh, Cornish and Breton Orthography, 600–800: the Evidence of Archaic Old Welsh,' *BBCS* 29: 20–86.

Snyder, Christopher, 2000, *Exploring the World of King Arthur* (London).

—— Forthcoming, 'From Aquileia to Camelot: Magnus Maximus and the Arthurian Tradition,' *L'Unicorno*.

Tierney, J. J., 1959–60, 'The Celtic Ethnography of Posidonius,' *Proceedings of the Royal Irish Academy*, 60C: 189–275.

Tolstoy, Nikolai, 1983–4, 'Merlinus Redivivus,' *Studia Celtica*, 18/19: 11–29.

Williams, Ifor, 1970, *Lectures on Early Welsh Poetry* (Dublin).

—— (ed. and introd.), 1972, *Armes Prydein ('The Great Prophecy of Britain') from the Book of Taliesin*, trans. Rachel Bromwich (Dublin).

—— 1980, *The Beginnings of Welsh Poetry*, ed. Rachel Bromwich (Cardiff).

Williams, J. E. Caerwyn, 1984, 'Gildas, Maelgwn and the Bards,' in R. R. Davies et al. (eds.), *Welsh Society and Nationhood* (Cardiff), 19–37.

Chapter 13: Conclusion

Anglo, S., 1961, 'The British History in Early Tudor Propaganda,' *Bulletin of the John Rylands Library*, 44: 17–48.

Colley, Linda, 1992, *Britons* (New Haven and London).

Ellis, Peter Berresford, 1985, *The Celtic Revolution* (Talybont).

Evans, D. Ellis, 1980–2, 'Celts and Germans,' *BBCS* 29: 230–55.

Davies, John, 1993, *A History of Wales* (London).

Davies, R. R. 1979, *Historical Perception: Celts and Saxons* (Cardiff).

Galliou, Patrick, and Michael Jones, 1991, *The Bretons* (Oxford).

Green, Miranda J., 1997, *Exploring the World of the Druids* (London and New York).

Hale, Amy, and Philip Payton (eds.). 2000, *New Directions in Celtic Studies* (Exeter).

Levy, F. J., 1967, *Tudor Historical Thought* (San Marino, CA).

Lewis, Henry (ed.), 1963, *Angles and Britons: O'Donnell Lectures* (Cardiff).

Piggott, Stuart, 1967, *Celts, Saxons, and the Early Antiquaries* (Edinburgh).

—— 1989, *Ancient Britons and the Antiquarian Imagination* (London).

Sims-Williams, Patrick, 1986, 'The Visionary Celt: The Construction of an Ethnic Preconception,' *CMCS* 11: 71–96.

Index